Experimental Psychology:
its scope and method
IV Learning and Memory

First published in English in 1970, the first chapter of the book is
concerned with conditioned reactions. Jean François le Ny discusses
ways in which conditioned reactions are acquired and the laws governing their function.

The second contributor, Gérard de Montpellier, looks at different types
of learning. The varying processes involved in both animal and human
learning are considered, together with some general factors and
mechanisms of learning. The third section of the book by Geneviève
Oléron deals with the phenomenon of transfer. Among the topics
included are the determination of transfer effects, transfer in perceptual-motor activities and explanations of transfer. In the final chapter,
César Florès examines memory, forgetting and reminiscence. The discussion covers methodology, the influence of material, the role of
practice, the part played by attitudes, motivation and emotive reactions
in the memory process, as well as the importance of organisation of
memory tasks on the part of the subject.

T0322749

Experimental Psychology:
its scope and method
IV Learning and Memory

Jean-François Le Ny,
Gérard de Montpellier,
Geneviève Oléron
and César Florès

Ψ Psychology Press
Taylor & Francis Group

LONDON AND NEW YORK

Experimental Psychology
its scope and method
edited by Paul Fraisse and Jean Piaget

IV Learning and memory
by Jean-François le Ny, Gérard de Montpellier
Geneviève Oléron and César Florès

Translated by Louise Elkington

Routledge & Kegan Paul   London

Translated from the French
TRAITÉ DE PSYCHOLOGIE EXPÉRIMENTALE
IV APPRENTISSAGE ET MÉMOIRE
© *1964 Presses Universitaires de France*
First published in Great Britain 1970
by Routledge & Kegan Paul Limited
Broadway House, 68–74 Carter Lane
London, E.C.4
Printed in Great Britain by
Western Printing Services Limited
Bristol
English translation
© *Routledge & Kegan Paul 1970*
SBN 7100 6653 8

Contents

Contents

CHAPTER 14   *César Florès*

MEMORY

Contents

Chapter 11

Conditioned Reactions

Jean-François Le Ny

The study of conditioning first arose from studies in physiology. In the course of his research into the function of the digestive glands, Pavlov became interested in so-called *psychic* secretion. Following the general tendency at that time, he refused to consider it from a psychological (i.e. subjective) standpoint. Later, seeing the weakness of objective psychology, which was in its infancy, he maintained that 'the physiologist ought to keep to his own route' and so he continued to present his findings and his general ideas as a 'theory of higher nervous activity'.

Today things have developed sufficiently for the main data on conditioning to be presented from an essentially psychological point of view, without this information losing any of its experimental and objective nature. The neurophysiology of conditioning forms a special subject which is beyond the scope of this chapter.

Pavlov started with the basic idea of *reflex* which he defined in this way: 'Every activity of an organism is a response, governed by laws, to the action of a specific outside agent.'

In psychology today, the same definition would probably be given for the term *reaction*. This is a wider term since it has no physiological restrictions. Conditioned reactions often overlap the strict conception of reflex, although they retain the same basic characteristics: they are *responses* of an organism to the action of an *external agent* and they obey certain laws.

1 Conditioned reactions and their acquisition

1 Classical conditioned reactions

(A) CONDITIONED SALIVARY REACTION

Pavlov and his collaborators studied salivary reactions, in particular. The animal they generally used in their experiments was a dog. First they would carry out a small operation on the dog so that its salivary passage ended outside its cheek. By inserting a small piece of equipment, they could measure with considerable accuracy the quantity of saliva secreted.

In this way they were able to observe two sorts of reaction: alimentary and protective. The latter occurred when a noxious substance (such as a weak solution of acid), which the organism tended to reject, was placed in the dog's mouth. Alimentary reactions were produced by food: Pavlov generally used meat powder, which he introduced into the dog's mouth by means of a tube, causing considerable secretion. We shall refer to these reactions more than to protective reactions.

As soon as it had recovered from its operation, the animal was adapted to the conditions under which the experiments were carried out: it was placed in a room away from all sounds, sights and smells that could affect it; it was completely alone in this room; the experimenter made all his observations and any intervention necessary from an adjacent room; no stimulation outside the scope of the experiment could come from this room; the dog was held still by a harness on a table. The real conditioning began when the dog had become accustomed to this situation. The experimenter then presented some form of stimulation, for example, a bell. This sound, like the other things in the dog's surroundings, produced no salivary secretion, so this was a *neutral stimulus* in relation to the reaction under observation. A second later a certain amount of powered meat was introduced into the dog's mouth. Then, after a few instants of latency, saliva was seen running out. This was the direct result of the mechanical and chemical action of the food on the buccal mucus.

This secretion was an *unconditioned reaction* and the powdered meat was the *unconditioned* or *absolute* stimulus of this reaction.

However, if this combination of neutral stimulus (the bell) and unconditioned stimulus (the meat) was repeated, saliva began to appear at the sound of the bell. If this combination of the two stimuli was presented repeatedly, the amount of secretion at the sound of the bell gradually increased. By about the fifteenth trial, the stimulus that had previously been neutral was as effective as the meat. It had become a *conditioned stimulus* and the salivation which it caused was a *conditioned reaction*.[1] After a while, the joint presentation of the two stimuli seemed to have no further effect on the situation; the C.R. was *stabilized*. So as to obtain a true picture, the meat was not administered in one trial and only the bell was used. As the latter still produced salivation in the absence of the unconditioned stimulus, it had obviously become a sort of substitute for the meat.

(B) CONDITIONS FOR THE ACQUISITION OF CONDITIONED REACTIONS

(*a*) Numerous experiments following the same schema, but using other forms of stimulation, have revealed that the nature of the stimuli is unimportant when it is a question of transforming them into conditioned stimuli. The fundamental condition is the temporal *contiguity* of the neutral stimulus and the unconditioned stimulus. If this condition is fulfilled, any external, neutral agent can produce a salivary response after a certain number of trials.

One particular experiment, carried out by Erofeeva (Pavlov, 1953), illustrates this point. Before giving the animal any food, Erofeeva gave it an electric shock on its skin. Naturally the animal was not indifferent to this electric stimulation, which produced a protective reaction shown mainly by motor activity. The electric shock was an unconditioned stimulus in relation to this motor activity, but it was a neutral stimulus in relation to the salivation, since it did not originally cause any secretion. After administering

---

[1] From now onwards, we shall make considerable use of the following abbreviations:
C.R. = conditioned reaction;
U.R. = unconditioned reaction;
C.S. = conditioned stimulus;
U.S. = unconditioned stimulus.

the electric shock in conjunction with the food several times, Erofeeva found that the electric stimulation no longer produced an obvious, protective reaction. On the contrary, it clearly produced a salivary reaction for which it had become the conditioned stimulus. The term 'neutral' stimulus should, therefore, be understood in relation to the reaction undergoing conditioning, since a stimulus can very well be neutral in relation to one reaction at the same time as being unconditioned in relation to another. As a rule,[1] this does not prevent the establishment of conditioning.

How can this contiguity of stimuli, which is essential for the formation of any C.R., be explained? The best situation is that in which the neutral stimulus slightly precedes the unconditioned stimulus. With the traditional Pavlovian technique, where stimulation usually lasts quite a long time, the neutral or conditioned stimulus is presented alone for several seconds. Then, while this is still acting, the unconditioned stimulus is presented. In this way, the two stimuli overlap. But this is not essential and the C.S. can perfectly well be stopped before or at moment when the U.S. is presented; all that is necessary is that the C.S. should be presented before the U.S. Several Americans have investigated the importance of this interval between stimuli, and it would seem that conditioning is more easily established when this interval lasts about 0·50 second (see Kimble, 1961). However, no systematic research has been carried out along these lines with salivary conditioning. Intervals of less than half a second can be used, and conditioning is possible even if the C.S. and U.S. are presented simultaneously. But the results of experiments carried out so far indicate that conditioned reactions cannot be obtained with certainty when the U.S. precedes the C.S. Possibly there is no such thing as backward conditioning, although some authors (for example, Asratian, 1959), citing experiments on temporary connections (described later), say that backward temporary connections can be established, but they are not as strong.

Although this contiguity of stimuli is the basic condition for

---

[1] However, the relative strength of reactions must be considered. If strong electric stimulation is administered, producing a very strong, protective reflex, it is impossible to transform it into a conditioned alimentary stimulus. If the trial lasts too long, it produces a conflict between reactions, which upsets the animal's nervous activity causing experimental neurasthenia.

the establishment of classical conditioned reactions, there are other, secondary conditions which, without being essential, can combine to assist or upset the result.

(*b*) First, *repetition* must be mentioned: one trial is rarely enough for the establishment of a C.R. Even if it does appear the first time, the stimuli usually have to be repeated several times before the C.R. appears in its full strength. Between this first appearance and the stabilization mentioned earlier there is an intermediary phase during which the C.R. grows in frequency, magnitude or rapidity, whichever applies. Each combination of stimuli accelerates this growth. In fact the presentation of the unconditioned stimulus *reinforces* the action of the conditioned stimulus. The meat powder is the conditioned alimentary reaction's *reinforcing* agent, which is, therefore, elaborated by the accumulation of a series of reinforcements. However, this repetition may not be necessary and conditioning may be achieved with the first combined presentation of stimuli. Conditioning in a single trial is not impossible. It depends on the reaction and the strength of the stimuli. The type of animal used is equally important. Conditioning is usually easier and quicker with animals higher up the biological tree.

(*c*) The *strength of the unconditioned reaction* is an important factor: if the animal is very hungry, all its alimentary reflexes, particularly salivation, will be stronger. Therefore it will be easier to elaborate the C.R., which will also be much stronger. Notes on experiments in Pavlov's laboratory often show the amount of saliva produced by the unconditioned stimulus so that the strength of the C.R. can be compared with that of the U.R. (Pavlov, 1953).

(*d*) The *intensity of the neutral stimulus* (which becomes the conditioned stimulus) also plays a part. If this stimulus is too weak, it will be difficult, or even impossible, to establish conditioning. However, once the C.R. is established, it will be stronger, the greater the intensity of the stimulus.

(*e*) *External stimuli*, which could cause some other activity in the organism, should be considered in conjunction with the previous condition. If, at the moment when the C.S. is presented, some other stimulation outside the experiment (for example, a noise, a movement or a smell) strikes the animal's receptive organs, the conditioning effect will be weakened and the reaction

5

will be less marked. Pavlov called this effect 'external inhibition', because it usually weakens the strength of the response. In order to avoid external inhibition, special conditions must be created: strict isolation from all parasitic stimulation, hence the creation of Pavlov's famous 'tower of silence'. This artificial environ‑ment does not mean that the phenomena themselves are arti‑ficial, since everything happens in the same way (albeit, with a little more complexity) for an organism in its natural surround‑ings. The care taken in the laboratory, aiming as it does at simplification and standardization of experimental conditions, has only methodological value.

(C) CONDITIONED VISCERAL REACTIONS

Several examples will be given later of the numerous reactions that have been conditioned in both humans and animals. Experi‑ments show that, no matter what basic U.R. is involved, con‑ditioning is always elaborated in accordance with the rules demonstrated by Pavlov in salivary reflexes. The extension of the study of conditioning to numerous visceral or neurovegetative reactions (Bykov, 1956) opened up new avenues for functional physiology and medicine. Not only does this research provide a way of explaining the influence of 'psychic' conditions on 'somatic' activity, but it also provides a basis for understanding certain psychological functions, particularly in the affective and emotional field.

The sort of stimuli that can be conditioned come not only from the external world (exteroceptive stimuli), but also from the internal organs (interoceptive and proprioceptive stimuli). For example, Aïrapetianz used stimulation of the stomach by irrigation of the gastric mucus as the stimulus for a salivary C.R. Water at a certain temperature flowed into the stomach by means of a fistula. It was immediately evacuated to prevent an increase of liquid in the organism, which could affect salivation. Food was presented to the animal after each stimulation of the stomach, and soon gastric stimulation alone produced salivation. However, considerably more joint presentations of stimuli were required for the establishment of a C.R. in this case than in the case of an exteroceptive stimulus. This seems to be a general rule for C.R.s with a visceral stimulus (Bykov, 1956). Various forms of

6

internal stimulation have been used as C.S. for conditioned reactions. These phenomena have provided a basis for research into interoceptors in various internal organs about which little is known from this point of view.

Not only visceral *stimulation*, but also *activities* belonging to this sphere, play a part in conditioning. Many reflexes such as gastric and biliary secretions, diuresis, cardiac, respiratory and vasomotor activity, peristalsis, gaseous changes, thermic reactions, etc. can all be conditioned in their different ways. We quote the example of Slonim's experiments on the metabolism

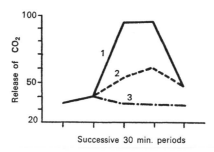

Fig. 1. Release of carbon dioxide at 30-minute intervals in a mouse. (After C. Bykov, *Le cortex et les organes internes*, Edit. Langues étrang., Moscow, 1956, p. 246.)

1. When the surrounding temperature varies; 2. Constant temperature, with C.S.; 3. Constant temperature, without C.S. (control).

of mice (Bykov, 1956). Outside the experiment the mice were kept at a temperature of 20°C. and their gaseous changes, particularly the production of carbon dioxide, were noted. During the experiment they were kept at 30°C. for two hours and then the temperature was lowered to 10°C. for half an hour. When this change was made, a bell was rung intermittently and an electric light went on. Under these conditions, there was an increase in the amount of carbon dioxide produced. If the temperature was maintained at 30°C., but the bell rang and the electric light went on when the temperature usually dropped, there was still a definite, but smaller, increase in the amount of carbon dioxide produced (Fig. 1).

2 Instrumental conditioning

(A) FIRST AND SECOND TYPES OF CONDITIONING

The extension of classical Pavlovian conditioning, referred to earlier, was accompanied by development in a different direction. Pavlovian laws and methods of analysis served as a model for the objective study of other forms of learnt transformation.

S. Miller and Konorski (1928) were the first to carry out experiments on these lines and their research led to important developments. The basis of their study was the fact that motor reactions in animals tend to be repeated if they lead to a pleasant situation, whereas they will be avoided if they lead to a situation which is painful or disagreeable for the organism. Thorndike's experiments emphasized this fact which is, in any case, taken for granted in the training of animals. Miller and Konorski used the classical, experimental situation of alimentary conditioning. Placing a dog on a platform, they induced artificial flexion of its paw by raising it themselves. Then they gave the dog some food. After doing this a number of times, they noted that the dog began to bend its paw spontaneously. If they continued to give the dog food after the paw movement, the movement became quicker and more frequent, so Miller and Konorski declared that the administration of food *reinforced* the paw action.

However, this experiment could be carried out in a different way. If, each time he raised the animal's paw himself, the experimenter placed acid, and not meat, in the animal's mouth, there was resistance to the movement. This happened whenever stimulation caused an unconditioned protective reaction. The dog would stretch its paw so as to avoid bending it. This seems to be *negative reinforcement* tending to bring about the disappearance of the reaction.

However, in accordance with the Pavlovian situation, both cases contain a classical, conditioned salivary reaction (either alimentary or protective). If, before it flexed its paw, the animal was given a signal (for example, a bell ringing),[1] then the bell would cause the paw movement and salivation *at the same time*

---

[1] This signal is not absolutely necessary. In its absence, the entire situation constitutes a conditioned stimulus.

after several trials reinforced by food. But these two reactions have different characteristics, summed up by Konorski (1948) as follows:

(*a*) In salivary conditioning, and indeed in all conditioning consistent with Pavlov's scheme, the C.R. is identical to the U.R. from which it is elaborated. This statement is perhaps not strictly accurate, but the differences between the C.R. and U.R. are very slight, and the basic phenomenon is still the change in stimulus provoking the reaction. In the experiments carried out by Miller and Konorski and in all similar cases, the reinforced stimulus and *response* differ from the reinforcing stimulus and its response. There need be no resemblance between them, and a reaction unconnected with food can be established with alimentary reinforcement.

(*b*) In classical conditioning, no distinction is made between different types of reinforcement nor, consequently, between the C.R.s themselves. However, in the experiments by Miller and Konorski, it was essential to know whether the reinforcement was *positive* (food), in which case the frequency and strength of the paw movement increased, or *negative* (acid), causing the disappearance of the reaction and the development of the opposite response.

(*c*) In conditioning of the Pavlovian type, the response can be any reaction on the part of the organism, whether autonomic (like salivation) or somatic (like a protective, motor reaction). However, it appears that new, conditioned responses can only be somatic reactions, so they can be compared to 'voluntary' movements.

All these differences led Miller and Konorski to make a distinction between two types of conditioned reflexes. The conditioned reactions studied by Pavlov belonged to the first group, while reactions of the type they had studied belonged to the second group. There have been many experiments involving the second type of reaction since the first experiment by Miller and Konorski in which they raised the dog's paw by means of a cord and pulley. It has been suggested that this method could hurt the dog and so produce a protective reaction. In fact the same response can be obtained if the experimenter bends the dog's paw with his hand and then gives it the food. This is the well-known trick of the dog that 'gives you its paw', one of the original forms of

9

animal training. Nevertheless, this method does pose one problem: does the C.R. really stem from a 'passive' movement by the animal, i.e. a movement provoked in an entirely mechanical way by the experimenter? This question remains unanswered, but there are reasons for supposing that a purely passive movement alone cannot result in a C.R.[1]

This problem has a more general side to it, namely whether or not the reaction is conditioned at its first appearance. Clearly in so far as it is a reaction, and not a stimulus, which is reinforced (followed by positive or negative stimulation), the animal must make this reaction at least once before it is conditioned; but how can this first reaction appear? There are several possible ways, other than mechanically-induced movement.

(B) SKINNER'S EXPERIMENTS

Skinner placed a starving rat in a box isolated from all external stimulation. A lever in this box worked a mechanism which dropped a ball of food into an eating trough on the wall. At the beginning of the experiment, there was nothing to induce the rat to press the lever, so considerable time elapsed before the first reaction appeared. This reaction appeared quite 'by accident' as a result of the animal's spontaneous behaviour, scurrying about the box and trying to climb the walls, etc. Once this first reaction had been achieved, it was positively reinforced by administering food to the rat. Each time the animal pressed the lever, the reaction was reinforced by food. In Skinner's experiment, the appearance of each reaction was automatically registered and the reactions were soon seen to appear more and more frequently. The time between them gradually diminished until the animal only stopped long enough to eat the ball of food. From this point onwards, the reaction was conditioned.

'Skinner's box' became a classical situation for conditioning experiments and Skinner himself later explored all its possibilities in detail (1938). Analysing the acquisition of this response under these conditions, Skinner (1935) declared that it was indeed conditioning. At the same time, and independently of Miller and Konorski, he came to the conclusion that there were *two types* of

[1] One can suppose that this mechanically-induced flexion of the paw provokes a proprioceptive reflex (Sherrington) and that it is this which is conditioned.

conditioning. Hilgard and Marquis (1941) adopted the name *instrumental*[1] for this second type of conditioning to distinguish it from *classical* conditioning of the Pavlovian type. They added to the differences already outlined by Miller and Konorski the fact that reinforcement *depends* on the performance of the response in instrumental conditioning, whereas this reinforcement (absolute stimulus) is given in every case in the classical situation, whether the C.R. has been performed or not. This dependence of reinforcement upon reaction is probably the most obvious feature of the instrumental situation. As we have already seen, Skinner's experiment represents one of the cases in which the reaction can be conditioned from its first appearance, since the reaction appears 'spontaneously' and 'by accident'. Even so the reaction must belong to the animal's repertoire so that there is a reasonable chance of its appearing in this situation. From this point of view, the animal's hunger (and the fact that it is shut up), producing considerable spontaneous activity, is an important factor. However, it is still possible to establish conditioning with reactions produced in a different way in the first place.

One way is 'instrumentalize' unconditioned, even complex, reflexes. For example, the unconditioned reaction of scratching can be provoked by putting a piece of cottonwool in a cat's ear. If these reactions are followed by the administration of food, they occur much more frequently than unconditioned responses.[2] Moreover, they are still produced in the absence of any absolute stimulation so the *unconditioned* reaction has been *conditioned.* Soviet experimenters submitted to similar treatment the reactions of snuffling, sneezing, barking, yawning etc. of a dog that had been soaked in water, but the original reaction does not seem to have been entirely reproduced. The conditioned reaction

---

[1] Skinner used the term 'operant' for the second type (first in his classification). But, in addition, this term (as opposed to 'respondent' behaviour) refers to a more complex distinction between reactions which are given in response to a stimulus setting them off and reactions which are 'emitted' by the organism. In our opinion, this distinction (although an interesting one) does not cover the difference between classical and instrumental conditioning. Proof of this is the fact (described later) that reactions which are obviously responsive in Skinner's classification (unconditioned reactions) can also be 'instrumentalized'.

[2] Thorndike was the first (1898) to realize that the natural movements of scratching and licking in dogs and cats can be increased, if these movements become the means by which an animal can open its cage.

tends to degenerate into a sort of outline, or even an 'imitation', of the unconditioned movement (Jankowska and Soltysik, 1958).

One last way of obtaining the first reaction on which to set up the C.R. is to use direct, electrical stimulation from points attached to the cortex. This produces motor action which can be followed by the administration of food (Loucks, 1935). Under certain conditions[1] the movement produced in this way can also be 'instrumentalized'. After a number of trials, the action is produced spontaneously without any electric stimulation.

To sum up, the way in which the first reaction is obtained does not matter very much. Mechanically-induced movements, spontaneous activity, unconditioned (or previously conditioned) reactions, and responses to direct, electrical stimulation can all be conditioned. The important thing is to follow the first reaction, no matter how it has been obtained, by *positive reinforcement* so as to increase its frequency, strength and rapidity. It is possible to take the same examples and show that by using negative reinforcement the reaction will become less frequent, slower and weaker, and even eventually disappear altogether. Although it is not essential, a conditioned stimulus calling for differentiation can be used. Reinforcement is only made in cases where the reaction has been preceded by a particular signal. This signal becomes the only thing which will arouse the reaction and, finally, in organisms capable of such differentiation, the reaction cannot be provoked in the absence of the signal. This can also be done without using a specific signal, in which case the whole situation is the conditioned stimulus.

(c) PROTECTIVE ESCAPE CONDITIONING

As we have already indicated, it is essential to know which type of reinforcement is used in instrumental conditioning. Positive reinforcement, which encourages the appearance of the reaction and increases its strength, is often referred to as a *reward*. However, negative reinforcement causes the decrease and eventual disappearance of the reaction and so this is described as a *punishment*.

[1] These conditions are still being investigated. We shall content ourselves with stating that in certain cases the movement produced by electrical stimulation cannot be conditioned.

Nevertheless, punishment does not always make the reaction disappear. Supposing an electrode is attached to a particular point on a dog's skin (for example, its ear) and enough current is passed through to cause painful stimulation; it is decided to stop the current as soon as the dog makes a specific movement, for example, flexes its right, back paw; if the current is applied repeatedly, the dog soon begins to flex its paw when the electric current starts. This is a familiar, learning process: the reaction becomes more frequent, more rapid and more vigorous until it reaches its maximum point. The same sort of experiment has been carried out with rats on electrified metal bars. The rats can only stop the unpleasant stimulation by jumping on a particular bar. This kind of conditioning, usually very effective, is called *escape* conditioning, since it allows the subject of the experiment to escape from unpleasant stimulation.

This kind of C.R. can be classified with instrumental C.R.s obtained by either a reward or a reciprocal method. Hunger can also be a disagreeable stimulation which food ends, at least temporarily. In both cases, the C.R. is elaborated on a need (hunger in one case, pain in the other) and the *reduction of this need* is a determining factor in the reinforcement of the C.R. (Hull, 1943). Experiments have shown that conditioned reactions can be elaborated on a variety of needs (hunger, thirst, sexual needs, exploratory tendencies of 'curiosity', pain etc.).

The four possible procedures for instrumental conditioning can be summarized as follows:

TABLE I

	Procedure		Result
1	S + M—meat	S—no meat	S→ M
2	S + M—el. current	S—no current	S→∼M
3	S—meat	S + M—no meat	S→∼M
4	S—el. current	S + M—no current	S→ M

S = stimulus (or situation); M = movement; — = followed by; → = sets off; ∼ = absence of
(After Konorski, 1948.)

Procedures 1 and 2 outline the experiments (described earlier) carried out by Miller and Konorski or by Skinner (with reward or punishment). Procedure 4 is the escape procedure. Procedure 3 has not been described and is only included in the table to complete the diagram. This procedure has been checked, but it does not have much experimental interest.[1] This table gives a general picture of the principal ways in which instrumental, conditioned reactions can be obtained. However, it does leave out one conditioned reaction which is of considerable, practical and theoretical importance.

(D) CONDITIONED AVOIDANCE REACTIONS

This type of reaction occurs in a situation, similar to that of escape, in which an animal receives an electric shock after a signal (for example, the sound of a buzzer). The signal and the current are separated by an interval of, say, 5 seconds, but the experiment is set up in such a way that, if the dog makes a particular movement *before* the electric shock, then this is not administered. This reaction enables the dog to *avoid* punishment, and not just to stop it or escape from it. Experiments have shown that C.R.s are easily learnt under these conditions. Obviously the problem of the response's first appearance remains; but, provided the response chosen for reinforcement belongs to the animal's repertoire and does not occur too infrequently, the response can be well and truly conditioned after only a limited number of reinforcements. From then onwards, as soon as the C.S. is applied, the animal flexes its paw (if this is the movement chosen) and, in this way, it never receives an electric shock.

However, this very fact presents serious problems. As we shall see in more detail later, a C.R. disappears when it is no longer reinforced. However, a C.R. of avoidance can be maintained for a considerable number of trials without reinforcement; the animal reacts and never receives any punishment. But, if the situation is altered slightly, making it impossible for the animal to be punished, it still goes on reacting. If the electric current is cut off, so that the animal cannot receive a shock even if it does not bend its paw, there will be no change in the animal's behaviour, because it has no way of 'realizing' that the situation has changed. This point has led to considerable research. Various

[1] An extinction procedure which is not typical.

authors (Konorski, 1948; N. E. Miller, 1948; O. H. Mowrer, 1960) have put forward the idea that conditioned avoidance rests on a double process: firstly, conditioning of fear is established, since the unconditioned reaction produced by the electric shock (or whatever unpleasant stimulation is used) is, after several trials, produced by the signal preceding the shock in the form of a conditioned reaction of fear. This constitutes the motivation or need on which is elaborated the motor reaction capable of meeting this need. Several experimental illustrations have been given of this schema.

Thus the parallel development of a cardiac (acceleration of the heartbeats) and a motor C.R. was studied (Soltysik and Kowalska, 1960; Soltysik, 1960) in the course of avoidance conditioning in a dog. The reinforcement was an electric shock, the C.S. was a buzzer and the reinforced reaction was the flexion of the paw.

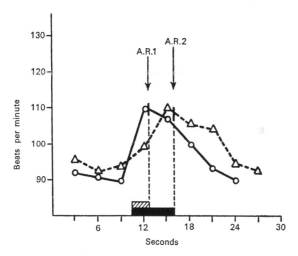

Fig. 2. Acceleration of heartbeats up to a constant rate before an avoidance reaction. (After S. Soltysik and M. Kowalska, *Acta Biol. Exper.*, 1960, **20**, 162.)

The avoidance response only occurs when the heartbeats reach about 110 per minute. Two groups of trials, divided up according to the latency of the avoidance reaction (about 2 seconds or about 5 seconds), are shown in the diagram. The latency is indicated by rectangles on the axis of the abscissae, also showing the duration of conditioned stimulus (which lasts until the avoidance response appears). The latter (A.R.) is marked by a vertical line. The heartbeats are counted in 3-second intervals.

The results show clearly the relationship between the acceleration of the heartbeats, which usually indicates fear, and the motor reaction. Figure 2 shows this relationship in connection with the latency of the avoidance reaction. This reaction only lasted until the heartbeats had reached a certain rate. The trials in which the avoidance reaction's latency was about 2 seconds and those in which it was about 5 seconds are shown in the graph by circles and triangles, respectively. The results all apply to the same dog. In addition, there was distinct cardiac deceleration after the instrumental C.R. which confirmed Konorski's idea that an avoidance reaction would inhibit the protective excitation (fear).

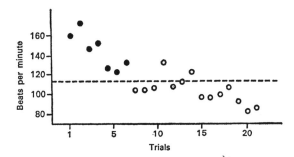

Fig. 3. Extinction of an avoidance reflex in a dog. (After S. Soltysik, *Acta. Biol. Exper.*, 1960, **20**, 176.)

Each circle represents a trial. The cardiac frequency is measured in 3-second intervals and the maximum taken for each trial. The black circles represent trials in which an avoidance response was observed, while the white circles represent trials in which there was no such response. The horizontal, dotted line represents the level of cardiac frequency (110 per minute) at which the C.R. appeared in response to the positive stimulus.

Fig. 3 shows the relationship between the cardiac reaction and the motor reaction in an 'extinction' situation.[1] The C.R. of avoidance almost disappeared when the heartbeats fell below the level of 110–115 per minute. With this dog the C.R., when it was elaborated, appeared at the same level.

This proves the close connection between a classical C.R.

[1] In fact this situation involves discrimination, since there is another conditioned stimulus which continues to be reinforced, but this distinction is not important here.

(acceleration of heartbeats) and an instrumental C.R. (paw movement) within an apparently homogeneous, conditioning situation. The first reaction (or the state that it reveals) can be regarded as a link in the chain leading to the second reaction.

An analysis of this apparently simple and common situation shows just how complex conditioning really is.

3 The elaboration of conditioned reactions in humans

Great prudence should be exercised in applying to humans the results of conditioned reactions studied in animals. There is no reason for believing that man's higher nervous activity is, by its nature, different from that of the more highly developed animals. Indeed everything seems to confirm their similarity, but man's psychic activity is infinitely more complex. Higher functions are superimposed on ordinary behaviour and control it. This explains why it is so difficult to obtain with any stability quite elementary, conditioned reactions in man. Man's awareness of different elements in a situation and the connections between them, the different interpretations that he can put on them, the motives that influence him, the attitudes he adopts and the decisions and 'strategies' (deliberate or otherwise) that he applies are all disturbing factors. To these should be added the relationship which is bound to exist between the human subject and the experimenter. For all these reasons, conditioning experiments carried out on humans cannot have the simplicity (which is, in any case, only relative) found in some experiments on animals. However, it is easier to experiment with children, because their intellectual development is not so advanced.

(A) SALIVARY CONDITIONED REACTIONS

In Pavlov's laboratory, Krasnogorski carried out conditioning of salivary responses in children. Saliva was collected in a small container fixed inside the mouth. Satisfactory results were obtained with young children, but beyond the age of 3 or 4 years the results became erratic (see Razran, 1933).

Razran (1936) attempted the elaboration of salivary C.R.s in adults (students). He placed rolls of dental cottonwool, which had been weighed beforehand, into his subject's mouth. This cottonwool was weighed again after a time to measure the amount of conditioned salivation. The amount of unconditioned salivation directly caused by the cottonwool was also checked. Razran found that the results of this method were unreliable. A determining factor was the subject's *attitude*, which could be affected by the instructions given. If the subject was told to associate the conditioned stimulus with the presentation of the food that he was going to eat. then conditioning was easily established. If, however, the subject was told to avoid this kind of association, conditioning was rarely obtained. Razran later (1939a) used this salivary technique again, but with better control of the subject's attitude. The subject was given false information about the object of the experiment. For example, he would be told that they were studying the effects of visual fatigue on digestion; he would then be asked to eat for periods of two minutes, during which a neutral stimulus would be presented a great many times. In this way, the subject was not aware of the experiment's objective, and Razran obtained positive results which confirmed the principal laws laid down by Pavlov.

(B) VISCERAL CONDITIONING

Visceral conditioning of the type described in animals has been obtained in humans.

Kourtsine and Sloupski carried out observations on a boy and girl, from the ages of 14 to 16, who had undergone an ablation of the oesophagus as a result of accidental burns, so it was possible to recreate the famous experiment of the 'imaginary' meal, first attempted by Pavlov, in which the subject ingests food that never reaches his stomach. With these young patients, Kourtsine and Sloupski found that the sound of the bell announcing the meal, accompanied by the clatter of the meal being prepared, caused abundant gastric secretion (Bykov, 1956; cf. Fig. 4). The conditioned stimuli were 'natural' ones, but they were effective, nevertheless. Similarly, an imaginary meal lasting a quarter of an hour produced considerable secretion for some time, with different characteristics for each type of food ingested (but not digested).

Slonim and Ponougaeva also discovered phenomena of thermic conditioning in humans very similar to those already found in animals. They studied respiratory changes in train drivers on trains between Leningrad and Ljubljana, a journey usually involving considerable variations in temperature. On this occasion, however, the temperature remained the same and they found that the gaseous changes were slighter on the return journey (back to Leningrad) than on the outward journey. In the first case, the signals received by the organism prepared it for a rise in temperature and not, as in the second case, for a drop in temperature. Other control experiments have confirmed their interpretation (Bykov, 1956).

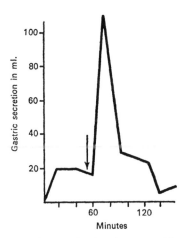

Fig. 4. Conditioned gastric secretion in a human subject. (From C. Bykov, *Le cortex et les organes internes*, Edit. Langues étrang., Moscow, 1956, p. 130.)

The arrow indicates the bell ringing and the table being laid.

Other important, visceral or neurovegetative conditioned reflexes are vaso-motor reactions, pulse rate, respiration, etc. Experiments carried out in this field show the existence and importance of conditioning phenomena. The conditions under which such reactions can be obtained are not always practicable (e.g. the salivary reaction quoted). Nevertheless, recent Soviet research has recorded some of these vegetative reactions in conjunction with other responses, in particular, with motor reactions. However, reactions which, without being very easily interpreted (there are very few of these), at least provide clearer *indications*

19

are preferable for the purposes of systematic research. Consequently salivary reactions in humans are rarely used. The two most common are eyelid reactions and electrodermal reactions.

(C) CONDITIONED EYELID REACTIONS

This reaction does present certain problems and various precautions have to be taken in its use. Many unconditioned stimuli cause this reaction, but the most commonly used is a puff of air blown on to the cornea. Mercury is then dropped into a tube and the strength of the unconditioned stimulus can be regulated by varying this drop. There are various ways of registering the response. Photography can be used, or the movement of a small indicator stuck to the eyelid can be measured by means of a potentiometer. However, the conditioned stimulus is usually a change in lighting on a luminous screen. This is better than putting a light on, for example, since the eye's adaptation to light must be carefully controlled.

The major difficulty is identifying these conditioned responses. The inertia of the eyelid reaction is so slight that it is easy to distinguish the C.R. from the unconditioned responses produced by the puff of air. If there is sufficient time between the C.S. and the U.S. (say, 500 m.secs.), the conditioned response should precede the U.S. so only those reactions that occur between the C.S. and the U.S. are recorded. However, some of these reactions cannot be conditioned: there may be spontaneous blinking in the intervening time. To avoid this, some researchers use an 'attention' signal before the C.S. when the subjects are instructed to blink. This minimizes the risk of a subject blinking in the few seconds after the signal. This in turn brings another problem: the signal may become a new C.S. and so the amount of time between the signal and the real C.S. must vary.

A study of reactions occurring between the C.S. and the U.S. shows that these are divided into two categories (Hilgard, 1931). In one category, called *alpha* responses, the eyelid closes very rapidly with very little latency (less than 100 m.secs.). This type usually appears in the first trial, but its frequency and magnitude decrease thereafter.[1] Responses with a higher latency do not

[1] In fact these are unconditioned responses produced by the conditioned stimulus, which is not strictly neutral in this case. If the experiment were to be

appear in the first trial and only develop gradually with the presentation of both C.S. and U.S. Only these responses can be conditioned, but another distinction must be made here. Some of these responses may be acquired voluntarily, since they are distinguished by a sudden, complete closing of the eyes which lasts until after the presentation of the unconditioned stimulus. This seems like a deliberate, avoidance reaction. Such reactions occur frequently with certain subjects, particularly if the U.S. is fairly strong. Other reactions occur gradually and erratically, and the subject tends to open his eyes before the U.S. These two types of reaction differ in their latency, since the first type appears between 200 and 300 m.secs. after the C.S., while the second type appears more than 300 m.secs. after it (Spence and Ross, 1959). Objective tests would seem to be necessary in order to avoid subjects who react voluntarily. It is obvious that the eyelid reaction, although widely used, does present considerable problems.

(D) ELECTRODERMAL CONDITIONED REACTIONS

Electrodermal (also known as psychogalvanic) reactions are widely used in conditioning. They can give an indication of the level of activation or affective tension, but this is incidental to their role in conditioning. These reactions can generally be conditioned without difficulty. The absolute stimulus is usually a fairly strong electric shock that the subject finds disagreeable, but not painful. The C.S. can be a sound, a light or any other external agent, but the unconditioned effect that it is likely to produce must be carefully controlled. More often than not, this stimulus has only to be presented alone a few times for it to become truly neutral. Its unconditioned effect disappears through familiarity. When this happens, it is presented again, but this time it is followed by the electric shock. Conditioning is usually established after a few trials only. However this can vary considerably from one person to another, apparently according to temperament. Anxious subjects tend to be conditioned more quickly than others, who may not be conditioned at all by the

carried out in darkness, there would be a risk of 'beta' responses with a slightly higher latency (120 to 240 m.secs.; Grant and Norris, 1947).

same strength of U.S. Conditioning may weaken[1] in some subjects and the C.R. disappear spontaneously in spite of reinforcement. The shock has, therefore, to be sufficiently strong to establish the C.R. and maintain it, although it has to be as weak as possible for obvious, ethical reasons. All these individual differences make it difficult to strike a balance.

Although it is strictly involuntary, a conditioned electrodermal reaction is not altogether independent of higher control. Here too, the attitude the subject adopts and the instructions he receives can affect the result. If the subject is told that there will be no more electric shocks (and if his previous experience leads him to *believe* the experimenter), the C.R. can weaken quite considerably. Secondary factors, such as the presence of the electrode through which the shock was administered, also play a part. If the electrode is taken away, the C.R. can weaken or disappear completely.

There are many other examples of classical conditioning in humans and they all lead to the same conclusion, i.e. the same general rules apply as for animals but all the complex conditions in a situation must be carefully analysed and controlled.

(E) INSTRUMENTAL CONDITIONED REACTIONS IN HUMANS

Psychological activity becomes more complex in this situation. This type of conditioning is directed towards a definite end that has already been classified as 'voluntary' behaviour in animals (Konorski), so, when a human subject is placed in a instrumental situation, the experimenter finds he is even more deeply involved in the field of voluntary activity. Skinner's box was really only a simplified version of Thorndike's 'problem box'. Every situation of this kind appears to a human subject as a problem to solve, and he obviously does this in a conscious and voluntary way, using previously acquired knowledge. Consequently all theorizing on this type of conditioning must be restricted to cases in which the subject is not already aware of the connection between the C.S., C.R. and the reinforcement. It is sometimes more effective to use

---

[1] This really stems from the unconditioned reaction produced by the shock (the absolute stimulus). If this gradually lessens through familiarity (cf. B. Cardu, 1954), the C.R. will naturally do the same thing.

subjects whose intellectual development (particularly in the use of words) is not too advanced.

Ivanov-Smolenski (1927) placed children in the following situation: the subject found himself alone in an empty room with a tube sloping down in front of him. The end of the tube had a glass cover. The experimenter, who watched the subject from the next room, provided some sort of neutral stimulus (a bell or a light) and then dropped a piece of chocolate down the tube. If the child squeezed a rubber bulb, he could lift the cover and take the chocolate: eventually he would learn to press the bulb when the signal went on. Using both normal and deficient children, Ivanov-Smolenski and his collaborators elaborated reactions which complied with the general laws of conditioning. However, it should be pointed out that, although he used a technique described as instrumental, Ivanov-Smolenski never made this distinction (generally recognized today) between the two types of conditioning situation.[1]

The method generally employed in Bekhterev's 'reflexology' studies (1926)[2] can also be included in this category. This method consists of giving a slight electric shock to the finger preceded by a signal. An attitude of avoidance, shown by a movement of the finger, develops. But it is very difficult to know whether this is *really* conditioning or voluntary behaviour. Moreover, if the subject feels that the experimenter is testing him, he can decide (courageously as he thinks) to keep his finger on the electrode. Pavlov himself severely criticized this method.

(F) 'VERBAL REINFORCEMENT' TECHNIQUE

Ivanov-Smolenski (1937, 1951, 1955; see also Povorinski, 1956) tried, in addition, to work out a more complicated procedure. His idea was to establish a conditioned schema of the simple, motor reaction of squeezing a rubber bulb. His point of departure was not an unconditioned reaction, but a previously conditioned reaction. When a subject is told to 'squeeze' a rubber bulb that he is holding in his hand, this verbal stimulus elicits a reaction of

[1] Ivanov-Smolenski did introduce another distinction between 'unconditiono-conditioned' and 'conditiono-conditioned' reflexes, depending on the nature of the basic absolute stimulus.

[2] It should be noted in passing that it is not correct to use the term 'reflex-ology' in connection with the work done by Pavlov and his school.

squeezing the bulb. This order (the absolute stimulus) can be preceded by a neutral stimulus, for example, a light. In Ivanov-Smolenski's opinion, this light normally became a C.S. eliciting the squeezing movement. In fact further reflection, confirmed by experiments (cf. Le Ny, 1960), shows that with adults everything depends on how the subject interprets the situation. Nevertheless, this method has produced some interesting results with young children, since it enables the relations between voluntary activity and verbal development to be studied in a genetic context (Luria, 1958). Although this method is based on classical conditioning, some experimenters do introduce instrumental reinforcement by saying 'Good' after the reactions they want to develop.

Although simple methods of instrumental motor conditioning are difficult to apply under laboratory conditions and have to be used with great care, there can be no doubt as to their importance. Failure is really caused by trying to interpret human activities, which are simple in appearance only, by means of psychological and physiological schemes that are too rudimentary. The fact that behaviour is easy to describe does not mean that it is easy to understand it psychologically. It is sometimes more profitable to apply a conditioned interpretation to one part or aspect of any complicated activity, temporarily ignoring other parts or aspects involving more complex processes. Many motor activities, or parts of these activities, are learnt in daily, psychological life through conditioned reinforcement.

(G) CONDITIONING IN THE VERBAL FIELD

Similar processes of conditioning occur in the verbal field. Only two illustrations will be given here (also see Chapter 26).

There is a rival theory to that of conditioning (as it is understood by Behaviourists of the S–R school) called the theory of *expectancy*. Humphreys (1939*b*) carried out the following experiment in order to defend this theory: his students were seated before two lights. After a preparatory signal, the left-hand light went on; this was the neutral stimulus. Five seconds later, the right-hand light went on; this was the absolute stimulus. The subjects' task was to guess whether the right-hand lamp would light up after the left-hand one. These guesses were the 'conditioned responses'. The idea was that the lighting of the right-hand lamp should provoke a certain response (which could be expressed verbally by the word "yes', for example). If the lighting of the right-hand lamp was *always* preceded by that of the left-hand one, then this became the signal, the C.S. for the response 'yes'. The subject could answer 'Yes' as soon as the left-hand lamp went on, thus anticipating the right-hand lamp going on.

If the 'yeses' given after the signal are counted, they start at about 50 per cent and reach 100 per cent after a certain number of trials (24 in Humphreys's experiments). With another objective in mind (about which we shall say more later), Humphreys added to the subjects 'conditioned' in this way a second group of subjects for whom the lighting of the left-hand lamp was only followed by that of the right-hand one in *50 per cent of the trials*. The situation had not changed basically. It had merely become a little more complicated. As Humphreys said, it was still a question of a 'situation akin to conditioning'. All the experiments involving this method demonstrated the same general laws.

Another situation, which is also 'akin to conditioning', is that of pairs of associated elements learnt by heart: for example, the word 'pencil', followed by the word 'table', is presented visually a number of times to the subjects. The sight of the word 'table' will evoke an identification response in the subject, which will be accompanied by an explicit response when he says 'table'. After several trials, the subjects will be able to say 'table' when they see the word 'pencil' before the word 'table' is presented to them. Other experiments using this method of anticipation follow the same schema, but they involve more than one pair of objects. The second object is the absolute stimulus which produces an absolute verbal response.[1] The first object is the neutral stimulus, which quickly becomes conditioned and evokes the anticipatory verbal response. A study of mnemonic mechanisms by this method has shown that the conditioning schema applies here (cf. Chapter 14).

A technique inspired by Skinner's methods (1957) was used recently to condition verbal behaviour. This consisted of re-inforcing certain aspects by a reward of a social nature. For example, Cohen, Kalish, Thurston and Cohen (1954) presented

---

[1] i.e. previously learnt.

subjects with 80 cards in succession, each card bearing a verb, currently in use, in the past tense. Under each of these words there were six pronouns, *I, We, He, They, She* and *You*, arranged at random in a different order each time. The subjects were asked to make up phrases using the verb shown and beginning with any one of the pronouns. The experimenter said 'Good' in a flat, neutral tone[1] to any phrase beginning with 'I' or 'We' to the subjects in the experimental group. He said nothing at all to the subjects in the control group. In this group the frequency of phrases beginning with 'I' or 'We' remained the same throughout, but their frequency in the experimental group increased quite considerably. Questions put to the subjects after the experiment revealed no awareness of the connection between the form of the phrases and their reinforcement. However, experimenters, who have repeated this type of experiment, are far from agreed on this point, and the role of awareness remains an important point for further investigation.

4   Temporary connections

Naturally the main feature of conditioning is the presence of a reaction, but does this reaction play an absolutely essential part in conditioning? Prokofiev and Zeliony (1926) were the first, using human subjects, to try following a neutral stimulus (the sound of a metronome) by another neutral,   but no longer unconditioned, stimulus (in this case, rhythmic stimulation of the skin). After a number of trials, they transformed the second stimulus into a C.S. by following it up with an unpleasant, electric stimulus causing a protective reaction. The stimulation of the skin, thus conditioned, began to evoke the protective reaction and it became clear that the *metronome also* evoked this reaction, meaning that it had been associated[2] with the cutaneous stimulation from the beginning, i.e. before the electric stimulation had been introduced. In Pavlov's laboratory, they called this

---

[1] Other experimenters prefered a vague sound like 'Hmm'.

[2] In fact the method used in this first experiment contained a mistake. The metronome and skin stimulation were used again after this second stimulus had been conditioned. Therefore the action of the first stimulus could be attributed to second-order conditioning (referred to later). This mistake rendered the results of the earlier research invalid and the phenomenon had to be re-established under the correct conditions.

phenomenon (which had been reproduced in humans on several occasions[1]) a *temporary connection.* This is sometimes considered to be the basis of the conditioned reaction itself, since the connection is fundamentally established between the two stimuli. Possibly the stimuli within the temporary connection are not indifferent to one another and, like all new stimuli, they give rise to an *orienting-investigatory reaction* which is conditioned and plays a role in transfer. This would apply, in particular, to the second stimulus.

Various authors, notably Brogden (1939, 1947) who called it *sensory* conditioning or preconditioning, have provided evidence of the existence of this phenomenon in both animals and humans. What have been called, perhaps rashly, 'hallucinations' (cf. Ellson, 1941, 1942; Dostalek, 1960) have been studied in the same situation, but a whole series of phenomena has still to be elucidated.

Electro-cortical conditioning, first produced accidentally by Durup and Fessard, can be included under the heading of temporary connections. The presentation of a light stimulus produces a reaction causing the alpha rest rhythm to cease in most people. A sound stimulus does not usually produce the same reaction, but, if it is followed several times by a light, the sound begins to interrupt the alpha waves. Electroencephalogram records indicate that a kind of sensory conditioning has taken place (Jasper and Shagass, 1941; Popov and Popov, 1954; Fessard and others, 1958).

Pseudo-conditioning. When an experimenter wishes to prove that conditioning has taken place, he must be on his guard against artifacts. If, in a given situation, a dog is given a series of fairly strong, electric shocks and if, at the same time, a series of neutral stimuli (for example, sounds) are presented at random (i.e. not in conjunction with the shocks), there is every chance that the dog will show fear, expressed by various reactions, when the sound alone is later presented again. This does not mean that the sound has become a C.S., since there was no systematic conjunction between it and the shock. In fact the whole situation

---

[1] Some Russians authors have denied that it is possible to establish a temporary connection between indifferent stimuli *in dogs*, since all their results were negative when they investigated this point (cf. Dostalek, 1960). However, most of the results obtained recently, using more precise methods, are positive.

is capable of evoking fear, and not only the sound, but any other stimulus could elicit this response. This is called 'sensibilization' or pseudo-conditioning. The second term refers, of course, to the critical stimulus which has not been truly conditioned.

This procedure is often used as a control to ensure that real conditioning has been established. If a neutral stimulus S_N produces a reaction after being presented with an absolute stimulus, but, if the same stimulus S_N also produces a reaction after a series of non-systematic associations in a given situation, the experimenter must be on his guard against possible pseudo-conditioning in the first instance.

2 Laws governing the function of conditioned reactions

So far we have been mainly concerned with the elaboration of conditioned reactions, which are generally considered to be responses learnt in accordance with one of the two schemes described: conditioned reactions of the classical or of the instrumental type. Conditioned reactions are distinguished by certain conditions necessary for their establishment. As we have already seen, these conditions can become so complicated in humans that it is difficult to find simple, conditioning schemes. Even after they have been established, conditioned reactions do not remain the same. They evolve in accordance with certain, well-defined laws and they may also display certain characteristics. There laws and characteristics must form part of any study of conditioning. After Pavlov had discovered conditioned reflexes and the conditions for their establishment, he used this discovery as a *method* for the investigation of what he called *higher nervous activity*. We shall now study the laws governing the *function* of conditioned reactions, once they have been elaborated.

1 *Extinction*

(A) We have already seen that reinforcement (absolute stimulus in classical C.R.s and reward or punishment in instrumental C.R.s) is an essential condition for the establishment of conditioning. It is also essential, if conditioning is to be maintained. In laboratory experiments, reinforcement is often omitted from certain trials in order to prove that the conditioned stimulus alone can produce the response, but this does not mean that the C.S. could go on acting in this way without reinforcement. In fact the omission of reinforcement in a given trial is a method of observation which may defeat its own object, since it is impossible to observe the situation in this way without changing it.

If all reinforcement is omitted, the change is radical. The conditioned reaction begins to weaken, its magnitude diminishes, its latency increases, and it occurs less and less frequently until it disappears altogether (Pavlov, 1953). Since the C.S. no longer produces any reaction, it would appear to have become a neutral stimulus as far as that particular reaction is concerned. This is the reverse of elaboration, *extinction*. The slower and more difficult the elaboration of the C.R. proves to be, the easier and quicker its extinction, and *vice versa*, so the extinction and the establishment of a C.R. are inversely proportional.

(B) The factors that play a part in the establishment of a C.R. also influence its extinction. In the case of salivary reactions, extinction will be easier if the period without food was shorter, meaning a weaker C.R. In general any lessening of the need or drive in a C.R. will have this effect. Similarly a stronger C.S., producing a stronger C.R., will make extinction more difficult (Pavlov, 1953). Finally, if learning involves a large number of reinforcements, an equally large number of presentations without reinforcement will be required to extinguish the C.R. *Resistance to extinction*, which can be measured by the number of trials without reinforcement required to extinguish a C.R., provides a valid indication of this C.R's strength. In fact, in its own way, it is a characteristic (like magnitude, latency, frequency, etc.) of a C.R. (cf. Williams, 1938; Perin, 1942).

(C) Should it be assumed that a stimulus which has been extinguished is really neutral (i.e. exactly the same as it was before conditioning)? Several facts seem to indicate that this is not so. In the first place, there is the effect produced by a parasitic stimulus, foreign to the situation (Zavadski's experiment, quoted in Pavlov, 1953): if an unexpected noise, something touching it or any disturbance (for instance, the experimenter's entry into the room) stimulates an animal to which a previously extinguished C.S. is presented, an unusual thing happens; instead of diminishing the C.R., the foreign stimulus strengthens it. Indeed, if the C.R. has just disappeared, the parasitic stimulus may revive it so the old C.S. cannot have become truly neutral, since it has retained its capacity to evoke the reaction. The parasitic stimulus restores this capacity to its full effect.

Another fact confirms this point: a neutral stimulus, which has been conditioned and extinguished, is presented again to the subject in conjunction with reinforcement; if this stimulus, inactive after extinction, has really become neutral again and is as ineffective as it was before conditioning, the same number of trials will be required to re-establish conditioning; but, in fact, far fewer trials will be needed to produce conditioning on the second occasion. In practice, a few trials only reactivate the inactive stimulus.

(D) SPONTANEOUS RECOVERY

One last phenomenon is even more characteristic of extinction. If a stimulus is not presented immediately after extinction of a C.R., it will be found to have completely recovered its effect when it is administered after a lapse of time. This stimulus, which has been successfully extinguished so that it no longer produces the C.R. and which has not been reinforced since the last (negative) trial, will be once more capable of evoking the C.R. This phenomenon of *spontaneous recovery* is very significant, since it proves beyond doubt that the temporary connection *extinguished* had not been *obliterated*, but had survived; it had simply been prevented from appearing. This fact provides the strongest argument in support of the theory (defended by Pavlov, 1953) that attributes extinction to *inhibition* which can stop a C.R., but which is likely to disappear in time.

Spontaneous recovery is itself governed by certain laws. The greater the interval which separates the new trial using the C.S. from the last extinction trial, the more complete the recovery (Ellson, 1938). If a C.R., spontaneously recovered in this way, is submitted to a series of trials using the C.S. without reinforcement, extinction will occur again and the C.R. will disappear. However, fewer tests will be needed to achieve this extinction. Spontaneous recovery can be produced again after a while, but the C.R. will be weaker and more easily extinguished. It is thus possible to produce several spontaneous recoveries, each successively weaker, and several extinctions, each successively easier.

However, if the C.S. is reinforced after spontaneous recovery, the situation described earlier recurs and the C.R. can easily be restored to its original level.

The facility with which spontaneous recovery can be achieved is obviously linked to the degree of extinction. If extinction is not fully accomplished and the C.R. is merely weakened, it will recover its original strength in part or in full. However, if the old conditioned stimulus is still applied without reinforcement after the extinguished C.R. has disappeared, there will be little or no recovery (Razran, 1939*b*). Extinction can, therefore, be made more thorough, even in the absence of any response. This 'superextinction', which brings the C.R. below zero, so to speak, is also an argument in favour of the Pavlovian interpretation of extinction by inhibition.

(E) EXTINCTION IN HUMANS

The results that we have set out so far were mostly obtained in conditioning experiments on animals, but the same results can be found in humans. Electrodermal or eyelid reactions disappear very quickly, if the absolute stimulus is not presented, in the same way as a dog stops salivating after several trials without food. The same thing applies to instrumental conditioning. When the mechanism for sending pellets of food into a Skinner's box ceases to function, the rat presses the lever less and less frequently until it gives up completely. In some French cities there are machines at bus stops which give you a numbered ticket showing your place in the queue. The ticket is obtained by pressing a bar and the machine, when empty, provides a situation similar to that in a Skinner's box. The psychologist can study the varying rate of extinction of the action of pressing the bar in people using the machine; and, if he returns the next day at the same time, he can observe its spontaneous recovery.

Of course many phenomena occur consciously in humans and so become more complex.

31

(F) EXTINCTION AND EFFORT

Mowrer and Jones (1943) carried out research into the part played by one, very controversial factor in extinction. They trained rats to press a lever in a Skinner's box. During training the lever was balanced by different weights, 5 grams, 42·5 grams and 80 grams. For the purposes of extinction, they divided the rats up into three groups. The weight was always 5 grams for the first group, 42·5 grams for the second and 80 grams for the third. They found that the heavier the weight was, the quicker the extinction. Solomon (1948) confirmed these results in a study also using rats. The rats had to leap over gaps of varying widths. The conclusion to be drawn from these results would seem to be that fatigue is an important factor in extinction. This resulted in a revival of the theory of extinction through fatigue (Miller and Dollard, 1941; Hull, 1943) against which Pavlov fought strongly. In this new form of the theory, fatigue was thought to generate 'reactive inhibition' leading to extinction.

Nevertheless, reflexes, which are not apparently tiring and which we can repeat thousands of times a day (provided that they are reasonably spread out), such as blinking, can also be effectively extinguished. This is equally true of most visceral reactions involving little effort.

Consequently effort should be regarded as a factor facilitating extinction, but not determining it.

(G) INTERMITTENT REINFORCEMENT AND PROLONGED
   EXTINCTION

We shall now return briefly to the problems of elaborating C.R.s. All the cases described so far have involved *constant* presentation of reinforcement, i.e. when a succession of repeated trials have led to conditioning, all these trials have been identical in that they have all been followed by reinforcement. However, a different procedure is possible. Reinforcement can be given *intermittently* only, with some trials reinforced and others not. If there is a definite system to the order of reinforcement, two things are learnt instead of one. For example, reinforcement and non-reinforcement can be alternated and an animal is capable of learning this alternation. More complicated systems can be

32

devised to establish an animal's capabilities in this type of learning.

A more interesting situation is that in which there is no system and reinforcement and non-reinforcement are distributed at random. There need only be a proportion or *ratio of reinforcement*; for example, 50 per cent of the trials can be reinforced in any order. The C.R. will still be established without difficulty and the final result will not be appreciably different from that obtained by constant reinforcement. The difference only becomes apparent in extinction.

Humphreys (1939*a*) was the first to demonstrate the existence of an interesting phenomenon in this situation. He conditioned eyelid reactions in three groups of subjects. Some received 100 per cent reinforcement and others received only 50 per cent reinforcement. The third group was a control group. There were 96 trials in all and the frequency of response was about the same in the first two groups. Extinction was then carried out with very different results. The reactions of subjects who had received constant reinforcement decreased sharply and stabilized at a much lower rate of frequency, whereas the decrease in the reactions of subjects who had received intermittent reinforcement was *slighter and much slower*. Humphreys (1940) obtained the same results with electrodermal reactions in humans. The situation recurs with the same results in the verbal anticipation method 'akin to conditioning' previously described (Humphreys, 1939*b*). Earlier experiments on animals had revealed the same phenomenon: extinction was always slower and more difficult after intermittent reinforcement than after constant reinforcement. Systematic studies (for example, Weinstock, 1954) have shown that the lower the percentage of previous reinforcement, the slower the extinction of the C.R. will be. These results have given rise to much theoretical debate. At first sight, a situation with intermittent reinforcement seems to be a long series of conditioning, partial extinction, re-conditioning, extinction, etc. If this were so, C.R.s which had received only 50 per cent reinforcement would already be partially extinct and real extinction (with no reinforcement at all) would be *more* rapid than in the case of C.R.s previously submitted to the same number of trials with 100 per cent reinforcement. In fact observation shows that the reverse is true. Various interpretations of this phenomenon have been put forward, but none have been satisfactorily substantiated.

2 *Generalization of stimuli*

(A) CONDITIONED GENERALIZATION

The discovery of this far-reaching and important phenomenon resulted from experiments carried out by Krasnogorski and M. K. Petrova (Pavlov, 1953). Their C.S. was stimulation of the skin in a particular spot. They found that stimulation of any other part of the skin in the same region as the original C.S. also produced a salivary reaction which was only slightly weaker than the normal C.R. The reaction grew weaker, the further the stimulation was from the original spot. Additional experiments all produced the same result: stimuli *which have never been reinforced* can evoke C.R.s in the same way as C.S. They combined all the traditional stimuli in Pavlov's laboratory (e.g. a metronome, a light, a whistle and tactual stimulation) in every possible way, using one as the C.S. and the other as a test stimulus, and they obtained the same result every time: the test stimulus produced a conditioned reaction which was equal to at least one-third of the original reaction (cf. Razran, 1949*a*).

It was also possible to establish quantitative relations by means of precise measurement. Using musical stimuli (notes of the scale), Pavlov demonstrated that their conditioning action became less effective, the further away the sounds were (either higher or lower in the scale) from the original C.S. Using sounds that could be physically measured in vibrations per second and collecting the saliva produced, Kupalov (1955) was able to draw a continuous curve which drops on either side of the original C.S. (Fig. 5). This relation between the strength of the reaction and the distance separating the C.S. from the other stimuli is called a *generalization gradient*. Many experiments have shown that such a gradient exists for the probability, the latency and the resistance of a response to extinction as well as for its magnitude. There is no difference between instrumental and classical C.R.s in this field. The important factor in generalization is always the *similarity* (or its reverse, the remoteness) between the stimuli tested and the original conditioned stimulus. This similarity can be expressed in various ways, but the best method is usually physical measurement of stimuli. The existence of generalization means that the parameters of stimulus and situation must be clearly defined in every conditioning experiment.

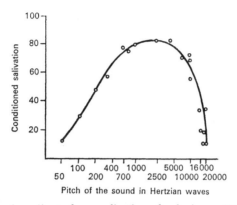

Fig. 5. Bilateral gradient of generalization of a dog's conditioned salivary reaction as a function of the sound C.S.'s pitch. (After P. S. Kupalov, *Fisiol. nerv. prots.*, 1955, p. 63.)

A particular type of similarity, connected with the intensity of stimuli, merits special mention, because it produces generalization effects that seem quite different from those noted elsewhere. In this case the absolute action of the intensity of the stimulus is combined with the generalization itself. Stimuli which are stronger than the original C.S. can produce reactions which are barely weaker (or even stronger) than the real C.R.s. On the other hand, with stimuli less intense than the original C.S., reactions are weak and diminish rapidly as the intensity decreases.[1] However this superposition of two distinct effects does not mean that this phenomenon is basically different from that produced by other forms of similarity.

There have been numerous experiments on generalization in humans. Hovland (1937a) started with electrodermal conditioning, using a pure tone made by a generator. He had previously obtained from a group of observers psycho-physical estimations resulting in the use of four stimuli separated by 25 differential

[1] In this connection a quantitative analysis of many experiments in Pavlov's laboratory can also be found in Razran's article (1949a).

gradations. He then conditioned half his subjects using a stimulus of 153 Hz and he tested stimuli of 468, 1,000 and 1,967 Hz. The other half of his subjects received the reverse treatment, the C.S. being the sound of 1,967 Hz. The overall results showed the existence of a generalized reaction, since all the stimuli produced the electrodermal conditioned response. A gradient can be drawn when the distance separating the sounds in differential subjective gradations is taken as the reference value.

Hovland also found a generalization effect when he varied the intensity of the sound stimulus (1937*b*) in this situation. Finally he came upon another, equally important phenomenon, discovered by Pavlov, namely *generalization of extinction*. This time he conditioned all four stimuli (using the same sounds as before). Each was presented six times in conjunction with an electric shock. At the end of this stage of the experiment, all four had become C.S.s and produced similar responses. He then extinguished one of the stimuli (either 468 Hz or 1,967 Hz) by presenting it 16 times without reinforcement. The other stimuli were not presented. When he had achieved extinction with the stimulus selected, he tested all four stimuli. He found that the C.R.s to all four stimuli had weakened and that the degree of weakening depended on the proximity of the stimulus tested to the previously extinguished stimulus. Clearly this stimulus had generalized the other three, even though these had never been presented without reinforcement. A generalization gradient can be drawn here.

(B) GENERALIZATION IN VOLUNTARY BEHAVIOUR

Generalization occurs in activities which are not strictly conditioned and which show conscious and voluntary features.

E. J. Gibson (1939), using tactual stimuli, Brown, Bilodeau and Baron (1951), using luminous stimuli in a visual-spatial dimension, and Le Ny (1957), using the same auditory stimuli as Hovland, all found characteristic generalization effects in voluntary reactions. For example, if a subject was instructed to press a key as soon as he heard a particular stimulus and not to respond to any other stimuli, these other stimuli still produced reactions. These 'wrong' reactions were distributed as a function of the similarity between stimuli, i.e. the nearer a stimulus was to the positive stimulus, the more incorrect responses it produced. The gradient of errors in this case is the same as a gradient of generalization and can be treated as such.

Generalization effects are usually found (Le Ny, 1961) in learning involving verbal anticipation (e.g. Hovland) where meaningless words are used as stimuli. Here similarity between words is purely a question of form and lies in the number of sounds or letters that the words may have in common. The same

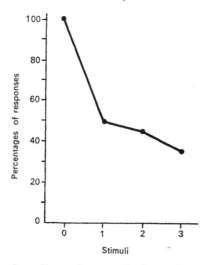

Fig. 6. Unilateral gradient of errors during voluntary discrimination when speed is required. (J. F. Le Ny, *Année psychol.*, 1957, **57**, 333.)
The stimuli are sounds equidistant in a range of tonal pitch.

multiple effects of generalization can be found in learning verbal elements (words or syllables) by heart. An analysis of errors (when subjects associate an element with an inadequate stimulus) shows that the more similar the incorrect stimulus is to the correct one, the more likely it is to evoke a response. In this type of situation, the law of generalization enables the researcher to predict and interpret many phenomena of memory.

(c) SEMANTIC GENERALIZATION

The major feature in generalization is similarity between stimuli, but all the examples given so far involve physical similarity and

37

there is another sort of similarity which can best be seen in the verbal field, namely similarity of meaning or sense.

It was discovered in Ivanov-Smolenski's laboratory, during experiments on children with the motor technique described earlier, that the efficiency of a stimulus could be generalized by means of its verbal name. If a C.R. was elaborated by means of a metronome, the word 'metronome' was capable of evoking the reaction. In the same way, a reaction conditioned by a blue light would be set off by the word 'blue' (Ivanov-Smolenski, 1937, 1955).

This generalization of the 'direct' stimulus (belonging to the 'first signal system', to use Pavlov's terminology) with the verbal stimulus (belonging to the 'second signal system') has its counterpart in the generalization of the verbal stimulus to the direct stimulus. Generalization also occurs between two verbal stimuli when the words have a similar meaning. Razran (1939) demonstrated *semantic generalization*, using his method of salivary conditioning in humans. Taking the words *style, urn, freeze* and *surf* as conditioned stimuli, he found greater generalization with their respective synonyms, *fashion, vase, chill* and *wave*, than with their homonyms, *stile, earn, frieze* and *serf*. This proved that semantic generalization is stronger than sensory generalization. In other words, similarity between the meaning of words is more powerful than any outward resemblance of form.

Razran (1949*b*) later showed that semantic generalization occurs not only between synonyms, but also between antonyms and between words of varying relationships of meaning, such as subordination, co-ordination, superordination and synecdoche. In all these cases, the test word which has not been reinforced is capable of producing a salivary response in the same way (albeit, to a lesser extent) as the conditioned stimulus to which it is related. The phenomenon of semantic generalization has played an important part in the emergence of objective interpretations of meaning in connection with theories of conditioning (cf. Le Ny, 1960*b* and Chapter 26).

3 Discrimination

(A) We have just seen how stimuli which have not been reinforced can still evoke a C.R., but it is possible to prevent this

38

happening. Using a dog, Pavlov demonstrated that a sound could be made into a stimulus capable of provoking a salivary C.R., while another stimulus, only one-eighth of a tone different, had no effect. Obviously there was discrimination (in this case, very precise discrimination) between the two stimuli. At first Pavlov thought that this discrimination could be established spontaneously by simple repetition of the C.S. with its reinforcement. This method does eventually consolidate the positive conditioned connection, but it does not eliminate generalization, although it does make it evolve. Stimuli differing from the C.S. could still evoke the C.R. after several trials. It seemed that the only way to obtain discrimination was to use contrast, i.e. sometimes presenting the conditioned stimulus followed by its reinforcement, and sometimes presenting the stimulus or stimuli to be rendered ineffective (Pavlov, 1953). A sound of 1,200 Hz must be presented repeatedly without reinforcement, while a sound of 1,000 Hz must be repeatedly reinforced, in order to make them into a *negative* stimulus (i.e. a stimulus which will not evoke the C.R.) and a conditioned stimulus, respectively. This method applies to both classical C.R.s and instrumental C.R.s. In order to obtain extremely precise discrimination (e.g. between 1,000 and 1,010 Hz), Pavlov (1953) demonstrated that it is better to start with very obvious and distinct discrimination, gradually moving nearer to the discrimination desired. The limits of an animal's discriminative ability, using a given sense, can be determined by this method.

(B) Conditioned discrimination follows certain well-defined laws. Some of these laws emphasize its resemblance to extinction. For example, the response to the positive C.S. is normally conditioned first and no negative stimulus is introduced in this phase. It is only introduced when the C.R. is established. Initially it will produce a reaction (caused by generalization), but lack of reinforcement gradually weakens this reaction until it disappears. If a parasitic stimulus is presented with the negative stimulus at this point, the reaction often reappears (Beliakov's experiment, in Pavlov, 1953). De-discrimination (or disinhibition) has taken place.

No systematic study has been made here of a phenomenon similar to spontaneous recovery; but it is a fact that, in conditioning laboratories where daily sessions are held, the first trial with a negative stimulus will often produce a reaction on one day, although the same stimulus produced no reaction at the end of the session on the previous day. The 'extinguished' reaction to the negative stimulus has reappeared spontaneously. Only when discrimination has been solidly established can this reaction be retained after a rest interval.

Record of an experiment carried out by Beliakov showing de-discrimination by a parasitic stimulus

Time	Stimulus (30 seconds)	Salivation in 30 seconds	
12.30	S+	3·5	Reinforced
1.00	S—	o	
1.20	S+	3	Reinforced
1.35	S— accompanied by smell of amyl acetate	2	

The stimuli S+ and S— are two sounds. The difference between them is one-eighth of a tone.

Another way to revive a reaction is to raise the organism's level of excitability. In the case of alimentary reactions, the animal has only to be left without food for a few hours and discrimination disappears. Hunger makes the reaction to the negative stimulus reappear. An injection of caffeine, raising the general level of excitability, has the same effect (Nikiforovski, in Pavlov, 1953).

However, the usual method is to establish the C.R. to the positive stimulus first. When this has been accomplished, the negative stimulus can be presented alone several times until its effect weakens. If the positive stimulus is presented again, the C.R. that it produces will, in turn, be weaker. The extinction of the negative stimulus has become generalized to the positive stimulus, clearly proving that the more closely the positive stimulus resembles the negative stimulus, the stronger the effect. All these facts have led to the conclusion that discrimination, like extinction, should be attributed to a process of *inhibition* which, without stopping the excitatory process caused by the (positive) conditioned stimulus, superimposes itself on this stimulus and hinders its action.

In psychology there are many discriminating situations which cannot properly be described as conditioned: for example, in perception, in motor activities such as reaction time in choosing, in verbal learning, in the solving of problems and in various intellectual tasks. Many of these situations resemble conditioned discrimination so closely that the laws governing the two seem very similar or even identical.

4 Delayed and trace conditioning

Discrimination and inhibition can also occur in the temporal sphere.

In classical experiments in Pavlov's laboratory, reinforcement is given shortly after the beginning of the C.S., generally while the latter is still acting. The interval between the beginning of the C.S. and the reinforcement can be increased, in which case the C.R. itself tends to appear later. For example, if the meat powder is given to the dog two minutes after the start of the C.S., the animal will only begin to salivate two minutes after the start of the C.S. This result is generally achieved only after considerable training during which the reaction becomes 'delayed', hence the name *delayed conditioning* given to this phenomenon. In the case of considerable delay, the animal has to be trained gradually, starting with short intervals which grow progressively longer.

In a similar situation, reinforcement is given a long time after the beginning of the C.S., which ceases in the intervening time. For example, a stimulus lasting 5 seconds is presented and 60 seconds after it begins reinforcement is administered. In this case too, the animal tends to respond at the moment when reinforcement should come; in other words, it adjusts the delay in its reaction to the delay in reinforcement. In fact what evokes the C.R. is not the stimulus itself, but its trace, so this is called *trace conditioning*. It seems as if the animal's ability to delay its reaction should be once again attributed to a process of inhibition. The way in which the delay gradually increases proves that it must be acquired in opposition to the animal's first impulse, which would be to react immediately after the presentation of the signal. Moreover, the presence of a parasitic stimulus during the interval can make the reaction reappear, so there is also disinhibition in this situation (Pavlov, 1953).

The phenomena of discrimination and trace reactions occur in the same form in instrumental conditioning, where they may even be combined. In an experiment done by Lawicka (1959), the animals had three feeding troughs in a work-room. Above each trough there was a buzzer. One of these would buzz for several seconds. This was a signal to the animal that it would find food in that trough, but the animal was tied on its platform and only released a few minutes later. Cats and dogs react well in this situation. Some dogs are capable of remaining quite calm, and even indifferent, for as much as ten minutes on their platform before going straight to the trough whose buzzer has sounded. Additional experiments have confirmed that the trace of the stimulus 'kept in reserve' evokes the correct action.

5 Conditioned inhibitors

A form of discrimination involving compositive stimulation has been used quite often in Pavlov's laboratory. An isolated stimulus (for example, a light) is first transformed into a C.S. by constant reinforcement. Then, on a number of occasions, it is preceded by another stimulus which is allowed to act alone for several seconds. For example, a subject hears the sound of a metronome for 30 seconds and, at the end of this time, a light goes on, but the sound of the metronome continues. This combination is not reinforced. In the first trials, the light (accompanied by the metronome) will still produce the C.R., but this will gradually disappear as the trials are not reinforced. Thereafter the light alone will still be an efficient C.S., but it will have no effect when it is preceded by the metronome. Pavlov called this a *conditioned inhibitor*: its presence inhibits the conditioned action of the light. To prove that this effect is really linked to a specific stimulus (the metronome), this stimulus has only to be applied with a different conditioned stimulus. If in a C.R. previously elaborated by mechanical stimulation of the skin on the same animal, the stimulus is preceded by the sound of the metronome, it is rendered ineffective straightaway and produces no salivation (cf. Pavlov, 1953).

The same procedure can be used with an instrumental reaction; for example, when the animal places its paw on the eating trough. In this case, the conditioned inhibitor produces behaviour denoting 'a lack of interest' on the animal's part. It will turn its head away, sit down and pay no marked attention to the C.S., as if this has already lost all significance.

This technique of conditioned inhibitors is quite often used (in preference to discrimination of similar stimuli), in laboratories following Pavlovian methods, to estimate the inhibitory capacity of an animal in preference to discrimination of similar stimuli.

6 Secondary conditioning

The forms of conditioning described so far are all simple forms, even though they may reveal fairly complicated phenomena from other points of view. In fact only avoidance conditioning seems to have involved a double process.

However, behaviour with several links in the chain can be created on the basis of simple conditioning. This is the case in conditioning of more than one order. Frolov produced the first example of such a phenomenon. He established a normal, alimentary-salivary C.R., using a metronome. Then he presented a new stimulus to the animal, a black square, followed repeatedly by the metronome, but he did not give it any food. After repeating this a number of times, he found that the black square produced salivation. He had thus established *second-order conditioning*, proved by the fact that the previously conditioned stimulus was the reinforcing agent, and not the meat. Nevertheless the second-order C.R. was weaker than the first-order C.R. (the normal C.R. produced by the metronome). Presumably two opposite processes are at work: in the second phase of the experiment, when the metronome is presented without any *primary* reinforcement (the meat), its effect tends to be extinguished, i.e. its reinforcing power, which should be transferred to the black square, tends to weaken with repetition. This makes second-order conditioning experiments difficult. Third-order conditioned reactions have been obtained in dogs, but beyond that extinction takes place faster than the transfer of the conditioned effect (Pavlov, 1953).

The phenomenon is of a slightly different character in instrumental conditioning, since the reinforcement is different, but its basic nature is the same. Wolfe (1936) and Cowles (1937) demonstrated this effect in monkeys. First the monkeys were taught to throw counters into a machine, which gave them a grape each time. The second phase consisted of a discrimination test: the animals had to make a choice out of 5 boxes, the reward being either a grape or a counter. In the first place, the frequency of the right choice was 93 per cent whereas it was 74 per cent in the second (obviously more than just chance), so the counter seemed to have become, to a lesser extent, a reward like the grape. This is usually called *secondary reinforcement* (rather than second-order conditioning) in order to emphasize that it is the reinforcing property which is conditioned and transferred from the primary reinforcement to a stimulus which had previously been neutral.

Extinction does cause certain problems here, but the laws governing the appearance of these problems do contain a means of lessening them. The method consists of intermittent reinforcement which, as we have already seen, increases resistance to extinction. In fact intermittent double reinforcement is usually employed. Zimmerman (1957) trained rats to run down a corridor towards their food when they heard a buzzer and a door in the box opened. He gradually introduced intermittent reinforcement, making the food accessible once every eight presentations of the stimulus only. He then trained the rats to press a lever in a Skinner's box and rewarded them intermittently with the sound of the buzzer and the door opening, but no food. This type of reinforcement was also intermittent. This method of intermittent secondary reinforcement with rats produced more than 2,000 actions of pressing the bar, while methods involving constant reinforcement only produced a few dozen such actions.

Obviously secondary (or more) reinforcement plays an important part in concrete, psychological life. The sight of food is almost as powerful a reinforcement as its actual ingestion. The lion-tamer, who uses both 'punishment' and 'reward' to train his animals, employs the sight of the whip as much as the whip itself to restrain them.

In the case of humans, nearly all reinforcement is secondary. Within the confines of the laboratory, secondary reinforcement, i.e. the experimenter's approval which need not even be expressed in so many words, often serves as the reward for the subjects taking part in the experiment. The extent to which the subjects appreciate this reward (which itself belongs to a complex social background) is a measure of their enthusiasm. This bears out earlier comments on how easily human conditioning is affected by various psychic factors. Just saying to a subject, 'You are going to get an electric shock' is reinforcement which, although weaker than the actual shock, is still quite effective. In fact electrodermal conditioning can be established in some subjects just by making this threat. The existence of language and symbolized thought make these phenomena very complex in humans, without making them any less real.

The importance of conditioned reactions. Conditioned reactions play a very important part in all man's psychological and psychic activity. The whole field of visceral reactions (with all their affective and emotional concomitants) has yet to be thoroughly explored from this point of view, but it certainly owes much of its complexity to conditioned reactions. In higher activities (voluntary, conscious, verbal and intellectual), certain recurring features seem to conform with the laws of conditioning. Consequently conditioning should not be regarded as a separate subject, but as something which penetrates to some extent into every psychological activity. Further discussion can be found in other chapters of this treatise.

Bibliography

ASRATIAN, E. A. (in Russian), 'Quelques problèmes de l'établissement des liaisons conditionelles et de la formation de leurs propriétés', *C.R. de la Ier session de la Société de Psychologie*, Moscow, 1959, pp. 106–108.

BEKHTEREV, W. (in Russian), *Principes généraux de réflexologie humaine*, Leningrad, G.I.Z., 1926.

BLOCH, V., 'Nouveaux aspects de la méthode psycho-galvanique ou électro-dermographique comme critère des tensions affectives', *Année psychol.*, 1952, **52**, 329–62.

BROGDEN, W. V., 'Sensory preconditioning', *J. exp. Psychol.*, 1939, **25**, 323–32.

— 'Sensory preconditioning of human subjects', *J. exp. Psychol.*, 1947, **37**, 527–40.

BROWN, J. S., BILODEAU, E. A. and BARON, M. R., 'Bidirectional gradients in the strength of a generalized voluntary response to stimuli on a visual-spatial dimension', *J. exp. Psychol.*, 1951, **41**, 52–61.

BYKOV, C., *Le cortex et les organes internes*, Moscow, édit. en langues étrangères, 1956.

CARDU, B., 'Facteurs physiques et facteurs psychiques de la réponse galvanique de la peau', *Année psychol.*, 1954, **54**, 345–56.

COHEN, B. D., KALISH, H. I., THURSTON, J. R. and COHEN, E., 'Experimental manipulation of verbal behavior, *J. exp. Psychol.*, 1954, **47**, 106–10.

COWLES, J. T., 'Food-tokens as incentives for learning by chimpanzees', *Comp. Psychol. Monogr.*, 1937, **14**, 1–96.

DOSTALEK, C., 'Rücklaufige zeitweilige Verbindungen zwischen sogenannten indifferenten Reizen', *Deutsche Gesundheitwesen*, 1960, **44**, 2151–9.

ELLSON, D. G., 'Quantitative studies of the interaction of simple habits: I. Recovery from specific and generalized effects of extinction', *J. exp. Psychol.*, 1938, **23**, 339–58.

— 'Hallucinations produced by sensory conditioning', *J. exp. Psychol.*, 1941, **28**, 1–20.

— 'Critical conditions influencing sensory conditioning', *J. exp. Psychol.*, 1942, **31**, 333–8.

FESSARD, M. A., GASTAUT, H., LEONTIEV, A. N., MONTPELLIER, G. DE and PIERON, H., *Le conditionnement et l'apprentissage*, Paris, Presses Universitaires de France, 1958.

GIBSON, E. J., 'Sensory generalization with voluntary reactions', *J. exp. Psychol.*, 1939, **24**, 237–53.

GRANT, D. A. and NORRIS, E. B., 'Eyelid conditioning as influenced by the presence of sensitized Beta-responses', *J. exp. Psychol.*, 1947, **37**, 423–33.

HILGARD, E. R., 'Conditioned eyelid reactions to a light stimulus based on the reflex wink to sound', *Psychol. Monogr.*, 1931, **41** (1).

HILGARD, E. R. and MARQUIS, D. G., *Conditioning and learning*, New York, Appleton Century Crofts, 1940.

HOVLAND, C. I., 'The generalization of conditioned responses: I. The sensory generalization of conditioned responses with varying frequencies of tone', *J. gen. Psychol.*, 1937, **17**, 125–48.

— 'The generalization of conditioned responses: II. The sensory generalization of conditioned responses with varying intensities of tone', *J. genet. Psychol.*, 1937*b*, **51**, 279–91.

HULL, C. L., *Principles of behavior*, New York, Appleton Century Crofts, 1943.

HUMPHREYS, L. G., 'The effects of random alternation of reinforcement on the acquisition and extinction of conditioned eyelid reactions', *J. exp. Psychol.*, 1939*a*, **25**, 141–58.

— 'Acquisition and extinction of verbal expectations in a situation analogous to conditioning', *J. exp. Psychol.*, 1939*b*, **25**, 294–301.

— 'Extinction of conditioned psychogalvanic responses following two conditions of reinforcement', *J. exp. Psychol.*, 1940, **27**, 71–5.

IVANOV-SMOLENSKI, A. G., 'Études expérimentales sur les enfants et les aliénés selon la méthode des réflexes conditionnels, *Annales méd. psychol.*, 1927, **85**, 140–50.

— (in Russian), 'Quelques faits nouveaux dans le domaine de l'étude de l'activité nerveuse supérieure de l'enfant', *Arkh. Biol. Nauk.*, 1937, **42**.

— 'Le travail en commun et l'interaction des deux systèmes de signalisation', from *Questions scientifiques, Psychologie, Activité nerveuse supérieure*, Paris, 1955.

— 'Les interactions du premier et du second système de signalisation dans quelques conditions physiologiques et pathologiques', *La Raison*, 1951, **2**, 54–67.

JANKOWSKA, E. and SOLTYSIK, S. (in Russian), 'Réflexes conditionnels moteurs élaborés à partir de réflexes inconditionnels moteurs au moyen d'un renforcement alimentaire', in (in Russian), *Mécanismes centraux et périphériques de l'activité motrice des animaux*, Moscow, Éd. Acad. Sc. U.R.S.S., 1960.

JASPER, H. and SHAGASS, C., 'Conditioning the occipital alpha rhythm in man', *J. exp. Psychol.*, 1941, **28**, 373–88.

KIMBLE, G. A., *Hilgard and Marquis' Conditioning and Learning*, New York, Appleton Century Crofts, 1961.

47

Bibliography

KONORSKI, J., *Conditioned reflexes and neuron organization*, Cambridge, Cambridge University Press, 1948.

KUPALOV, P. S. (in Russian), 'La généralisation des liaisons conditionnelles dans l'analyseur auditif', *Fisiol, nerv. prots.*, 1955, 61–3.

LAWICKA, W., 'Physiological mechanism of delayed reactions: II. Delayed reactions in dogs and cats to directional stimuli', *Acta Biol. exper.*, 1959, **19**, 199–220.

LE NY, J. F., 'Généralisation d'une attitude dans une épreuve de temps de réaction', I and II, *Année psychol.*, 1957, **57**, 11–21 and 329–37.

— 'Conditionnement et signification', *Année psychol.*, 1960, **60**, 71–86.

— 'A propos de la méthode dite du "renforcement verbal" chez l'homme adulte, *Année psychol.*, 1960, **60**, 371–5.

— 'Généralisation et discrimination d'un stimulus verbal dans un apprentissage stochastique chez des enfants', *Année psychol.*, 1961, **61**, 79–96.

— *Le conditionnement*, Paris, Presses Universitaires de France, 1961.

LOUCKS, R. B., 'The experimental delimitation of neural structures essential for learning: The attempt to condition striped muscle responses with faradization of the sigmoïd gyri', *J. Psychol.*, 1935, **1**, 5–44.

LURIA, A. R., 'Le rôle du langage dans la formation des processus psychiques', *La Raison*, 1958, **22**, 3–25.

MILLER, N. E., 'Studies of fear as an acquirable drive: I. Fear as motivation and fear reduction as reinforcement in the learning of new responses', *J. exp. Psychol.*, 1948, **38**, 89–101.

MILLER, S. and KONORSKI, J., 'Sur une forme particulière des réflexes conditionnels', *Bull. S. Biol.*, 1928, **99**, 1155–8.

MONTPELLIER, G. DE, 'Le processus de conditionnement et les faits de conditionnement indirect', *Année psychol.*, 1951, **50**, 429–40.

MOWRER, O. H., *Learning and behavior theory*, New York, John Wiley & Sons, 1960.

— JONES, H. M., 'Extinction and behavior variability as function of effortfulness of task', *J. exp. Psychol.*, 1943, **33**, 369–86.

PAVLOV, I. P., *Leçons sur l'activité du cortex cérébral*, Paris, Legrand, 1929.

— *Les réflexes conditionnels*, Paris, Alcan, 1932.

— *Leçons sur le travail des hémisphères cérébraux* (series), Paris, Éd. des 'Cahiers de Médecine soviétique', 1953.

— *Œuvres choisies*, Moscow, édit. en langues étrangéres, 1954.

— *Typologie et pathologie de l'activité nerveuse supérieure*, Paris, Presses Universitaires de France, 155.

PERIN, C. T., 'Behavior potentiality as a joint function of the amount of training and the degree of hunger at the time of extinction', *J. exp. Psychol.*, 1942, **30**, 99–113.

POPOV, N. A. and POPOV, C., 'Observations neuro-électro-encéphalographiques sur les réactions corticales chez l'homme: II. Les réflexes conditionnés électro-corticaux chez l'homme', *Année psychol.*, 1954, **54**, 323–43.

POVORINSKI, I. A., 'La méthode d'étude des réflexes conditionnels moteurs avec renforcement verbal', summarized in *La Raison*, 1956, **14**, 89–112.

PROKOFIEF, G. and ZELIONY, G., 'Des modes d'associations cérébrales chez l'homme et chez les animaux', *J. de Psychol.*, 1926, **23**, 1020–8.

RAZRAN, G., 'Conditioned responses in children', *Arch. of Psychol.*, 1933, **148**, 1–112.

— 'Attitudinal control of human conditioning', *J. Psychol.*, 1936, **2**, 327–37.

— 'A quantitative study of meaning by a conditioned salivary technique (semantic conditioning)', *Science*, 1939*a*, **90**, 89–91.

— 'The nature of the extinctive process', *Psychol. Rev.*, 1939*b*, **46**, 264–97.

— 'Stimulus generalization of conditioned response', *Psychol. Bull.*, 1949*a*, **46**, 337–65.

— 'Semantic and phonetographic generalizations of salivary conditioning to verbal stimuli', *J. exp. Psychol.*, 1949*b*, **39**, 642–7.

SKINNER, B. F., 'Two types of conditioned reflex and a pseudo-type', *J. gen. Psychol.*, 1933, **12**, 66–77.

— *The behavior of organisms*, New York, Appleton Century Crofts, 1938.

— *Verbal behavior*, London, Methuen and Co., 1957.

SOLTYSIK, S. and KOWALSKA, M., 'Studies on the avoidance conditioning: I. Relations between cardiac (type I) and motor (type II) effects in the avoidance reflex', *Acta Biol. exper.*, 1960, **20**, 157–70.

— 'Studies on the avoidance conditioning: II. Differentiation and extinction of avoidance reflexes', *Acta Biol. exper.*, 1960, **20**, 171–82.

SOLOMON, R. L., 'Effort and extinction rate: a confirmation', *J. comp. physiol. Psychol.*, 1948, **41**, 93–101.

SPENCE, K. W. and ROSS, L. E., 'A methodological study of the form and latency of eyelid responses in conditioning', *J. exp. Psychol.*, 1959, **58**, 376–81.

THORNDIKE, E. L., 'Animal intelligence: an experimental study of the associative processes in animals', *Psychol. Monogr.*, 1898, **2**, 4.

WEINSTOCK, S., 'Resistance to extinction of a running response following partial reinforcement under widely spaced trials', *J. comp. physiol. Psychol.*, 1954, **47**, 318–22.

49

Bibliography

WILLIAMS, S. B., 'Resistance to extinction as a function of the number of reinforcements', *J. exp. Psychol.*, 1938, **23**, 506–21.

WOLFE, J. B., 'Effectiveness of token-rewards for chimpanzees', *Comp. Psychol. Monogr.*, 1936, **12**, 1–72.

ZIMMERMAN, D. W., 'Durable secondary reinforcement', *Psychol. Rev.*, 1957, **64**, 373–83.

Chapter 12

Learning

Gérard de Montpellier

Introduction. The notion of learning

1. What does it mean, to learn? Although a variety of answers have been given to this question, it seems to be generally accepted that, from a functional point of view, learning is the systematic modification of behaviour in a recurring situation.

If it is assumed that all behaviour is a 'reaction' to 'stimuli' which make up the physical situation, it follows that learning occurs when a reaction alters in a specific way as a result of repetition of a stimulating situation, or of 'previous contact with a given stimulating situation'.[1] Learning can be defined more briefly, but perhaps a little ambiguously, as dependent upon prior experience of a given situation.[2]

Such a functional definition of learning doubtless implies certain consequences from the structural point of view, i.e. from the point of view of the processes and mechanisms which enable the observer to modify reactions systematically.

The various problems occurring here will be examined in greater detail later, but it is immediately obvious that if the systematic modification of a reaction results from repetition, i.e. from the previous experience of a stimulating situation, some

[1] Mourad, 1943, p. 89.
[2] This agrees with another definition put forward by various authors. For example, according to McGeoch, learning occurs whenever the change in performance results from practice (1949, p. 3); according to Osgood, where there is selective modification of a response when the same situation is repeated (1953, p. 299); according to Spence, when there is a definite change in behaviour, following successive experience of the same situation (1956, p. 25).

trace of this must be left in the organism. The nature and mechanism of this trace have to be elucidated in order to explain or 'understand' the phenomena of learning.

If 'memory' is assumed to be the process which enables these traces to exist, i.e. the retention of previous experience, it must be part of every phenomenon of learning.

2. In practice many authors have found this functional definition, with all its structural implications, too broad to describe learning phenomena.

Certain systematic changes in reactions resulting from repetition of the same stimulating situation, for example, sensory adaptation or fatigue, are not usually considered to be learning phenomena.[1]

From the functional point of view, the *adaptive* nature of the change seems to some authors to be the prominent feature of learning.[2]

It would appear that two restrictive criteria should be added to the principal criterion. In the first place, a modification in reaction must be relatively durable to qualify as learning. Secondly, any such change must show a variation in quality or range, such as a change in the form or structure of the reaction or its eventual production by new stimuli. A variation in intensity or quantity, i.e. an increase in speed, a reduction in effort, etc., is not enough.

From a structural point of view, these two qualifications result in the exclusion from the field of learning of all modifications in reactions resulting from changes concerned only with the receptor organs (e.g. summation of excitation or sensory adaptation) or the reactor organs (muscular fatigue). In actual fact all these modifications last only a short time and generally affect only the intensity of the reaction.

Thus only modifications affecting the receptor and effector

---

[1] For example, according to Hunter, learning is any progressive change in behaviour which cannot be attributed either to fatigue or to modifications in the effector or receptor systems (1934, p. 467).

Hilgard has described learning as the appearance or change of activity resulting from the exercise of, or the reaction to, a situation, unless this change can be attributed to inborn, reactive tendencies, to maturation or to certain temporary conditions of the organism caused by fatigue, drugs, etc. (1956, p. 3).

[2] For example, Piéron regards learning as an adaptive modification of behaviour during repeated tests (1951, p. 20), while Thorpe sees it as an adaptive modification of individual behaviour resulting from experience (1956, p. 49).

systems in their anatomical and functional connections, i.e. the central nervous system, belong to the field of learning. Consequently the form of memory which makes the phenomenon of learning possible is not merely the persistence of excitation or the effect of a reaction, i.e. the existence of isolated traces, but an *associative memory*, a type of retention corresponding to the formation of clusters or syntheses of traces and involving the receptor mechanisms in their connections with the effector mechanisms.

3. While this functional and structural description of the phenomena of learning is generally accepted, there are widely differing opinions on the nature of the mechanisms and processes at work in learning. These are the processes which occur in the establishment and preservation of the clusters of traces to which we have just alluded. Since these processes cannot be directly observed, they have to be inferred and so they give rise to hypotheses and theories that cannot be substantiated easily.

Some of these theories will be examined later, but first we should like to describe what actually happens in learning and the various forms these events take.

1 Different types of learning

There are several ways in which the events occurring in learning can be classified.

We shall first provide a brief review of the different types of learning that can be observed in animals, before examining methods of learning in human behaviour.

Animal learning

1 Reactions of habituation

The first kind of learning, which can be observed even in very low forms of life, is the gradual reduction, or even temporary disappearance, of a clearly reflex reaction when a particular stimulating situation is repeated. A good example of this is the withdrawal reaction in certain gasteropods (both salt-water and fresh-water molluscs) when sudden darkness follows light. This reaction gradually diminishes until it disappears altogether when darkness occurs again (Piéron, 1910).

Similar phenomena, resulting from various types of stimulation of relatively moderate intensity, have been observed throughout the zoological tree, from unicellular organisms upwards.[1]

At first sight, these phenomena resemble the phenomena of sensory adaptation (reduction of sensibility in organs exposed to a source of excitation) or fatigue (reduction of efficiency in reaction mechanisms), but the resemblance is only superficial. The decrease and arrest of the reaction often occur very quickly, as the result of a few presentations of the stimulus or a few reactions, and new stimuli, reaching the same receptor organs and setting in motion the same reaction mechanisms, can be completely effective.

These phenomena of habituation or accommodation seem to demonstrate a negative aspect of the adaptive nature of learning phenomena, giving rise to the occasional use of the expression *negative adaptation*.

2 Conditioned reactions

Conditioning is often considered to be the prototype of elementary learning in both men and animals.

Conditioning covers a wide field, but it is used here in its 'classical' sense to describe the situation illustrated by Pavlov's experiments.

(*a*) The basic phenomenon illustrated by these experiments is the transfer of the power to excite a specific reaction from an absolute (unconditioned) stimulus to a stimulus which is initially neutral, but which becomes effective when it is presented in conjunction with the absolute or unconditioned stimulus.

In this case, the systematic modification of behaviour by repetition of a situation does not consist of a real change in the reaction, but rather of a substitution of stimulus *vis-à-vis* a specific response; or, if this new stimulus initially produced a specific response, it consists of a substitution of response *vis-à-vis* a specific source of stimulation.

[1] Humphrey, 1933.

This transfer is illustrated by the following schema: in which

S₀ = conditioned stimulus;
Sᵤₙₒ = unconditioned stimulus;
r = initial response to conditioned stimulus;
R = unconditioned response.

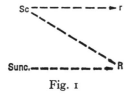

Fig. 1

This phenomenon has been demonstrated in various forms (muscular or glandular reactions) on all levels of the zoological scale, including the lowest.[1]

Nevertheless, as several authors have noted,[2] there is rarely perfect transfer of response. The reaction evoked by the conditioned stimulus is not usually identical to that evoked by the unconditioned stimulus. More often than not, a completely different reaction appears and establishes itself, in which case the following schema applies:

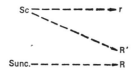

Fig. 2

Although it is distinct from the response R to the unconditioned stimulus, the new response R' does have a connection with the appearance of this stimulus. It usually bears a preparatory relationship to this stimulus, placing the organism in a better position either to receive or avoid it.

(*b*) There are two complementary aspects of conditioning phenomena which also seem to involve learning in the negative form described in connection with habituation or accommodation. In conditioning, the original reactions provoked by the new

[1] Conditioning has even been found in protozoa (Métainikov, 1912 and 1914; Plavilstchikov, 1928).
[2] Wever, 1930; Britt, 1935; Warner, 1932; Rey, 1936; Zener, 1935.

stimuli gradually disappear, so this negative learning seems to be the reverse of positive learning; the original reaction disappears as the stimulus starts to evoke a new reaction.

This phenomenon appears particularly clearly when the initial reaction to the conditioned stimulus is a well-defined one. The stimulus already possesses a high biological value for the organism.

Examples of classical situations of negative learning appeared in studies made many years ago. Möbius (1873), using pike, and Triplett (1901), using perch, both observed reactions of withdrawal and indifference towards gudgeon in the same aquarium after the pike and perch had suffered the unpleasant effects of colliding with a glass partition which initially separated them from their prey.

Transferred reactions, produced by conditioned stimuli, also gradually disappear when the unconditioned stimuli are no longer presented. In other words, transferred reactions are only maintained when the situation is faithfully repeated.

Some authors regard this phenomenon, described as *experimental extinction*, as the opposite of positive learning; the conditioned reaction gives way to a new, but less clearly defined, reaction of arrest or lack of interest. More simply, it may be a phenomenon of 'unlearning', a return to the reaction preceding that of conditioning. Either way, this phenomenon is an important aspect of the learning process.

3 Discrimination reactions

Yerkes's apparatus for discrimination between two or several stimuli (1917), as used in animal psychology, constitutes a situation akin to that of conditioning in which the conditioned reaction differs quite widely from the unconditioned reaction, although this situation involves a reaction of choice, since there may be several alternatives.

The apparatus (see Fig. 3) consists of a sort of central chamber opening into two side compartments adjacent to it. The two stimuli to be discriminated are placed near the exits leading to the side compartments. There is an attractive bait in one of these compartments. The other is empty or contains a device which can administer an electric shock. The stimuli are never in the same place in two consecutive trials. Sometimes they are placed near one exit and sometimes near another. The location of the food and the device for administering an electric shock, if used, alters in the same way.

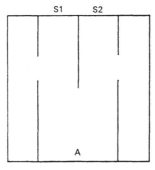

Fig. 3

The absolute or unconditioned stimuli (food, shock) and the conditioned stimuli (light, sound, etc.) all produce clearly defined, but quite distinct, reactions.

The responses normally evoked by the food and the shock are to approach and eat the former and to avoid and flee from the latter, while the response produced by the discriminated stimulus consists of moving in a particular direction after the choice has been made. The direction taken probably has something to do with the position of the 'absolute' stimulus, but this is through a reaction which is definitely not a complete replica of that produced by the absolute stimulus.

4 Reactions of acquired spatial orientation

The maze situation has probably produced most observation of phenomena of acquisition and learning in animals.

The maze is a more complex discrimination situation in which there are possible alternative responses at each fork along the way (see Fig. 4). At each point, the form of the alternative is rigidly linked to an absolute spatial localization of specific qualitative aspects and, consequently, of directions to take and directions to avoid. In Yerkes's apparatus, these directions are connected only with the qualitative aspect of the stimuli to be

57

discriminated and do not depend upon the absolute position of the stimuli in the apparatus. However, there is no basic difference in principle between the two situations. The food or bait is like an absolute stimulus which naturally produces a reaction of approach and absorption, while the specific sensory aspects along the way, especially at the points where a choice has to be made, are like conditioned stimuli that finally produce specific reactions of choice of direction and of approach. These reactions partially resemble the reactions produced by the absolute stimulus.

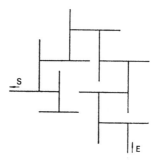

Fig. 4

In both types of situation (discrimination apparatus and maze), the reaction, which appears and is established as a function of repetition of the same stimulating situation and which can be regarded as a conditioned reaction *vis-à-vis* the absolute stimulus (food or electric shock), is a partially new reaction. It is not an absolute replica of the reaction produced by contact with the absolute stimulus, but it is still the reaction normally evoked 'at a distance', so to speak, by the stimulus (approach, retreat, etc.).

5   Reactions in instrumental conditioning and training

Some situations give rise to the appearance and gradual establishment, in animals, of modes of reaction. These can still be regarded as conditioned reactions in the widest sense of the term, but they are really new reactions, since the organism has never revealed them before nor have the 'absolute' stimuli (food, shock, etc.) ever produced them before, not even 'at a distance'.

(*a*) Miller and Konorski (1928, 1934, 1937) described reactions of this sort as 'type II conditioned reflexes' in order to distinguish them from the classical conditioned reaction.

The phenomenon observed is as follows: an auditory stimulus, such as a note on the piano, is presented a certain number of times before the performance (either passive or provoked by appropriate excitation) of a firm movement by a dog, for example, withdrawal of its paw. This auditory stimulus eventually produces the motor reaction itself when this is followed by a second stimulus, such as food.

According to these two authors, a new type of reflex is established within a more general situation which conforms to the schema of classical conditioning (see Fig. 5). If the food is the

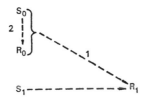

Fig. 5 (After Konorski and Miller, 1937.)

absolute stimulus for the salivary response, all the excitation (auditory from the piano and kinaesthetic from the actual performance of the movement) must together constitute a complex conditioned stimulus *vis-à-vis* the salivary response. A second conditioning will then form within the first: the auditory stimulus will become the conditioned stimulus, not only for the salivary response, but also for the motor response which it will produce from then onwards. The motor response will no longer be merely part of a complex of conditioned stimuli *vis-à-vis* the salivary reaction, but also a conditioned response to the auditory stimulus.

As far as features peculiar to conditioned reactions are concerned in this second type of conditioning, Miller and Konorski noted that the reaction should give rise to proprioceptive excitation and should be an essential condition for attaining or avoiding the absolute stimulus.

They also observed that, contrary to classical conditioning, the conditioned reaction is never identical with the unconditioned reaction to the absolute stimulus.

Type R

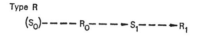

Type S

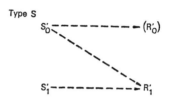

Fig. 6. (After Skinner, 1938).

(*b*) Skinner (1935, 1937, 1938) described and analysed a situation, similar to that of Miller and Konorski, to which considerable study has been devoted.

This situation is illustrated by the following phenomenon: a rat, placed in a cage in front of a lever, learns to manoeuvre this lever by pushing it down when the manoeuvre will obtain food for him.

According to Skinner (see Fig. 6), the reaction in this situation is an 'operant' reflex, i.e. not linked to a specific stimulus, but 'emitted' spontaneously by the organism. This reflex gives rise to type R conditioning in which the reinforcing stimulus (absolute) bears a 'relationship of contingency' to a response. A 'respondent' reflex, i.e. linked to a specific stimulus, would produce type S conditioning in which the (absolute) reinforcing stimulus would bear a 'relationship of contingency' to another (conditioned) stimulus.

The basic difference between the two types of conditioning lies in the fact that the reinforcing or absolute stimulus is accompanied, in the one case, by a reaction and, in the other, by a stimulus. This would explain why classical conditioning is only possible where there is 'respondent' behaviour, since 'operant' behaviour has no identifiable stimulus.

Skinner noted a second difference which other authors,

notably Hilgard and Marquis (1940), see as the external distinction between the two types of reflex. This difference concerns the presentation of the reinforcing stimulus: in the first case, obtaining the food does not in any way depend upon the salivary reaction, while in the second case it depends upon pressing the lever. Thus, one type of reflex is independent of the presentation of the reinforcing stimulus, whereas the other depends upon it.

For this reason, type R conditioning, involving 'operant' behaviour, has usually been drescribed as 'instrumental conditioning' since the studies of Hilgard and Marquis (1940), because the reaction is needed either to obtain or to avoid the absolute or unconditioned stimulus.

(*c*) Various learning situations in animals fit easily into the schemes set up by Skinner and Miller and Konorski. Situations in which the animal has to learn a device for opening a door or hidden cupboard (by pressing a pedal, undoing a latch, pulling a string, etc.) all belong to the first scheme. So-called 'training' situations, involving one or several artificial movements that have to be induced initially either passively or by means of suitable stimulation (later abandoned), all belong to the scheme set up by Miller and Konorski.

This learning mechanism is more complex than that of simple classical conditioning, but it cannot be entirely separated from the latter.

6 Reactions of 'intelligent' learning

In all the examples of learning phenomena so far mentioned, the appearance and establishment of modified or transferred reactions are not usually achieved 'in one go,' but gradually through a series of repetitions or successive trials.

However, phenomena of adaptation to new circumstances or conditions, involving a relatively abrupt acquisition of a reaction, have been described in animals. Acquisition did not necessarily take place right away, without previous trials, but the right adaptation was obtained 'in one go', apparently without any gradual acquisition.

We should like to refer here particularly to the type of behaviour observed by Köhler (1917) in chimpanzees. The same behaviour has also been described by others[1] and does not seem to belong exclusively to higher animals.[2]

This type of modification in behaviour has been compared with the type described earlier and has been called by some authors 'an intelligent reaction' or a reaction of 'intelligent learning'. 'Something' is definitely acquired which was not present initially. Otherwise adaptation would be immediate as in the case of innate adaptation or adaptation resulting from prior learning. Nevertheless, because of its abruptness, this sort of adaptation seems to imply a process different from that found in the examples of learning quoted earlier.

We shall have cause to return to this point when we examine theories or interpretations of learning. From a descriptive point of view, the only different feature of this mode of learning is its suddenness, which produces a curve of acquisition that drops abruptly. However, this feature may vary considerably in a complex situation, making it difficult to identify this mode of acquisition.

Human learning

The modes or types of acquisition already observed in animals can also be found in humans, but in new forms and with new features. This applies to motor and verbal acquisition, in particular.

1 The conditioning process

The phenomena of conditioning, particularly of classical conditioning, in humans have been the subject of much study and experiment.

Conditioning of the salivary reaction (Lashley, 1916; Krasnogorski, 1926; Razran, 1935), of the plantar reflex (Shipley, 1932), of the patellar reflex (Wendt, 1930) and of the pupillary reflex (Cason, 1922; Hudgins, 1932) have all been achieved.

However, the reactions most frequently studied are the

---

[1] Yerkes, 1927, 1928; Guillaume and Meyerson, 1930, 1931, 1937; Bierens de Haan, 1931, 1934.

[2] Hsiao, 1919; Maier, 1929; Tolman and Honzik, 1930; Buytendijk and Fischel, 1931; Caldwell and Jones, 1954.

psychogalvanic reactions,[1] in particular, the eyelid reflex[2] and the retraction reflex of a limb (hand or finger),[3] under the effect of a painful excitant, such as an electric shock.

In some cases, it proved possible to observe the phenomenon of transference, in accordance with the classical schema of Pavlovian conditioning. In other cases, notably those involving a retraction or avoidance reaction, the form taken by the conditioned reaction seemed to be somewhat different from that provoked by the absolute stimulus, although it did reveal some features of adaptation in relation to the advent of the absolute or unconditioned stimulus.

Certainly the descriptive formula for conditioning in its widest sense can easily be applied to a whole host of reactions acquired in the course of human existence, from the very first transference observed in young children right up to the preparatory reactions, anticipating daily events in our lives, which are usually very different from those arising when the events in question actually occur (for example, taking an umbrella or stick before going out, switching a light on in a room before going in, taking the key out before reaching the doorstep, etc.).

One point made by several authors[4] in connection with conditioning experiments in humans is the importance of 'attitudes', which are either adopted spontaneously or induced by the instructions given, to the development of the process. These attitudes can facilitate conditioning, but they can also hinder or inhibit it. Very often they make conditioning less stable and more variable than it would be in an animal, because a man is far more able to alter his own attitude to a stimulus presented to him and this is outside the experimenter's control. These attitudes affect, favourably or otherwise, every form of human learning, not only conditioning.

2 Perceptual learning

Modification of a reaction, which characterizes conditioning phenomena, is based on one of two things happening: either there

[1] Switzer, 1933; Jones, 1928; Menzies, 1937; de Montpellier and Colle, 1939.

[2] Hilgard, 1931; Hilgard and Campbell, 1936; Reynolds, 1945.

[3] Bechterev, 1913; Wolfe, 1930, 1932; Razran, 1934, 1935; de Montpellier and Colle, 1939.

[4] Razran, 1936; Hilgard and Humphrey, 1938; Grant, 1939; Miller, 1939; de Montpellier and Colle, 1939.

is a substitution of response *vis-à-vis* a particular source of excitation, producing a form of reaction not initially evoked by it, but really belonging to the unconditioned or absolute stimulus; or a new response appears which is distinct from that provoked by the absolute stimulus, but which reveals features preparatory to the imminent arrival of this stimulus. Reactions of the glandular or muscular type, and possibly of the verbal type, may 'respond' to stimulation given in a sensory form, but their modification does not necessitate corresponding modifications in the sensory or perceptual field. When a bell ringing produces a salivary reaction in either humans or animals, it may have acquired a new significance, but this does not mean that it has appeared in a new phenomenal form.

We shall take 'perceptual learning' to mean the systematic modification of perceptual or phenomenal aspects of a system of physical stimulation which is repeated in an identical form.

(A) These modifications in phenomenal aspects can be regarded as 'reactions' to systems of physical stimulation. They 'establish contact' between the physical stimulation and the organism, and this contact gives birth to the 'percept' or phenomenal datum. It is really a question of finding a phenomenological definition of perception, since the perceptual reaction in this sense is situated on a strictly individual and subjective level and, as such, is uncommunicable.

However, in an objective conception of psychology, the percept can only be considered as an inferred variable, as an intermediary between the stimulus and an obvious, discriminatory response which is, in a way, its expression.

This being so, modification of an obvious, differentiating response (usually a verbal reaction of a symbolic nature), when the same stimulating situation is repeated, should constitute the criterion for perceptual learning. However, in so far as the existence of characteristic, phenomenal data can be inferred from an objective, differentiating reaction, this data can 'recur', not in its individual singularity, but in its abstract, transindividual structure.[1]

(B) In what *form* do these modifications or changes appear?

The answer is probably that all systematic modification of a perceptual reaction consists basically of a gradual change in the

---

[1] Michotte, 1959.

structural aspect of the phenomenal data, but this can happen in several ways.

(*a*) Reduction of thresholds as a function of practice, i.e. judgement of existence replacing judgement of non-existence, in the case of the absolute threshold, and judgment of difference replacing judgment of identity, in the case of the differential threshold.

Reduction (as a function of practice) of the aesthesiometric threshold for a double contact (Mukherjee, 1933), of the visual acuity threshold (Wilcox, 1936; McFadden, 1941; Bruce and Low, 1951), of the auditory acuity threshold (Humes, 1930), of the differentiating threshold (relative discrimination) for luminosity (Gavini, 1962), for tonal pitch (Wipple, 1903; Smith, 1914; Seashore, 1939; Wyatt, 1945; Oakes, 1955) and for distance (Wolfe, 1923; Woodrow, 1938) can all be classed in this first group.

(*b*) Perception of details or new aspects in complex systems of stimulation as a function of practice: for example, locating a particular instrument in an orchestra or a detail in a complex scene or a new aspect of an ambiguous figure.

(*c*) Recognition or identification of structures presented in conditions which render perception difficult (shown by the appearance of previously used verbal responses): for example, in the case of tachistoscopic presentation (Renshaw, 1942), presentation in a bad light (Seward, 1931; Bevan and Zener, 1952) and presentation with, or just after, similar structures (Gibson and Gibson, 1955; Phaub and Caldwell, 1959). In all these cases, performance improves as a function of practice.

(*d*) Reduction of perceptual illusions, in particular the Müller-Lyer illusion (Crosland, Taylor and Newson, 1929; Köhler and Fischback, 1950; Noelting, 1960).

(C) However these changes do not result from the action of the same *factors*.

Some appear to be caused by gradual and systematic modifications of the receptor mechanisms (in their broadest sense), including perceptual attitudes in the form of fixation, attentive concentration, passage from a syncretic to an analytic attitude, etc. Piaget underlined the importance of one of these factors, namely, changes in peripheral or central 'centring' of the receptor mechanisms in complex situations.

Other factors probably result from earlier experience and finally bring about a structural reorganization or modification of some aspects of the initial, perceptual situation.

(*a*) This can happen in various ways. The previous experience may be that of previous *perceptions*, resulting from earlier, similar systems of stimulation.

The experiments carried out by Gottschaldt (1926), Braly (1933), Djang (1937) and others, in which perception of a complex figure followed presentation of simpler figures which occurred as elements of the complex figure, revealed the extent of the influence of earlier perceptions. The experiments showed that the extent of the influence depends on the 'structure' or internal organization of the figure. Thus, the less unified a complex figure is, the greater the influence of the earlier perceptual experience.

Henle (1942) demonstrated rather cleverly the action of this experience when structural conditions are neutralized. He presented letters of the alphabet, which were upright on one side and reversed (mirror image) on the other, to his subjects in conditions of reduced perception (peripheral or tachistocopic vision). The figures had the same structure in both cases, but they differed from the point of view of familiarity or experience. The results showed a significantly higher percentage of correct reproductions for the upright figures than for the reversed ones.

The experiments carried out by Wallach, O'Connell and Neisser (1953) on three-dimensional perception provide examples of the appearance of new structures as a result of earlier experience. In these experiments, the flat projection of a wire cube, which initially looked like a flat figure, could be seen as a three-dimensional figure when the projection was preceded by presentations revealing the three-dimensional nature of the cube (the cube was shown rotating).

(*b*) Previous experience can have less direct and immediate effect in the form of *conceptions* or *hypotheses*, resulting from general knowledge previously acquired by the subject. The action of this general experience gave rise to the notion of perception, defended by E. Brunswik (1943), that systems of physical stimulation would only provide, through direct data, an 'indication' of interpretation (which would, in any case, only be probable) as a function of the subject's earlier, rationalized experience.

(*c*) Previous experience can also act in the form of *suggestions* or *information* given to the subject during repeated presentations of the same system of stimulation. Work carried out by Luchins (1945) showed that, where stimulation could give rise to several perceptual structures, suggestions of a social nature could be a determining factor in the subject's perception of the structure involved.

(*d*) Finally, previous experience can be that of *actions* performed by the subject in the course of successive presentations of the initial situation. For example, Kilpatrick (1954) used Ames's distorted rooms and showed that a subject, who first perceives the room as normal from a particular observation point, eventually 'sees' it as distorted after he has performed certain actions, such as throwing a ball towards a light in the room, or tracing a line along the far wall with a stick, etc.

Although all the examples of perceptual learning quoted contain modifications of response during repetition of the stimulating situation, the factor of previous experience does not act in the same way in each case.

In some cases, the perceptual modifications are the result of changes in the perceptual mechanisms themselves during repetition. Previous experience can still probably be referred to in this instance since how perception occurs in a specific trial depends on how it occurred in a earlier trial. In any case, this is previous experience of the *same stimulating situation.*

However, in other cases, modification results from the influence of earlier experience of *situations different* from the present stimulating situation. In these cases, the influence of earlier experience involves a process of memory or retention, i.e. of traces affecting the actual contents of perceptions, conceptions, information or actions preceding the perceptual reaction.

3 Sensori-motor learning

We shall include in this section those learning phenomena in which the modification of reaction consists of an adjustment or adaptation of a pre-existent reaction, to new perceptual conditions, involving either the establishment of new sensorimotor coordinations or an increase in precision or subtlety in the schemes or coordination already existing.

Basically acquisition affects the relationship between perceptual or sensory data and reaction processes of a motor nature. Phenomena of acquisition belonging to this group, in which the perceptual or sensory data is of an essentially kinaesthetic or proprioceptive nature, will be dealt with separately under the heading of motor learning.

A classical example of the acquisition of new sensori-motor coordinations occurs in *mirror drawing*. The reaction required of the subject consists of tracing with a stylet held in the hand the outline of a drawing seen in a mirror. In these conditions, the directions taken by the tracing should be the reverse of the indications provided by visual perception on the basis of earlier experience. At first the reaction is hesitant and clumsy, but it increases in precision and speed as the experiment goes on. The acquisition of visual-motor coordinations when wearing spectacles which reverse or alter the visual location of objects in the spatial field (Stratton, 1897; I. Kohler, 1951) falls into the same category.

In some cases, the sensori-motor coordinations are not, strictly speaking, new, but they have to function within unaccustomed conditions of speed, precision and mobility in the reaction field. Learning situations involving sighting targets, throwing balls or darts at targets, chasing moving targets, etc., all belong to this category. The last situation, in particular, has been the subject of many studies, using various devices, the best known being that of Seashore (1928), consisting of a gramophone record with a small, metal target with which the end of a stylet held in the hand has to remain in contact, while the disc goes round.

Reactions in writing, typing, playing the piano or violin, or in reaching objects described by conventional signals—for example Van der Veldt's experiments (1928) in which subjects had to touch one or several objects when syllables or words identifying them appeared (see Fig. 7)—all involve the establishment of new sensori-motor coordinations, since the visual aspects of the signal is gradually associated with a particular motor reaction whose rapid and precise evocation depends upon the extent to which this association or connection has been set up.

However, the performance of these reactions has another aspect which produces true motor learning. In practice, these reactions rarely occur in isolation, but in fairly long series which quickly form organizations or structures of a motor nature. From this point of view, they really belong to the field of motor learning.

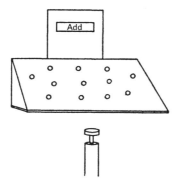

Fig. 7. (After Van der Veldt, 1928.)

4 Motor learning

As already stated, this section covers learning situations in which the reactions are connected to sensory constituents of basically kinaesthetic or proprioceptive origins.

The most obvious examples of situations of this kind are those in which the differentiating sensory constituents have an exclusively kinaesthetic origin, i.e. result solely from the actual performance of the movements in the reaction.

These situations occur mainly in maze learning with a stylet, in which hollow paths are tracked with a stylet held in the hand, or in mazes of raised wire (Miles), where the path is tracked with the finger. Both experiments are carried out blindfold.

However, they can also occur in learning in typing or playing the piano or violin, when blindfold, or in learning to hit targets (experiments by Van der Veldt (1928), McNeill (1934) and de Montpellier (1935)) either with the eyes closed or with the eyes fixed on a point above or outside the reaction area.

In all these cases, the sensory control of the reactions has a kinaesthetic origin. The other sensory data, in particular those relating to the field of vision, if present at all, only act as indications or signals in the production of a specific type of reaction.

In all these cases, learning results in the establishment of a kinaesthetic 'form' or structure. For, as we have already noted, motor reactions which follow each other in succession together form unified organizations like those characterizing other perceptual forms.

This is particularly noticeable in the forms of the spatial trajectories corresponding to these reactions, and is shown by cinematographic records of the experiments referred to earlier.[1] Photographic records, obtained by Marey's methods (see Fig. 8) show the evolution of the trajectories' forms during the practice period. Cohesive and unified reactions gradually replace the initial reactions of sighting the targets. These original reactions, isolated from each other and only succeeding each other because they follow the order of the targets, are gradually combined into uniform and inclusive, kinetic structures. The trajectories also become unified. The rectilinear or angular parts of the initial trajectories are replaced by curves drawn at fairly uniform speeds.

This phenomenon of integration, producing true motor 'forms' as a result of practice, also occurs in the examples of learning given earlier (typing, writing, playing the piano or violin) as well as in sporting activities such as skating and swimming.

Motor learning is not radically different from sensori-motor learning. In both cases, the motor or reactive aspect of acquisition is attached to a sensory aspect and depends upon it for its actual development. But, while this sensory aspect is external in one case, it becomes proprioceptive in the other. The actual performance of the reaction produces this sensory aspect which in turn controls the movement. This control by the sensory aspect cannot be exercised on the motor aspect corresponding to the same elementary reaction: a certain lapse of time is needed for the causal process to take effect. In fact, as the reaction unfolds, each phase of its performance sets off and controls the new phase in its sensory aspect. Seen in this light, the execution of the motor 'form' acquired under these conditions corresponds to a chain of sensori-motor processes.

[1] de Montpellier, 1935.

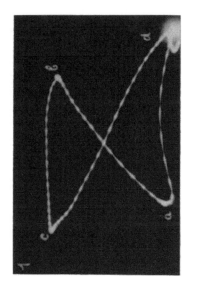

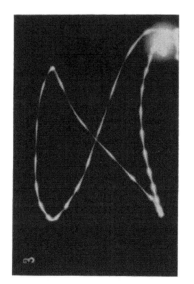

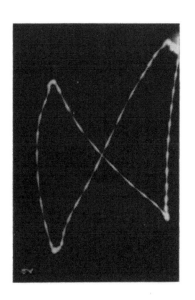

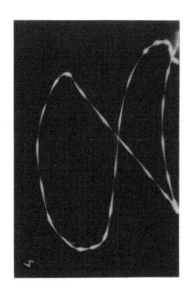

Fig. 8

5   *Verbal learning*

(A) LEARNING VERBAL SERIES

This type of learning consists of being able to recite in a particular order a series of verbal terms, either in the form of meaningful words or phrases (as at school), or in the form of nonsense syllables, which has been the classical method in psychology laboratories since Ebbinghaus began his studies in 1885. The terms are usually presented either aurally or visually, and the reaction consists of reproducing the series 'from memory'.

Learning verbal terms does bear a certain similarity to motor learning. The terms have to be pronounced which means that movements, accompanied by appropriate proprioceptive excitation, are made and reactive 'forms' or structures of a motor nature are constituted. The series is a chain of elements and each element plays the role both of response and of stimulus.

However, the proprioceptive sensory aspect of an articulated element is the same as its auditory sensory aspect. A reaction of articulation can be provoked by sensory excitation which is both proprioceptive and auditory, so this cannot really be called motor learning.

When the material is meaningful, the connections between the successive elements are naturally assisted by the meaning, so they are really pre-established connections.

In some cases, the terms or elements are presented in pairs, and learning consists of being able to give one of the elements in a pair when presented with the other. There is no question of a kinaesthetic chain, because the inductive term is always presented aurally or visually and the induced term, expressed verbally, is just a simple, isolated response.

(B) LANGUAGE LEARNING

Meaningful verbal terms may be learnt in series or in pairs, but they may also be learnt alone, i.e. as terms of *language*, when their importance lies in their meaning. This acquisition of meaning is an important aspect of the whole problem of learning. What does this type of acquisition consist of and how is it effected?

We shall not examine these questions in detail, since they are the subject of another chapter in this treatise. Language learning normally takes place during childhood and belongs more properly to the sphere of genetic and child psychology. We shall confine ourselves to noting that, from a descriptive point of view, the acquisition of the meaning of verbal terms (which form the elements of a language) involves the acquisition of referential relations between these terms or elements and objects or happenings in the cognitive field.

From a genetic point of view, these relations are of a purely associative nature, initially at any rate. A word refers to an object just as a signal refers to the object signalled, simply because the two events follow one another in the experiment; but these relations soon acquire a new, symbolic character which is the mark of true language. The word no longer merely accompanies the object; it symbolizes or represents it.

Acquiring verbal meaning, which is understanding terms of language in their symbolic sense, is an acquisition which seems to depend on specific aptitudes characterizing human intelligence.

Acquisition of the use of verbal terms, which entails articulation, is largely achieved by imitation. However, as this is probably only one of the forms taken by the process of learning, an understanding of the mechanism of this process is required in order to obtain a satisfactory explanation of this type of acquisition in both its aspects. Several authors have noted this fact.[1]

6 'Intelligent' learning

We have already referred to the possible existence of reactions of intelligent learning in animals, shown by the relatively abrupt changes in reactions in order to adapt to new conditions and surroundings. The same feature appears in humans, but in both cases it represents an exterior sign of intelligent behaviour, rather than a mark of learning in the strict sense of the word.

However, certain situations produce reactions which can be regarded as half-way between learning behaviour and intelligent behaviour or true, 'intelligent learning' behaviour. These are situations in which the subject has to discover a 'concept' or 'principle', i.e. a general or abstract structure or 'form' appearing

[1] Guillaume, 1925; Miller and Dollard, 1941.

in different ways in a series of individual presentations. This succession of presentations, bringing into play previous experience, is an essential feature of these learning situations, while comprehension of the abstract 'principle' or structure, implicit in the adapted reaction, is definitely a sign of intelligent behaviour. However, the change in the reaction does not always present an 'all-or-nothing' character, any more than it did in the reactions of 'intelligent learning' in animals described earlier. The change is sometimes progressive, producing a rising learning curve, even in the case of relatively simple 'principles' or structures.

(A) The first type of structure in this class occurs in various situations which have one common feature, i.e. the presence of a particular element. The classical experiments carried out by Hull (1920) into the formation of concepts are an example of this. In these experiments, complicated pseudo-Chinese characters were presented in succession to the subjects. Each character possessing a radical aspect in common with others in the series was followed by a specific syllable (for example, *oo, yer, fid*, etc.), pronounced out loud. The subjects' task was to give the syllable corresponding to a particular character and then, if possible, to extend this response to new characters possessing the same common feature. It has been pointed out[1] that learning in this kind of situation depends basically on attributing a vocable to a specific element, common to several objects.

In other situations, particularly the situation studied by Smoke (1932), the common feature lies, not in a common element, but in a structure of identical spatial outlines, for example, where the same syllable accompanies circles with two dots, one inside and the other outside the outline. Other features of the figures do not matter.

(B) The situations studied by Drever (1934), and later by Borchgrave (1957), are similar to those described in (A) above. The subject had to discover a common feature (two acute angles) in certain geometrical figures belonging to a series of 30 figures presented in succession. The experimenter acknowledged each response negatively or positively until the subject found the key.

The situations studied by Pollet (1946) belong to the same group. Pollet presented five nonsense terms simultaneously to

[1] Osgood, 1953.

73

the subject, who had to discover which one was supposed to correspond to a French word, presented elsewhere. The subject's choice was again acknowledged positively or negatively. The criterion for the 'right' terms was decided in advance, for example, those ending in an *s*, those containing two particular letters, etc.

Some of the situations studied by Heidbreder (1924, 1947, 1948) under similar conditions are comparable to those of the second type in so far as they concern concepts of concrete objects, such as human figures, buildings, trees, etc. Situations involving spatial forms like circles, crosses, etc. can be included in this group.

Situations involving the perception problem of the 'form in itself' can also be included. This problem has been the subject of considerable research both in animals and in children.[1] A series of a particular form, for example, a triangle, varied systematically, is presented among a collection of various figures. If the subject repeatedly chooses the triangular form, in spite of the variety before him, there is said to be perception of the triangular form 'in itself'.

(C) Other situations, involving more abstract structures, have been studied in research related to that just mentioned. In some of these situations (Ree, 1946; Heidbreder, 1946, 1947, etc.), the feature common to a series of objects (directly perceived or represented verbally) was the fact that these objects all belonged to the same class or category designated by a nonsense syllable, but defined in a more abstract way in that the similarity between members of a classification was very general, even purely functional (for example, groups of animals, vegetables, colours, abstract numbers, etc.).

One situation, related to that of numerical structures, involves the so-called 'odd one out'. This has given rise to considerable research, first in animals[2] and then in children.[3] The situation entails the formation of groups of objects which vary from presentation to presentation as far as their qualitative aspects are concerned, but which always contain one 'odd' object among all the other similar objects. The subject has to contrast the single

---

[1] Fields, 1931; Gellermann, 1933; Andrew and Harlow, 1948; de Lannoy, 1962.
[2] Klüver, 1932; Robinson, 1933; Rey, 1935; Spaet and Harlow, 1943.
[3] Szentkereszty, 1956.

'odd' object with the quantity of similar ones, and this must be done on a relatively high level of abstraction, since the qualitative aspects of both the single object and the other objects vary constantly.

All these situations involve the learning process in that the acquisition of an invariable 'concept' or 'principle' is effected by means of a series of presentations, ranging over a wide field and so implying the action of previous experience.

The problem of the mechanism of these acquisitions and of the nature of an invariable 'concept' or 'principle' has to be investigated against the background of all the theoretical interpretations of the learning process.

2 Factors and mechanisms of learning

The learning process appears in a variety of forms, from a descriptive point of view.

What factors and mechanisms are involved in this process? Although, in accordance with the definition contained in the previous section, this variety of form presents a certain unity, it also indicates that the factors and mechanisms are likely to be equally varied. Consequently a strictly uniform interpretation of this process is not likely to be possible.

Of course, various factors and interpretations of them have already been put forward, but no single one of these interpretations applies to all that happens in learning. As for the factors, their importance and the part they play vary in different forms of learning. In addition, their mode of action can appear in different ways, giving rise to varying interpretations. This also means that it is difficult to consider them independently, so we shall try to describe them within in their particular theoretical context.

1 Practice

First we should like to consider briefly one general aspect of acquisitions effected in learning, namely their progressive nature, which is linked to the condition of practice. Some authors have not even considered this as a factor.

Acquisition is not usually accomplished in one single trial, i.e. one presentation and one reaction. It is established gradually, each repetition of the situation leading to an improvement in performance until a satisfactory level of efficiency is reached.

(A) Repetition of both situation and reaction, i.e. practice, seems to be an essential condition for many acquisitions in which the situation or reaction is slightly more complex. However, many authors do not consider that this condition constitutes a real factor in learning on the grounds that repetition, as such, does not bring about a progression in the quality of the performance. It merely enables true factors to work.

Thorndike (1931, 1932) demonstrated, by means of numerous experiments, the extremely limited effect of frequency of repetition, i.e. of practice, as such.

In one of these experiments (1931, p. 8), the subjects had to trace a line (four inches long) a great many times (3,000 reactions divided up into 12 sessions). In each session, the lines actually traced varied in length and the frequency of the various lengths divided up to form a Gaussian curve. However, the dispersion of the curve was the same for each session: the variability was not reduced, although, in accordance with the law of frequency, the most frequently performed reactions must have dominated increasingly, so leading to a reduction in variability as a function of the degree of practice.

In another experiment (1931, p. 13), the subjects' task was to complete a large number of words beginning with two letters at the rate of 240 per day for 14 days. Some of these words were repeated a great many times, sometimes as often as 28 times, but the subjects did not always respond to them in the same way. Those that finally dominated and became fixed in the last work period were not necessarily those that had appeared most frequently in the first period. On the contrary, they tended to be the simplest and most rapidly performed reactions.

It would seem, however, that practice should be regarded as a true factor in motor learning, since repetition of the reaction does appear to be a direct and essential factor in the progress of the performance. As many authors have noted, motor skill is acquired by practice. This is probably because the sensory control of such reactions has a kinaesthetic origin, and so depends on the actual performance, the structure of which is exclusively motor in other respects.

(B) The progressive nature of most acquisitions involving practice can be shown in the form of a diagram or *learning curve*.

These curves are constructed by placing on abscissae the repetitions or consecutive trials and on ordinates the acquisition achieved in each trial, measured either by the quantity of material acquired or by the number of incorrect reactions or mistakes.

The shape of the curve is either of positive or negative gradient, depending on the nature of the measurement. Curves increase and decrease in irregular ways, but, in general, they average out into three types (e.g. those obtained by Vincent's method): positive acceleration (increasing gain), negative acceleration (decreasing gain) or sigmate shape (S-shaped). The last two occur most frequently and the sigmate curve generally appears when acquisition starts at zero.

Various mathematical formulae have been proposed for these curves: an exponential function (Hull, 1943) and a more complex function applying to the sigmate curve (Culler, 1928; Thurstone, 1919, 1930). These exponential formulae, which take into account the speed of the curve's gain and its limit, seem to be the best for empirical data, although this application is only approximate.

Occasionally a learning curve can follow a completely different pattern. After an initial, steady course (often chance), the curve may rise or fall suddenly to the level of correct adaptation. These curves are often produced by 'intelligent' learning (described earlier) in both humans and animals. They have been regarded as an indication of a learning mechanism different from that producing curves which increase or decrease steadily.

(C) When learning calls for prolonged practice, the following question arises: is it better to 'mass' this practice, which means repeating the trials one immediately after the other, or to space it out, leaving gaps between consecutive trials?

This question of *distribution of practice* has been the subject of considerable study. Generally speaking, spacing out the trials seems to provide the most favourable conditions for the exercise, from the point of view both of the number of repetitions required to reach the learning criterion and of the quantity of work accomplished in a given period.[1] This is the substance of a law

[1] Piéron (1913), learning numbers; Lorge (1930), mirror drawing; Doré and

known as *Jost's law* (1897) which states that, with two associations of equal strength, but unequal age, repetition increases the strength of the older more than that of the younger.

It is worth noting that this fact corresponds to a law of optimum: the best conditions for fixation seem to be obtained when the time interval is neither too short nor too long. The absolute length of this interval lies between 1 minute and 24 hours[1] depending on the nature of the material and the reaction performed. In general, the less meaning the material has, the shorter the interval should be. In other respects it varies according to the length of the trials and of the work period: the optimal interval seems to be at least as long as the work period.[2]

Interpretation of this fact has given rise to various hypotheses. On the one hand, it has been assumed that the fixation process is not instantaneous,[3] but goes through a phase of maturation following presentation of the situation or performance of the reaction. On the other hand, it can be assumed that a process of fatigue develops, in some cases anyway, giving rise to a partially refractory period as far as any new presentation or reaction is concerned. This would justify a rest period between presentations, but the interval ought not to exceed a certain time on account of the inevitable action of forgetting. If the interval is long enough for forgetting to develop, all the benefit gained from maturation and the possibility of eventual recovery will be lost.[4] The value of the optimal interval will be worked out by balancing the opposing action of these various factors.

(D) If practice cannot be considered to be a factor, but only a condition of learning, it still appears to be a real factor in the case of acquisition taking the form of habit.

Establishment of habit is characterized by automatism of reaction, i.e. objectively by features of stereotype and fatalism in the development of the action and subjectively by the absence of any conscious control on the part of the subject. Habit can only be established by frequent repetition of both a 'stimulating' situation and a given response to that situation. Research into

---

[1] Piéron, 1934.   [2] Lyon, 1914; Travis, 1939; Hovland, 1940.
[3] Müller and Pilzecker, 1900; Piéron, 1934.   [4] Cook, 1944.

Hilgard (1937), tracking reactions; Kientzle (1946), tasks consisting of writing letters of alphabet upside down.

this problem[1] has shown that the reaction is not repeated identically. It changes and evolves systematically and it is precisely this fact that qualifies it as a form of learnt or acquired reaction. However, this evolution slows down and the reaction assumes the fairly sterodyped aspect of a reflex action as the exercise is repeated. Consequently repetition seems to be a decisive factor in this case.

2 Interpretative theories

Many interpretative concepts have been formulated as to the mechanism of learning and the nature of the processes and factors involved.

If learning phenomena imply the existence of processes of connection or organization of traces of earlier experience, i.e. a certain kind of associative memory, the nature of such processes and their functional mechanism can obviously be interpreted in different ways.

If the classical schema of Watsonian behaviourism, whereby all behaviour should be regarded as a reaction to stimulus (both of which can be observed objectively), is accepted, the traces of prior experience must be studied in accordance with the same schema, i.e. as systems of traces of a purely phsyiological nature, linking the receptor and effector processes in the form of S–R type connections.

If, however, behaviour is regarded as being determined by a variety of internal factors, as well as by external stimuli, the traces of prior experience must give rise to much larger, associative organizations or syntheses, in addition to sensori-motor connections. These organizations will include not only specific modes of reaction, but also traces of things which happened earlier and which refer to or depend upon each other. It would certainly be more difficult to define these in purely physiological terms.

3 The theory of conditioned reflexes

This theory, which seems to be the simplest and most physiological interpretation of certain events occurring in learning,

[1] Van der Veldt, 1928; de Montpellier, 1935.

belongs to the first type of interpretation mentioned, although it complies, in part only, with a strict conception of the S–R schema.

(A) This theory was elaborated by Y. Pavlov in order to explain what happens in conditioning. He and other authors later expressed the view that it could be extended to other forms of learning.

This theory refers to excitation and inhibition, on the one hand, and to irradiation and concentration, on the other, as representing states or, more precisely, dynamic processes of the higher nervous system. The action of stimulus can produce a process of excitation or inhibition and this process can either be irradiated or concentrated in particular points. In addition, processes of irradiation and concentration can alternate in a zone, particularly when the level of excitation or inhibition varies. Irradiation occurs when the level is very low or very high and concentration occurs in between. Alternation of processes of excitation and inhibition can also take place, causing reciprocal induction.

The transfer of stimulating power (*vis-à-vis* a particular reaction) from an effective stimulus to an initially neutral stimulus can be explained as follows: when excitation processes of unequal intensity (under the influence of appropriate stimuli) develop in two or several points of the hemispheres, irradiation occurs in such a way that excitation from the points of least intensity tends to concentrate on the point of maximum intensity. This 'drainage' of the excitation processes takes place through the nervous channels linking the points in question. There is a sort of 'clearing-a-way' process in these channels which may cause a decrease in synaptic resistance[1] with the result that the response belonging to the unconditioned stimulus is evoked by the new, initially ineffective stimulus alone.

This can be represented as the following schema:

$$S_c \quad - \quad C_{rc} \quad - \quad C_{e_{init}} - R_{init}$$
$$|$$
$$S_{unc} - C_{runc} - C_{e_{unc}} - R_{unc}$$

S_c = conditioned stimulus;
S_{unc} = unconditioned stimulus;
C_{rc} = receptor centre of the conditioned stimulus;

[1] Pavlov, 1955, p. 9.

C_{runc} = receptor centre of the unconditioned stimulus;
$C_{e_{init}}$ = effector centre of the initial reaction;
$C_{e_{unc}}$ = effector centre of the unconditioned reaction;
R_{init} = initial reaction;
R_{unc} = unconditioned reaction.

The process of 'clearing-a-way' takes place between the receptor centres of the conditioned and unconditioned stimuli, thus making possible the transfer of excitation *vis-à-vis* the unconditioned reaction. Pavlov saw this as the essential phenomenon of learning.[1] Of course, the stimulatory power of the new stimulus is only temporary in the absence of the unconditioned stimulus. Repeated alone, this new stimulus will produce inhibition in the corresponding cortical, receptor centre (experimental extinction and differentiation). This process of inhibition may also irradiate round it, producing conditioned inhibition.

A problem arises since conditioning results in the production of a reaction by a new stimulus, thereby creating a new stimulus–response relationship. One hesitates to group this with the other S–R theories, since the basic process which enables transfer to take place is, in fact, the establishment of a new communication between the receptor centres of the two stimuli. A connectionist schema of the S–S type would probably define this process better.[2]

The only condition considered as necessary by the theory for the establishment of the new connection is the temporal contiguity of the two processes of stimulation. In fact the necessity of this condition is the origin of the name given to this type of learning. Obviously this interpretation is limited to examples of conditioning which conform to the transfer schema in which the conditioned reaction is the same as the unconditioned reaction. It can hardly be extended to examples of instrumental conditioning nor, *a fortiori*, to those of more complex learning in which it is no longer a question of the transfer of a pre-existent response to new stimuli, but rather of the appearance and fixation

---

[1] Pavlov, translated Anrep, 1927, p. 385; Pavlov, translated Baumstein, 1955, pp. 36 and 128.
[2] The definition of conditioning given by Hilgard and Marquis (1940, p. 48), in which conditioning is considered as 'an experimental procedure giving rise to the establishment of simple, associative connections between specific stimuli and responses', seems to depart from the Pavlovian conception and to have been influenced by the general schema of the behaviourist conception.

of an entirely new response. It is even a little difficult to apply this interpretation to examples of classical conditioning in so far as the conditioned response differs from the unconditioned response.

(B) Watson (1914, 1919) was the first psychologist to consider the process of conditioning as the prototype of the mechanism of learning and the formation of habits in humans.

Following the classical schema of behaviourism, he saw conditioning as the establishment of a new S–R connection, but he probably regarded this as the expression more of the phenomenon of transfer on the behavioural level than of a underlying, physiological process. The condition of contiguity is not specifically included in this definition. In any case, it would have to be understood in a new way, since the terms of the connection have altered. On the other hand, the factors of *frequency* and *recency* are used to explain the fixation of a reaction.

These factors have been the subject of considerable critical discussion. Frequency has been called a preliminary condition rather than a real factor, and the results of many experiments do seem to minimize its importance.[1]

Recency, in the sense that Watson understood it, is more a condition for reproduction or evocation than for fixation: when a repeated situation gives rises to various reactions, the most recent reaction (the last in the series) tends to be reproduced. However, this statement is surely an expression of the law of forgetting which is the weakening of a trace as time passes.

(C) Guthrie (1930, 1935, 1959) is one of the present-day psychologists who considers that most examples of learning can be reconciled with the principles of Pavlovian conditioning. However, the schema of behaviourism underlying this interpretation is not exactly the same as that of Watson; it is more a question of 'molar' behaviourism in the sense Tolman gave to this word.

Behaviour is a reaction to stimuli, but the latter are defined as 'cues', i.e. perceived signals, which the organism locates in a given system of physical variables, while a reaction is an 'act' or unified collection of movements distinguished by its *pattern* and by its result.

This being so, learning, i.e. conditioning, consists of the

[1] Thorndike, 1931, 1932.

establishment of a chain of connections between signal-stimuli (located by the subject) and *patterns* of movements, dependent only on the condition of contiguity.

This is the only essential condition. Frequency and repetition of the situation or reaction are not directly essential: for, according to Guthrie, a connection is always completely established at the first combined occurrence of stimulus and response. Consequently experimental extinction and all forms of weakening in the reaction, when stimuli are repeated, are not the result of inhibition, but of the establishment of new reactions incompatible with those that disappear (interference). This conception does have the merit of being very simple, but it is difficult to agree that temporal contiguity is the sole factor necessary for the formation of new connections, since the most elementary observation shows that any stimulus acting at the moment when a response appears does not acquire the power to produce precisely that response. We are told that an element or aspect of a physical situation becomes 'stimulating' as a 'signal', but as a signal of what?

(D) Konorski (1948, 1950) made important changes in Pavlov's theoretical concept. These changes defined the processes of excitation and inhibition, and attempted to enlarge this concept's field of application by including examples of a new type of condition, type II conditioning, very similar to that described by Skinner (1938) as 'operant' reflexes, and by Hilgard and Marquis (1940) as instrumental conditioning.

These examples can appear in different forms. Konorski, like Hilgard and Marquis, divided them up into four different categories. They are, of course, all distinguished by the fact that, contrary to what occurs in the Pavlovian situation, the presence of the unconditioned stimulus (often called the reinforcing stimulus) is dependent upon the actual performance of the reaction, i.e. the reaction has a truly instrumental character *vis-à-vis* the stimulus.

According to Konorski, the basic process in classical conditioning consists of the formation of new functional connections between the centres of the conditioned and the unconditioned stimuli by a modification in the synaptic processes. These processes can cause stimulating or inhibiting connections, depending on whether the excitation from the effector centre (conditioned stimulus) coincides with the activity or cessation of activity in the receptor centre (unconditioned stimulus).

In the case of type II conditioning, Konorski stated that synaptic connections are established between the cortical centres of the conditioned stimulus and the centres of the motor reaction. These connections can be stimulating or inhibiting, depending on whether the reaction results in the abolition or the maintenance of a state of general excitation in the motor cortex. Excitation or inhibition are produced either by a reduction of activity in the alimentary centre, due to the absence of food, or by an increase of activity in a defensive centre, due to the presence of a noxious stimulus. As a result of the state of general excitation in the motor cortex, the centre of proprioceptive excitation arising from the reaction becomes similar to an unconditioned centre and acquires the temporary ability to form synaptic connections with the centres of the unconditioned stimuli.

This conception, like that of Pavlov, applies only to cases of transfer in classical conditioning, i.e. cases in which the conditioned and unconditioned reaction are alike.

In the case of type II conditioning, the process of general excitation in the motor cortex to which this theory refers seems a rather curious condition for the formation of a new reflex, although it may simply be the expression of a relatively high level of motivation (need) which is linked to the existence of positive or negative unconditioned stimuli. The latter certainly applies to all conditioning,[1] but it does not seem to be confined to the motor zone of the cortex.

4   The theory of the reinforcement of connections

According to this interpretation, the learning process consists not so much of the establishment of new connections, but of the differential reinforcement of certain connections between stimuli and responses which existed before the intervention of factors of appropriate reinforcement, such as Thorndike's 'effect' factor and C. Hull's 'need-reduction'.

The main object of Thorndike's conception is to explain the

---

[1] This condition, which is not really mentioned at all in Pavlov's works, should be noted here, since it plays an essential role in theories reviewed later.

preferential fixation of certain reactions to the exclusion of others in selective learning by 'trial and error'. Conditioning phenomena in the classical sense remain outside the explanation. Hull's concept, however, attempts to interpret all types of learning on the same basic principles.

(A) Thorndike felt that the notion of connection could only be defined in a functional and probable sense: 'There is a connection between stimulus S and response R when the probability of R appearing after S is greater than zero' (1932, p. 19). On the other hand, he barely defined the process of connection from a physiological point of view: a connection is 'any activity, state or condition of the neurons' (1933, p. 475).

(*a*) The essential factor in the reinforcement of a connection is expressed in the law of *effect*. One statement of this was: 'When a modifiable connection between a situation and a response is made and accompanied or followed by a satisfying state for the organism, the strength of the connection is increased: when it is made and accompanied or followed by a disagreeable state, the strength of the connection is diminished' (1913, p. 4). Later (1931), he limited the factor of effect to its positive aspect; the disagreeable state does not necessarily diminish the strength of a connection, whose intensity may sometimes even increase slightly.

What constitutes a satisfying state? Thorndike attempted to give an objective definition of this as a function of observable features of behaviour: 'By satisfying state, one means a state that the organism does not try to avoid, but rather tries to reach and maintain; by disagreeable state, one means a state that the organism tries to avoid' (1913, p. 123).

Thorndike demonstrated the existence and role of positive effect in various experiments. For example, in one experiment the subjects were presented with a series of 200 Spanish words. Each Spanish word was followed by 5 English words, one of which was the translation of the Spanish word. The subjects' task was to discover which of the 5 words corresponded to the Spanish word. The experimenter acknowledged each word 'right' or 'wrong'. The list was presented 12 times.

The table overleaf[1] shows the pattern of results of 5 subjects for one of the 200 Spanish words. The numbers are those

[1] 1931, p. 32.

of the words chosen in the 12 consecutive presentations, the correct word being no. 2 in each case:

	1	2	3	4	5	6	7	8	9	10	11	12
N	5	3	5	3	5	4	1	2	2	2	2	2
P	3	5	4	4	2	2	2	2	2	2	2	2
Ra	4	2	2	3	2	2	2	2	2	2	2	2
Ro	4	1	1	2	2	2	2	2	2	2	2	2
St	3	3	2	1	5	1	5	2	1	2	3	2

Obviously the correct word was chosen more and more often after it had been positively acknowledged.

The absence of any negative effect, lessening the intensity of the connection, came to light in the same experiments. For example, in the experiment we have just described, a note was made of the cases in which the correct word, out of the 200 words presented to 9 subjects, was chosen in the second or third trial (correct choice in the first trial was not included in order to avoid cases in which the connections already had a certain intensity caused by prior influences), and 20 such cases were retained. Cases in which the same incorrect word was selected in the second or third trial were also noted, and a further 20 cases were retained. The influence of the two correct or incorrect choices on the frequency of the correct or incorrect choices (given incorrect response) in subsequent trials was then examined.

With one subject, for example, in the trial immediately following the two correct choices, there were 18 correct choices and 2 incorrect ones, when mere chance would have produced 4 correct choices and 16 incorrect ones out of a total of 20. In the trial immediately following the 2 incorrect responses (same choice), there were 10 choices of a different response, whereas chance would have produced 16.

The results of the group of 9 subjects were as follows: the percentage of cases in which a correct response in trials 2 and 3, 3 and 4 or 2 and 4 was followed by a correct choice in the next trial was 70, while chance would have produced 20, so the positive influence of an agreeable effect was 50 per cent. The percentage of cases in which an incorrect response (the same one) in trials 2 and 3, 3 and 4 or 2 and 4 was followed by a different response in the next trial was 73, whereas the percentage resulting from chance would have been 80, so the positive influence of a disagreeable effect was 7 per cent.[1]

(*b*) How does effect act on a connection in order to reinforce it? This question touches on the actual nature of the mechanism involved in the process of reinforcement.

The mechanism is that of a 'confirming reaction', but this is not the evocation (on the level or representation or recollection) of a given response and the agreeable or disagreeable effect following it, i.e. interior repetition of the stimulus-response sequence followed by effect. This mechanism is immediate and direct. Effect automatically provokes an increase in the connection's intensity which lies entirely outside the subject's consciousness. In other words, a confirming reaction is a physiological phenomenon of an existing nervous process influencing the previous state of the organism. It does not necessarily have a psychological counterpart. Moreover, Thorndike did not conceal the fact that the nature of its action might be vague.[2]

Two groups of examples are used to support this mode of interpreting a confirming reaction. These are examples of unconscious learning and of the spread of effect.

(α) *Unconscious learning* consists of the formation of S–R connections, distinguished by an increase in the frequency of response, when the subject does not know either to which feature of a situation he is responding (ignorance of the stimulus) or how he responds to a given situation (ignorance of the response).

The following experiment is an example of the first type: the subject is presented with a series of 100 cards, each bearing four lines numbered from 1 to 4, measuring 5 cm. In addition, each card has a special feature (one line may be thicker than the others, or may have a little mark across it, etc.) enabling the experimenter to identify the rewarded response. For example, when the card has a line with two marks, line no. 2 has to be acknowledged positively; when the card has a badly drawn line on it, line no. 1 has to be acknowledged, and so on. Naturally the subject is not told of this connection between the card and the rewarded response. He is simply asked to compare the four lines and say which one he thinks is the longest. The differences are often very small, and so the subject has to guess initially.

[1] Thorndike, 1931 p. 41.   [2] 1935, p. 40.

After each choice, the experimenter indicates 'right' or 'wrong', according to whether the subject's response meets the criterion of a good response, or not. Some subjects find the key to the system and, of those who do not, some make no progress at all, while others make a little progress. Eight subjects progressed from a total of 362 correct responses in the beginning to 432 at the end of the presentations, a gain of 19·6 per cent.

An example of the second type occurs in the experiment with Spanish words, already described. The subject has to choose the corresponding English word out of several presented to him, but this time his choice has to be accompanied by a motor reaction consisting of underlining the word chosen. As soon as he has done this, the experimenter says 'right' or 'wrong' and the subject goes on to the next line. The acknowledgment system is constructed in such a way that the right word occupies positions 1, 2, 3, 4 and 5, from left to right, 10, 15, 20, 25 and 30 per cent of the time respectively. Under these conditions, a satisfying effect is linked not only to the choice of certain words, but also to the action of choosing a word situated at the extreme right-hand end of the line and to the reaction of underlining it there. The series of 200 words is presented 16 times to the subjects. Immediately afterwards, the subject takes a test containing 100 different words, in which reactions are neither punished nor rewarded. After the final test, the experimenter makes sure that the subject still has not noticed the unequal distribution of the right word. Only the results of students who have noticed nothing during the experiment count.

The following results are obtained: out of 8 subjects, the average number of words underlined, from the first to the last test, is from 28 to 19 for position 1 and from 12 to 21 for position 5, so the reaction has a tendency to localize itself in the position where positive effect acts most frequently.

(β) The phenomenon of the *spread of effect* consists of an increase in the reinforcement of penalized connections adjoining the connection (both in time and space) which undergoes the action of positive effect. The nearer the penalized connection is to the rewarded connection, the more marked the increase.

Thorndike came across this phenomenon in serial learning experiments. In one of these experiments,[1] a list of words was

[1] 1933.

read to the subject. Immediately after each word, the subject had to respond by choosing a number, and this choice was acknowledged either 'right' or 'wrong' by the experimenter, in accordance with a pre-arranged system. The list was presented several times, but it was too long for the subject to be able to remember how he reacted in previous presentations. An analysis of the responses to each word shows that the rewarded responses were more numerous than unrewarded ones and also that penalized responses were repeated more frequently, the nearer they were to a rewarded response. This happened too often for it to be mere coincidence. Repetition diminished from its maximum next to the rewarded response, until it was practically non-existent 5 words away.

Here are the aggregate results from 15 experiments of this type: with zero as reference, the percentage of repetitions of a penalized response 5 or more units away from a rewarded connection in the trial following the rewarded response gains 10 times what a penalized response 5 units away gains, 9 times what a penalized response just before it gains and 2·5 times what a penalized response just after it gains. The latter gains the most from the action of the spread of effect, i.e. from an indirect action of effect.

(c) On which connection does effect act directly? Thorndike introduced the notion of *belongingness* (1932, p. 76; 1935, p. 59): effect acts directly on those connections bearing a relationship of belongingness to it. What does this mean? How does something belong to a connection? Sometimes Thorndike seemed to define belongingness as temporal contiguity between effect and connection (1935, p. 59); on other occasions (1935, pp. 51–52), a stronger link of an intrinsic nature seemed to be implied, with effect appearing to be a consequence of the response, i.e. linked to the response by a causal relationship similar to that existing between the taste and the actual presence of food in the mouth, for example, or between the capture of prey and the leap made to reach it.

Such internal belongingness is certainly different from that resulting from mere temporal contiguity, but Thorndike emphasized that the subject must not be aware of this relationship. Moreover, although the factor of belongingness is important, the phenomenon of spread shows that it is not a necessary condition of reinforcement.

(*d*) Although effect is the essential factor in the formation of connections, Thorndike listed several secondary factors favouring the establishment of connections. The first is a factor of belongingness which exists, in certain cases, between the two parts of a connection prior to reinforcement: for example, the belongingness between subject and verb in a statement. However, this belongingness, resulting as it does from a pre-existent connection, is probably not really a new factor. It merely shows that a connection can reach a certain level of intensity more easily if it already exists initially.

Other factors mentioned by Thorndike are those of identifiability, i.e. facility of differentiation between stimuli, and of availability, i.e. facility of performance of reaction. These two factors are certainly auxiliary conditions in the establishment of connections.

(*e*) This conception has been the subject of some criticism.

(α) In the first place, it is difficult to see the nature of the mechanism of a 'confirming' reaction as a direct and automatic process, independent of all subjective awareness of what occurs in the connection. Is there retroactive influence of one physiological process upon another; but, if so, how can this influence suddenly result in the reinforcement of an earlier process? Thorndike admitted that the nature of this confirming mechanism was unknown, and he even went so far as to describe it himself in psychological terms![1]

(β) What about the two groups of examples quoted by Thorndike to support the idea of the direct and automatic action of reinforcement?

As far as unconscious learning is concerned, the facts do not seem to agree and various interpretations are possible. Some of Thorndike's experiments produced different results when they were repeated by other experimenters.

For example, the experiment of the cards with lines on was repeated by Pollet (1946), with two groups of 40 and 50 subjects. The results were entirely negative. The average percentages of 'correct' responses showed no improvement from beginning to end.

However, Pollet also repeated the experiment using words

---

[1] It seems to accept it, say "yes", or O.K. to it, endue it with acceptability . . .' (1932, p. 316).

chosen and underlined as corresponding to Spanish words, with results similar to those obtained by Thorndike: of 12 subjects (out of 27), who had not noticed the unequal distribution of the 'right' words, the choices for columns 4 and 5 were from 16·5 to 22 per cent (first to last test) and from 17·5 to 26·5 per cent (from first to sixteenth presentation of 200 words). There was an increase, but the reaction in question was, of course, a simple motor one, automatic, always the same, and this could produce a habit of a localized reaction, due to the law of frequency, i.e. practice, as happens in motor learning.

In other experiments, first carried out by Thorndike[1] and later repeated by Pollet (1946), as in various learning situations of the same type in which it was a question of discovering a 'principle',[2] an improvement in performance, i.e. learning, was noted before the discovery of the principle involved. Indeed, in some cases there was an improvement without the principle ever being discovered. However, this does not seem to constitute indubitable proof of unconscious learning. As Pollet (1944), Szentkerenszty (1956) and de Borchgrave (1957) have shown, progress could result from a partial and gradual discovery of the principle involved, i.e. the subject starts by perceiving isolated aspects or elements of the solution.[3]

(γ) Phenomena of the spread of effect, where it has proved possible to confirm their existence, have also been subjected to various interpretations. If the tendency really is to repeat connections situated near a rewarded connection more often than those situated farther away, it does not necessarily follow that these more frequently repeated connections are directly and immediately reinforced by the action of the reward.

[1] Experiments involving word completion, for example (1932). The subject is presented with a list of incomplete words, i.e. words in which one or several letters are replaced by dots. The subject's task is to complete the words by replacing the dots with letters. After a preliminary series, the experimenter tells the subject that certain words only will be 'right', without telling him the basis for this. The experimenter evolves his own system: for example, a dot after *a* should be replaced by a *v*, a dot after a *b* by an *e*, etc.

[2] Drever, 1934; Pollet, 1946; de Borchgrave, 1957.

[3] These results do not mean that any form of unconscious learning is impossible. Some forms of sensori-motor and motor learning appear to be unconscious, since modifications in reaction very often occur outside the control of the subject and without him being aware of them. However, it must not be assumed that they occur without the existence of cognitive data of a sensory nature.

Nutting (1941, 1953) demonstrated that connections situated near a rewarded connection do not produce any more precise recollection of associated terms than those situated elsewhere in the series, which would seem to indicate that these connections are no better formed than the others. Take the example of the following experiment: the subject is presented with a list of 40 everyday words, each word accompanied by 5 foreign words. He has to select one of these foreign words as corresponding to the inductive word. His choice is rewarded or punished in accordance with a pre-arranged scheme. Slightly different instructions are given to the subject after the first presentation of the list. He is asked to repeat the word he gave previously in response to each stimulus word. The percentage of correct replies is compared with the two categories of penalized responses: those placed between two rewards or just before or just after a reward, and those situated 2, 3, 4 or 5 units away from the rewarded connections. The results of 16 experiments of this type, using 500 subjects and involving 21,170 connections, showed 48 and 50 per cent correct replies, respectively.

However, Nuttin (1953) also demonstrated that the tendency to recollect a penalized connection as a rewarded one is strongest when this connection is situated close to a connection which was rewarded in an earlier presentation. For example, in the experiment of choosing foreign words to go with words in the mother tongue, when the subjects (11 groups totalling 358 subjects) were asked, in the second session, to repeat for each stimulus word the response given and the sanction received (either right or wrong), the percentage of responses remembered as rewarded, but actually punished, was higher for responses very close to a rewarded connection (just before or just after it) than for responses farther away (at least 3 units away). The percentages were 27 and 22, respectively. The difference is not enormous, but it is significant. This is a new sort of spread, spread in the process of recalling the sanction received, but it does not mean that connections close to a rewarded connection have been reinforced in preference to others. It simply means that the rewarded point tends to irradiate a whole zone and to oust the trace of penalization from the memory. Nuttin also found that the subject could often remember the response he gave, but was uncertain about which sanction it received.

Nuttin felt that these two facts combined (spread and hesitation about the sanction) could result in the subject repeating the responses that he remembered giving near a successful choice because of the aura of success surrounding this choice. But this would mean that effect acted as the indicant of 'what had to be done' to accomplish the task, rather than direct and automatic reinforcement of certain connections.

Zirkle (1946) demonstrated that the tendency to repeat a response, previously given close to a rewarded reaction, still appears when the presentation order of stimuli in connections around this rewarded connection is altered from trial to trial. Obviously spread of effect acts on the actual performance of the response, rather than on the connection.[1]

(δ) Consequently the process of a *confirming reaction* does not seem to be direct and automatic. How can this process be explained? The answer seems to be as a process of information. It seems to act not as an affective factor (i.e. producing an agreeable or disagreeable state) but as an indicant of what must be done or not done to accomplish the task. Effect is not an absolute factor, but a relative one, i.e. relative to the task: it is determined by the successful performance of the task.

This explains why the influence of effect is more marked, the more precise the information given. Repeating Thorndike's experiment of drawing lines of a given length blindfold, Cason and Trowbridge (1937) compared four experimental conditions:

Condition 1: no indication followed reaction;

Condition 2: reaction followed by nonsense syllable;

Condition 3: reaction followed by sanction 'right' or 'wrong', depending on whether length of line fell within certain limits;

Condition 4: reaction followed by statement of precise length of line.

The results, in percentages of correct reactions, were as follows: 13·6 per cent for Condition 1, 5·1 per cent for Condition 2, 22·6 per cent for Condition 3 and 54·8 per cent for Condition 4. The more information was given, the more precise the reactions. The poor results obtained under Condition 2 were probably due to the effect of distraction caused by the introduction of a completely new factor.

---

[1] See M. H. Marx (1956) and Fältheim (1956) for the work done on the phenomenon of the spread of effect or the 'Thorndike effect' and its interpretation.

This also explains the part played by the factor of belonging-ness between connection and effect (to which Thorndike referred), although it cannot be precisely defined. Effect only acts on those responses and their possible determinants which are part of the system constituting the task. Obviously it is a question of internal belongingness and not just of concomitance or contiguity.

Finally, this explains the privileged action of positive effect in learning reactions, i.e. in 'open-task' reactions, to use Nuttin's terminology (1953). In this case, the subject *knows*, or is almost certain, that some of his reactions (those sanctioned positively) should be acquired and retained, for they will have to be repro-duced and evoked later. However, in the case of a 'closed' task, i.e. an operation which does not constitute a learning activity, positive effect no longer has any privileged action *vis-à-vis* negative effect. Nutting demonstrated this fact in a series of important experiments (1953).

For example, a series of cards showing groups of objects or individuals of the same type (flock of sheep, line of trees, row of houses, etc.) was presented to his subjects,[1] who were asked to estimate how many objects there were on each card. Their responses were acknowledged 'right' or 'wrong' in accordance with a prearranged pattern (half were acknowledged positively and half negatively). At a second session, the subjects were not presented with the cards, but were reminded of them, and then asked to repeat the response they gave at the first session for each card. The percentage of correctly recalled responses was almost the same for both rewarded and penalized responses: 48·1 and 48·3 per cent respectively.

In another, similar experiment, each card presented bore a pair of capitals drawn in large letters. There were 12 different pairs of capitals and each pair recurred 12 times, but each time they were drawn in different sorts of letters, so that a total of 124 pairs were presented. The subject's task was to say whether the space covered by one letter was larger or smaller than that covered by the other letter. In actual fact, they both occupied about the same amount of space. The judgement of the subject, who had to say one letter or the other, was acknowledged 'right' or 'wrong' on the same pattern as before (6 of the 12 pairs were rewarded, and

---

[1] Five groups of subjects totalling 321 subjects.

6 penalized). At the second session, the experimenter said the first letter of the 12 pairs followed by 'smaller than', where he saw from his notes that the subject had usually judged the first letter to be smaller than the second, and 'larger than', where the opposite applied. The object was to see whether the recall of the second letter would be facilitated by pairs which had been positively acknowledged 12 times in comparison with pairs negatively acknowledged 12 times. The percentages of correct second letters, calculated on the results of 6 groups of subjects totalling 444 individuals, were again practically the same: 40·4 and 42 per cent. The difference is not significant and would seem to be opposite of the hypothesis. Therefore it seems in order to conclude that positive effect does not act in a privileged way under these conditions of performance without learning.

However, in learning conditions like those in Thorndike's experiments, the task remains 'open', so that the sanctions or acknowledgments can exercise their function of information or integration, by incorporating data into the system of tension created by the task.

Nuttin compared the action of sanctions in 'open' and 'closed' tasks in one of his experiments. The experiment was carried out with the aid of a Michotte kinesimeter. One group (A) performed a 'closed' task: the subjects were simply asked to make a movement of a given distance (indicated by the position of a mobile obstacle, moved in each trial) with their eyes closed. The experimenter acknowledged each movement 'right' or 'wrong', depending on how far it deviated from the angle of the obstacle's original position. The subjects were warned in advance that they would have to perform a series of reactions of this type. The second group (B) carried out an 'open' task: the subjects had to learn to repeat the same movement, after they had, by knocking against the mobile obstacle, found out its size. In actual fact, both groups made the same movement, since the experimenter put the obstacle back in the same place each time. The only difference was that the movement made by the subjects in group A, though followed by sanctions, was not integrated into a task as it was in group B. The results showed that the mean angle of distance from the obstacle was smaller for subjects in group B than for subjects in group A (81 degrees for group A, 58·8 degrees for group B).

(ε) Various authors seem to agree that negative effect acts on learning.[1] It could probably act initially in the form of positive effect *vis-à-vis* a response which is antagonistic or opposed to the penalized response. For example, a withdrawal reaction, produced by negative effect, would lead to positive effect, i.e. rescue or deliverance, which would reinforce the connection between situation and withdrawal reaction.

Negative effect can also give information *vis-à-vis* a given response and so be the reinforcing agent of the connection. Tolman, Bretnall and Hall (1932) showed that, in stylet maze-learning with the administration of an electric shock for either correct or incorrect responses, learning was achieved more rapidly in the first case than in the second. These authors considered that the role of effect was to accentuate perceptually the features of correct or incorrect responses.

Nuttin (1953) also demonstrated that, under certain conditions, a negatively acknowledged response (which could be used in the accomplishment of a later task) might be better integrated, and so better preserved, than a response which was positively acknowledged, but not integrated. A subject was shown a series of cards bearing letters of the alphabet. On the back of each card there was a number. The subject had to say the letter and guess the number. The experimenter said 'good', if the number was right; but, if the number was wrong, he turned the card over and showed the subject the number that he should have said. The subject was told: 'The object of the experiment is to see how many times you have to be shown the cards before you guess the right number. Each time you guess correctly, I will put the card on one side, since we will no longer need it'. This was the preliminary part of the experiment designed to show the subject what it was all about. The main part of the experiment involved a new series of 11 cards. The sanctions system was so arranged that the replies to 5 cards were always 'good'. In the case of the other 6, the experimenter turned the card over immediately after the subject's response, unless the subject actually gave the number of the back of the card, but this rarely happened. However, if it did, the experimenter said 'good'. In the third session, the subject was asked to recall the

[1] Thorndike, 1932; Tolman, Bretnall and Hall, 1932; Wallach and Henle, 1941; Nuttin, 1941, 1943.

exact number for all the cards presented to him a second time. This number was the 'rewarded' number or, in the case of the cards for which he gave the wrong response, the number on the back. To summarize, there was positive sanction (reward) which was also an indication to the subject that he need take no more interest in that reaction, and there was negative sanction (punishment) which showed the subject that he must remember that response, since it provided him with a means of accomplishing the rest of the task successfully.

The results, obtained from three groups of subjects totalling 264 individuals, ate shown in the following table:

	Positive sanction	Negative sanction	't'
Exp. I (N = 16)	29 %	37 %	1·18
Exp. II (N = 186)	26·1%	31·6%	2·55
Exp. III (N = 62)	28·1%	37·2%	3·43

In all three cases, the percentage of numbers remembered correctly is higher after negative acknowledgment than after positive acknowledgment, although the figures are only significant for groups II and III.

In addition, it could be argued that negative effect caused the formation of a connection between the situation and the response which led to this result, but this connection did not appear in the form of a reaction, since the performance of a reaction would have constituted positive effect. This would lead to the distinction, upon which some authors[1] have insisted, between the notions of learning and of performance. Thorndike did not make this distinction which, in any case, hardly applies to this theory, since the connection here is defined as the probability of a response in the presence of a situation. The connection has to be seen as a link between the process of excitation and of reaction to the potential state, as it were (on a neural plane, for example). This connection only makes its appearance in behaviour after the substitution of a positive effect for a negative one, but it is formed long before it actually appears. Consequently positive

[1] Lashley, 1929; Williams, 1929; Elliot, 1930; Tolman, 1932, 1934; Hull, 1951, 1952; Nuttin, 1953.

effect would be the necessary factor for performance, but not for learning.

(B) C. Hull (1943, 1951, 1952) attempted to systematize and define very precisely the theory of the reinforcement of connections. At the same time, he tried to include everything that occurs in learning and, in particular, in conditioning.

(*a*) Like Thorndike, Hull regarded learning as the formation of connections between stimuli and responses. But he saw these connections as persistent states of the organism (1943), established between receptor and effector processes on the level of the central nervous system and corresponding to the well-known notion of habit ($_{s}H_{R}$). He did not explain these states more fully. They are 'hypothetical constructions', intervening as intermediary variables between stimuli and responses and shown (on the behavioural level) by the 'tendency', i.e. probability, of a stimulus to evoke a reaction.

The essential condition for the establishment of these connections is similar to that of Thorndike's effect, but Hull called it more vaguely a 'factor' or 'agent' of reinforcement. It was no longer defined as an agreeable state (*satisfier*), but as a process of *need reduction*, so the reinforcement mechanism implies the existence of an initial need and its subsequent reduction.[1] The presence of this need is signalled to the organism by afferent excitation (*drive stimulus*).

The only condition required for reinforcement to act and give rise to a connection is temporal contiguity between a reaction and the action or trace of the action of a stimulus, on the one hand, and between this double occurrence and the reduction of a need, on the other. The law of 'primary reinforcement' described this fundamental mechanism as follows: 'When an effector activity acts in temporal contiguity with an afferent impulsion or the persistent trace of such an impulsion, and when this combination of events is so intimately associated in time with the decrease of stimulation corresponding to a need, there is a resultant increase in the tendency of the stimulus to evoke this reaction subsequently' (1943, p. 80).

---

[1] Need reduction, since it constitutes a generalization of Thorndike's law of effect, can occur in two ways: either by the presence of a stimulus of a positive nature meeting a pre-existent need or by the suppression of a stimulus of a negative nature (noxious) entailing the disappearance of the need caused by the presence of this stimulus.

There is a corollary to this law of primary reinforcement, that of 'secondary reinforcement' by virtue of which any stimulus, which gives rise to a receptor activity (afferent impulsion) acting at the same time, or almost the same time (not more than 20 seconds between them), as a need-reduction process, can acquire reinforcing power. This law seems to have been introduced in order to extend the mechanism of reinforcement to cases in which need reduction is only produced after a relatively long and complex period of activity greater than that of the primary reinforcement.

(*b*) The strength of the reinforcement and, consequently, of the connection depend on various *factors*. Hull attempted to explain their role by a quantitative formulation of their mode of intervention.

In Hull's interpretation, the strength of a reinforced connection depends, first of all, upon the number of trials or presentations of the situation during which reinforcement took place. The function linking the strength of the connection to the number of reinforcements had an exponential aspect expressed by the equation $_sH_R = M(1 - e^{-iN})$ in which M is the limit of possible strength under given experimental conditions, N is the number of reinforcements, i is an empirical constant representing the speed with which the function reaches its maximum and e is the basis of natural logarithms. This equation is a function of growth in which the increase is always a constant fraction of the remaining available potential.

The limit of strength that could be reached by a connection under given conditions would itself be a function of various factors, so these could also be considered as factors of a connection's strength.

The first factor of this type would be the size or quantity of reinforcement. A connection's limit of strength would be a function of this factor following the exponential relationship: $M = M_o(1 - e^{-kw})$, in which M_o is the limit of strength possible under optimal conditions, e expresses the quantity of reinforcement and k is the constant growth rate.

The second factor would be the interval of time separating reaction from reinforcement. The limit of a habit's strength would also be a function of this factor following an exponential, but negative, relationship: $M = M_o e^{-jt}$, in which t is the interval of time and j the constant growth rate.

This relationship expresses the law of the 'reinforcement gradient' according to which a reinforcement's strength decreases as a function of the time separating the reaction from the moment when need reduction occurs. This phenomenon is, on the whole, the same as Thorndike's spread of effect.

Finally, the limit of a habit's strength would also be a function of the interval separating the appearance of the stimulus (new or conditioned) in the new connection from the response (or, in some cases, from the duration of the action of the conditioned stimulus).

This function also has a negatively exponential aspect: $M = M_o e^{-ut'}$, in which t' is the interval of time between stimulus and response or the duration of stimulus action, and u is the constant growth rate.

The final equation expressing a connection's strength as a function of these various factors would be:

$$_sH_R = M_o(1 - e^{-iN})(1 - e^{-kw})(e^{-jt})(e^{-ut'})$$

(*c*) We have seen that need intervenes in the process of a connection's formation, since the reinforcement factor acts in the form of need reduction. But need can intervene in another way, as an agent bringing about a formed connection, i.e. as a performance factor which transforms habit from the mere ability to act into the actual action. In conjunction with a connection's strength, need strength gives rise to *excitation* or *reaction potential*, $_sE_R$, which would be a multiplicative function of these two factors:

$$_sE_R = f(_sH_R \times D).$$

In fact, this potential would depend on other factors, as Hull subsequently pointed out[1] in the following equation for the reaction potential: $_sE_R = f(D \times V_i \times K \times _sH_R)$, in which not only need strength and connection strength figure, but also strength of stimulus and of motivational value of the object intervening in the reinforcement process.

However, excitation potential is subject to a reverse action springing from the actual performance of the reaction. Far from being a factor of progress, the performance of a reaction would engender inhibition with a direct and indirect (conditioned)

[1] Hull, 1952.

effect on this same reaction. This would produce a sort of inhibition potential I_R, which would increase with the effort expended in the reaction and with the number and proximity of repetitions, but which would gradually disappear when the reaction ceased to be produced. This potential must be abstracted from that of the excitation or *effective* reaction, following the formula: $_s\bar{E}_R = {_s}E_R - I_R$, from which it is possible to predict performance.

(*d*) Hull's concept is probably the most precise and systematic attempt that has been made to explain learning on the basis of connections formed between stimulus and responses by means of a single, general process in which reinforcement is caused by need reduction.

This concept is wider than that of Thorndike. On the one hand, it applies to everything that takes place in learning and conditioning as well as in selective learning 'by trial and error'. On the other hand, the action of both positive and negative effect can be interpreted identically by means of the need-reduction process: in both cases, organic tension is lowered either by the positive reaction of approaching and obtaining something or by the negative reaction of fleeing from and avoiding something.

(α) Nevertheless this theory does have certain grave deficiencies. Firstly, as with Thorndike's concept, it is difficult to understand the reinforcing action. Why and how does need reduction manage to reinforce a pre-existent stimulus–response connection? Neither from a physiological nor from a psychological point of view is the mechanism of such reinforcement specifically explained.

This mechanism is all the more difficult to understand, for apparently the only condition required for its operation is temporal contiguity between connection and need reduction, but this condition does not seem to take into account established or reinforced connections. The connection which is formed or reinforced is not just any connection preceding need reduction, but those connections which lead, directly or indirectly, to this need reduction. Thorndike saw this problem and tried to solve it by introducing the belongingness factor between connection and effect, but even this notion is absent from Hull's theory.

(β) Furthermore the law of frequency linking a connection's strength to the number of reinforcements cannot always be verified. It has been demonstrated that, as far as strength of conditioning and resistance to extinction are concerned, partial or intermittent reinforcement can produce equally good, and sometimes better, results than continual reinforcement.[1] Similarly, in the case of stimuli of a negative or noxious nature,[2] conditioning resulted in the fixation of relatively durable escape reactions after only a few trials of reinforcement by need reduction.

(γ) The formation of connections seems to be possible without reinforcement by need reduction, for example, in the case of *latent learning*. Blodgett (1929), Tolman and Honzik (1930) and Reynolds (1945) all found that rats placed without food in a maze for a certain number of trials were not appreciably slower in acquiring the habit (judged by number of trials required to find correct route or by average number of errors) than animals who had found food in the endbox from the beginning. The acquisition of the habit is hardly evident during the trials without food; but, once food is present, the curves are very similar (see Fig. 9),

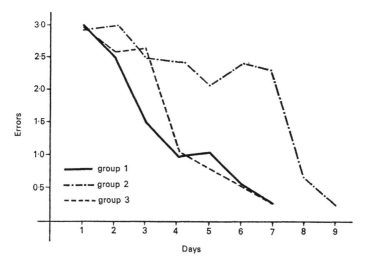

Fig. 9. (After Blodgett, 1929.)

[1] Humphreys, 1939, 1940, 1943; Finger, 1942: Mowrer and Jones, 1945; Sheffield and Temmer, 1951. Also see Jenkins and Stanley, 1950; Lewis, 1960.
[2] Solomon and Wynne, 1950.

so learning, which is the formation of connections (but not, perhaps, of connections between stimuli and responses), took place during the trials without need reduction.

Other observers,[1] using apparatus with one choice-point (simple T-maze with two endboxes), observed that, when appropriate motivation was introduced, animals were quite capable of adapting their reaction (choice of a particular direction) to the presence of an object which they had previously encountered in earlier trials, without motivation *vis-à-vis* this object or without any identifiable motivation at all.

In this situation, there is choice and fixation of a reaction, without any previous reinforcement by need reduction of the connection which eventually exists between this reaction and the stimuli provoking it.

(δ) The process of secondary reinforcement is also a weakness in the theory. This process appears to involve a phenomenon of associative connection between need reduction and a stimulating situation which occur almost simultaneously. This is a new type of connection, quite distinct from the S–R type and more like the S–S type (in so far as need reduction can be likened to a source of stimulation), but which is established without reinforcement, unless need reduction is both one of the conditions and the reinforcing agent for the connection. In fact, the law of secondary reinforcement lacks any clear explanation of the mechanism bringing about its establishment.

(C) Spence (1956, 1960) is one of the foremost exponents of Hull's theory today, but he partially dissociates himself from Hull's definition of a reinforcing agent. He defines this simply and empirically as an event following a reaction which increases the probability of the reaction's susequent appearance. Such an event probably implies the existence of needs on the part of the organism, but not necessarily a process of need reduction.

Moreover, he does not consider that the reinforcing agent plays a part in the formation of true habit (H), but only in the determination of the strength of the effective excitation potential ($\bar{E}$) through the intermediary of the motivational value of goal-object (K), following the formula: $\bar{E} = H \times (D+K) - I$, factor K depending on the number of experiments with the goal-object,

[1] Meehl and MacCorquodale, 1948; Thistlethwaite, 1951, 1952; Walker, 1952; Bendig, 1952; Johnson, 1952; Northon and Kenshalo, 1954.

the length of the chain or responses and the duration of the reinforcement interval.

However, Spence has pointed out that need reduction is an important factor in classical and instrumental conditioning with a negative or noxious stimulus.

(D) STATISTICAL OR STOCHASTIC THEORY OF LEARNING

This description of Hull's theory must be followed by a review of the attempts to interpret the learning process in terms of stochastic processes, i.e. series of events possessing a certain probability of appearance.

Models of this sort have been set up by Estes (1950, 1959), Bush and Mosteller (1951) and Jonckheere (1958).

These models usually involve a learning schema conceived in terms of connections between stimuli and responses. In addition, at any rate in the case of the authors mentioned, they involve a 'molecular' or 'atomistic' concept of learning.

For example, Estes (in common with Mosteller and Bush) feels that various aspects or elements of a situation are capable of exercising the function of stimulus to a certain type of response, quite independently of one another. In each trial or presentation of the total situation, certain elements become stimuli and are thus connected with the response following a law of 'all or nothing'. The response's probability increases thereafter as a function of repetition of the situation. A growing number of elements are linked to this response, and learning actually lies in this systematic change in a given response's probability of appearance.

However, in a situation in which the number of elements likely to become stimuli, and so form connections with a given reaction, diminishes with frequency of presentation of the situation, the amount of increase in the response's probability also gradually diminishes with each trial, producing a 'growth' function (similar to that suggested by Hull) established from the base equation: $\rho n + 1 = \rho n + \theta(1 - \rho n)$ (in which θ is understood as a proportional constant between 0 and 1, representing the connection probability, presumed to be equal, of various stimuli, n being the trial number), since $\Delta\rho = \theta(1 - \rho)$.

The first requisite for the establishment of connections

between stimuli and responses is probably contiguity. As Guthrie indicated, the neutral stimulus must be given at the moment when a response is performed, in order to become the stimulus of this response.

But these new connections also require a certain reinforcement condition. From 1951 onwards, Mosteller and Bush introduced into the base equation for operation, which determines the probability of a response, two parameters, one relating to the positive influence of reward and the other relating to the negative influence of punishment or expenditure of energy connected with the performance of a response. Estes, on the other hand, referred only to the condition of contiguity in his earlier works, although subsequently he too referred to a reinforcement factor, notably in the collection of studies published in 1959.[1] However, the nature of this factor is no more clearly defined than that of stimuli and responses. The agent of reinforcement is a concomitant or subsequent event, also producing an increase in the response's probability, which should consequently be introduced as a factor into the equation giving the reaction's probability of appearance. Estes (1959, p. 460) seems to compare this event to a stimulus–response system distinguished by two conditions: firstly, responses evoked by stimuli in this system should not interfere with the response whose probability of appearance is sought; secondly, the action of stimuli in this system should cease immediately after the performance of this response. Other authors[2] see reinforcement as linked to the result, and particularly to the success, of the reaction as far as the subject's task is concerned (agreement with the subject's forecast, for example).

Obviously these statistical interpretations apply directly to serial learning: successive discrimination, mazes, verbal series of syllables, words, motor reactions, etc. Yet these interpretations appear to encounter considerable difficulties in the case of learning which is both more complex and more unified, i.e. situations which cannot be broken up into elements or aspects likely to be connected separately, as partial stimuli, with a particular kind of reaction.

[1] Estes, 1959.   [2] Bush and Mosteller, 1951; Jonckheere, 1958.

Gérard de Montpellier

5 The theory of 'expectancy' or formation of cognitive syntheses

(A) According to this theory, expounded principally by Tolman,[1] the learning process lies essentially in the formation of synthetic units or structures of the *gestalt* type between cognitive data. On the strength of these syntheses or structures, the appearance of certain events or objects causes the imminent occurrence of other events or objects to be 'expected', depending on the existence of certain attitudes or reactions on the part of the organism.

(*a*) Tolman used the expressions *sign-gestalt-expectations* or *field-expectancies* or *means-end-readiness* to describe these structures. For this reason, the theory has often been called the theory of expectancy. Basically these structures comprise three stages or parts: a signal event, a signalled event and a behavioural passage from signal to signalled. A *sign-gestalt-expectation*,[2] according to Tolman,[3] is equivalent to expectancy on the part of the organism that 'this' (the signal) will give rise to a specific operation (the behavioural passage) leading to 'that' (the signalled event). This being so, learning must consist of the formation or reformation of expectancies of this sort under the effect of acquired experience and as a result of efficiently performed reactions.

In addition to the preliminary condition of performance (i.e. of the sequence of signal-reaction-signalled events), the conditions or factors in the formation of these systems of expectancy are: firstly, the conditions for the formation of *Gestalten*, in particular the condition of internal belongingness and continuity as well as that of contiguity or spatial-temporal proximity; secondly, the condition of motivation or drive which implies the presence of need and set, but not the process of need reduction. Nevertheless Tolman has admitted that a principle of reinforcement or effect exists in the sense that expectancy can be confirmed or disabled by experience, but this applies equally to events producing a negative response of avoidance or escape or a positive response of approach.

---

[1] Tolman, 1932, 1934, 1936, 1948, 1949, 1955, 1959.
[2] The *sign-gestalt-expectation* has been expressed by MacCorquodale and Meehl (1953) in the formula $S_1R_1S_2$ with which Tolman seems to agree (1959).
[3] Tolman, 1934.

(*b*) What, for Tolman, are the factors or conditions of performance, i.e. the factors intervening when a specific reaction is evoked in a given situation and at a given moment? This problem of *performance*, which has already appeared in Hull's theory, becomes particularly acute in Tolman's theory, due to the absence of a specific, associative connection between the signal-stimulus and the reaction leading to this signalled object or event. MacCorquodale and Meehl (1953) managed to detail the subject more precisely in their attempt to formulate Tolman's theory on the basis of Hull's equations. The reaction potential of response R_1 in the presence of S_1 would be a multiplicative function of the strength of expectancy $S_1R_1S_2$ and the valence of the object 'expected' S_2: $S_1ER_1 = f(S_1R_1S_2)(V_{S2})$. As for the valence, this would be a multiplicative function of the need and the cathexis[1] of the object S^2: $V = f(D \times C)$.

Tolman himself has tried to explain this point in his later works.[2] Performance is an 'act', accomplished by movements and accompanied by reflexes, but only defined and distinguished by the environment-organism changes it provokes, and not by these movements and reflexes. Performance depends on a variety of things: firstly, on four types of independent variable, namely existing stimuli, earlier sequences of the $S_1R_1S_2$ type, existing needs and their corresponding objects, and innate or acquired individual differences; secondly, on three types of intermediary variable (inferred process), namely discriminative dispositions which enable an organism to distinguish certain aspects or dimensions in a complex, stimulating situation, expectative dispositions which act in such a way that, by reacting specifically to certain discriminated stimuli (signals), an organism expects or is prepared for the occurrence of other specific stimuli, and appetitive dispositions, i.e. 'demanding' certain objects, which act in such a way that, because of specific needs, certain objects appear with a motivational value or positive valence in relation to these needs.

The temporary value of these intermediary variables may be determined from the temporary values of the independent

---

[1] The cathexis of an object is its ability to reduce a need. Other authors have seen this as a growth function (negative acceleration) of the number of times the object and the accomplished response, aroused by the object, occur together.

[2] Tolman, 1955, 1959.

variables, so that any specific performance must be seen as the result of the activation of specific dispositions or sets, arising from these three types of variable in the form of a unified process which is discriminative, expectative and appetitive.

In fact, a specific performance would only exist initially as a tendency, represented in 'behaviour space' by a vector, whose direction and size would determine the direction and strength of the actual performance that could be expected.

In practical terms, this vector would be the result of the following factors:

(1) Strength of the needs in relation to the objects;

(2) Strength of the positive or negative valences of the drive-objects;

(3) Strength of the needs opposed to the effort to be extended in the reaction leading to or away from the drive-objects;

(4) Strength of the negative valences relating to this effort;

(5) Strength of the expectancies about the result of the action in relation to the drive-objects and the effort to be made in order to reach or avoid them.

As Tolman himself has noted (1955, 1959), these factors (determining the performance vector) partially resemble those occurring in Hull's equations defining the excitation or reaction potential.[1] In both cases, performance is a function of the needs and motivational value of the objects. The difference between them appears more clearly in the case of habit, which is a system built on the basis of earlier experience. Hull regards this system as a connection of the S–R type, while Tolman sees it as an expectancy of the S–R–S type.

The principal examples quoted by Tolman to support his theory are those in which performance does not consist of a specific motor reaction linked by a connection to equally specific stimuli, and those of latent learning.

The latter certainly provide an argument in favour of a theory which does not make reinforcement by need reduction an essential condition of learning. But they also favour a concept which sees in learning, above all else, the establishment of cognitive syntheses or structures between given events or objects on a perceptual or representational level. If performance can occur, when motivation is present, without previous practice, the fundamental

[1] See de Montpellier (1959).

process in learning cannot be that of the formation of stimulus–response connections. It must, in fact, consist of the formation of connections or syntheses between 'cognitive' data which will subsequently be put to good use in a performance.

Tolman quoted many other examples, mostly taken from research in animal psychology, to support this concept.

For example, maze learning in rats seems to involve the formation of systems of spatial relations, rather than of specific motor structures. An animal who has learnt how to run through a maze correctly is equally capable of swimming through it correctly.[1] If the animal's motor behaviour is profoundly disturbed after surgical intervention (removal of certain sections of the spinal cord), it can still take the right route through the maze and reach the end without mistake.[2] In this sort of learning, the general direction of the goal is often acquired before the details[3] of the route, and this general direction will be retained even after considerable alterations to the route the animal has to follow.[4]

Tolman, Ritchie and Kalish (1946) attempted a direct comparison between the formation of a motor habit (learning a specific movement) and that of a spatial habit (learning specific localization). The apparatus used consisted of two raised paths intersecting to form a cross (see Fig. 10). At the end of one of the arms, there were two identical chambers containing the bait.

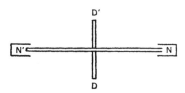

Fig. 10. (After Tolman, Ritchie and Kalish, 1946.)

The ends of the other arm provided alternative starting points. The rats were divided up into two groups: one group had to learn to choose, in each trial, the path leading to the chamber on the right (or left) of the subject; the other group had to learn to choose the path leading to a chamber in a specific, spatial position.

[1] MacFarlane, 1930.   [2] Lashley and Ball, 1929.   [3] Dashiell, 1930.
[4] Lashley, 1929; Honzik, 1933; Tolman, Ritchie and Kalish, 1946.

By alternating the starting point, a motor habit was imposed on one group and a spatial habit on the other. The results of this experiment indicate that the second habit was acquired more easily than the first. The 8 animals in the second group attained the learning criterion in less than 8 trials, while 5 of the 8 animals in the first group had not attained it after 72 trials. On the contrary, they acquired the habit of always going towards the same chamber even though they only found food in it half the time.

This experiment has been repeated, under slightly different conditions, by other experimenters.[1] Their results do not entirely agree, but they do seem to favour Tolman's interpretation.

(*c*) Although the phenomena of classical and instrumental conditioning can be interpreted by either of these two theories (Pavlov's conception is, nevertheless, probably closer to Tolman's theory than to Hull's), examples of indirect conditioning seem to support Tolman's theory.[2]

These phenomena consist basically of the production of certain reactions by stimuli which have never been linked with them, but which have been linked with certain stimuli rendered effective *vis-à-vis* these reactions during earlier conditioning. Here is an example of this type of situation described by Shipley (1933): using human subjects, he first achieved conditioning in which the eyelid reaction, usually produced by a tap on the cheek, was produced by lighting a lamp in front of the subject. He then established conditioning in which the tap on the cheek acquired the value of a conditioned stimulus *vis-à-vis* the motor response of withdrawing the finger, which had originally been provoked by an electric shock. As a result, most of the subjects withdrew their finger when the lamp went on. Obviously the interpretation of these results calls for some experimental control. The experimenter must make sure that the light does not initially

---

[1] Thompson and Thompson, 1949; Tolman and Gleitman, 1949; Blodgett, McCutchan and Mathews, 1949; Webb, 1951; Hill and Tune, 1952; Galanter, 1955; Gleitman, 1955.

[2] On the same subject, also see Rozeboom (1958), who considers that, in classical as in instrumental conditioning, the functional dependence of behavioural effects produced by the new or conditioned stimulus *vis-à-vis* the effects produced by the unconditioned stimulus constitutes the actual object of acquisition.

produce the motor response. In addition, he must check that both phases of the experiment are absolutely necessary.

The results of these experiments have been explained more fully and been generally verified by other research of the same sort. Repeating Shipley's original experiment, Lumsdaine (1939) obtained identical results: the light alone, in the critical trials, provoked the motor reaction in most of the subjects. However, Lumsdaine found that the withdrawal movement only occurred if the eyelid reaction also appeared. In other words, the light simulus produced two reactions at once.

Various other experimenters[1] carried out this experiment under simpler conditions. After a combined presentation of two stimuli (for example, sound and light), conditioning was established in which one of the two stimuli acquired the function of conditioned stimulus *vis-à-vis* an unconditioned stimulus (electric shock), after which the second stimulus was presented alone. This stimulus, in turn, provoked the conditioned stimulus without ever having been previously linked with it by a connection resulting from direct conditioning.

If the process of stimulus generalization is eliminated as the mechanism producing a reaction in this way (and the results of various control experiments do seem to be fairly conclusive on this point), the functional equivalence of the stimuli used in the first phase of the experiment seems to be involved. But, as Birch and Bitterman (1951) noted, this would mean comparing the conditioning process to a phenomenon of sensory integration.

(*d*) Interesting as it is, Tolman's theory also reveals certain deficiencies.

In the first place, the actual notion of expectancy is rather equivocal. In fact, expectancy is considered both as an intermediary variable, not directly observable, but inferred from features supplied by an analysis of behaviour, and as an 'immanent determinant of behaviour', i.e. as an objective feature of behaviour. This equivocality probably stems from some development in the author's thinking. Judging from his later works, he seems to be saying that expectancy is basically a variable inferred from certain aspects (notably, the preparatory aspect) of the reaction (1955, p. 316).

---

[1] Prokofiev and Zéliony, 1926; Brogden, 1939, 1942, 1947; Karn, 1947; Silver and Meyer, 1954.

Gérard de Montpellier

However, in spite of Tolman's statement (1936, p. 102) that introspection does not enter into the definition of this variable, it seems very difficult to deny that the specific nature and positive significance of such a process lead, in the end, to an introspective analysis. This may not cancel out the system's value and interest, but it does perhaps make it impossible to consider it as a formula of strict behaviourism.

In addition, it seems difficult to apply this conception to certain things that occur in learning. In some cases of elementary conditioning (for example, the patellar reflex), the conditioned reaction has no preparatory feature. And how can the notion of expectancy be applied to incidental or unconscious learning or, for that matter, to motor learning? Moreover Tolman himself admitted that there is more than one kind of learning and that motor learning is a special form of learning (1949).

(B) The theory defended by Woodworth (1958) is very similar to Tolman's concept.

According to Woodworth, the basic process in learning is once again the constitution of a cognitive structure which affects the surrounding events, objects and aspects when these appear to the organism in succession. As a result, this structure takes on a sequential form. The organism learns that event S_1 is followed by another S_2, and so on. The events become signals for one another and the reactions that they provoke are a function of this signalization. Each one prepares the organism for the following event. However, this simple succession in time is not sufficient for the constitution of such structures. Some of these events must correspond to existing needs and reinforce the value of the signal by evocation of the appropriate reactions.

The formula for a structure formed in this way (employing the usual notations S and R) would be: $S_1R_1-S_2R_2$ (as compared with Tolman's formula: $S_1R_1S_2$). This represents the structural unit formed. Stimulus S evokes response R_1, in preparation for the occurrence of S_2 which, in turn, evokes the final reaction R_2. A basic relationship of a cognitive nature is established between the first sensori-reaction group S_1R_1 and the second S_2R_2. The existence of strictly specific connections between the two groups is not implied.

(C) Guillaume's name should be mentioned in connection with authors who support a cognitive theory of learning.

In fact, this author (1947) stated that the fundamental transformations taking place in learning occur on the level of perceptual and cognitive processes, particularly in the form of the acquisition of signal value by certain events or objects. Changes in behaviour are only the effect, in the form of reactions, of these cognitive acquisitions and transformations. This applies not only to intellectual, sensory or sensori-motor learning, but also to cases involving the formation of real motor habits. These habits involve the constitution of kinaesthetic structures, veritable kinetic melodies, which are captured and 'understood' by the proprioceptive sensitivity as being similar to other perceptual structures. But, in this case, there is no gap between the cognitive and the executive aspects. The actual reaction is perceived as a structure.

6 O. Mowrer's 'reconsidered' two-factor learning theory

Initially, Mowrer proposed and defended a double interpretation[1] of events occurring in learning, according to which events in conditioning or 'signal' learning consisted of a process of substitution of stimulus *vis-à-vis* a given response under the effect of contiguity, whereas events in selective or problem-solving learning consisted of a process of substitution of response *vis-à-vis* a given stimulus under the effect of reinforcement by need reduction. Today, however, he defends[2] a concept which is much closer to that of Tolman and whose dual nature is considerably reduced.

The phenomena of selective learning and problem solving and of the formation of habits by 'trial and error', like those of classical conditioning, involve the acquisition of new significance by certain internal or external stimuli (stimulus-excitants). This acquisition of significance is revealed by emotional attitudes and reactions, such as anxiety or hope.

However, this acquisition is accomplished through a reinforcing process which appears in two different forms, producing two types of reaction: in the case of repeated concomitance with a factor bringing need reduction (positive stimulus) and corresponding to an 'agreeable' experience, any active stimulus (either external or internal) will acquire a significance conducive

[1] Mowrer, 1950, 1951.   [2] Mowrer, 1956, 1960.

113

to the recurrence of this experience (positive reaction of obtaining or approaching something); in the case of repeated concomitance with a factor producing an increase of need (negative or noxious stimulus) and corresponding to a 'disagreeable' experience, any internal or external stimulus will acquire a significance tending to prevent the recurrence of this experience (negative reaction of escape or avoidance).

Consequently, these positive or negative reactions must be the result of the acquisition of these significances, brought about by the intervention of the factor of contiguity, on the one hand, and of reinforcement through need reduction, on the other.

Nevertheless, the fact that these reactions must result from the positive or negative significance acquired by the stimuli-signals can only be partially explained, even by the author.

7   C. Osgood's theory of 'mediation'

This theory seems to be an attempt to reconcile events in conditioning and selective learning and the theories of both Tolman and Hull.

(A) The learning process is, to Osgood (1935), the acquisition of significance by certain stimuli and the appearance of certain instrumental reactions, resulting in a modification in the organism's relationship with its environment. These two fundamental features represent two successive stages in the accomplishment of the overall process, the first stage exercising a function of *mediation vis-à-vis* the second.

How does this happen? The acquisition of significance lies in the ability that certain stimuli acquire to evoke the same reactions, or the so-called 'detachable' parts[1] of these reactions, as those immediately produced by other stimuli (stimulus-objects), i.e. becoming the signal for a stimulus-object means evoking the reaction (or detachable part of it) normally produced by this object. But, although these transferred or detachable reactions are 'responses', they are also 'stimuli', since they actually give rise, directly or indirectly, to characteristic, proprioceptive excitation. In this capacity, they play a mediatory role between the stimulus-signals and instrumental reactions, modifying

---

[1] This notion of a 'detachable response' is the same as Hull's 'fractional anticipatory goal-response' (Hull, 1930).

Learning
relations between the organism and its environment by eliciting
these reactions, in their turn'[1]

(B) Under what conditions are the acquisition of significance
and production of instrumental reactions effected? Conditions
for the acquisition of significance are, firstly, temporal contiguity
between the stimulus-signals and stimulus-objects and, secondly,
a reinforcement process brought about by the action of the
stimulus-objects *vis-à-vis* certain needs of the organism.

Conditions for the production of instrumental reactions are,
firstly, the action of the reactions to the stimulus-signals giving
rise to auto-stimulation and, secondly, a reinforcement process
resulting from the motivational properties of these reaction-
stimuli. Reinforcement occurs in so far as the instrumental
reactions bring about a reduction in needs shown by these very
properties of the reaction-stimuli. Consequently there is reinforcement in both stages, causing a waterfall effect. The reaction-
stimuli finally gain their motivational properties from the motivational value of the stimulus-objects *vis-à-vis* certain needs of
the organism.

This being so, the changes characterizing learning would
affect both aspects, although they principally affect the mediatory
process (acquisition or loss of significance) in most classical
conditioning situations, while instrumental reactions are hardly
affected at all. In selective learning by 'trial and error', the
changes affect both the significance of stimulus-signals (i.e. the
mediatory process) and instrumental reactions, new responses
generally being acquired and fixed by their successful accomplishment through the intervention of a reinforcement mechanism in
the form of the reduction of a pre-existent need. Only the
mediation reactions, and not these new reactions, should resemble at least partially the responses produced by the stimulus-
objects. Osgood regards this similarity as the significant feature
of the stimulus-signals.

(C) This attempt to reconcile a variety of factors, interesting
as it is, still presents certain problems. In the first place, the
nature of the mediatory process is somewhat equivocal. It is
supposed to be a process of acquiring significance, i.e. the

[1] Osgood uses the notion of a *pure stimulus act*, i.e. an act whose sole function
is to be a stimulus. Hull introduced this idea to account for the cognitive and
deliberate nature of some reactions.

formation of cognitive syntheses on a representational level, and a 'reaction', usually non-instrumental of a viscero-glandular type, evoked by stimulus-signals. Consequently this reaction, rendered perceptible by the organism by means of appropriate, proprioceptive excitation, must also be a stimulus for instrumental reactions. But how can instrumental reactions, which are usually motor reactions on a relatively high level of adaptation, be the effect of viscero-glandular reactions, which are of an emotional nature and on a low level of adaptation? Perhaps the two sorts of viscero-glandular and instrumental reactions are 'effects' (on a reactional plane) of cognitive syntheses produced in some other way. If this is the case, what does the process of mediation consist of?

In addition, viscero-glandular reactions provoked by stimulus-signals do not always produce proprioceptive excitation, so how can they be stimulatory *vis-à-vis* instrumental reactions?

Finally, the mechanism of the reinforcement process is not adequately explained as far as the acquisition of significance is concerned. It appears to be a question of secondary reinforcement at this stage. But is this reinforcing power acquired by the stimulus-signals (in accordance with Hull's theory) or by reaction-stimuli which must, therefore, be the expression of states of tension or need (anxiety) that can be reduced (in accordance with Mowrer's theory)?

8 *J. Piaget's theory of 'equilibration'*

Piaget interpreted learning in the perspective of his general conception of the development of behaviour.

He regarded learning, in the strict sense of the word, as acquisition by means of previous experience without any direct, systematic control by the subject. This differs from acquisition by simple perception or immediate comprehension (*insight*) and from a process of induction in which there is some control.

In Piaget's view, learning can affect either the subject's actions, as in the case of the acquisition of habits, or properties or laws concerning objects, as in the case of perceptual learning or discovery of a law of alternation or of the 'odd one out' in a group of physical things.

In both cases, the learning phenomenon appears in the form

of a change in behaviour. However, this change does not result either from the establishment of new stimulus-response (SR) connections or from new, entirely cognitive syntheses or structures of the S–S type, but from the transformation of a *schema of action* of a sensori-motor nature (or cognitive-reactional nature) whose initial tendency is to assimilate objects by incorporating them into a canvas of behaviour; this can be transformed by the effect of a compensatory tendency to accommodate itself to these objects (when the latter resist assimilation) as a result of the action's success, i.e. satisfaction of a pre-existent need.

The assimilatory phase of this process can give rise to a learning phenomenon in the form of a reaction transfer (as occurs in conditioning) when the reaction produced by the unconditioned stimulus becomes a new stimulus.

Nevertheless, the transfer is not produced by an association of conditioned and unconditioned stimuli, but in the assimilation of the new stimulus to the unconditioned S–R scheme, already in existence, i.e. in its active incorporation into a prior, sensori-motor organization. Consequently it is a question of an S–SR connection between a stimulus and a schema (to use the same symbolism, even though assimilation is not an association), and not of an S–S or S–R connection.

On the other hand, the accommodation phase is a more general form of learning process in that the actual reaction schema is altered by the success of a reaction method in producing satisfaction of a need, i.e. of experience which becomes previous experience *vis-à-vis* a subsequent situation.

Moreover, this motivational factor is also involved in the phenomena of transfer or generalization of the assimilatory phase, since only objects capable of satisfying the particular need in the schema are assimilated to a previous schema. This need is nothing more nor less than 'the conative or affective aspect of a schema in so far as it demands the objects it can assimilate', as Piaget wrote (1958, pp. 46–47). Consequently it is not necessary to refer to factors other than motivation, since this factor is included in the complementary processes of assimilation and accommodation.

However, if motivation does act through reinforcement, external reinforcement must be distinguished from internal reinforcement, since one results from the successful outcome of an action, while the other results from a necessary success corresponding, from a cognitive point of view, both to a simple value of the object's use and to an insight value.

Nevertheless, the structural or cognitive aspect must not be separated any further from the dynamic or conative aspect characterizing the schema. The two aspects are fundamentally linked and are complementary to one another.

Finally, and this seems to be the whole point of the theory, when there is discordance between a schema and an object or situation, which is implicit in a learning situation, a certain equilibrium is established between assimilation, i.e. the distorting incorporation of an object in order to submit it to the initial system, and accommodation, i.e. the modification of the schema itself in order to apply it to the object, 'all resultant accommodation and differentiation of schema consisting by definition of compensatory reactions in response to disturbances (in comparison with earlier schemas) which make the variation in the initial schemas necessary' (1958, p. 50). This equilibrium increases with the level of learning achieved. It is very unstable in learning at a low level, but it attains considerable stability in the constitution of logico-mathematical structures.

This theory also encounters the problem of performance. Which of the various schemas in existence will, in fact, be used at any given moment? In the case of compatible schemas, their actualization 'will be effected as a function of old co-ordinations or of new ones constructed in their place' (1958, p. 47). In the case of incompatible schemas, the one involving maximum gain and minimum loss will be activated. Once again, this must be understood as a balance of gains and losses resulting from accommodation. Thus the problem of performance is posed in terms of strategy, but at the same time it is resolved by a process of equilibrium.

Piaget's interpretation of learning probably requires some further elucidation on certain points, but it has the incontestable merit of gathering together into a coherent whole the principal facts discovered in the field of learning, and of placing the learning process among all the other processes affecting the development of behaviour.

This conception also reconciles, to some extent, the theories of Hull and Tolman in that it includes the mechanism of reinforcement by need reduction as well as the notion of cognitive structures.

9 *J. Nuttin's theory of the interdependence of cognitive, dynamic and reactional processes*

The concept of learning put forward by J. Nuttin (1953), which has certain similarities to Piaget's theory, is developed within the framework of a wider theory of human behaviour on the basis of important experimental research carried out by the author. Reference has already been made to this work.

The notion of motivation or drive, based on that of need, is the focal point of this doctrine of human behaviour; but, in Nuttin's theory, the dynamic process of need is not so much a state of the organism, which can be defined and considered in isolation, as a requirement or necessity that this process should possess certain forms of 'behavioural contact with the environment' (p. 434). Just as a perceptual or cognitive aspect of an object generally has a functional or operational aspect ('grasping' an object on the level of practical awareness, is, in fact, how the object is used), so need must also involve the realization of a particular method of action or operation *vis-à-vis* environment.

Thus the behaviour or reaction should be regarded both as a prolongation of the perceptual process on an operational level and as 'the concrete form created and taken by need as it passes from its intra-organic existence to its functional existence in the subject's world' (p. 435), i.e. as a prolongation of need on the same level of action.

Moreover, in the case of humans, these forms of behavioural contact with environment also occur cognitively, i.e. the schema of behavioural relations established on the level of action prefigures fairly clearly on the level of awareness in the form of a task or project. But 'at the moment when need appears, the cognitive scheme of these relations to be established does not coincide with the structure of relations which actually exist between the organism and its environment' (p. 435). This discordance results in a 'cognitive structure under tension' of the 'need-project' (p. 435).

Consequently learning is precisely the function 'which occurs when need passes from its intra-organic form to its functional realization in the world' (p. 437). This is accomplished in two ways: firstly, by 'the incorporation into a system of persistent need' (p. 425) of certain behavioural relations between the subject and the world, which must result in the constitution of the functional aspect shown by the world and its objects. This mode of learning occurs in 'open-task' situations which probably represent normal conditions of human activity. All the past experiences that have 'interested' the subject, both as cognitive and as reactional data, are fixed and retained by means of this mechanism of incorporation into a system of persistent need.

However, the passage made by need 'from its infra-organic form to its functional realization' in behaviour can also occur automatically by the 'canalization of need into a successful behavioural form' (p. 439) which has actually reduced the need tension. This form of learning prevails when the cognitive elaboration of need and behaviour is slight, notably in 'closed-task' situations where the essential agent for fixation is the process of need reduction. Nevertheless, in both cases, 'the fundamental principle of learning seems to be a form of incorporation of the behavioural response or of the datum perceived in the subject's dynamic system' (p. 441).

The problem of performance recurs, since evocation and use of these acquisitions should also be related, not to a stimulus connected with the response, but to the needs. 'Learnt behavioural responses, as well as awareness of the world and of objects in it', wrote the author, 'constitute within us traces of behavioural relations which are integrated or incorporated into the subject's system of needs. . . .' In fact, 'the successful behavioural schema can become a concrete form of need itself: a vague and undifferentiated need is reborn in the form of a behavioural need, i.e. as a tendency to activate the group of behavioural relations into which it is canalized. . . . As for acquired cognitive elements, they are also incorporated into a system of needs or into an orientation of interests, so that it becomes obvious that the activation of the dynamic system in question also actualizes the cognitive data integrated into it' (p. 450).

'To sum up, an actual state of need, task or affectivity *ipso facto* brings about the activation or actualization of behavioural and cognitive schemas which have been incorporated into this dynamic system in previous experience' (p. 451).

Thus, just as there is a 'close link between cognition and behavioural forms' (p. 451), there is a close link between behavioural and cognitive forms and motivation.

This is obviously an attempt to bring together the three fundamental processes of awareness, need and action involved in human behaviour or, to be more precise, an attempt to formulate an analytic theory which would emphasize the fundamental interdependence of the cognitive, conative and executive aspects of this behaviour. Nevertheless, it is basically a dynamic theory of conduct and learning.

This interpretation bears some resemblance to that put forward by J. Piaget, at least as far as the learning process is concerned. The dual mechanism of learning, incorporating cognitive data relating to objects and behaviour into a system of persistent need and canalizing need into successful, behavioural forms, brings to mind the complementary action of the processes of assimilation and adaptation, in learning phenomena, to which J. Piaget referred. Piaget's notion of schema is close to that of need, as Nuttin understood it, since a schema involves a tendency, arising from need, to function in a specific way, just as need calls for a schema of behavioural contact. The principal difference is that the accent is placed more heavily on the dynamic aspect of the process in Nuttin's theory.

This theory greatly favours the retention of behaviour as a basic unit, together with a fairly simple picture of how it functions, particularly in the case of learning phenomena. Everything that occurs in acquisition can be interpreted by it in the same way, and it also accounts for the variable degree (in individual cases) of the cognitive aspect of the different processes at work.

Conclusion

To conclude this review of the principal interpretations of the mechanism and nature of learning, no new theory of these phenomena will be proposed, but the following suggestions are made:

    1. The basic process at work in learning is that of the formation (through previous experience and, consequently, through

memory) of *syntheses* or *structures* of elements or occurrences resulting from an organism's receptive and reactional activity.

These syntheses are of three types: cognitive, sensori-motor and kinaesthetic.

Cognitive syntheses, which are connections or organizations of data from the perceptual or representative field, probably occur most frequently. They have already been found in phenomena of classical conditioning, qualitative discrimination, acquired spatial orientation and intelligent learning, both in animals and in humans, as well as in perceptual and verbal learning.

Sensori-motor syntheses, corresponding to connections or organizations of sensory and motor data, occur, in the case of animals, in phenomena of training and in certain phenomena of instrumental conditioning and, in the case of humans, in sensori-motor learning in general.

Kinaesthetic or motor syntheses, which are connections or organizations of purely proprioceptive data, are characteristic of true motor learning and are probably only encountered in humans.

2. These structures are brought about by the action of two conditions: an essential, objective condition, called *belongingness* and an auxiliary, subjective condition, namely *motivation* or *drive*.

Belongingness appears in two forms: external belongingness, in the form of *contiguity* (in time and space) of occurrences or elements making up the syntheses; and internal belongingness, in the form of *continuity*, i.e. the intrinsic necessity for a connection to exist between elements or occurrences, particularly through similarity or continuation.

Motivation results from the presence of *needs*, which can be satisfied or reduced by certain forms of action *vis-à-vis* elements or objects belonging to syntheses, although this does not always happen. In fact, the existence of need, and not its reduction, is the auxiliary, motivational condition.

3. The establishment of these syntheses or structures gives rise to various *effects* on the level of observable performances or reactions.[1]

In the case of cognitive syntheses, the first effect (when specific

---

[1] In fact, the existence and features of the structures formed can be inferred from these observable performances or reactions.

elements in the syntheses possess a high motivational value, i.e. correspond adequately to existing needs) is probably the production of emotional reactions by elements, which were neutral initially, belonging to new syntheses. These reactions appear in the form of hope or fear, etc., as well as in the form of different, concomitant reactions of an organic nature (circulatory and respiratory changes, etc.).

A second effect (sometimes occurring simultaneously, but usually occurring later in similar situations) of instrumental, motor reactions of obtaining or avoiding elements or objects, having a high motivational value, by initially neutral stimuli.

Where syntheses involve verbal elements or terms, presented visually or auditively, the appearance of one of the elements can also give rise to a reaction in which the subjects say one or other of the elements in the synthesis. This verbal reation is also the effect of a prior cognitive structure.

Where syntheses involve elements partially or wholly motor (sensori-motor and kinaesthetic syntheses), the reaction is naturally of a motor type. In addition, in the case of kinaesthetic syntheses, the actual performance of an element or part of a synthesis can produce the next element or part, so the stimulus can also be a reaction.

4. The *condition for the performance of reactions* is, first and foremost, the existence of previously constructed syntheses; but motivation also intervenes here at the performance stage in what seems to be not just an auxiliary but an essential way.

Performance depends on needs existing *vis-à-vis* elements of a high motivational value, which make up syntheses, or *vis-à-vis* tasks in reactions, for example, the task of speaking in verbal learning. These needs cause the evolution of the syntheses from their functional level within the organism to the level of a reaction. There reactions appear as behavioural methods of need satisfaction or need reduction. Consequently, although need reduction may not be necessary for the formation of syntheses, it is very necessary for their performance.

In fact, the interaction of two sorts of factors (previous structures and need) is the only condition which actually determines the production of the performance. The need 'actualizes' the previously constituted structure in the form of a behavioural reaction which leads to the reduction or suppression of the tension possessed by the need. This structure, formed by the intervention of previous experience, provides the specific features of the reaction arising from need. These features relate and are appropriate to a particular situation.

5. If syntheses are not exclusively cognitive, *unconscious learning* can occur in the sense of the formation of connections or syntheses between elements which are not given 'cognitively', although this does not mean that they may not be given sensorially.

In so far as the condition of motivation is only auxiliary and not essential, *latent* or *incidental learning* may also occur. This is learning in which there is no drive affecting the establishment of connections as such, or, in other words, learning without a learning task. There are many examples of this in everyday life, in addition to those furnished by experimental research with both animals[1] and humans.[2]

6. The prolonged exercise of syntheses of a sensori-motor or kinaesthetic nature often produces a kind of reaction showing fairly marked features of automatism and stereotype. This is called a motor habit.

It represents a later stage in the development of new syntheses in which the properties of a reflex reaction recur. At this stage, motivation, like reflex, often plays a considerably reduced role; but the factor of performance or practice is essential.

---

[1] See p. 101.   [2] Saltzman, 1953; Stevenson, 1954; and others.

Bibliography

ANDREW, G. and HARLOW, H. F., 'Performance of a macaque monkey on a test of the concept of generalized triangularity', *Comp. Psychol. Monogr.*, 1948, **19**, 3.

BEKHTEREV, V. M., *La psychologie objective*, Paris, Alcan, 1913.

BENDIG, A. W., 'Latent learning in a water maze', *J. exp. Psychol.*, 1952, **43**, 134-7.

BEVAN, W. and ZENER, K., 'Some influences of past experience upon the perceptual thresholds of visual forms', *Amer. J. Psychol.*, 1952, **65**, 434-42.

BIERENS DE HAAN, J. A., 'Werkzeuggebrauch und Werkzeugherstellung bei einem niederen Affen', *Zeit. Vergl. Physiol.*, 1931, **13**, 640-95.

— 'Versuche über die Verwendung der Kiste als Schemel bei einigen Procyoniden (wasch- und nasenbären) nebst einigen Bemerkungen über das concrete Verständnis der Tiere im allgemeinen', *Zeit. Psychol.*, 1934, **131**, 193-216.

BIRCH, H. G. and BITTERMAN, M. F., 'Sensory integration and cognitive theory', *Psychol. Rev.*, 1951, **58**, 355-61.

BLODGETT, H. C., 'The effect of the introduction of reward upon the maze performance of rats', *Univ. Calif. Publ. Psychol.*, 1929, **4**, 113-34.

— MCCUTCHAN, K. and MATHEWS, R., 'Spatial learning in the T-maze. The influence of direction, turn and food location', *J. exp. Psychol.*, 1949, **39**, 800-9.

BORCHGRAVE, C. DE, *L'apprentissage inconscient dans la découverte d'un principe*, Louvain, degree thesis, 1957.

BRALY, K. W., 'The influence of past experience in visual perception', *J. exp. Psychol.*, 1933, **16**, 613-43.

BRESSON, F., 'Perception et indices perceptifs', in *Logique et perception. Études d'épistémologie génétique*, vol. VII, Paris, Presses Universitaires de France, 1958, 156-85.

BRITT, J. H., 'Tonal sensitivity in the white rat', *J. comp. Psychol.*, 1935, **19**, 243-63.

BROGDEN, W. J., 'Sensory pre-conditioning', *J. exp. Psychol.*, 1939, **25**, 323-32.

— 'Test of sensory pre-conditioning with human subjects', *J. exp. Psychol.*, 1942, **31**, 505-17.

— 'Sensory pre-conditioning with human subjects', *J. exp. Psychol.*, 1947, **37**, 527-39.

BRUCE, R. H. and LEW, F. N., 'The effect of practice with brief exposure techniques upon central and peripheral visual acuity and a search for a brief test of peripheral acuity', *J. exp. Psychol.*, 1951, **41**, 275–80.

BRUNSWIK, E., 'Organismic achievement and environmental probability', *Psychol. Rev.*, 1943, **50**, 255–72.

BUGELSKI, B. R., *The psychology of learning*, New York, Holt, 1956.

BUSH, R. R. and MOSTELLER, F., *Stochastic models for learning*, New York, Wiley, 1955.

BUYTENDYK, F. J. J. and FISCHEL, W., 'Versuch einer neuen Analyse der tieriechen Einsicht', *Arch. Neerland. Physiol.*, 1931, **16**, 449–76.

CALDWELL, W. E. and JONES, H. B., 'Some positive results on a modified Tolman and Honzik insight maze', *J. comp. physiol. Psychol.*, 1954, **47**, 416–18.

CASON, H., 'The conditioned pupillary reaction', *J. exp. Psychol.*, 1922, **5**, 108–46.

— TROWBRIDGE, M. H., 'An experimental study of Thorndike's theory of learning', *J. gen. Psychol.*, 1937, **7**, 245–60.

COOK, T. W., 'Factors in massed and distributed practice', *J. exp. Psychol.*, 1944, **34**, 325–34.

CROSLAND, H. R., TAYLOR, H. R. and NEWSON, S. J., 'Practice and improvability in the Müller-Lyer illusion in relation to intelligence', *J. gen. Psychol.*, 1929, **2**, 290–306.

CULLER, E., 'Nature of the learning curve', *Psychol. Bull.*, 1928, **25**, 143–4.

DASHIELL, J. F., 'Direction-orientation in maze learning by the white rat', *Comp. Psychol. Monogr.*, 1930, **7**, 1–72.

DE LANNOY, J.-D., 'La perception de la forme en elle-même', *Journ. Psychol. norm. path.*, 1962, **59**, 59–74.

DJANG, S., 'The role of past experience in the visual apprehension of masked forms', *J. exp. Psychol.*, 1942, **30**, 1–22.

DORE, L. R. and HILGARD, E. R., 'Spaced practice and the maturation hypothesis', *J. Psychol.*, 1937, **4**, 245–59.

DREVER, J. I., 'The pre-insight period in learning', *Brit. J. Psychol.*, 1934, **25**, 197–203.

ELLIOTT, M. A., 'Some determining factors in maze performance', *Amer. J. Psychol.*, 1930, **2**, 315–17.

ESTES, W. K., 'Toward a statistical theory of learning', *Psychol. Rev.*, 1950, **57**, 94–107.

— and others, *Modern learning theory*, New York, Appleton Century, 1954.

— 'The statistical approach to learning theory', in Koch, *Psychology. A Study of a Science*, vol. II, New York, McGraw-Hill, 1959, pp. 380–491.

FÄLTHEIM, A., *Learning, problem-solving and after-effects*, Uppsala, 1956.

FIELDS, P. E., 'Studies in concept formation: I. The development of the concept of triangularity by the white rat', *J. comp. Psychol.*, 1931, **11**, 326-66.

FINGER, F. W., 'The effect of varying conditions of reinforcement upon a simple running response', *J. exp. Psychol.*, 1942, **30**, 53-68.

GALANTER, E. H., 'Place and response learning: learning to alternate', *J. comp. physiol. Psychol.*, 1955, **48**, 17-18.

GAVINI, H., 'Apprentissage et transfert dans le seuil différentiel de luminance', *Bull. C.E.R.P.*, 1962, **11**, 13-24.

GELLERMANN, L., 'Form discrimination in chimpanzee and two year old children', *J. genet. Psychol.*, 1933, **42**, 3-27.

GIBSON, E. J., 'Improvement in perceptual judgments as a function of controlled practice', *Psychol. Bull.*, 1953, **50**, 401-31.

GIBSON, J. J. and GIBSON, E. J., 'Perceptual learning: differentiation or enrichment', *Psychol. Rev.*, 1955, **62**, 32-41.

GLEITMAN, H., 'Place learning without prior performance', *J. comp. physiol. Psychol.*, 1955, **48**, 77-9.

GOTTSCHALDT, K., 'Ueber den Einfluss der Erfarhung auf die Wahrnehmung von Figuren', *Psychol. Forsch.*, 1926, **8**, 247-60.

GUILLAUME, P., *L'imitation chez l'enfant*, Paris, Alcan, 1925.

— MEYERSON, I., 'Recherches sur l'usage de l'instrument chez les singes: I. Le problème du détour', *J. Psychol. norm. path.*, 1930, **27**, 177-236; II. 'L'intermédiaire lié a l'objet', *ibid.*, 1931, **28**, 481-555; III. 'L'intermédiaire indépendant de l'objet', *ibid.*, 1934, **31**, 499-554; IV. 'Choix, correction, invention', *ibid.*, 1937, **34**, 425-48.

— *La formation des habitudes*, Paris, Alcan, 1936.

GUTHRIE, E. R., 'Conditioning as a principle of learning', *Psychol. Rev.*, 1930, **37**, 412-28.

— *The psychology of learning*, New York, Harper, 1935.

— 'Association by contiguity', in Koch, *Psychology. A Study of a Science*, New York, McGraw-Hill, 1959, pp. 158-95.

GRANT, D. A., 'The influence of attitude on the conditioned eyelid response', *J. exp. Psychol.*, 1939, **25**, 33-346.

HEIDBREDER, E., 'An experimental study of thinking', *Arch. Psychol.*, 1924, **73**.

— 'The attainment of concepts: IV. The process', *J. Psychol.*, 1947, **24**, 93-138.

— 'The attainment of concepts: VI. Exploratory experiments on conceptualization at perceptual levels', *J. Psychol.*, 1948, **26**, 193-216.

HENLE, M., 'An experimental investigation of past experience as determinant of visual form perception', *J. exp. Psychol.*, 1942, **30**, 1-22.

HILGARD, E. R., 'Conditioned eyelid reactions to a light stimulus based on the reflex wink to sound', *Psychol. Monogr.*, 1931, **41**, 1-50.

Bibliography

— CAMPBELL, A. A., 'The course of acquisition and retention of conditioned eyelid responses in man', *J. exp. Psychol.*, 1936, **19**, 227–47.
— HUMPHREYS, L. G., 'The effect of supporting an antagonistic voluntary instruction on conditioned discrimination', *J. exp. Psychol.*, 1938, **22**, 291–304.
— MARQUIS, D. G., *Conditioning and learning*, New York, Appleton Century, 1940.
— 'Methods and procedures in the study of learning', in Stevens, *Handbook of Experimental Psychology*, New York, Wiley, 1951, pp. 517–67.
— *Theories of learning*, New York, Appleton Century, 1st edn., 1948; 2nd edn., 1956.
HILL, C. W. and THUNE, L. E., 'Place and response learning in the white rat under simplified and mutually isolated conditions', *J. exp. Psychol.*, 1954, **43**, 289–97.
HONZIK, C. H., 'Central control in the maze learning of rats', *J. comp. Psychol.*, 1933, **15**, 95–132.
HOVLAND, C. I., 'Experimental studies in rote learning theory': VI. 'Comparison of retention following learning to same criterion by massed and distributed practice', *J. exp. Psychol.*, 1940, **26**, 568–87.
— 'Human learning and retention', in Stevens, *Handbook of Experimental Psychology*, New York, Wiley, 1951, pp. 613–89.
HSIAO, H. H., 'Experimental study of the rat's insight within a spatial complex', *Univ. Calif. Publ. Psychol.*, 1929, **4**, 57–70.
HUDGINS, C. V., 'Conditioning and the voluntary control of the pupillary light reflex', *J. gen. Psychol.*, 1933, **8**, 351.
HULL, C. L., 'Quantitative aspects of the evolution of concepts', *Psychol. Monogr.*, 1920, **123**.
— 'Knowledge and purpose as habit mechanisms', *Psychol. Rev.*, 1930, **37**, 511–25.
— *Principles of Behavior*, New York, Appleton Century, 1943.
— *Essentials of Behavior*, New Haven, Yale Univ. Press, 1951.
— *A Behavior system*, New Haven, Yale Univ. Press, 1952.
HUMPHREY, G., *The Nature of learning*, London, Kegan Paul, 1933.
HUMPHREYS, L. G., 'The effect of random alternation of reinforcement on the acquisition and extinction of conditioned eyelid reactions', *J. exp. Psychol.*, 1939, **25**, 141–58.
— 'Extinction of conditioned psychogalvanic responses following two conditions of reinforcement', *J. exp. Psychol.*, 1940, **27**, 71–5.
— 'Measures of strength of conditioned eyelid responses', *J. gen. Psychol.*, 1943, **29**, 101–11.
HUMS, J. F., 'The effect of practice upon the upper limit for tonal discrimination', *Amer. J. Psychol.*, 1930, **42**, 1–16.

Bibliography

HUNTER, W. S., 'Learning': IV. 'Experimental Studies of learning', in *Handbook of General Experimental Psychology*, Worcester, Clark Univ. Press, 1934, pp. 497–570.

JENKINS, J. G. and SHEFFIELD, F. D., 'Rehearsal and guessing habits as sources of the "spread" of effect', *J. exp. Psychol.*, 1946, **36**, 316–30.

JENKINS, W. O. and STANLEY, J. C., 'Partial reinforcement: a review and critique', *Psychol. Bull.*, 1950, **47**, 193–234.

JONES, H. E., 'Conditioned psychogalvanic responses in infants', *Psychol. Bull.*, 1928, **25**, 183–4.

JONCKHEERE, A. R., 'Modèles stochastiques et apprentissage', in *Logique apprentissage et probabilité. Études d'épistémologie génétique*, vol. VIII, Paris, Presses Universitaires de France, 1959, pp. 139–72.

JOHNSON, E. E., 'The role of motivational strength in latent learning', *J. comp. physiol. Psychol.*, 1952, **45**, 526–30.

JOST, A., 'Die Assoziationsfestigkeit in irher Abhängigkeit von der Verteilung der Wiederholungen', *Zeitschr. Psychol.*, 1897, **14**, 436–72.

KARN, H. W., 'Sensory pre-conditioning and incidental learning in humans', *J. exp. Psychol.*, 1947, **37**, 540–4.

KIENTZLE, M. J., 'Properties of learning curves under varied distributions of practice', *J. exp. Psychol.*, 1946, **36**, 187–211.

KILPATRICK, F., 'Two processes in perceptual learning', *J. exp. Psychol.*, 1954, **47**, 362–70.

KIMBLE, G. A., *Hilgard and Marquis' Conditioning and Learning*, 2nd edn., New York, Appleton Century, 1961.

KLUVER, H., *Behavior mechanisms in monkeys*, Univ. Chicago Press, 1932.

KOHLER, I., *Über Aufbau und Wandlungen der Wahrnehmungsveld*, Vienna, Roher, 1951.

KÖHLER, W., *Intelligenz Prüfungen an Menschenaffen*, Berlin, Springer, 1917.

— FISCHBACK, J., 'The destruction of the Müller-Lyer illusion in repeated trials', *J. exp. Psychol.*, 1950, **40**, 267–81, 398–410.

KONORSKI, J. and MILLER, G., 'Nouvelles recherches sur les réflexes conditionnels moteurs, *C.R. Soc. Biol.*, 1934, **115**, 91–6.

— MILLER, G., 'On two types of conditioned reflexes', *J. gen. Psychol.*, 1937, **16**, 264–7.

— *Conditioned reflexes and neuron organization*, Cambridge Univ. Press, 1948.

— *Mechanisms in learning*, in Symp. Soc. Exp. Biol., no. 4, Cambridge Univ. Press, 1950, pp. 409–31.

KRASNOGORSKI, N., 'Die letzten Forschritte in der Methodik der Erforschung der Bedingten Reflexe in Kindern', *Jahrb. f. Kindernk*, 1926, **114**, 256–69.

Bibliography

LASHLEY, K. S., 'The human salivary reflex and its use in psychology', *Psychol. Rev.*, 1916, **23**, 446–64.

— *Brain mechanisms and intelligence*, Univ. Chicago Press, 1929.

— BALL, J., 'Spinal conduction and kinaesthetic sensitivity in the maze habit', *J. comp. Psychol.*, 1929, **9**, 71–106.

— 'Learning. Nervous mechanisms in learning', in *Foundations of Experimental Psychology*, Worcester, Clark Univ. Press, 1929, pp. 456–96.

LE NY, J.-FR., *Le conditionnement*, Paris, Presses Universitaires de France, 1961.

LEWIS, D. J., 'Partial reinforcement: a selective review since 1950', *Psychol. Rev.*, 1960, **57**, 1–28.

LORGE, I., *Influence of regularly interpolated time intervals upon subsequent learning*, Teach. Coll. Contr. Educ., 1930, no. 438.

LUCHINS, A. S., 'Social influences on perception of complex drawings', *J. soc. Psychol.*, 1945, **22**, 279–96.

LUMSDAINE, A. A., 'Conditioned eyelid responses as mediating generalized conditioned finger reactions', *Psychol. Bull.*, 1939, **36**, 650.

LYON, D. O., 'The relation of length of material to time taken for learning and the optimum distribution of time', *J. educ. Psychol.*, 1914, **5**, 1–9, 85–91, 155–63.

MACCORQUODALE, K. and MEEHL, P. E., 'Preliminary suggestions as to a formalization of expectancy theory', *Psychol. Rev.*, 1953, **60**, 55–63.

MACFARLANE, D. A., 'The role of kinaesthesis in maze learning', *Univ. Calif. Public. Psychol.*, 1930, **4**, 277–305.

MAIER, N. R. F., 'Reasoning in white rats', *Comp. Psychol. Monogr.*, 1929, **6**, 1–93.

MARX, M. H., 'Spread of effect. A critical review', *Genet. Psychol. Monogr.*, 1956, **53**, 119–86.

MCFADDEN, H. B., *Three studies in psychological optics*, Duncam, Okla. Optometric Extension Program, 1941, 1–26.

MCGEOCH, J. A., *The psychology of human learning*, New York, Longmans Green, 1942.

MCNEILL, H., *Motor adaptation and accuracy*, Louvain, édit. Inst. Sup. Phil., 1934.

MEEHL, P. E. and MACCORQUODALE, R., 'A further study of latent learning in the T-maze', *J. comp. physiol. Psychol.*, 1948, **41**, 372–96.

MENZIES, R., 'Conditioned vaso-motor responses in human subjects', *J. Psychol.*, 1937, **4**, 75–120.

METALNIKOW, S., 'Les infusoires peuvent-ils apprendre à choisir leur nourriture?', *Arch. f. Protistenk*, 1914, **34**, 60–78.

MICHOTTE, A., 'Réflexions sur le rôle du langage dans l'analyse des organisations perceptives', *Actes Congr. intern. Psychol.*, Brussels, 1957.

MILLER, G. and KONORSKI, J., 'Sur une forme particulière de réflexe conditionnel', *C.R. Soc. Biol.*, 1928, **99**, 1155–7.

MILLER, J., 'The effect of facilitory and inhibitory attitudes on eyelid conditioning', *Psychol. Bull.*, 1939, **36**, 577–8.

MILLER, G. A. and DOLLARD, J., *Social learning and imitation*, New Haven, Yale Univ. Press, 1941.

MÖBIUS, K., 'Die Bewegungen der Tiere und ihre psychischer Horizont', *Sohr. Naturw. Ver. Schl.*, 1873, **1**, 113–30.

MONTPELLIER, G. DE, *Les altérations morphologiques des mouvements rapides*, Louvain, Inst. Sup. Phil., 1935.

— COLLE, J., 'Réactions conditionnées volontaires et involontaires', *Arch. psychol.*, 1939, **27**, 134–56.

— *Conduites intelligentes et psychisme chez l'animal et chez l'homme*, Louvain, Ed. Inst. Sup. Phil., 1946 and 1949.

— 'Conditionnement et apprentissage', in *Le conditionnement et l'apprentissage*, Symposium Assoc. psychol. scientifique de Langue francaise, Paris, Presses Universitaires de France, 1958, pp. 107–51.

— 'Théories de l'apprentissage et conditions de la performance', *Année psychol.*, 1959, **59**, 107–16.

MOURAD, Y., *L'éveil de l'intelligence*, Paris, Alcan, 1940.

MOWRER, O. H. and JONES, H. M., 'Habit strength as a function of pattern of reinforcement', *J. exp. Psychol.*, 1945, **35**, 293–311.

— *Learning theory and personality dynamics*, New York, Ronald Press, 1950.

— 'Two-factor learning theory: Summary and comment', *Psychol. Rev.*, 1951, **58**, 350–4.

— 'Two-factor theory reconsidered with special reference to secondary reinforcement and the concept of habit', *Psychol. Rev.*, 1956, **63**, 114–28.

— *Learning theory and behavior*, New York, Wiley, 1960.

MUKHERJEE, K. C., 'The duration of cutaneous sensation and the improvement of its sensible discrimination by practice', *J. exp. Psychol.*, 1933, **16**, 339–42.

MÜLLER, G. E. and PILZECKER, A., 'Experimentelle Beiträge zur Lehre vom Gedächtnis', *Zeitsch. Psychol.*, 1900, **1**, 1–288.

NOELTING, G., 'La structuration perceptive de la figure de Müller-Lyer en fonction de la répétition, chez l'enfant et chez l'adulte', *Arch. de Psychol.*, 1960, **37**, 311–413.

NORTON, F. T. and KENSHALO, D. R., 'Incidental learning under condition of unrewarded irrelevant motivation', *J. comp. physiol. Psychol.*, 1954, **47**, 375–7.

Bibliography

NUTTIN, J., *De wet van effekt en de rol van de Taak in het leerprocess*, Louvain, Diss. Doct., 1941.

— *Tâche, réussite et échec*, Louvain, Univ. Publ., 1953.

OAKES, W. F., 'An experimental study of pitch naming and pitch discrimination reactions', *J. genet. Psychol.*, 1955, **86**, 237–59.

OSGOOD, CH., *Method and theory in experimental psychology*, New York, Oxford Univ. Press, 1953.

OSGOOD, CH. F., *Motivational dynamics of language behavior. Nebraska Symposium on Motivation*, Lincoln, Univ. Nebraska Press, 1956.

PARREREN, C. F., *Psychologie van het leren*, Arnhem, W. de Haan, 1960.

PAVLOV, I. P., *Conditioned reflexes*, translated. Anrep, London, Univ. Press, 1927.

— *Typologie et pathologie de l'activité nerveuse supérieure*, translated Baumstein, Paris, Alcan, 1955.

PHAUB, M. R. and CALDWELL, W. E., 'Perceptual learning: differentiation and enrichment of past experience', *J. gen. Psychol.*, 1959, **60**, 137–47.

PIAGET, J., 'Apprentissage et connaissance', in *Études d'épistémologie génétique*, vol. VII, pp. 21–67; vol. X, pp. 159–88, Paris, Presses Universitaires de France, 1959.

PIÉRON, H., *L'évolution de la mémoire*, Paris, Flammarion, 1910.

— 'L'habitude et la mémoire', in *Nouveau Traité de Psychologie*, vol. IV, Paris, Alcan, 1934, pp. 67–136.

— 'Recherches expérimentales sur les phénomènes de mémoire', *Année psychol.*, 1913, **19**, 91–193.

— *Vocabulaire de psychologie*, Paris, Presses Universitaires de France, 1951.

PLAVILSTCHIKOV, N. N., 'Observations sur l'excitabilité des infusoires', *Russ. Arch. Protist.*, 1928, **7**, 1–24.

POLLET, R., *Le problème de l'inconscient dans l'apprentissage*, Louvain, Diss. Doct., 1946.

PROKOFIEF, G. and ZÉLIONY, G., 'Des modes d'associations cérébrales chez l'homme et chez les animaux', *J. Psychol. norm. path.*, 1926, **23**, 1020–8.

RAZRAN, G. H. S., 'Conditioned withdrawal responses with shock as the conditioned stimulus in adult human subjects', *Psychol. Bull.*, 1934, **3**, 143.

— 'Conditioned responses: an experimental study and a theoretical analysis', *Arch. Psychol.*, 1935, **191**, 1–124.

— 'Attitudinal control of human conditioning', *J. Psychol.*, 1936, **2**, 327–37.

RENSHAW, G., 'The visual perception and reproduction of forms in tachistoscopic methods', *J. Psychol.*, 1945, **20**, 217–32.

REY, A., 'Choix adapté précédant la prise de conscience', *Arch. Psychol.*, 1935, **25**, 157–78.

REYNOLDS, B., 'A repetition of the Blodgett experiment on "latent learning" ', *J. exp. Psychol.*, 1945, **35**, 504–16.

ROBINSON, E. W. A., 'A preliminary experiment on abstraction in a monkey', *J. comp. Psychol.*, 1933, **16**, 231–6.

ROZEBOOM, W. W., 'What is learned? An empirical enigma', *Psychol. Rev.*, 1958, **65**, 22–33.

SALTZMAN, E. J., 'The orienting task in incidental and intentional learning', *Amer. J. Psychol.*, 1953, **66**, 593–7.

SEASHORE, R. H., 'Stanford motor skills unit', *Psychol. Monogr.*, 1928, **39**, 51–66.

— 'Work methods: an often neglected factor underlying individual differences', *Psychol. Rev.*, 1939, **46**, 123–41.

SEWARD, J. P., 'The effect of practice on the visual perception of form', *Arch. Psychol.*, 1931, **20**, no. 130.

SHEFFIELD, F. D. and TEMMER, H. W., 'Relative resistance to extinction of escape training and avoidance training', *J. exp. Psychol.*, 1950, **40**, 287–98.

SHIPLEY, W. C., 'Conditioning the human plantar reflex', *J. exp. Psychol.*, 1932, **15**, 422–6.

— 'An apparent transfer of conditioning', *J. gen. Psychol.*, 1933, **8**, 382–91.

— 'Indirect conditioning', *J. gen. Psychol.*, 1935, **12**, 337–57.

SKINNER, B. F., 'Two types of conditioned reflex and a pseudo-type', *J. gen. Psychol.*, 1935, **12**, 66–77.

— 'Two types of conditioned reflex: a reply to Konorski and Miller', *J. gen. Psychol.*, 1937, **16**, 272–9.

— *The behavior of organisms*, New York, Appleton Century, 1938.

SMITH, F. O., 'The effect of training in pitch discrimination', *Psychol. Monogr.*, 1914, **16**, no. 69.

SMOKE, K. L., 'An objective study of concept formation', *Psychol. Monogr.*, 1932, **49**, no. 191.

SPAET, I. and HARLOW, H. F., 'Solution by rhesus monkeys of multiple sign-problems utilizing the oddity-technique', *J. comp. Psychol.*, 1943, **35**, 119–32.

SPENCE, K. W., 'Theoretical interpretations of learning', in Stevens, *Handbook of Experimental Psychology*, New York, Wiley, 1951, pp. 690–729.

— *Behavior theory and conditioning*, New Haven, Yale Univ. Press, 1956.

— *Behavior theory and learning*, New York, Prentice Hall, 1960.

SOLOMON, R. L. and WYNNE, L. C., 'Traumatic avoidance learning: the principal anxiety conservation and partial irreversibility', *Psychol. Rev.*, 1954, **61**, 353–85.

STEVENSON, H. W., 'Latent learning in children', *J. exp. Psychol.*, 1954, **47**, 17–26.

STRATTON, G. M., 'Vision without inversion of the retinal image', *Psychol. Rev.*, 1897, **4**, 341–60, 463–81.

SWITZER, S. A., 'Disinhibition of the galvanic skin response', *J. gen. Psychol.*, 1933, **9**, 77–100.

SZENTKERESZTY, M., *L'expérience de l' 'espèce unique' chez les enfants de 8 à 12 ans*, Louvain, degree thesis, 1956.

THISTLETHWAITE, D., 'A critical review of latent learning and related experiment', *Psychol. Bull.*, 1951, **48**, 97–129; 1952, **49**, 61–71.

— 'Condition of irrelevant incentive learning', *J. comp. physiol. Psychol.*, 1952, **45**, 517–25.

THORNDIKE, E. C., *Educational Psychology*: II. *The psychology of learning*, New York, Teachers' College, 1913.

— *Human learning*, New York, Century, 1931.

— *Fundamentals of learning*, New York, Teachers' College, Columbia, 1932.

— *An experimental study of rewards*, New York, Teachers' College, Columbia, 1933.

— 'A theory of action of the after-effect of a connection upon it', *Psychol. Rev.*, 1933, **40**, 435–9.

— *The psychology of wants, interests and attitudes*, New York, Century, 1935.

THORPE, W. H., *Learning and instinct in animals*, London, Methuen, 1956.

THURSTONE, L. L. A., 'The learning curve equation', *Psychol. Monogr.*, 1919, **114**.

— 'The learning function', *J. gen. Psychol.*, 1930, **3**, 469–93.

TOLMAN, E. C. and HONZIK, C. H., ' "Insight" in rats', *Univ. Calif. Public. Psychol.*, 1930, 4, 215–32.

— HONZIK, C. H., 'Introduction and removal of reward and maze performance of rats', *Univ. Calif. Public. Psychol.*, 1930, **4**, 257–75.

— *Purposive behavior in animals and men*', New York, Century, 1932.

— BRETNALL, E. P. and HALL, C. S., 'A disproof of the law of effect and a substitution of the laws of emphasis, motivation and disruption', *J. exp. Psychol.*, 1932, **15**, 601–14.

— 'Operational behaviorism and current trends in psychology', *Proc. 25th Ann. Univ. South Calif.*, 1936, 89–103.

— 'Theories in learning', in Moss, *Comparative Psychology*, New York, Prentice Hall, 1934, pp. 367–408.

— RITCHIE, B. F. and KALISH, D., 'Studies in spatial learning: I. Orientation and the short-cut', *J. exp. Psychol.*, 1946, **36**, 13–24; 'II.

Place learning versus response learning', *J. exp. Psychol.*, 1946, **36**, 285–92.

— 'Cognitive maps in rats and men', *Psychol. Rev.*, 1948, **55**, 189–208.

— GLEITMAN, H., 'Studies in spatial learning: VII. Place and response learning under different degrees of motivation', *J. exp. Psychol.*, 1949, **39**, 653–9.

— 'There is more than one kind of learning', *Psychol. Rev.*, 1949, **56**, 144–55.

— 'Principles of performances', *Psychol. Rev.*, 1955, **62**, 315–26.

— 'Principles of purposive behavior', in Koch, *Psychology. A Study of a Science*, vol. II, New York, McGraw-Hill, 1959, pp. 92–157.

THOMPSON, M. E. and THOMPSON, J. B., 'Reactive inhibition as a factor in maze learning': II. 'The role of reactive inhibition in studies of place learning versus response learning', *J. exp. Psychol.*, 1949, **39**, 883–95.

TRAVIS, R. C., 'Length of the fraction period and efficiency in motor learning', *J. exp. Psychol.*, 1939, **24**, 339–45.

TRIPLETT, N., 'The educability of the perch', *Amer. J. Psychol.*, 1901, **12**, 354–60.

VAN DER VELDT, J., *L'apprentissage du mouvement et l'automatisme*, Louvain, Inst. Sup. Phil., 1928.

WALKER, E. L., 'Drive specificity and learning: demonstration of a response tendency acquired under a strong irrelevant drive', *J. comp. Psychol.*, 1952, **44**, 596–603.

WALLACH, H. and HENLE, M., 'An experimental analysis of the law of effect', *J. exp. Psychol.*, 1941, **28**, 340–9.

— O'CONNELL, D. N. and NEISSER, U., 'The memory effect of visual perception of the three-dimensional form', *J. exp. Psychol.*, 1953, **45**, 360–8.

WARNER, L. H., 'An experimental search for the "conditioned response"', *J. genet. Psychol.*, 1932, **41**, 91–115.

WATSON, J. B., *Behavior: An introduction to comparative psychology*, New York, Holt, 1914.

— *Psychology from the standpoint of a behaviorist*, Philadelphia, Lippincott, 1919.

WEBB, W. B., 'A study in place and response learning as a discrimination behavior', *J. comp. physiol. Psychol.*, 1951, **44**, 263–8.

WENDT, S. R., 'An analytical study of the conditioned knee-jerk', *Arch. Psychol.*, 1930, **18**, 1–97.

WEVER, E. G., 'The upper limit of hearing in cats', *J. comp. Psychol.*, 1930, **10**, 221–34.

WILLIAMS, K. A., 'The reward values of a conditioned stimulus', *Univ. Calif. Public. Psychol.*, 1929, **4**, 31–55.

Bibliography

WILCOX, W. W., 'An interpretation of the relation between visual acuity and light intensity', *J. gen. Psychol.*, 1936, **15**, 405–35.

WIPPLE, G. M., 'Studies in pitch discrimination', *Amer. J. Psychol.*, 1903, **14**, 289–304.

WOLFE, H. M., 'On the estimation of the middle of lines', *Amer. J. Psychol.*, 1923, **34**, 313–58.

— 'Time factors in conditioning finger-withdrawal', *J. gen. Psychol.*, 1930, **3**, 372–8.

— 'Conditioning as a function of the interval between the conditioned and the original stimulus', *J. gen. Psychol.*, 1932, **7**, 80–103.

WOODROW, H., 'The relation between abilities and improvement with practice', *J. educ. Psychol.*, 1938, **29**, 215–30.

WOODWORTH, R. H. and SCHLOSBERG, H., *Experimental Psychology*, New York, Holt, 1954.

WOODWORTH, R. S., *Dynamics of behavior*, New York, Holt, 1958.

WYATT, R. F., 'Improvability of pitch discrimination', *Psychol. Monogr.*, 1945, **58**, no. 267.

ZENER, K., 'The significance of behavior accompanying conditioned salivary secretion for theories of the conditioned response', *Amer. J. Psychol.*, 1937, **50**, 385–403.

ZIRKLE, G. A., 'Success and failure in serial learning: I. The Thorndike effect; II. Isolation and the Thorndike effect', *J. exp. Psychol.*, 1946, **36**, 230–6, 302–15.

YERKES, R. M., 'Methods of exhibiting reactive tendencies characteristic of ontogenic and phylogenic stages', *J. Anim. Behav.*, 1917, **7**, 11–28.

— 'The mind of a gorilla', *Genet. Psychol. Monogr.*, 1927, **2**, 1–193; 375–551; *Comp. Psychol. Monogr.*, 1928, **5**, 1–91.

Chapter 13

Transfer

Geneviève Oléron

Man exists in time and so his activities must follow each other in succession. Everyday experience shows that, in some cases, the succession of two activities facilitates the execution of the second, whereas, in other cases, this succession of activities may cause problems. Accomplishing a task is never a matter of indifference, and an individual always acquires something that he can use to advantage or disadvantage in a similar task.

Whenever one activity affects another following it (either by facilitating it or interfering with it), there is said to be *transfer*. This is a basic, but very complex, phenomenon, since it applies to all acquisitions and methods of action.

As Sandiford pointed out (1928), all education is based on the existence of phenomena of transfer. The educator's object is to teach a child or an adult principles and methods for dealing with specific tasks in different situations. From 1901 onwards, Thorndike and Woodworth carried out a series of experiments in order to verify a theory of transfer applicable to teaching. This theory of identical elements, which has, in fact, been questioned, stated that adaptation to new situations must be facilitated by the existence of the same elements (taking this term in its widest sense) in the earlier situations, previously experienced, and in the new situations.

Learning itself is based on transfer (Husband, 1947; Fergusson, 1954). In fact, learning is only possible when the acquisition effected in the first trial is transposed to the second, that of the second to the third, and so on. In this particular case, the successive tasks are identical and transfer usually appears as facilitation. However, learning is the subject of a separate chapter, so there is no need to consider this aspect of transfer here.

Can the mechanisms intervening in transfer be defined? Can one measure the effects of facilitation and interference? Can their determinants be analysed? Is it possible to draw up laws by which effects of transfer from one situation to another can be predicted from precise data characterizing both situations? This chapter is an attempt to answer these questions.

Systematic study leads to the abandonment of the very complex perspectives of education, even though these were the original basis of studies in transfer (see Kingsley, 1946, for a review of these problems). Experimental research, whose object is the strictly controlled manipulation of variables, may by oversimplifying the problems, distort them. Contemporary studies are actually the result of much earlier work, which emphasized the necessity for precise detailing of elementary factors before attempting to understand their multiple interactions.

All the work reviewed here arose from theoretical or applied research. Orata outlined this work in 1941 and Oléron (G.) made a partial review of it in 1955. No single transfer theory is generally accepted today. Thorndike's theory (1903), known as the theory of 'identical elements', accounts, by the very generality of its expression, for much of what happens in transfer. On the other hand, Osgood's model (1949, 1953) systematically presents the role of similarity in phenomena of transfer. However, neither seems to account for all that happens, and other theories (in relation to learning) have been put forward.

So-called 'proactive' transfer phenomena will only be studied here in the sense of how one task influences another. The term proactive is the opposite of retroactive. The latter refers to the effects of a task which intervenes between the acquisition of a task and the recall or relearning of this task, as demonstrated by Hovland (1951). The transfer or proactive phenomenon is a hypothetical concept and its existence is only inferred from effects seen in situations or tasks which succeed each other. The nature of transfer will be discovered by the study of its qualitative and quantitative effects.

1 Determination of transfer effects

1 Features of transfer effects

(A) NATURE OF TRANSFER

(*a*) *Direction taken by effects.* When the execution or learning of a task produces an improvement in the efficiency of the task following it, the transfer effects are called *positive*, since there is *proactive facilitation*. This concept of facilitation refers not to any specific process but to an improvement in efficiency only. This is shown by more correct responses or fewer errors or faster responses or any other criterion of progress.

If the influence of the acquisition of the first task causes reduced efficiency in the second task, the transfer effects are called *negative*, and there is *proactive inhibition* or *interference*. It is tempting to make a distinction between these two negative effects by applying the term 'inhibition' for those cases in which there is a reduction in the number of correct or incorrect responses, while retaining 'interference' for those in which responses, previously learnt in the first task, intervene in the second in the form of intrusions. This distinction is difficult to make, because some intrusions remain implicit. In practice, this distinction is made in very few studies and the terms inhibition and interference are used indiscriminately in all cases in which there is a reduction in the level of efficiency in the second task.

Most research into transfer has been on the effects of facilitation. When Orata (1941) was preparing his resumé, he found that 78 per cent of the research on transfer concerned the effects of facilitation, while only 22 per cent was on interference. This has led to the idea of transfer as the same as facilitation, whereas, in fact, it is only one of the possible effects of one task upon another.

The effects of proactive interference have been the subject of recent studies, particularly those by Gagné, Baker and Forster (1950) in sensori-motor adaptation tests, and of Bugelski (1948) and Underwood (1949) in mnemonic tests.

It is often very difficult, in an analysis of results, to dissociate positive transfer effects from negative ones. Only the end result is measured; but sometimes, during the second learning session, positive and negative transfer effects do not act in the same way, so it is possible to separate them.

In the various works quoted later, a distinction will be made between positive effects of facilitation, negative effects of inhibition or interference and no effect at all (zero). This zero effect can also result from a state of equilibrium existing between negative and positive effects.

(*b*) *Transfer effects are not static, but dynamic.* They evolve with the passage of time, and so their appearance depends on the length of the interval between successive tasks.

(*c*) *Transfer effects depend on the degree of acquisition in the first task.* Murdock (1960) demonstrated this fact, which will be referred to later.

A distinction must be made between a negative transfer effect at the beginning of the second task and a 'warming-up' effect (Thune, 1950). This 'warming-up' effect can look like a temporary, negative effect of transfer.

(B) EXAMPLES OF TRANSFER

(*a*) An experiment carried out by Martin (1915), and described by Woodworth (1949, p. 271), illustrates the different effects of transfer and their complexity.

The author was investigating how training in crossing out words containing both *a* and *t* in an English text affected efficiency in various, similar tests. The results obtained in the second task in four situations only are given below in Table I. These situations were very similar, but positive, negative and even zero, transfer effects appeared.[1]

Obviously the transfer effects were not simple. Positive transfer for speed appeared in situations I and III. In these two

---

[1] Two things, speed and accuracy, were used to calculate gains in efficiency, the criteria of the existence of transfer. Gains were calculated by taking the difference in speed and accuracy between the results of an experimental group with prior learning and those of a control group with no previous learning (groups equal before training).

The 'speed' was estimated from the number of correct elements crossed out (words or letters). The percentage of the number of elements actually crossed out compared with those that should have been crossed out gave the 'accuracy'.

situations, the subjects crossed out the same letters *a* and *t* in both tasks. However, transfer was zero for accuracy in situation I and very negative in situation III. Foreign words were used in the first case, and series of letters in the second. In the second case, it would appear that, trained by the first task to cross out words containing *a* and *t*, the subjects went too rapidly through the succession of letters, because they were used to looking through groups of them. Consequently there were many omissions.

TABLE I

| Second tasks | Gains and losses in | | | |
Crossing out	Speed Average	P.E.	% Accuracy Average	P.E.
I. Words with *a* and *t* in a Spanish prose	+6·44 words	0·38	+ 1%	1·92
II. Words with *e* and *s* in a Spanish prose	+0·02 words	0·36	+ 6%	2·11
III. Letters *a* and *t* in a series of mixed letters	+4·91 letters	1·25	−16%	1·30
IV. Letters *e* and *s* in a series of mixed letters	−3·89 letters	1·78	− 3%	0·75

(Taken from Martin (M.A.), *Arch. of Psychol.*, 1915, **32**, 42 and 44.)

On the other hand, there was no transfer for speed in situation II and negative transfer in situation IV. For accuracy there was 6 per cent transfer in situation II. The fact that the subjects had to cross out new letters obliged them to concentrate as much in situation II as in the first task, and this meant greater accuracy. However, situation IV was too difficult and transfer was negative for both speed and accuracy.

This example of very similar transfer situations producing very different effects shows that the habits acquired are both general and specific. In this case, not only was a general, discrimination skill acquired but there must have been a positive effect in each transfer situation. This skill was also specific: the *a*'s and *t*'s were crossed out, causing interference and, consequently, negative transfer.

(*b*) *Transfer as a function of the length and nature of training.*

Murdock (1960) has shown that transfer depends on the duration of training in the first task, but that it may also depend on the nature of the first task in comparison with that of the second.

Murdock compared the effect of verbal training on the performance of a perceptual-motor task with that of motor training on the same task. For this comparison, a group of subjects learnt to associate six nonsense syllables NOV, FAM, GUL, WIS, HOB and PEB with six luminous figures on a panel. Another group learnt to associate six different reaction keys with the same figures.

This preliminary training enabled both groups of subjects to learn to discriminate the six luminous figures by associating each of them with a different response, verbal in one case and motor in the other. In order to compare transfer effects, the two groups then took a test, using a star-shaped discrimimeter. This apparatus consists of a panel showing the stimuli and a table of responses. There is a slot for each figure (Fig. 1).

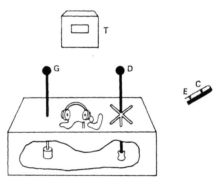

Fig. 1. Simplified schema of Duncan's star-shaped discrimimeter (1953). This apparatus consists of a vertical panel T on which stimuli can be presented (luminous or any other visual stimuli). The response table has two levers. The right-hand lever D, which is the essential part of the apparatus, can be moved into any of the notches in the star. The star has six arms in the figure, but this varies in different versions of the apparatus. Each notch has two points of contact: E at the beginning of the notch registers errors and C at the end registers correct responses. Lever G makes a single point of contact possible. A pair of earphones enables the experimenter to transmit instructions or sound stimuli. (After Duncan (C.P.), *J. exp. Psychol.*, 1953, **45**, 2.)

Taking different standards of success as training criteria (see Table II), Murdock demonstrated that transfer from verbal learning was greater than that produced by motor learning. The difference was greater the higher the level of success achieved in the first learning.

TABLE II

Learning criterion Number of correct responses out of 6 in the last trial	Number of trials needed to reach the learning criterion	
	Motor learning	*Verbal learning*
1	2	2
2	3	5
3	6	5
4	9	8
5	18	13
6	34	24

(Taken from Murdock, *Amer. J. Psychol.*, 1960, **73**, 357.)

In both cases, two trials were sufficient to produce a correct response. Nine trials with motor learning and 8 with verbal learning were required to obtain 4 correct responses. To obtain 6 correct responses 34 and 24 trials were required respectively. The Mann-Whitney test showed that statistically verbal learning was, on the whole, more efficient than motor learning. In a subsequent experiment, the author showed that this effect was due to better discrimination of the figures in verbal learning. This is possibly because associated verbal responses are better differentiated than motor responses.

2   Methodology

(A)   EXPERIMENTAL PLANS

(*a*) *Basic plan.* An experimental study of transfer requires the experiments to be elaborated in accordance with a definite plan. Volkmann (1858) was the first to propose an adequate method.

One basic principle that can be stated with certainty is that any change in efficiency in the second task must be caused by prior activity, so efficiency with the previous task must be compared with efficiency without it.

The basic plan from which different versions can be established is as follows: let B be the task in which transfer is studied and A be the task causing this effect. The results of an experimental group E must be compared with those of a control group C (B_E and B_C being their results in task B). These groups, which should be about equal, take tests A and B in accordance with the following schema:

	1st task	*2nd task*	*Results*
Experimental group E	Task A	Task B	B_E
Control group C	Rest	Task B	B_C

A comparison of results confirms that, if $B_E > B_C$, the transfer effect is *positive*, and there is proactive facilitation. If $B_E = B_C$, the transfer effect is *zero*. If $B_E < B_C$, the transfer effect is *negative*, and there is proactive interference or inhibition.

The overall influence of task A can be studied by means of this experimental plan. In order to study the role of a specific variable in task A, there have to be as many experimental groups as this variable has levels of variation.

If A_1, A_2 and A_3 are three versions of task A, the plan becomes:

Groups	*1st task*	*2nd task*	*Results*
E_1	Task A_1	Task B	B_{E1}
E_2	Task A_2	Task B	B_{E2}
E_3	Task A_3	Task B	B_{E3}
C	Rest	Task B	B_C

A comparison of the different groups E_1, E_2 and E_3 shows the influence of the variable on transfer. The direction and rate of transfer can be established from the control group.

(*b*) *This plan poses two problems.* (α) The control group and the experimental group must have equal ability to perform task B. For this purpose, the subjects can take a test very similar to task B, and then be divided up into equal groups E and C on the basis of their results.

	1st task	2nd task
Pre-test P ⟨ Group E →	Task A	Task B
Group C →	Rest	Task B

Task P, which is similar to B, can give rise to transfer, particularly if it is fairly long. Of course it can be assumed that, since groups E and C are equal, they undergo the same proactive effects following P. The only problem is that, in the case of group E, task P acts on task A first, and then on task B; but, in the case of group C, the proactive effect of P acts directly on task B.

Consequently this proactive effect must be rendered as negligible as possible by making P a short test, which precedes the transfer experiment quite considerably.

(β) The second problem is that of 'warm-up', which does not affect task B in exactly the same way for both groups. This effect appeared very clearly in Hamilton's experiment (1950). Hamilton systematically varied the length of the rest period between two equivalent learnings of a list of paired associates (numbers and adjectives). The two learning sessions were held with intervals of 10, 20, 40, 60, 120, 180 and 240 minutes between them. Fig. 16. (p. 204) shows that the decrease in efficiency during the second task bore an inverse relation to the increase in the length of the interval. In order to compensate for the 'warm-up' effect, during the rest period, the control group can perform a neutral task (X), which bears no resemblance to either task A or task B. Presumably the performance of this neutral task will 'warm-up' group C without causing any proactive effects. Thune (1958) emphasized how difficult it is to achieve these conditions.

The effect of this task X can be compared with that of the so-called rest. In fact, a subject is never completely inactive during this rest period. More often than not, he is engaged in tasks that it is very difficult to control (Osgood, 1953; Murdock, 1957). The experimental plan will be:

		1st task	2nd task
	Group E	Task A	Task B
Pre-test	Group C	Task X	Task B
	Group C'	Rest	Task B

A comparison of groups C and C′ will show the 'warm-up' effect.

(*c*) *Comparison of transfer effects*. Of the various problems arising in the study of transfer, the one which occurs most frequently is that of ascertaining whether transfer effects are the same from test A to test B or test B′; tests B and B′ are, therefore, closely comparable. Martin's experiment (1915) illustrated this problem.

Therefore, ignoring these secondary effects, the experimental plan becomes:

		1st task	2nd task
	Group E	Task A	Task B
Pre-test	Group E′	Task A	Task B′
	Group C	Rest	Task B
	Group C′	Rest	Task B′

The transfer rates of task A to tasks B and B′ can be studied and compared by reference to the control groups.

(*d*) *Reversibility of transfer effects*. One frequently recurring problem is that of whether transfer effects are reciprocal between tasks A and B.

This simple problem is posed by all situations in which the subjects have to carry out two successive, independent tasks in order to establish whether they both equally favour the training of the task which follows. This can be done quite simply by following this plan (in which a counterbalance appears):

		1st task	2nd task
Pre-test P	Group E_1	Task A	Task B
	Group E_2	Task B	Task A

In this case, the experimental groups E_1 and E_2 serve as control groups for each other.

Andreas, Green and Spraag (1954) found that there was no reciprocal transfer effect between two tests in which a luminous target and a mobile spot had to be brought together by manual control. In one test, the spot had to follow the mobile target, and, in the other, the spot's mobility had to be compensated for in order to keep it and the target together.

Nor was there any reciprocal, transfer effect between two tests involving the distribution of cards, one with cards coloured blue, red, green and yellow, and the other with cards bearing symbols. The latter were printed in such a way that they had neither top nor bottom, nor back nor front. The transfer effect from the distribution of the cards with symbols to that of the coloured cards was greater than the other way round. The distribution of the symbols involved a discrimination process which, while it was very elementary (discriminating V, T, Z and D), was still more complex than that required for the discrimination of of colours.

(*e*) *Transfer effects and relearning*. Transfer effects can also be studied in relearning the second task, and the following plan is easily established from the preceding ones:

		1st task	2nd task	3rd task
	Group E	Task A	Task B	Task B
Pre-test	Group C_1	Task A	Rest	Task B
	Group C_2	Rest	Task B	Task B

This plan takes into account the delay before relearning, which can have an effect distinct from those effects arising from first learning task B (group C_1).

Not only effects of transfer, but also those of forgetting and reminiscence, can easily be analysed from a comparison of the results obtained in the performance of task B by the different groups.

Thus, with the aid of these experimental plans, the influence of different variables can be studied in task B, which undergoes transfer, as well as in task A, where transfer originates. Obviously temporal determinants are very important in the establishment of any experimental plan, i.e. duration of the task, especially the first one, and the time interval between the performance of the two tasks. These effects will be discussed later.

(B) MEASUREMENT OF TRANSFER

Murdock (1957) has emphasized how important it is to seek a valid, and therefore efficient, measurement of transfer effects in order to obtain general laws, rather than a mere description of phenomena. Nevertheless, the problem is a difficult one, since the method of evaluating the amount of transfer should not depend upon a specific unit of measurement used in a particular experiment (seconds or minutes measuring the time needed for the accomplishment of a task, the number of successes, etc.).

Transfer is usually measured in percentages, which are independent of the unit of measurement.

In addition, the results of the control group must be compared with those of the experimental group, so the rate of transfer is also a comparative measurement. The simplest formula is that first proposed by Gagné, Forster and Crowley (1948).

$$\text{Percentage of transfer} = \frac{E-C}{C} \times 100.$$

This formula is valid in cases in which the positive transfer effect takes the form of an increase in the original figures (number of successes, for example).

If there is a decrease in errors or in the performance time of a task, which also shows a positive transfer effect, the formula becomes:

$$\text{Percentage of transfer} = \frac{C-E}{C} \times 100.$$

However, this formula is not altogether satisfactory, since the maximum percentage of transfer, thus expressed, tends towards infinity when E is greater than C. On the other hand, the result is zero when the efficiency of both groups is identical: $C = E$. This formula only expresses correctly the negative transfer effect which can vary from o to -100 per cent.

Gagné and others (1948) criticized this formula. As most research had been on positive transfer effects, they proposed a new formula in which the maximum, positive transfer effect would be 100 per cent, but the maximum, negative effect would be $-\infty$. This formula is:

Percentage of transfer: $(E-C)/(T-C) \times 100$ (*2a*), if the figures stand for successes;

Percentage of transfer: $(C-E)/(C-T) \times 100$ (*2b*), if the figures stand for mistakes.

In formula (2*a*), T is the maximum number of successes that can be expected in the performance of the task. This number can be theoretical if it is possible to estimate *a priori* the number of successes possible (number of words learnt, number of correct connections established between stimuli (signals) and motor responses). But this figure can be obtained experimentally in cases in which the theoretical limit cannot be fixed by logical deduction, i.e. cases in which the task is too difficult to be done by just anybody.

In formula (2*b*), T is the minimum number of errors.

Murdock (1957) noted that the formulae (2*a*) and (2*b*) of Gagné and his collaborators (1948) give percentages which vary as a function of the figures of both the control group and the experimental group, and that the transfer rate depends particularly upon the difference between the control group's figure and the maximum possible figure T. If this difference is too great, the variations in E must be considerable in comparison with C to produce a high percentage.

Since this formula is not balanced for both negative and positive transfer effects, Murdock has proposed the following formulas:

$$\text{Percentage of transfer} = \frac{E - C}{E + C} \times 100 \ (3a)$$

in which E and C are successes, and

$$\text{Percentage of transfer} = \frac{C - E}{C + E} \times 100 \ (3b)$$

in which E and C are mistakes.

In fact, these formulae present a variation of -100 per cent to $+100$ per cent, and they do not feature a calculation of the maximum number of successes or errors.

Table III overleaf shows the values obtained, using the three formulae given above, in a theoretical example.

(c) TRANSFER EFFECTS IN LEARNING CURVES

Very often transfer effects appear between two learning tests, and the existence of this transfer can be established by comparing the two learning curves. Nevertheless, this is always a difficult comparison to make.

TABLE III

Transfer percentages calculated from the number of successes on the basis of three different formulae.

Number of Successes			*Formulae*		
E	C	T	$\dfrac{E-C}{C}\%$	$\dfrac{E-C}{T-C}\%$	$\dfrac{E-C}{E+C}\%$
20	0	20	$+\infty$	$+100$	$+100$
15	5	20	$+200$	$+ 67$	$+ 50$
10	5	20	$+100$	$+ 33$	$+ 33$
5	5	20	0	0	0
5	10	20	$- 50$	$- 50$	$- 33$
5	15	20	$- 67$	-200	$- 50$
0	20	20	-100	$-\infty$	-100

(Taken from Murdock (B.B.), *Psychol. Bull.*, 1957, **54**, 323.)

Of course, transfer can be studied by counting the number of trials required to reach a fixed criterion of success for both tasks. In this case, one of the formulae given in the previous section can be used.

The successes in both learning tests can also be compared trial by trial. The evolution of transfer can then be analysed from the different figures obtained in each trial.

The transfer effect can appear in the changes in the learning curve as well as in the variation in the final result. Woodworth and Schlosberg (1954) illustrated this fact by an example in which they considered the variation in the curve's growth rate.

Fig. 2 shows the results of the control group and the experimental group.

The learning equation is as follows:

$$z - y = (1 - F)^n(Z - A).$$

Z is the practical level that can be reached;
A is starting level; $Z - A$ is the extent of possible development;
F is the growth rate of this development.

In the example quoted, F is 1/5 for the control group and 2/5 for the experimental group, so the transfer rate is 44 per cent.

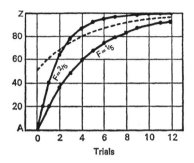

Fig. 2. Possible transfer effects in a learning curve

The curve called F = 1/5 shows the progress of a control group. The one called F = 2/5 assumes that the speed of learning has been doubled by some preliminary learning: it starts from the same base level, but grows twice as fast towards the final level. The dotted curve assumes that the difference in the time taken to reach the final level has been halved at the beginning by preliminary training, although F retains the same value (1/5) as for the control group.

In comparison with the theoretical curve, the dotted curve would save 3·1 trials on reaching each level with 44 per cent of the number of trials needed by the control group. (After Woodworth (R.S.) and Schlosberg (H.), *Experimental Psychology*, New York, Holt, 1954, p. 738.)

2 Transfer in perceptual-motor activities

1 *Transfer effects relating to receptor acitivity*

Taking into account an individual's relations with the outside world only, any situation in which he finds himself can be outlined as follows: he receives stimulation by means of his sensory receptors, and, through the different effectors at his disposal, he responds to this stimulation in a more or less appropriate manner. Consequently a transfer effect is possible between receptors, whether these belong to the same sensory modality (*intrasensory transfer*) or to different modalities (*intersensory transfer*).

(A) TRANSFER ON THE RECEPTOR LEVEL AND TRANSFER
IN PERCEPTION

Perceptual skill depends partly on the reception of elementary sensory messages and partly on their integration. These messages are identified by a small number of indications or cues.

A study can be made of how much training and practice facilitate different, simple or complex, perceptual activities.

(*a*) *Intrasensory transfer.* Studies made many years ago revealed the increase that can occur in the discriminative abilities of different receptors belonging to the same sensory modality.

In 1858, Volkmann published a study of tactile discrimination (measured with an aesthesiometer). He found that (α) sensitivity increased after repeated exercise on the same cutaneous surface; (β) there was a comparable increase in sensitivity on the corresponding surface area of the other arm; (γ) this transfer was temporary and very localized.

Dresslar (1894) and, more recently, Mukherjee (1933) demonstrated that these transfer effects on the level of cutaneous reception only occur between corresponding contralateral surfaces. This seems to confirm Volkmann's contention that the effect must depend upon a central process. Boring (1920) put forward the hypothesis that these facilitation effects were caused by training of the perception. Two points have to be made here: this activity certainly makes a subject learn to use unfamiliar, perceptual cues, but the transfer effect is clearly due to facilitation through cortical interconnections, since it is very localized.

Hulin and Katz (1934) found tactile, perceptual transfer in a complex, discrimination test. Children with normal sight, who knew nothing of the Braille alphabet, learnt certain letters blindfold by touching them with the fingers of their right hand. The same children had then to distinguish these letters from other letters, using their left hand. There was at least 88 per cent transfer. Of course this is a complex form of discrimination, since the children initially learnt, not only to perceive groups of points, but to associate these with letters. Nevertheless, what was specifically transferred from the right hand to the left was the tactual recognition of structures of points already learnt.

Franz and Laymann (1933) demonstrated a facilitation effect from one eye to the other in the discrimination of forms.

The consecutive, figural effect obtained when the perceptual activity of one sensory organ follows the activity of another can be regarded as a transfer effect. The first perception influences the second, even though the same receptor may not be involved.

Gibson (J. J.) (1933) found a consecutive, figural effect in the perception of curved lines going from the right eye to the left. This effect is based on the functioning of central, receptive interconnections and on the diffusion of sensory stimulation.

(*b*) *Intersensory transfer.* Is perceptual activity in one direction affected by training in another? Meyer (1953) presented a review of all the work on the subject of interaction between simultaneous activities of the senses.

What happens when the activities occur in succession? Here is an account of three studies which, among others, investigated intersensory transfer in tasks of varying complexity.

Gaydos (1956) made two groups of 43 subjects learn the names of flat forms with rounded contours. They resembled triangles or ellipses, or they had very indeterminate shapes. In the first learning session, one group learnt to name these forms by touching them without seeing them, while the other group learnt to name them by seeing them without touching them. In the transfer situation, both groups had to recognize the forms by means of the sense that had previously been inactive, i.e. sight for one group and touch for the other.

In both cases, there was intersensory, perceptual transfer. Comparing the number of trials for a correct name, there was a gain of 74 per cent from sight to touch and of 84 per cent from touch to sight. The latter result, which surprised the author, seems to be due to the effort made by the subject to picture the forms that he touched. Perceptual transfer must be due to the establishment of complex schemes, elaborated when acquisition of the form's name took place.

Sinha and Sinha (1960) obtained a very different result in successive learnings, by sight and touch, of an identical maze schema, i.e. the visual and the tactual maze made the subject turn to left or right the same number of times and in the same order. There was a manual T-maze for touch and, for sight, two cards were placed in front of the subject, who had to say whether he chose left or right. There were as many choices to make in this situation as there were changes of direction in the manual maze. There was a gain of 57·16 per cent from visual training to tactual learning, while the gain was 78·6 per cent from touch to sight. In the latter case, it can be assumed that the spatial disposition of the tactual maze enabled the subject to establish a scheme, common to both tasks, with a greater degree of differentiation on account of all the secondary, kinaesthetic landmarks. In addition to the number of alternatives and their order, which also occur in visual learning, these landmarks provided a schema of positions in relation to the body itself.

The following hypothesis can be made: the task furnishing the most highly organized schema is the one which subsequently produces (no matter what sensory modality is involved in acquisition) the highest degree of transfer effect on the other modality.

Transfer can also stem from the existence of a scheme of contrast likely to affect perceptual activity. The consecutive, figural effect, in which visual and kinaesthetic perception are made to differ, can be explained in this way. In Jaffre's experiment (1956), the tactile-kinaesthetic estimation of the height of an object accompanied a visual estimation of it. In the so-called saturation phase inducing the consecutive effect, the individual held the object and looked at an enlarged picture of it. In the second phase, controlling the saturation effect, the subject looked at an exact representation of the test-object, whose height he had to estimate. He underestimated it.

The fact that reading words helps one to hear them can be explained by intersensory transfer. Presumably a close connection occurs between a written word and its sound. One recalls the other, since they are different expressions of the same thing. Postman and Rosenzweig (1956) demonstrated that the recognition threshold for nonsense syllables is lower for audio-discrimination after visual learning. The effect is much less marked in the reverse situation. The availability of phonemes seems to depend more on reading the words. People pronounce to themselves what they read more than they picture in writing what they hear. The two situations are not reciprocal. We speak before we write.

(B) TRANSFER AND DISCRIMINATIVE LEARNING

Most motor and cognitive activities make people distinguish between relevant elements and those which are only secondary, or even irrelevant. They learn to take no notice of certain indications or cues and to distinguish them clearly from the others.

When people cross a street, they try to see whether a car is coming. One important cue that they pick out is the speed of an advancing vehicle, and they learn to estimate this speed. The colour of the car and its make are easily evaluated data, but these they ignore. There are so many things appealing to people's senses that they only take notice of those which are relevant to the present task.

This selection usually operates through the association of responses with stimuli. In the previous example, people cross the street when they estimate that a vehicle will take longer to reach a certain point in the road than they will.

The handling of machines must involve the establishment of continuous connections between signals in the environment (dial of a machine, for example) and the movement of handles and levers. Such discriminative activity also occurs in learning paired associates.

The object of discrimination is to isolate these cues, and also to modify the subjective effect of similarity between various elements. In particular, it weakens the process of generalization of both stimulus and response.

The problem is to discover how transfer effects affect the discrimination of adequate or inadequate cues, which, incidentally, play a very important role in Tolman's theory of learning (1951).

Numerous experiments with both animals and humans confirm the existence of this transfer of differentiated cues. Here are several examples.

(*a*) *Selection of adequate cues and transfer.* In Graham's experiment (1943), a rat learnt to press a lever in a Skinner's box when there was silence. The absence of any sound stimulation became the effective cue in this case. This discrimination of silence was transposable, for the rat, trained in a Skinner's box, also became more active under the same conditions in maze learning. The author demonstrated that silence alone was really the source of the development of activity, for the transfer effect also appeared when maze learning came first. Silence, in this situation, was a cue which the animal differentiated from all other sounds in its environment.

Lawrence (1949) showed how general this is, in animal behaviour, by repeating these experiments with different cues.

What happens in the case of humans, whose level of integration of stimuli in the elaboration of behaviour involves more complex schemes?

In a discrimination task in which the subject had to select an 'adequate' cue from inadequate ones, Ecksirand and Wickens (1954) demonstrated, on the one hand, the selective effect of transfer which enables the subject to discriminate one cue from others; and, on the other hand, the relationship between the force of this effect and the nature of the cues selected.

In the second learning test, the subjects had to associate different shapes, colours and sizes with reaction keys. This is a classical test for perceptual-motor associations. The adequate cues in this test were either shape or colour, and the inadequate cue was size. Initially the authors had used three situations:

(α) With group A, shape and colour were reinforced equally (this group was to serve as a control group);

(β) With group C, colour was reinforced for half the subjects, and shape for the other half;

(γ) With group D, the size of the stimulus was reinforced (inadequate stimulus).

Table IV shows the number of trials required to reach the criterion of success chosen for the second learning session. The most efficient subjects were those who had previously learnt to discriminate the relevant dimension. However, the most effective pre-training was in colour rather than in shape. Comparison with the control group revealed the positive effect of a saving of 7·85 trials for colour and 3·75 for shape.

Similarly, the negative effects in the results of group D, trained with the inadequate cue, were higher when followed by perception of colour rather than by perception of shape.

Presumably the selection of 'size' made the subject consider shape as a secondary criterion, while ignoring colour. Thus inadequate cues in the first learning task were not equally neglected, and their limitations on the transfer lever varied according to the strength of their connection with the adequate one.

TABLE IV

| | Nature of the stimulus used for the different groups in the 1st learning session | | |
Nature of the adequate stimulus in the 2nd learning session	D (size)	A (colour and shape)	C (colour or shape)
Colour	28	24·10	16·25
Shape	17·25	15·85	12·10

(Taken from Ecksirand and Wickens, *J. exp. Psychol.*, 1954, **47**, 276.)

(*b*) *Role of inadequate cues and transfer.* Obviously, in most situations, inadequate cues exist alongside an adequate cue. At the same time, they play different roles *vis-à-vis* this adequate cue.

Using animals, Babb (1956) carried out a systematic study of the role of reinforcement of the adequate stimulus in learning prior to transfer. He found that the role of this cue depended on the frequency of its association with the adequate cue during learning. If the degree of association was 30 per cent, the presence of this cue in the transfer situation provoked interference; so the inadequate cue was a disturbing cue. If the degree of association was 50 per cent, the transfer effect was zero. It became positive, if the adequate and inadequate stimuli were associated in 70 per cent of the cases; so the inadequate cue reinforced the principal stimulus.

The results of this experiment emphasize the role of reinforcement in the effectiveness of transfer when learning cues. However, Bitterman, Federsen and Tyler (1953) have shown that reinforcement plays a different role according to the duration of learning. If learning was short, discrimination of the inadequate cue, at the moment of transfer, was facilitated by familiarity. However, if training was prolonged, the rats learnt not to differentiate the two cues, which were both 50 per cent reinforced.

157

Consequently, in the transfer test, when the rats had to learn to distinguish between these cues which had become confused, there was inhibition and a negative, transfer effect.

These studies prove that, in the case of animals, there is transfer of the selection of cues, and that this depends on the conditions of reinforcement under which it is effected. This seems to establish relatively simple laws between strength and duration of reinforcement and transfer of discrimination.

The same thing applies to human behaviour. Restle (1959) demonstrated that cues present in the first learning task could become neutral, if not reinforced.

The task consisted of dividing up into two categories groups of five letters arranged so that three, always the same three, were first, third and fifth in each group. The subjects had no prior knowledge of the principle behind the classifications. The cue was *a*, if X or Y were in the second position, and *b*, if V and W were in the fourth position. Thus the groups of letters could have both cues or one or the other. There were three different tasks in the first learning sessions.

Task A consisted of grouping in category 1 stimuli in which X occupied the second place and in category 2 those in which Y occupied this position. Only cue *a* was adequate in this task. In task B, cue *b* was adequate, and the grouping depended on the letters V and W.

In task A+B, category 1 was the one in which X and W occupied respectively the second and fourth positions in the groups of letters, while category 2 was that in which Y and V occupied these positions. Fig. 3 shows the learning and transfer curves. Groups I and II learnt task A or task B for 25 trials. Groups III and IV learnt task A+B for 25 trials. Classification was twice as fast when there were twice as many cues, and the efficiency of these two groups was greater than that of groups I and II.

However, from the transfer point of view, it appears that groups III and IV, trained in task A+B, were less efficient in task A or task B than the groups which had carried on learning them. However, the degree of familiarity with each of the cues was about the same for all groups.

The negative transfer effect found in groups III and IV was due to the fact that these subjects had to neutralize one of the two adequate cues in their first learning task. Neutralization is an active phenomenon, and not a passive one.

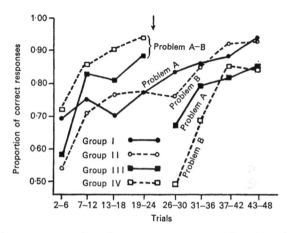

Fig. 3. Average proportion of correct responses as a function of training trials for groups I, II, III and IV

The arrow shows where transfer began for groups III and IV. Trials 1 and 25 were eliminated. (From Restle (F.), *J. exp. Psychol.*, 1959, **57**, 11.)

This research showed that the selection of cues, which are adequate *vis-à-vis* a given activity, is transferable. One aspect of an object becomes relevant, irrespective of the task. Concomitant, inadequate cues can either facilitate or hinder a task, depending on how frequently they occur concomitantly. These effects of facilitation or interference are a function of the length of preliminary training in differentiation of cues.

(*c*) *Transfer of discrimination and verbalization.* Miller and Dollard (1941) presumed that prior association of a word or name with a stimulus must favour its subsequent differentiation.

This facilitation, arising from association with a verbal cue, must be distinguished from that caused by learning verbally a symbolic or descriptive scheme of the task to be performed.

Arnoult (1953) tested this hypothesis in the field of perceptual tasks (discrimination of shapes). In the first learning task, the subjects learnt to associate letters with each of the shapes that had to be differentiated in the second task. These shapes had irregular surfaces with rounded contours. No positive, transfer effect was found for subjects trained in this way. The reason for this was insufficient training, since the first task was only practised until 70 per cent of correct responses, in the association of letters and shapes, had been obtained. Under these conditions, complete differentiation by name was not accomplished. Indeed it could even (at a weaker level) have provoked a negative transfer effect through proactive interference, as happened in Babb's experiment (1956).

Robinson (1955) treated this same hypothesis in an original way. The transfer task consisted of distinguishing between two fingerprints, presented simultaneously, which might be identical or different. In the training task, the author formed three groups: group D learnt to associate gangsters' names with the prints by an anticipatory method; group E learnt to associate the word 'cop' with five prints and the word 'robber' with the other five; group S–D merely looked at the ten prints, and decided whether they were identical or not. Only the control group N–P–T took the transfer test.

The following results show positive transfer in the decrease both in the number of errors and in the latency of the responses.

TABLE V

| Group | Errors | | Latency |
	Average	Standard Deviation	Average
D	4·34	0·79	33·04
E	4·30	1·14	35·25
S–D	3·88	1·17	31·82
N–P–T	5·15	0·79	39·82

(Taken from Robinson (J.S.), *J. exp. Psychol.*, 1955, **49**, 113.)

Once again, the hypothesis of Miller and Dollard was not verified, because the transfer effect seems to have been caused by familiarization with the stimuli, since group S–D was quicker and more accurate than groups D and E.

The relative superiority of group S–D seems to have been caused by a form of discrimination learning. Consequently, in the case of adults, words cannot be said to be an efficient aid in specifically perceptual tasks.

Is this true of young children of 3 and 4 years? Words are a very real and active part of children's development. They learn to associate words with objects. Their syncretism is such that all the elements connected with any object are so many cues, which should facilitate discrimination. Cantor (1955) proved this in a facial discrimination test. In the first task, a group of children learnt to associate a name with each of the faces; another group learnt to associate the same names with other faces, which would not be used in the transfer test. The children in the control group simply looked at the faces that were used in the transfer test.

In the transfer situation, a double-choice discrimination test (the faces were presented in pairs, some of them representing a reward), the subjects with previous verbal association were more efficient. This applied to groups whose average age was 3 years 6 months as well as to those of 4 years 6 months.

The hypothesis made by Miller and Dollard was also confirmed in perceptual-motor tasks performed by adults. Here are three examples.

Goss (1953) compared the effects of three training situations. In one, a verbal-association situation (V–L), the subjects learnt to associate four nonsense syllables with four light stimuli of varying intensity. In another (S–D) the subjects learnt to distinguish between these stimuli by paired comparison. In a visual-observation situation (S), the subjects merely looked at these stimuli. In situation V–L learning continued (depending on the group) until a success rate of 9, 11 or 12 out of 12 (i.e. 100 per cent) was achieved. In situations S–D and S training tests equalled the number of presentations of stimuli in situation V–L.

The transfer test consisted of the association of a particular reaction key with each of the light stimuli. Table VI shows that the number of trials without error, in a given time in the transfer situation, was higher in the case of pre-training by verbal association (V–L).

This indicates that more is at work than the effect of mere familiarity with the stimuli, as was the case in situations S–D and S. The number of errors shows the same tendency.

Other experiments have shown that preliminary learning by verbal association is more efficient, the more complete learning is.

TABLE VI

Situation	V–L		S–D				S			Control
Degree of previous learning (number of successes)	9	11	100%	9	11	100%	9	11	100%	*Nothing*
Number of trials without errors (average)	31	32	36·3	29·8	29·9	31·1	28·2	27·9	23	18·9
Number of errors (average)	21·2	19·8	14·4	24·3	24·4	22·5	27·9	28·5	36·7	44·3

(Taken from Goss, *J. exp. Psychol.*, 1953, **46**, 243.)

Macek (1957) has proved (by means of a test with a star-shaped discrimimeter) that there is positive transfer between preliminary verbal association and a perceptual-motor test when the first task is learnt up to a 57 per cent level of success. The transfer effect is zero when the success level is only 33 per cent.

Batting (1956) compared the transfer effects of two learning tests on a similar, perceptual-motor test learnt subsequently.

One of the first tasks, a verbal-association test S, only involved discrimination of stimuli, while the other (SR) involved a description of the motor responses to be performed later (i.e. symbolic learning). These two pre-training tests were very different, and so their effects bore on different aspects of the task. Both were more efficient, the simpler the task. The transfer effect from verbal association was zero when there were three or four connections to establish, but positive when only one or two connections had to be learnt.

Presumably, when the task is simple, verbal association is effective and produces positive transfer by differentiating the stimuli to which it relates. The transfer effect is higher, the greater the similarity between stimuli and the greater the degree of reinforcement of the association.

The following hypothesis can be made: the association of a stimulus with a specific word diminishes the tendency of the stimulus to generalization whereby very similar stimuli provoke the same response. Le Ny (1959) showed how, by associating widely separated letters of the alphabet with various notes, a subject's estimation of the tonal difference between these notes could be affected. He concluded: 'Finally, this experiment shows the relative nature of unconditioned similarities presumed to be absolute, such as tonal pitch, and the way in which these can be disturbed by learning, which is, after all, very simple and very short.' He had demonstrated a transfer effect of discrimination.

2 Transfer effects on the effector level

(A) BILATERAL TRANSFER

Bilateral transfer occurs when the effector activity of a limb (foot or hand) changes as a result of training a contralateral limb.

(*a*) *The facts.* Weber (1834) was probably the first author to point out that children trained to write with their right hands were subsequently more skilful at mirror-drawing with their left hands. Fechner reported the same fact in 1858, together with similar observations.

The earliest, systematic studies were those made by Scripture, Smith and Brown (1894) and Davis (1898, 1900) of tests in dynamometry, tapping and accuracy.

Swift (1903) demonstrated the effect of bilateral transfer in a game of cup-and-ball. Munn (1932) repeated this test in a more systematic way. The subjects in the experimental group worked with their left hands for 50 trials, then with their right hands for 500 trials, and, finally, again with their left hands for a further 50 trials. The subjects in the control group worked in the same way as those in the experimental group, but without any training on the right hand. A comparison of results in the last 50 trials led to the following conclusions:

(α) There was a positive effect of bilateral transfer. The experimental group was more skilful than the control group. The experimental group's gain on the two series of tests using the left hand was 61·1 per cent, while the control group's gain was 28·5 per cent.

(β) All the results of the subjects in the experimental group showed this gain. Gains were greatest in the case of those subjects whose spontaneous skill was least marked.

The classical test for the study of bilateral transfer is mirror-drawing. Starch (1910) demonstrated positive transfer when a subject was trained to trace a drawing in a mirror with his right hand, and then to do the same thing with his left hand. Incidentally, tracing with the left hand is easier from left to right when it has been learnt from right to left with the right hand. The two hands work symmetrically quite spontaneously in relation to the medial plane.

Ewart (1926) described this phenomenon in detail, and Bray (1928) demonstrated bilateral transfer between hand and foot as well as between hands. He compared results obtained with pre-training on the right hand with those obtained when the subjects' only means of knowing of any change in motor coordination was by looking in a mirror. The success rate of these subjects, who worked with their left hands only, lay between that of the control group, who worked solely with their left hands, and that of the experimental group with bilateral transfer (Fig. 4).

Consequently this experiment showed that bilateral transfer was not just due to knowledge of the movement required to compensate for the mirror-image. It seems to have resulted from a perceptual-motor adjustment of the sort that would occur, if the mirror were used to detect the track to follow by progressive adjustment, creating new automatisms, without any explicit awareness of the laws of reflection and their consequences. This training of perceptual-motor co-ordination can be transmitted to any one of the limbs, but the educability of sensori-motor co-ordination varies considerably from one subject to another, as indeed do their affective reactions to any obstacle encountered in the task.

Cook (1933, 1935) took up this problem in a series of extremely systematic studies. In a very ingenious mirror-drawing test with a stylet (which could be used either by hand or foot), the subjects had to trace, by means of specular vision, the raised outline (Fig. 5) of a star, whose six tracks extended beyond their twelve intersections. This was the first test. The other test consisted of following an irregular maze. In the first task, both time and errors were noted, but, in the second task, simply the time required to track through the maze was recorded.

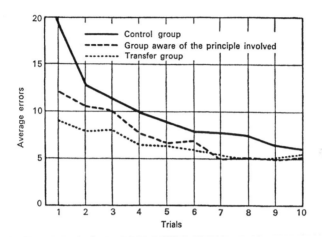

Fig. 4. The curves show the average errors of the control and experimental groups in trials during bilateral transfer. (After Woodworth (R.S.) and Schlosberg (H.), *Experimental Psychology*, New York, Holt, 1954, p. 742.)

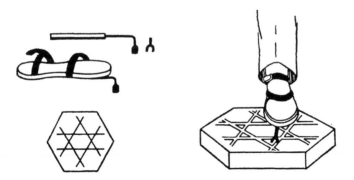

Fig. 5. Maze in the shape of a raised star which can be tracked with the foot, using a special sandal, or with the hand, using a stylet. (Adapted from a figure in Cook (T.W.), *J. exp. Psychol.*, 1933, **16**, 146.)

Prior to these specular experiments, Cook had taught his subjects to use the stylet to trace the star by direct vision, either by hand or foot. The subjects then took the series of tests shown in the table below.

TABLE VII

	Training (E)		Transfer tests (T)	
Group A	Right hand	Left foot	Right foot	Left hand
Group B	Left hand	Right hand	Left hand	Right foot
Group C	Left hand	Right foot	Left hand	Right hand
Duration	10 trials in 10 days	3 trials	3 trials	10 trials

In calculating the rate of transfer, Cook took into account the preliminary training. The rate of transfer was $(Ef - E_1)/(T_1 - E_1)$ per cent, in which E_1 and Ef were the success rates in the first and last training trials. T_1 was the result of the first transfer trial. Cook's main conclusions (1935) were: (α) *Positive* bilateral and homolateral (hand–foot on the same side) transfer do exist; (β) The rate of transfer depends on whether the limbs are symmetrical or not. Transfer rates decrease in the following order: between symmetrical limbs (hand–hand, foot–foot), between homolateral limbs (right hand–right foot, left hand–left foot), between cross-members (right hand–left foot); (γ) The transfer rate increases as an absolute figure, the higher the degree of initial training; (δ) The relative rate of transfer increases with the level of success attained in the first learning test; (ϵ) The transfer effect is permanent (i.e. maintained throughout the second learning test), at any rate, in the case of homolateral and symmetrical limbs.

In Cook's view, this transfer effect arises from a specific, sensori-motor acquisition, independent of any speculative knowledge of techniques to apply and of emotive adaptation.

However, a recent study by Zaidi (1956) shows how frustration can alter effects of bilateral transfer in a mirror-drawing test. A control group underwent training, prior to transfer, without any comment from the experimenter, whereas an experimental group received his critical comments. Although, at the end of this preliminary training, great care was taken to ensure that standards of acquisition were identical in both groups, the experimental group proved less efficient in the transfer test than the control group. Presumably the state of frustration, caused by the critical comments, developed a generalized reaction of inhibition, which appeared mainly when the new task was being performed.

(*b*) *Psycho-physiological explanations of bilateral transfer.* Daily and simultaneous training of the various receptor organs, particularly eyes and ears, is such that connections and conditioning are constantly being established. One eye covered up undergoes reactions of adaptation (alteration in convergence) provoked by the activity of the other eye.

However, in the case of hearing, experiments by Rosenzweig and Sutton (1958) have revealed interaction on the level of sensory relay. This is contrary to the findings of Kemp, Coppée and Robinson (1937), who discovered interaction of impulses from the two ears on the level of the lateral lemniscus.

Lashley's experiment (1924) with monkeys illustrated the central source of motor regulation between limbs. By means of surgery, it was possible to isolate the left motor area from the right without too much injury. The monkey was then trained to use its right hand. Next the right motor area was destroyed. When the monkey had almost recovered the use of its left hand, it repeated the task with this hand. The monkey then worked better with its left hand than if it had not undergone preliminary training.

Woodworth concluded (1949, p. 260): 'Such learning, from what we know of the brain, can extend over a large area of the cortex, in the pre-motor, parietal and occipital regions'. Transfer shows that both hands are capable of using the same cerebral mechanism to a high level. Recent research on the brain has underlined the extreme complexity of the connections between the cerebral hemispheres and the ability of one limb to adapt itself in order to replace another. Neurological explanations are valid in the case of elementary reactions, but they do not entirely explain this complex adaptation. Lashley and Wade (1946) treated this subject of generalization of response in accordance with Pavlov's theory. This approach was taken up and developed by McGeoch and Irion (1953, p. 327), who connected the process of bilateral transfer directly with the mechanisms of response generalization, or rather with those of the mediatory instrument of response. They felt that a clear distinction must be made between generalization of response, based on some generalizing property within the organism, and generalization of response, based on a mediatory process involving prior learning. The first is primary generalization of response, while the second is secondary generalization.

(*c*) *Bilateral transfer as an experimental method.* Bilateral transfer has become a method of research, since it apparently results in the intervention of connections on the cortical level.

Kimble (1952) demonstrated reactive inhibition *Ir*. This develops in the course of learning and, in accordance with Hull's theory, is definitely of a central nature, since it is transferable. For the purpose of this demonstration, Kimble made use of Koerth's tracking apparatus (1928) in which a needle has to be kept on a small target fixed to a rotating disc. Two groups of subjects participated in the experiment. One, the experimental group, performed 30 trials of 10 seconds, without interruption, with their left hands, and then had the benefit of 5 minutes' rest.

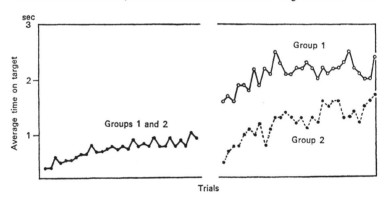

Fig. 6. Average time on target during preliminary learning with both groups using left hand together, and during transfer learning with group 1 using right hand after a rest and group 2, also using right hand, but without a rest. (After Kimble (G.A.), *J. exp. Psychol.*, 1952, **43**, 392.)

During this period, reactive inhibition (which had developed during the previous trials) should disappear. This group then performed 30 trials of 10 seconds each with their right hands.
168

The control group worked in the same way, but with no rest period between learning sessions.

The results in these graphs show that the experimental group was more efficient than the control group. Reactive inhibition *Ir*, evident in the results of both groups, did develop, but it could just as easily disappear, witness group 1's results. This reactive inhibition must have been central, since it affected the activity of the subjects' left hands, although it developed as a result of their right hands' activity.

(B) TRANSFER AND PERCEPTUAL-MOTOR ADAPTATION IN COMPLEX TASKS

One of the problems in working machines is that of the transfer of training acquired. In fact learning on one type of machine, and the education received, should mean rapid adaptation to other, similar machines.

Such training involves the progressive integration of effector reactions to stimuli that appear either simultaneously or in a specific order (which may or may not be predictable). The establishment of automatisms, conditioned to the appearance of signals, may cause either facilitation or interference.

(*a*) *Transfer of habits acquired in daily life.* People adapt themselves to complex tasks by means of all the skills required by their daily life. As Gibbs (1954) pointed out, elementary schemas of responses are established and these schemas are subsequently combined together.

Lewis and Sheppard (1951), using a firing device, did not find that just any arrangement of the controls sufficed. There was a 'natural' way of positioning them which favoured learning. These facilitation effects appear to stem from acquired, sensori-motor habits.

Schwartz, Norris and Spragg (1953), using a revolving device, found that the greatest degree of accuracy was obtained when the left-hand control handle was in the frontal plane, while the right-hand one was in a plane parallel to the medial plane. However, the co-ordination of gestures depended upon the nature of the task to be accomplished. The similarity of methods of response (position of the control levers and regulating buttons) did not necessarily result in positive transfer, if stimuli were different.

169

Andreas, Green and Spragg (1954), while studying two adjustment devices, noticed that opposite positions greatly facilitated learning two tests which, at first sight, appeared very similar. In the 'track' task, the subject had to keep an index finger in constant contact with a moving spot by means of two handles. This was a tracking test (Fig. 7). In the compensation

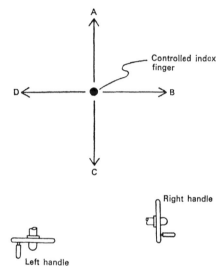

Fig. 7. This figure shows the path followed by an index finger controlled by turning two handles. The arrows show the direction taken by the finger when the controls were arranged 'naturally'. In the tracking test, A shows that the movement in that direction was caused by turning the right handle clockwise, B shows that it was caused by turning the left handle clockwise, and C and D show movements caused by turning the right and left handles anti-clockwise, respectively. (After Andreas (B.G.), Green (R.F.) and Spragg (S.D.S.), *J. Psychol.*, 1954, **37**, 175.)

('comp') task, the subject had to keep a spot over a reticule. The experimenter controlled this spot, moving it all the time, and the subject had to compensate for this movement (Fig. 6). The tracking task always appeared to be easier, although the movements were the same. The controls normally[1] best suited to the 'track' task was not best for the 'comp' task. In the latter case,

---

[1] 'Normal' means whichever position of the controls that is natural for the tracking task.

the subjects had to try and keep the spot still, while they were under the impression that they were pursuing the spot with the reticule. Consequently the controls, which were not normally suitable for the tracking task, proved to be the most efficient in the compensation task.

(*b*) *Transfer and change of arrangement.* What happens when a subject is moved to an arrangement which is not normal after training with a normal arrangement?

Andreas, Green and Spragg (1954) found that transfer depended on the tasks to be performed with the new mechanisms. As in the previous experiment, the subjects took a transfer test by moving from a 'tracking' situation to a 'compensation' situation, or *vice versa*, on the same apparatus.

The authors then set up four transfer situations by combining normal arrangements with abnormal ones for both tasks. Four groups of 23 subjects performed both tasks in the following order:

TABLE VIII

	Order of tasks with control condition	
Group	*1st task*	*2nd task*
I	Normal 'track'	Normal 'comp'
II	Normal 'comp'	Normal 'track'
III	Normal 'track'	Abnormal 'comp'
IV	Abnormal 'comp'	Normal 'track'

Fig. 8 gives the results. Only group III showed any significant amount of transfer. There was slight, positive transfer in group I. In the other two groups, there were slight, negative effects, but these were not statistically significant. Consequently the arrangement of the handles and the way they were turned were only important as a function of their role in adjustment.

(*c*) *Transfer and the interchange of control arrangement.* This problem often occurs in everyday life today. The controls of a a new machine may be the opposite way round to those on an-other machine. Driving a car involves learning to co-ordinate feet and hands as well as to avoid certain synkinetic movements (pressing with one foot, while releasing the other). The clutch, brake and accelerator occupy specific positions. A driver's confusion can well be imagined if he had to drive with the positions of the pedals changed round.

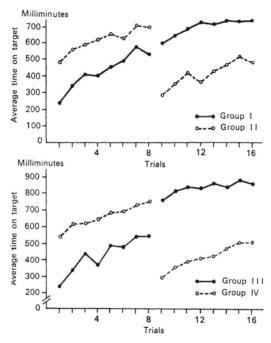

Fig. 8. Average time that contact was maintained with the spot by the different groups I, II, III and IV during training trials (1 to 8) and transfer trials (9 to 16). (After Andreas (B.G.), Green (R.F.) and Spragg (S.D.S.), *J. Psychol.*, 1954, **37**, 178.)

Duncan (1953) discovered (by means of a star-shaped discrimimeter) that the interchange of connections between signals and corresponding keys in two consecutive learning sessions provoked a positive, transfer effect which was, in all cases, greater, the smaller the number of changes for a constant number of connections.

Lewis and Sheppard (1950) obtained very similar results with Mashburn's apparatus. This device comprised three groups of signals arranged in three different ways: a horizontal line, a vertical line and a curve. Stimulation was provided by lighting one of the signals (red) in one of the three arrangements. The subject's response was to light one of the signals (green) in a group arranged in exactly the same way as the corresponding stimulation and situated just beside or just below it. By means of pre-established connections, each of the three groups of signal-responses could be linked to each of three control devices (two pedals and a column like the joy-stick of an aeroplane). One of the signals in a group would light up, depending upon the amount of pressure on the pedals and the angle of the joy-stick.

Various transfer situations could be obtained with this device by interchanging connections between consecutive learning tasks. Every situation produced positive, transfer effects, notwithstanding a temporary increase in the number of errors, i.e. subjects corrected their mistakes much more quickly at the beginning of the second learning task than at the start of the first task. They had become adapted to the type of task, and had found out the way in which to learn it.

Using these results, the conclusion can be drawn that the following information is required to predict transfer effects: (α) the subjects' spontaneous tendencies to regulate their own actions; (β) the standard of difficulty of consecutive tasks; (γ) the mechanisms of co-ordination involved in the integration of perceptual and motor activity.

3   Explanations of transfer

In order to explain the phenomenon of transfer in complex tasks, it is apparently necessary to know what motor, perceptual, cognitive, etc. processes are involved. There are two possible approaches to this sort of research, and an author's choice in this matter depends, during the development of psychology, very largely on what type of theory he subscribed (or subscribes) to. One possibility is to assume the existence of identical or similar processes, relevant to the accomplishment of consecutive tasks, in which case the accent will be on an analysis of these processes. The other possibility is to assume that tasks with identical or similar elements oblige the individual to use identical or similar psychological processes, in which case the emphasis will be on a preliminary analysis of the tasks.

Nevertheless, explanations of transfer are still subject to a knowledge of various, adapted and effective, psychological processes provoked by the tasks performed. Problems are mainly caused by the dynamic and evolutional nature of these processes and their interaction.

To put it more simply, research into explanatory principles of transfer can be divided up into two general currents. One current, global and structural, is more interested in determinants relating to the activity of the individual, and explains transfer by a learnt attitude, by the ability to use lessons learnt earlier, or simply by the fact that the same methods or principles apply to different tasks. As McGeoch and Irion (1952) pointed out, different modalities of transfer, which it is normally difficult to dissociate, can thus be distinguished. Various accounts by different authors use the same examples to show the existence of processes which are distinct from one another.

The other current, which is analytical, considers determinants in a behaviourist perspective. The similarity of tasks seems to be essential, and is analysed in terms of stimulus–response associations. This similarity stretches from the identity of elements in a situation, or of responses, to their complete heterogeneity, and is based on the establishment of generalization gradients. An examination will now be made of experiments illustrating both these approaches.

1 Explanation by activity of the individual

(A) TRANSFER OF LEARNING ATTITUDES TO LEARNING IN DIFFERENT ACTIVITIES

Attitude is orientation in the choice and organization of perceptual, affective and cognitive means. 'Learning to learn' puts all these selected means to work.

Deese (1958, p. 228) pointed out that the development of 'a learning attitude can be distinguished by the emergence of an attitude of a higher order, formed by the one common component which is reinforced in a certain number of habits at a lower level'. Every discrimination problem can be regarded as a habit on an elementary level, i.e. in a double-choice, discrimination test, transfer consists of the habit of altering the second choice when the first is incorrect.

As Montpellier (1936) expressed it, 'what is transposed is not an association or a succession of elementary associations, but rather an attitude of response, a way of seeing the same sort of solution for different problems'.

All that seems to distinguish transfer of 'attitude' from that of 'learning to learn' is the degree of complexity of the processes at work. Nevertheless, a distinction is always made.

(*a*) *Perceptual and discriminative activities.* In Harlow's experiments (1950), a monkey had to learn to find the correct response in a series of double-choice, discrimination tests. The same stimuli were used throughout the series, but, in each test, only one of the two stimuli presented was the right one which would produce a reward for the monkey.

At the beginning of the series, the animal always chose the stimulus that had previously been rewarded or the one occurring in the same place as the correct one in the previous test. This attitude of perseverance gradually diminished as training proceeded. Eventually the monkey realized that, if his first choice was wrong, he should choose the other stimulus. The animal had learnt to change its mind, and this attitude became independent of the nature of the stimuli and of any connections between them.

Riopelle (1953) confirmed this transfer of attitude in successive, discrimination tests which were complicated by the attitude to be adopted. For 63 days, he studied the behaviour of four monkeys as they made their selections. Each day, an animal had to solve four problems, one of which was presented the opposite way round during the session. Riopelle noted that the monkeys learnt the discrimination problems, including the problem in its reversed form, more and more quickly. Initially this reversed problem was learnt more quickly if there was some little time separating it from the original problem. However, as the days went by, he was able to reduce the amount of time separating them. Hayes and Thompson (1958) obtained very similar results when they repeated this experiment with young children.

(b) *Sensori-motor activity.* Transfer of attitude is also spoken of in the sensori-motor field, although 'learning to learn' does seem to apply more to the acquisition of all the complex processes together.

In a perceptual-motor test, Duncan (1958) showed that this process is not the same as practice. Practice, which also entails some facilitation, only affects the actual speed of performance of co-ordinations developed in learning. Speed is due to repetition, which makes identical gestures automatic. There is also a rise in inhibition in the production of a response by a signal.

Different programmes of association of visual stimuli could be used in this perceptual-motor, adjustment test (star-shaped discrimimeter). Training lasted for 2, 5 or 10 days with 1, 2, 5 or 10 programmes a day, but the amount of practice was the same for all subjects, i.e. 20 trials of a fixed length, no matter how many programmes were used each day. The results showed that training with several programmes was more efficient than training with only one programme (where the factor of practice predominated). Duncan also discovered that variety of training was more effective than length of training. There was no interaction between these two factors. In training with different programmes, no matter how incomplete, the subject learnt to adapt himself, to know when to change and to find methods of exploration in order to discover the exact associations more quickly.

These results can be related to experience in everyday life. The driver of a car who has only driven one vehicle for many years is, in fact, a less accomplished driver than one who has driven a variety of cars for the same length of time.

(c) *Mnemonic activities.* The progressive improvement in learning speed in various, similar, successive tests has been explained by transfer of learning attitude and training.

Marx (1944) demonstrated the increase in the speed with which rats can cross a series of similar mazes (Fig. 9.). The rats learnt how to tackle a maze. Husband (1931) demonstrated something similar in maze-learning by humans. The individual learnt to retain a spatial-temporal scheme. In preliminary training, the subjects had to learn to perfect, often almost unconsciously, a technique for learning by which they would be able to avoid initial stumbling in the first task. This effect is clear from various experiments which distinguish it from other processes that might also explain, without any question of real transfer, the facilitation noted.

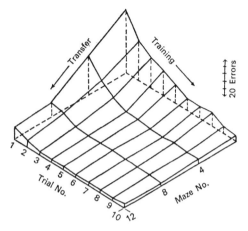

Fig. 9. Cumulative effects of transfer

The 25 rats perform 10 trials on a maze the first day, 10 trials on another maze the second day, and so on for 12 days. The mazes are similar structures in the form of a T. This three-dimensional drawing shows the training curves for each of the mazes: these are the lines descending to the right. The transfer lines show the degree of progress in each trial for each maze. (After Marx (M.H.), *Comp. Psychol. Monogr.*, 1944, **18**, 16.)

Ward (1937) demonstrated transfer in learning series of non-sense syllables. Each individual perfected his own mnemonic technique, although he might himself be unaware of his exact method. Thune (1950) showed clearly that transfer really occurred in every learning trial, and that this was quite different from the warm-up effect. The latter effect appeared at the same time as a certain amount of proactive inhibition caused by acquisition of the preceding list of syllables. Fig. 10 shows the transfer effect. The curves all have the same shape, but their different heights show that subjects learnt to learn more quickly each day.

(*d*) *Cognitive activity*. The experiment carried out by Di Vesta and Blake (1959) had a similar basis. It demonstrated the importance of the attitude of seeking a task's guiding principle. Transfer does not, in fact, stem from knowledge of this principle, but from the attitude of looking for it. In this experiment, the principle of the first task was not the same as that of the second.

Subjects in the RWP group discovered the law determining a response from the instructions and reinforcement given to them.

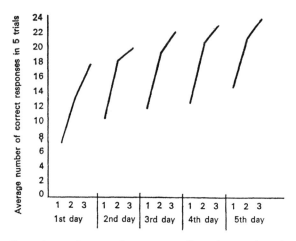

Fig. 10. Learning to learn and warm-up effects in rote learning. There were three different lists for each day for five days. (After Thune (L.E.), *J. exp. Psychol.*, 1951, **42**, 252.)

Their task was to find the figure associated with a word when this figure was the number of letters in the word. The subjects in group RNP only had to associate a word with the word presented when correct responses were confirmed. The subjects in group PRR also learnt to associate a figure with a word, but their responses were acknowledged right or wrong at random.

The transfer test consisted of completing a verbal expression suggested by a verb or adverb. Fig. 11 shows that group RWP, who knew that a rule existed, were more successful than the other two groups, so transfer must stem from *the attitude of looking for a law.*

McGeoch and Irion (1952) pointed out that learning to learn results, not only from the transfer of general methods of approach to a problem and the technique of acquisition, but also, at least partially, from learning how to re-adopt very swiftly the adapted attitude or type of behaviour required for the situation (Ammons, 1947).

This transfer process, which can be attributed to the means used by an individual to accomplish a task, is very global. A

better anlysis could probably be obtained with a deeper knowledge of the mechanisms involved. However, this global nature
will always remain for a subject who is given tasks to perform,

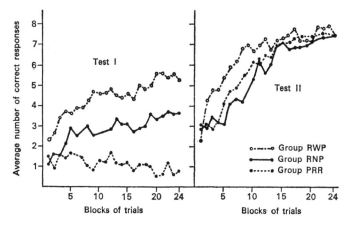

Fig. 11. Curves showing average number of correct responses for three
groups: RWP, Confirmation of correct responses and knowledge of law
determining them; RNP, Confirmation of correct responses only; PRR,
Random reinforcement of correct or incorrect responses, during two tests
(training I and transfer II). (After Di Vesta (F.J.), Blake (K.), *Amer. J.
Psychol.*, 1959, **72**, 60.)

without the means or the time to analyse them. A subject will be
more efficient, the more appropriate the principles and methods
he can find through his attitude developed by learning to learn,
and the deeper his understanding of these principles and methods.

(B) TRANSFER OF PRINCIPLES AND METHODS

Obviously, if two tasks are based on the same principles, the
effective means of performing them will be the same. In this
case, the accomplishment of the first task facilitates the execution
of the second. Education is largely based on teaching general
principles which enable an individual to discover means of
adapting himself to different situations.

Judd's point of view was: 'Mental development consists of
equipping an individual with the ability to think abstractly and
formulate general ideas. Transfer of training can act when this

goal has been achieved, since it is the nature of generalization and abstraction to extend beyond the specific experiences from which they spring'.

A knowledge of the principle involved does not necessarily lead to the discovery of the most efficient method of solving the problem or carrying out the task. Everything depends upon the generality of the principle and the specificity of the method. Thus the principles on which statistical trials are based are very different from the specific methods used to apply a particular, statistical test. The more abstract the principle, the more distinct its method of performance will be, and the less effective it will be on the plane of transfer from the level of concrete realization.

Consequently some studies are mainly concerned with demonstrating the importance of a knowledge of principles in transfer, while others emphasize the influence exerted by a knowledge of methods. Nevertheless, the two problems are interdependent and are in the same continuum from the general to the specific.

(*a*) *Transfer and knowledge of principles.* This question will be considered in relation to various activities.

(α) *Knowledge of principles in aiming tasks.* One of the first experimental studies in this field was carried out by Judd (1908). He demonstrated that aiming a dart at a submerged target in a pool of water was affected by a subject's knowledge of the laws of light refraction. Two groups of subjects were trained equally, but these laws were only explained to one group. Learning continued until the subjects in both groups reached the same standards of success. In the transfer test, the water-level was altered, and those subjects who knew the principle of light refraction were more successful than those who did not.

Hendrick and Schroeder (1941) repeated Judd's experiment, but they found that the group with knowledge of the principle were more skilful right from the start, and so, *a fortiori*, they were more successful in the transfer test.

Other experiments have verified the role played by a knowledge of principles in transfer. Forgus and Schwartz (1957) and Miller and Slebodnich (1958) demonstrated that the training obtained in mending an electronic device, which was assembled in accordance with fairly general principles, was more efficient than the training obtained in repairing different and very specialized, electronic devices. This experiment merely repeated, in a more up-to-date context, the experiment carried out by Cox (1933) on manual skill in fitting electric light bulbs into their sockets.

(β) *Transposition tests based on the existence of the transfer of a relation between two elements.* Transfer of principle is definitely involved in this situation (cf. Chapter 22). In an initial discrimination test, a subject learns to choose a stimulus out of a pair or a group of stimuli. This stimulus bears a certain relation to the other; for example, it is bigger, less luminous, etc. In order to find out whether this relation has been learnt, the subject is asked in the second task to choose again the stimulus bearing the same relation to the others as the previous one learnt (Kuenne, 1946; Oléron, 1957).

(γ) *Knowledge of principles and transfer in solving problems.* Like a number of other authors, Katona regarded transfer of principles as a fundamental process in the solving of problems. In a majority of cases, this does depend on a general principle that has to be applied to concrete situations. There is 'generalization', i.e. 'a general idea formulated can be present in the form of a constituent common to various, specific contents' (Katona, 1940, p. 56).

Sometimes, in geometrical problems, only the principle of construction (ruling a straight line or drawing a circle, for example) has to be learnt in order to solve the problem.

Katona demonstrated the influence exerted by an understanding of the principle in two sorts of task. One task consisted of card tricks and the other of transforming figures, made of short, straight lines (written test) or matches (manipulation test), into new figures. They had to break up the given figure and create a new one (cf. Chapter 22). The major problem encountered by the subjects was how to re-use, in a different way, in a new figure, an element of the figure originally given to them. The arrangement of the different elements made the subjects feel that each element could only play one role, i.e. the one it played in the first figure. Katona (1940) compared transfer from blindfold training with that from understanding the principle. The results shown in Table IX provide a resumé of the transfer effects noted in different tests of varying difficulty. Of course transfer depended in the difference in the degree of difficulty (or similarity) between the first and the second task, as well as on understanding the principle.

TABLE IX

1st task	% of degree of transfer in different tests				
Straightforward learning	0·3	7	16	21	24
Learning with an understanding of the task	63·0	89	90	92	107

(Taken from Katona, *Organizing and Memorizing*, 1940, p. 129.)

Sandiford (1928, p. 293) also found that, if learning consisted solely of mechanical training, transfer effects were in the region of zero, but transfer resulting from learning with an understanding of the principle involved was in the region of 100 per cent.

Katona also obtained this 100 per cent transfer rate, and he demonstrated that, once a subject had grasped the principle for solving a problem (a card trick, for example), he was better equipped to solve other, similar problems subsequently than if he had merely learnt the solution by heart in applying a particular method. 'It has often been said that the establishment of mechanical habits is the opposite of transfer', Katona wrote, underlining the difference between 'application', which is simply the use of a particular method to perform a task, and 'carrying over', which is the transfer of more general principles.

Table X gathers together the results of several experiments with card tricks in which Katona compared transfer as a function of conditions for accomplishing the first task. The comprehension group knew the principle of the card trick. The memorization group learnt by heart how the cards had to be placed in order to perform the trick.

These results show that transfer effects varied with methods used. They were negative for the memorization group, since 82·3 per cent of the subjects were less successful in the second task than in the first. Perseverance in applying the method previously learnt was probably the reason, since it created automatisms. The various, specific elements acquired would hinder the discovery of a more general principle which would be the only effective one in this transfer test. Katona concluded that 'subjects should not learn the solution to problems, but they ought to acquire a knowledge of what is different and what comes from the material specifically learnt'. The subject must find out what is the basis of the generalization of the principle.

TABLE X

Learning situation	Percentage of subjects for each type of transfer effect		
	Positive	Zero	Negative
Comprehension group (N = 107)	33·8	30·8	36·4
Memorization group (N = 85)	3·6	14·1	82·3

(Taken from Katona, *Organizing and Memorizing*, 1940, p. 130.)

In the comprehension group, transfer effects varied with individuals, positive for some and negative or zero for others. Some individuals can and others cannot apply a general principle to other, similar tasks.

It is not enough just to know the principle or principles governing a task. An individual must be able to put these principles into practice. This is very important from an educational point of view, and the following experiment would justify the practical application of principles, if such justification were necessary. In a multiple-choice test, Kittle (1957) made his subjects choose certain words out of others presented simultaneously. One group of subjects was told of the principle behind the correct choice, another group was partially informed of it, while a third group was given no information at all. By means of adapted training, all three groups attained the same standard in preliminary training. In the transfer test which followed, the most efficient group was the one whose members had been only partly informed of the principle. They had tried to find out all the principles involved, and so had been less passive in the first task than those who already possessed all the relevant information.

(*b*) *Transfer and knowledge of methods.* If an individual

183

possesses the necessary ability, knowledge of principles can lead to the discovery of efficient methods for the performance of tasks. This efficiency also appears if, in the absence of principles, methods suitable for a certain type of task are shown to the subject. Therefore, if the same methods are applied to similar tasks, there will obviously be positive transfer from one task to another. However, this can only happen when the tasks are very similar.

In learning lists of nonsense syllables, each individual perfects a method of mnemonic acquisition which, in most cases, leads to the establishment of associative connections, either between the stimuli themselves or between these stimuli and other elements already acquired. The individual is trained to establish connections, and the transfer of methods partly explains the transfer of 'learning to learn'.

Woodworth (1925) demonstrated the part played by different methods in memory training. Three groups of students took part in the experiment: one, the control group, only took the pre-test and the transfer trial; another group, called a 'practice' group, spent 3 hours (8 sessions in 4 weeks) memorizing poetry and nonsense syllables; the third group had the same amount of practice on the same exercise, but they were given advice on how to do it (for example, learn the syllables in groups, check what you have learnt, follow a particular rhythm, try and retain images and symbols, etc.). This third group was the most efficient one in the transfer test. Woodworth (1954) finally asked himself: what had been transferred? 'The subject improves his technique, adapts himself to the task and gains confidence. All the results obtained in these studies on memory confirm James's original conclusion that the improvement of memory lies in better methods of memorization'.

Katona (1940), followed by Hilgard, Irvine and Whipple (1953), compared three ways of learning how to perform card tricks successfully: (α) Explanation of the principle behind the trick; (β) Presentation of the cards in their relevant order; (γ) Use of pieces of paper as guides to this order. In a transfer test, the first and third methods appeared to be the most efficient.

However Luchins (1942) obtained a negative effect in his experiments, since his subjects persevered in the application of one method and, in so doing, neglected a much simpler method.

Consequently transfer of specific methods only produces

positive transfer when the tasks are very similar. Otherwise mechanical training can prove a hindrance to the acquisition of more general methods.

(*c*) *Transfer and verbal and non-verbal schematization of tasks.* Training can also be effected by means of a verbal description of a task or a written schematization of it. Both cases involve an abstract expression of the main elements in the task and their relations. This is a specific case of symbolic presentation of the method and of the connections to be established between stimuli and responses.

Gagné and Forster (1949) investigated the question of whether training with a paper-and-pencil test produced any improvement in learning in a test of perceptual-motor associations. These associations consisted of relating four reaction keys, two for each hand, to four green and red lights. The reaction keys bore no topological relation to the lights. The appearance of a red light at the bottom of the panel corresponded to a reaction by the left hand on key 1; a green light at the top corresponded to a response by the right hand on key 2, etc. This could easily be schematized and the task could be shown symbolically in drawings. Written training, by writing down the response to a signal (reproduced schematically), enabled the subjects to respond more quickly and more accurately in the actual task. This effect appeared as the subjects discovered the connections and learnt them. Obviously the part of a task involving sensori-motor co-ordination is only secondary in a simple task of this kind.

Baker and Wylie (1950) found that verbal training describing the action required by a task facilitated learning that task. Training consisted of 8 or 24 trials, depending on the experimental group (the subjects learnt to associate one-right with top-red, two-left with bottom-green, etc.). Only the 24-trial training produced efficient transfer in the actual task. This training favoured a reduction in the generalization of response or stimuli, producing a situation similar to the one occurring in discrimination learning. In a test of the same type, Batting (1956) demonstrated that facilitation due to verbal training decreased with the complexity of the task. There is probably a limit to an individual's ability to memorize connections that occur both on the verbal and on the perceptual-motor level.

2 Explanation of transfer by an analysis of similarity between tasks

(A) A FEW COMMENTS ON SIMILARITY

Transfer effects can only exist when there is a certain similarity between situations. The term 'situation' embraces both the task and the activity necessary for its accomplishment.

The various studies mentioned in the previous section all emphasize the importance of the subject's activity in the discovery and acquisition of attitudes, methods and principles. However, it is also possible to show how the task itself determines the type of activity involved and to investigate the question of whether systematic changes in the task produced systematic transfer effects.

Hull (1943), McGeogh and Irion (1952) and Osgood (1946) have all tried to establish laws of transfer, within this context, by means of an analysis on the behaviourist, stimulus–response pattern in which a subject's activity consists of establishing connections between certain stimuli and the corresponding responses. The individual himself is of secondary importance. This approach seems to be justified in tasks in which there is only one specific connection but, in many cases, although the direction of a connection is known, its actual content is not, since intermediary associations, which are often an important part of the subject's activity, may intervene.

However, an analysis in terms of stimulus–response has enabled experimenters to study, in greater detail, the part played by certain elementary factors of similarity occurring in the relatively simple association tasks which occur in many forms of human activity.

A study of transfer in a behaviourist context means that a method of measuring the degree of similarity must be found.

(*a*) *Measurement of similarity*. Noble (1957) felt that similarity could not be measured, the problem being that only 'psychological' similarity, as perceived by the subject, is important. But psychological and physical similarity are not the same thing. The latter can be measured with instruments, and degrees of likeness between stimuli can be established. However, an individual does not perceive stimuli in the same way as a measuring

186

device, and his perceptual interpretation depends, not only on his discriminative ability, but also on his knowledge, his attitude and the situation in which he is placed.

Nevertheless, a working definition of this similarity can be attempted with the aid of objective criteria (see Florès, 1957). The experimenter: (α) himself classifies stimuli as a function of their similarity, based on objective features (common elements); (β) appeals to judges to classify these stimuli; (γ) taking the notion of similarity as a generalizing tendency (similar stimuli produce the same response), he places stimuli (presumed to be similar) in order as a function of the number of responses (produced by them) identical to the response provoked by the stimulus with which they are being compared (Gibson, 1940; Osgood, 1946).

(*b*) *The establishment of degrees of similarity in actual research.* The role of similarity has been studied, for the most part, in learning paired associates by the anticipatory method.

The task consists of associating a 'response' element with a 'stimulus' element. In the first trial, the response word must be presented after the stimulus with which it should be associated. In subsequent trials, the subject should reply to the stimulus with the response word. If he fails, he is presented with the response word, and so on. Sensori-motor learning of the type carried out by Duncan (1953) and Van der Veldt (1928) falls into this category. In the case of Van der Veldt's work, all the means for making the motor responses were placed before the subject, who had to find the correct associations.

Nevertheless, in all these situations, in which the main activity is learning connections between stimuli and responses, the parts played by stimulus and response are not the same. In verbal learning, stimuli are presented to the subject who recognizes them, but does not need to memorize them. However, he must learn the responses. In some sensori-motor tasks, the responses are present and do not need to be learnt.

More often than not, the whole repertoire of responses must be acquired in addition to the connections.

It is easy to see how much similarity, both of stimuli and of responses, can vary, and to imagine the sort of transfer situations which result. These transfer situations can be grouped into two categories:

(α) Similarity of stimuli and responses. In this situation, the connections in the first and second task are formed between similar elements, the connections being similar. There are three possible cases here:

Identical stimuli and similar responses in both tasks;
Similar stimuli in both tasks and identical responses;
Similar stimuli and responses in both tasks.

This is illustrated by the schema of Woodworth and Schlosberg (1954) in Fig. 12.

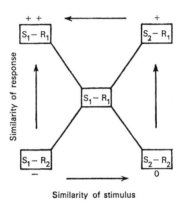

Similarity of stimulus

Fig. 12. This diagram gives a theoretical calculation of transfer effects, counting variations in stimulus or response or both from one task to another similar one. S_1–R_1 in the middle represent the initial task, while the other tasks on the outside are those performed secondly. The signs by each of these tasks stand for transfer effects. The transfer effect predicted for S_2–R_1, after learning S_1–R_1, is positive; while that for S_1–R_2 is negative. The arrows joining the second tasks show the way in which transfer effects would vary in a similar task placed between two others (S_1 and S_2 are stimuli and R_1 and R_2 are responses). (After Woodworth (R.S.) and Schlosberg (H.), *Experimental Psychology*, New York, Holt, 1954, p. 754.)

(β) Identical connections between stimuli and responses in both tasks. There are two possible cases here:

Reversal of connections when stimuli in the first task become responses in the second, and *vice versa*;
interchange of connections between stimuli and responses in the second task.

(B) THE ROLE OF SIMILARITY OF STIMULI AND
RESPONSES IN TRANSFER

(a) *The development of transfer theories based on this simi-*
larity. (α) Wylie (1919) made a distinction between the role of
stimuli and that of responses in transfer. He considered that
there was positive transfer when an old response (first task) was
associated with a new stimulus in the transfer test, but that
negative transfer must appear when an old stimulus (first task)
had to be associated with a new response. This theory arises from
the differing roles of stimulus and response.

(β) There has been an attempt to explain transfer effects by
similarity based on Pavlov's theory of the generalization process,
as systematized by Hull (1939–1943). This theory supposes that
any stimulus similar to a given stimulus tends to evoke the
response previously associated with this given stimulus. If R is
associated with S, and if S_a is similar to S, the presentation of S_a
will evoke R. This process of generalization can also apply to the
response. Learning an S–R connection means that, if R_a is
similar to R, R_a can also be given as the response. The more
similar R_a is to R, the more probable this response will be.
While generalization of stimulus is fairly obvious and easily
demonstrable, generalization of response has been studied less
often. It has been demonstrated by Underwood and Hughes
(1950) with pairs of adjectives and nonsense syllables as stimuli.
A classification of responses showed a generalization effect in
accordance with the three dimensions of similarity of the
adjectives used: synonyms, homonyms and antonyms. Goss
(1953), Duncan (1955) and Brown, Carke and Stein (1958) all
found a comparable effect in sensori-motor, co-ordination tests.

If the principle of generalization is held to be valid for both
stimulus and response, it should be possible to predict that
positive, transfer effects will appear in all situations in which
similar responses are produced by constant stimuli, and, *vice*
versa, in situations in which identical responses correspond to
similar stimuli, so at least the role of stimulus and response is the
same in the connection. However, as Wylie pointed out, this is
not so.

(γ) Osgood (1950), inspired by current experiments, established what he called 'a transfer and retroaction surface'. The

object was to describe learning situations in which similarity of both stimuli and response varied (Fig. 13.).

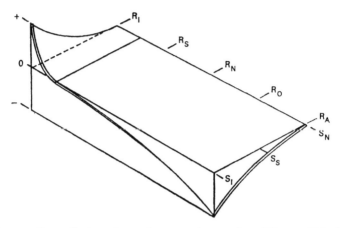

Fig. 13. Osgood's transfer and retroaction surface. The medial plane shows the zero effects; the axis of similarity of response is the length of the solid and the axis of similarity of stimuli is its breadth. The vertical axis indicates the rate and sign corresponding to the transfer effects. (After Osgood (C.E.), *Psychol. Rev.*, 1949, **56**, 140.)

This 'surface' is a three-dimensional figure. One of the axes represents the rate of transfer, another the variations in similarity between stimuli and a third variations in similarity between responses. Predictions become simple with this figure. All one has to do, for a given value of stimulus, is to cut the surface on a perpendicular plane to the axis of the stimulus corresponding to this value, and then find the variations in the transfer rate when the similarity of response varies.

Presumably, in the extreme positions, the transfer effect must be positive, for identical stimuli in both tasks, when responses are very similar, but must become negative when this similarity of response decreases.

How accurate are the predictions of this figure? It does not take into account either degree of familiarity, complexity of responses to be learnt or the standard of acquisition achieved in first learning the S–R connections, which affects their subsequent influence on the transfer test by varying the strength of the generalization. Nevertheless, it is a valuable attempt at systematization.

(*b*) *Two experiments of fundamental importance to an assessment of the role of similarity.* The first, Bruce's experiment (1933), served as a partial basis for Osgood's model, while the second was an experiment carried out by Bugelski and Cadwallader (1956) in order to verify the soundness of Osgood's model. Reference will be made to both experiments later in this section.

(α) Bruce's experiment (1933) was a classical transfer situation with two consecutive tasks consisting of learning paired associates, and he investigated the extent to which learning the first list affected learning the second. The two lists did bear a certain similarity to each other. The different aspects of this similarity are shown in the left-hand column of Table XI. Bruce used different combinations of variations of stimulus and response. For example, transfer condition 'identical S_1S_2– different R_1R_2' meant learning S_1R_1 pairs in the first instance, followed by S_1R_2. Similarly, 'different S_1R_1–identical R_1R_2' meant S_1R_1 pairs in the first instance, followed by S_2R_1 pairs.

Bruce selected four standards as criteria of acquisition in the first learning task. These corresponded to the number of trials. o shows the absence of any preliminary learning, since the subjects in the control group only learnt the second list. They were the reference group. Standards 2, 6 and 12 are the experimental groups who took 2, 6 and 12 trials in the first learning session.

Table XI overleaf provides a resume of data and shows the transfer results.

This table shows the percentage calculated, in each situation, by comparing the number of repetitions required to learn the second list of paired associates with the number required to learn the same list without any preliminary training. Values below 100 are the positive effects, while those above 100 are the negative effects.

(β) The experiment carried out by Bugelski and Cadwallader (1956) included 16 transfer situations. Table XII shows the different combinations of systematic variations in stimulus and response in the pairs of associated elements.

In this experiment, stimuli were figures whose degrees of

TABLE XI

Transfer conditions between the two tasks		1st task (examples)	2nd task (examples)	Transfer effects as a function of number of trials in 1st learning			
				0	2	6	12
S_1S_2 identical	R_1R_2 different	ceq kiv	ceq zam	100	117	116	109
S_1S_2 identical	S_1R_1 similar	bij bic	bij tab	—	101	90	90
S_1S_2 identical	S_2R_2 similar	mir ped	mir mig	—	127	123	102
S_1S_2 identical	R_1R_2 similar	tec zox	tec zop	—	102	101	80
S_1S_2 different	R_1R_2 identical	lan gip	fis gip	—	115	83	63
S_1R_1 similar	R_1R_2 identical	soj sog	nel sog	—	103	81	77
S_2R_2 similar	R_1R_2 identical	zaf qer	qec qer	—	66	56	40
S_1S_2 similar	R_1R_2 identical	bes gor	bef gor	—	84	64	44
S_2S_2 different	R_1R_2 different	xal pom	cam lup	—	100	108	84
S_1S_2 similar	R_1R_2 similar		Not investigated by Bruce				
S_1S_2 similar	R_1R_2 different						

(Taken from Bruce, *J. exp. Psychol.*, 1933, **16**, 347.)

similarity had been defined by Gibson (1941) as identical, similar, Osgood) of similar, neutral or opposite degrees of similarity.

TABLE XII

Transfer situations		Trials required to learn 1st list		Trials required to learn 2nd list	
		Average	σ	Average	σ
S identical	R identical				
	R similar	7·67	2·11	6·89	1·45
	R neutral	8·11	3·11	6·44	2·22
	R opposite	7·33	2·58	6·22	1·87
S similar	R identical	7·11	2·28	3·44	1·26
	R similar	6·11	2·02	6·44	2·11
	R neutral	6·44	1·50	5·67	1·70
	R opposite	8·44	3·13	6·44	2·17
S slightly similar	R identical	6·33	1·41	3·78	0·63
	R similar	6·67	2·40	4·89	0·99
	R neutral	6	1·76	4·67	1·94
	R opposite	5·77	1·31	6	1·82
S neutral	R identical	7·22	1·81	5	1·56
	R similar	8·44	2·45	4·67	0·94
	R neutral	8·33	3·56	5·89	2·47
	R opposite	7·33	2·71	5	1·36
Control group		7·67	2·83		

(Taken from Bugelski and Cadwallader, *J. exp. Psychol.*, 1956, **52**, 362.)

(*c*) *Analysis of results of experiments and conclusions on the part played by degrees of similarity.* (α) *Different or similar stimuli and identical responses in both tasks:* All the work on this question confirms Wylie's hypothesis and the model set up by Osgood. Transfer effects are positive when stimuli are different and responses identical in both tasks.

Yum (1931) verified this law by means of two different experiments. The task consisted of learning pairs of associated elements. In one experiment, the stimuli were nonsense syllables, while they were sketches in the other. In both experiments, the stimuli used in the second task bore a certain similarity to those used in the first task. Similarly, the responses were meaningful in both tasks.

TABLE XIII

2nd task	Percentage of recall after one trial
Experiment with words	*Experiment with sketches*
Identity	50·15	84·62
Similarity:		
1st degree	32·56	64·53
2nd degree	11·27	49·15
3rd degree		45·30
4th degree		36·32

(Taken from Yum, *J. exp. Psychol.*, 1931, **14**, 75, 78.)

This shows that the level of recall was higher, in the second task, the greater the degree of similarity. In fact, the transfer effect varied in proportion to the similarity. Gulliksen (1932) and Gibson (1941) obtained similar results with lists of pairs of words associated with drawings. Bruce's experiment also showed the same effect, which increased with learning the first list (Table XI).

Bugelski and Cadwallader (1956) obtained the same result (Fig. 14 illustrates the numerical results given in Table XII). The positive transfer effect decreased proportionately to the similarity of the stimuli, in accordance with Osgood's model.

Nobody seems to have carried out sensori-motor experiments of this type. However, in driving a motor car, for example, transfer effects are positive. In fact, stimuli are always different or more or less similar on the roads, while responses (manipulation of pedals and steering wheel) are identical. The positive transfer effects are obvious.

(β) *Identical stimuli and different responses in both tasks:* Wylie (1919) predicted that the transfer effect should be negative in this situation. Osgood's model qualified this assumption by showing that the effect is positive if responses are very similar, but becomes negative as dissimilarity increases (cf. Fig. 13.).

In fact, experimental results are even more complex, and depend on the nature of the tasks. Results from verbal tests will be considered first, followed by those produced by sensori-motor tests.

In a mnemonic verbal test, Morgan and Underwood (1950) demonstrated a zero transfer effect, which became positive as similarity between responses increased, in tasks of learning 12 pairs of adjectives. Underwood (1951) discovered that facilitation appeared in the second task, in spite of an increase in the number of intrusions (responses from the first task appearing in the second). These intrusions were more numerous, the greater the similarity, and they depended on the stage to which learning was pursued in the first task.

Contrary to what they expected, Porter and Duncan (1953) also found a positive effect in learning pairs of adjectives. They explained this, not by a process of generalization, but by the fact that the subjects had simply learnt the method. Mandler and Heinemann (1956) confirmed this.

Bruce's studies (1933) (Table XI) show a positive effect, while,

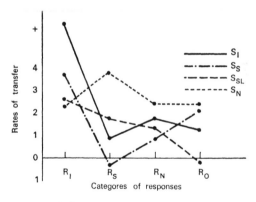

Fig. 14. Curves traced from results obtained by Bugelski (B.R.) and Cadwallader (T.C.), *J. exp. Psychol.*, 1956, **52**, 362.

The variation in the similarity of response in the second task is shown on the abscissae: R_1, response identical to that in the first task; R_S, similar response; R_N, neutral response; R_0, opposite response. Each curve corresponds to the variation in transfer effects for a given stimulus, in the second task, associated with one or other of the previously mentioned responses: S_1, simulus identical in the first task; S_S, similar stimulus; S_{SL}, slightly similar stimulus; S_N, neutral stimulus.

in the case of Bugelski and Cadwallader, the transfer effect was slight and relatively constant, no matter how high or low the degree of similarity. The effect would be greater if the response in the second task was neutral in relation to that in the first task.

The problem seems to remain: the results of experiments in the verbal field favour positive transfer when stimuli are identical and responses different. Clearly they do not confirm Osgood's model.

However, in the sensori-motor field, the work done by Van der Veldt (1928) confirmed the absence of interference in a transfer test in which the subject learnt to associate different motor responses (manipulation of keys) with word stimuli. When the first task had been thoroughly learnt, and when, at the start of the second task (in which responses were different), the level of alertness and attention was very high, there was no interference. The well-learnt task had become too specific. All the individual stimuli elements had been learnt sufficiently well, and the whole of the first task had become sufficiently integrated for there to be no intrusion by the first connections learnt into the performance of the second task.

Nevertheless, if there is any inhibition at the start of the second task, the first task is, as it were, broken up, and one of its elements, which also belongs to the second task, will evoke the motor response associated with it in the first place; although, as Van der Veldt (1928, p. 332) pointed out, the tendency to make movements consistent with the first task is rare. 'On the other hand, we have observed a very clear gradation in the frequency of the tendency to perform the movement learnt. When the movement required by the reaction in the new experiment is quite different from the movement learnt (for example, a verbal reaction instead of a manual one), there is practically never any tendency to move the arm. However, when the new experiment also involves a manual reaction, this tendency appears and is more pronounced, the closer the new movement is to the old one.'

This experiment by Van der Veldt seems very interesting, because it emphasizes the influence exerted by the degree of acquisition if connections between stimuli and responses as well as the importance of the attitude created by something specifically learnt. Due to this attitude, elements in the first task

196

(stimuli or responses) play a very special role, but they can also be used in a totally different way in another task. This involves a completely different attitude, so that the roles played by the same element do not interfere with each other. The attitude becomes more important than the similarity of the elements in the task.

(γ) *Simultaneous variations in stimuli and responses:* the transfer effects in these cases appear to be negative.

Bruce's results (Fig. 14.) show zero effects mainly when stimuli and responses are similar in both tasks.

(c) SIMILARITY WITH CHANGES IN CONNECTIONS
 BETWEEN STIMULI AND RESPONSES AND TRANSFER

In the following experiments, the stimuli and responses are always the same, but their connections are not. The similarity lies in this identity of stimuli and responses in the two successive tasks.

(*a*) *Interchange of stimulus–response connections.* Schematically, the experiments can be reduced to the following formula: let S_a, S_b, and S_c be stimuli in the first task associated with responses R_a, R_b and R_c respectively, with the connections becoming S_a–R_c, S_b–R_a and S_c–R_b in the second task, for example.

This problem often occurs in life today: for example, a classification is altered, and position-indicators are no longer linked in the same way to the elements classified. The same thing happens when the controls of an apparatus are interchanged.

If Thorndike's theory of identical elements is valid, this transfer situation should presumably produce positive effects of facilitation, since the elements in both tasks have a certain durability. The results in verbal tests are not the same as those in perceptual-motor tests.

(α) *Verbal tests:* Porter and Duncan found a negative, transfer effect when they compared successive learning tasks, involving series of paired adjectives, with interchanged connections. In order to show this effect, they compared learning the second list with learning a control list in which new responses were associated with the stimuli. Mandler and Heineman (1956), studying the same phenomenon, used association of numbers with groups of three consonants. They obtained the opposite result, i.e. positive transfer. The explanation would seem to lie in the actual nature of the material used. We obtained a positive effect when we repeated the experiment of Porter and Duncan with nonsense syllables.

This effect was weaker when all the subjects in both the experimental and the control group had preliminary training in the response elements. Thus, when elements to be learnt are not known to the subjects before the experiment, there is a positive transfer effect due to the fact that the control group, who serve as a reference, have to learn, not only the connections, but also the response elements in the second task. This additional difficulty in the control group's task prevents the appearance of any negative effect from interchange of connections when comparisons are made.

Besh and Reynolds (1958) also repeated the experiment of Porter and Duncan, but they controlled the warm-up effect. In this experiment, all three groups of subjects learnt the whole of list A–B (12 pairs of adjectives). Then each group learnt a list composed of three sorts of paired associates, some involving changes in connections (A–B_R), others new connections (A–C). The stimuli were the same in both cases. The third sort of paired associates consisted of entirely new stimuli (D–C). The experimental plan counterbalanced all secondary effects, since all the stimuli A in the original list were included in every possible connection.

Of the three groups of subjects, learning A–B_R produced the smallest number of correct responses in the 6 trials.

TABLE XIV

	Number of correct responses		
		Situations	
Groups	D–C	A–C	A–B_R
I	69·27	53·18	48·73
II	58	55·91	49·45
III	53·36	40·36	40·45
AVERAGE	60·21	49·82	46·21

(Taken from Besh (N.F.), Reynolds (W.F.), *J. exp. Psychol.*, 1958, **55**, 555.)

However, the subjects had prior knowledge of both stimuli and responses, which were taken from a list compiled by Melton and Saffier. The authors pointed out that their experiment placed learning elements A–B$_R$ and A–C in the same context, so to speak. In learning list A–B$_R$, there was double competition in the association of old responses with old stimuli (resulting from the first connections established) and in the fact that the old responses B$_R$ recalled one another, since they were all part of the same group in the first learning session. Consequently there was an effect of response generalization which did not exist in learning list A–C. This would explain the negative transfer.

The conclusion can be drawn that any change in connections between stimuli and responses brings a negative transfer effect in verbal learning tasks.

(β) *Interchange of connections between perceptual-motor tests:* The results are not as clear or as coherent in this field. Gagné, Baker and Forster (1950) found a negative transfer effect when they interchanged connections between two coloured stimuli (red and green) and two responses (consisting of pressing two buttons, one on the right and one on the left). If the resemblance between stimuli was increased, the negative effect became greater on account of the generalization effect.

Duncan (1953), in a more complex test, obtained a different result. Using the star-shaped discrimimeter shown in Fig. 1. (IV, p. 142), he obtained 720 variations by combining the stimuli with the different positions. He used 25 of these. Each subject learnt 6 connections in the first task. In the second task, 2, 4 or 6 connections were altered.

A comparison of the three groups' results in the second task with the results of a group that had only taken the first test showed clear positive transfer. This effect resulted from what the subjects had learnt of the method used. A comparison of the different results of these three groups showed that the positive effect was greater, the greater the alterations in the connections. These changes in connections brought considerable interference, which was greater, the shorter the first learning task.

Hauty (1953) obtained positive transfer with a device similar to that used by Gagné, Baker and Forster (1950): this effect was stronger when the spatial distribution of the response keys was the opposite to that of the stimuli (4 luminous stimuli were placed in the 4 corners of a square on a vertical panel, while 4 response keys were placed in the same positions on a horizontal panel). If the arrangement was orthogonal, the positive effect was less marked. Obviously similarity in the arrangement of stimuli and responses introduces an additional factor, independent of the nature of the connections established.

(*b*) *Forward and backward connections in transfer.* The actual direction of a connection must be considered. Thus, when a stimulus-response association S–R is learnt, a connection is established in the S→R direction. This is called a forward connection. However, it is possible for an individual to associate R with S on account of a previous connection in the opposite direction S←R, R being equally associative in reverse. Even if S always precedes R in the acquisition of the connection, S←R is still regarded as a backward connection between S and R. Consequently two versions of the connection co-exist when an S–R pair is learnt. Do they have the same effect in a transfer situation?

The first step is to find out whether the acquisition of a connection A→B, in which A is the stimulus and B the response, facilitates learning connection B→X, in which B becomes the associative stimulus. Harcum (1953) compared the number of trials required by each of four experimental groups and a control group to learn, as a second task, a new list of 8 pairs of nonsense syllables, arranged as shown in Table XV. The subjects learnt the list until they achieved two trials without mistakes.

Transfer was positive in all these situations, with the exception

TABLE XV

Groups	Transfer conditions		Changes
	1st learning	*2nd learning*	
C I	A→B	L→M	S and R different
C II	A→B	A→*m*	S identical R different
C III	A→B	*n*→B	S different R identical
E I	A→B	B→*x*	R stimulus R different
E II	A→B	G→A	S different R response

(Taken from Harcum (E.R.), *Amer. J. Psychol.*, 1953, **66**, 623–4.)

of C II in which it was zero. This exception conforms with the law (quoted earlier) relating to transfer between situations in which stimuli are identical and responses different. However, the B→*x* connection did not cause interference, but slight facilitation, since transfer was positive in this case. This was greater in E II in which the stimulus became the response, so element A had been partially learnt. It can be concluded from this that connections are established in both directions (A→B and B→A) in the first learning task. However, the positive transfer found in C I was much greater than that in any of the other situations. Presumably one of the elements in the first learning task played a different role in the second, and created a certain amount of interference. If this were not so, the results of the other groups would be at least equal to those of group C I.

Murdock (1958) confirmed these facts. Acquisition of backward connections does take place in the first learning task, and these connections interfere with any new connections acquired. This interference, which varies in the first 4 trials in learning the second list, appears to reach its peak in the second trial.

4 Other determinants of transfer

1 Influence exerted by the length of time between tasks

It has already been indicated that transfer effects evolve with the passage of time. Consequently the *time interval* between the first and second tasks is an important factor. The study of this factor is closely linked to the study of forgetting, since it is really a question of finding out to what extent a particular element acquired can be used subsequently. Various studies have shown that forgetting depends on the nature and number of tasks interpolated.

In order to study the effect of the time interval as such, it would be necessary to ensure that no other activity could interfere with the activity under observation, and also that the influence exerted by time really depended on the level of acquisition in the first task. It is easy to imagine how many experiments would be needed to reach any definite conclusions, particularly in view of the wide variety of possible transfer situations.

Nevertheless, there are studies which at least provide indications. Bunch and Rogers (1936) studied the influence of the time interval (0, 1, 7 and 14 days) on transfer in learning on T-shaped mazes by rats. Taking the *time* required to learn the second maze as their measure of efficiency, they found that transfer was zero when there was no interval between tasks. Transfer was positive after 1 and 7 days, but it became negative after 14 days. Taking the *number of trials* required as the criterion, the positive transfer effect of the first learning task was still considerable, but the rats performed the trials less quickly.

TABLE XVI

	% of transfer	
Interval between tasks	*Trials*	*Time*
0 day	+16	+ 6
1 day	+55·5	+31
7 days	+48	+30
14 days	+23	−42

(Taken from Bunch (M.E.), Rogers (M.), *J. comp. Psychol.*, 1936, **21**, 168.)

Bunch and MacCraven (1936) investigated the same problem in humans with mental mazes. In the first maze, the subjects learnt to associate the letters A to J with the numbers 1 to 10. In the second maze (the transfer test) they had to associate the letters K to T with the numbers 11 to 20. Naturally the order of the numbers was not the same as that of the letters. The second maze was learnt after intervals of different lengths for each group: 2, 14, 30 or 90 days. The results showed that there was positive transfer, no matter how long the interval (the differences do not signify variability of results). This transfer would be 28 per cent counting the number of trials, 42 per cent counting the length of time and 40 per cent counting errors. After the same intervals of time, there was a decrease in the efficiency of recall of the first task. This is an interesting result, since it emphasizes the fact that the essential factor in transfer is possession of the skill needed to learn a certain type of task. This skill is quite distinct from the acquisition of specific elements. Bunch and MacCraven (1938) confirmed these results in rote learning 10 pairs of nonsense syllables. They ascertained that the transfer effects were stable after 0, 2, 14 and 28 days.

Consequently the results are not the same for humans as they are for rats. Does time play the same role in humans and does the skill acquired by a rat disappear more quickly?

Gladis (1960) studied the role of time in a task that should have produced positive transfer in children of 8, 10 and 12 years. The subjects learnt 5 pairs of associated words, each of 4 letters. The second task contained the same response-words, but the stimuli were different. With the children aged 8 years, there was negative transfer which increased with the time interval (0, 2 or 14 days). In case of the children aged 10 and 12 years, transfer was positive and increased in accordance with their age. This study, which confirms all the work done by Bunch and his collaborators, seems to underline the importance of the integration of the skill acquired to the efficiency of transfer.

Osgood has pointed out the contradictions in the role of time intervals between these studies and those carried out by Ray (1945). Ray assumed that a negative transfer effect must reach a peak before decreasing, and he quoted the variation in discrimination with the lapse of time. There is clear differentiation between individual items after learning the first task. As time passes, the variation in the retention of these items will not be exactly the same as the variation in the skill to discriminate them. Proactive interference reaches its maximum point when discrimination between items is hazy, although memorization is still efficient. From this moment, however, the two phenomena weaken and the negative transfer effect diminishes, so that there is no longer any competition as far as the second task is concerned. Ray confirmed his hypothesis by means of lists of associated elements (identical stimuli and different responses), as shown in Fig. 15.

However, to obtain this result, Ray calculated the transfer effects on the first 5 trials only, and not on the whole learning session, as Bunch and MacCraven (1936, 1938) and Gladis (1960) did.

Hamilton (1950) continued the study of short intervals, from 8 seconds to 4 hours, in learning series of paired associates of nouns and adjectives. Under these conditions, he found that the rate of positive transfer between two successive learning tests decreased as the interval increased (Fig. 16). This decrease was greatest after an interval of 1 hour, and remained unchanged for

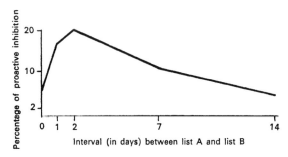

Fig. 15. Proactive inhibition (measured by the number of correct anticipations after one-fifth of learning) as a function of the interval of time between lists A and B. (After Ray (W.S.), *Amer. J. Psychol.*, 1945, **58**, 523.)

all longer intervals. However, as Hamilton noted, this effect must depend on the degree of acquisition in the first learning task and on the nature of this task. The author blamed this decrease on the warm-up effect.

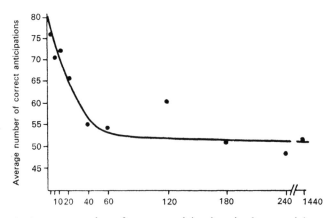

Fig. 16. Average number of correct anticipations in the ten trials on test-lists after rest periods of varying lengths following the warm-up lists. The dots represent the average for each experimental group under one of the rest conditions. The dot above 1,440 is taken from data given by Thune. (After Hamilton (C.E.), *J. exp. Psychol.*, 1950, **40**, 616.)

Duncan and Underwood (1953), in a perceptual-motor test, showed that transfer was stable after 24 hours, but very slight after 214 months; but relearning remained more rapid than initial learning. The authors regarded this as proof of the development of proactive inhibition.

From these studies, it can be provisionally concluded that the influence of time on transfer effects depends: (1) On the integration of the skill acquired, which itself depends on the subjects' development; (2) On the evolution of curves of forgetting, both of skill acquired and of specific elements; (3) On the similarity of the tasks; (4) On the moment when these effects are examined in a transfer task, since a time interval's effect reaches its peak at the beginning of the second task.

2 Degree of training before transfer

Research into the influence of the length of training in the first task has shown that the transfer effect tends to become positive, the longer this training lasts (corresponding to more complete mastery of the task). With little training in the first task, transfer is negative or zero. When training is increased, transfer becomes zero, and then positive. However, there is no linear or proportional relationship between variation in transfer and in training. But interference effects (shown by intrusions) vary as a function of training, and usually reach and drop away from a maximum point.

In the experiment with verbal learning of paired associates (shown in Table XI), Bruce (1933) demonstrated that transfer varied according to whether training consisted of 2, 6 or 12 trials in the first task. The effects tended to become positive in different transfer situations. For example, from an S_1–R_1 situation to an S_2–R_2 situation: (α) If S_1 and S_2 are similar and R_1 and R_2 identical, positive transfer increases; (β) If S_1 and S_2 are similar and R_1 and R_2 different, negative transfer decreases, and would presumably cancel itself out, if the preliminary training were continued; (γ) If S_1 and S_2 are different and R_1 and R_2 identical, transfer (negative after a short preliminary training of 2 trials) becomes positive with 6 trials, and is even stronger with 12 trials.

Atwater (1953) and Mandler and Heineman (1956) confirmed all these facts (cf. Fig. 17), with the exception of cases in which there is an alteration in connections between stimuli and responses which are identical in both tasks. Underwood (1951), in an experiment described earlier, showed that positive transfer increased with training and greater similarity between responses.

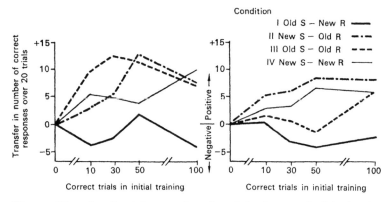

Fig. 17. Transfer of training as a function of the degree of original training expressed in the frequency of correct responses in 20 transfer trials. The figure on the left gives the results of a verbal learning test, and the figure on the right those of a motor test. The curves are comparable. (After Mandler (G.), Heinemann (S.H.), *J. exp. Psychol.*, 1956, **52**, 42.)

He also established that the effect of interference (shown by intrusions) was greater when the preliminary training was of average length. This leads to the hypothesis that the strength of the first training is such that it prevails, in the ensuing conflict between the two systems of responses, in spite of any inhibitory processes. This only happens when there is considerable similarity. When training is longer, there is greater differentiation of responses in the first task, and this weakens the effects of similarity. When similarity is slight, intrusions are almost non-existent, regardless of the degree of training.

Murdock (1958) insisted on the diminution in the generalization effect when initial training was more prolonged.

The same situations appear in perceptual-motor tests. Gagné and Forster (1949) used a task which consisted of associating four reaction keys with four light signals. There was no spatial connection between stimuli and responses. Training was with paper and pencil (8, 16, 24 and 48 trials). Positive transfer was maximum with training of 16 trials. It was noted, however, that a difference (as a function of the degree of training) only appeared from the tenth trial onwards in the second task, and not, as Atwater thought, from the beginning of the task. There were more intrusions for all the groups between the tenth and twentieth trials in the second task. Sears and Hovland (1941) pointed out that the two systems were of equal strength at that moment.

Duncan (1953), in the experiment described earlier (IV, p. 199), showed that positive transfer increased with training in the first task, and was stronger, the greater the similarity between tasks. There was no relationship between the amount of training and the similarity. Mandler (1954) obtained similar results from a task in which the subjects had to associate manipulation of keys, arranged in the shape of a hexagon, with letters of the alphabet. There were three versions of the situation in the second task: (1) New stimuli and old responses: transfer was positive and increased with training; (2) Old stimuli and new responses: transfer, zero with little training, became negative and then positive, as training increased; (3) Old stimuli and old responses, with different connections: there was no transfer.

The author himself agreed that these results confirmed the work done by Siipola and Israel (1933) on the transfer of code learning.

In conclusion, the effects noted, when the degree of training in the first task is varied, seem to lead to a better understanding of the complex mechanisms of transfer. They also emphasize the distinction between effects that result from interference and those that arise from proactive facilitation.

Bibliography

AMMONS, R. B., 'Acquisition of motor skill: I. Quantitative analysis and theoretical formulation', *Psychol. Rev.*, 1947, **53**, 263–81.

— 'Acquisition of motor skill: II. Rotary pursuit performance with continuous practice before and after a single rest', *J. exp. Psychol.*, 1947, **37**, 393–411.

ANDREAS, B. C., GREEN, R. F. and SPRAGG, S. D. S., 'Transfer effects between performance on a following tracing task (modified S.A.M. two hand coordination test) and a compensatory tracking task (modified S.A.M. two hand pursuit test', *J. Psychol.*, 1954, **37**, 173–85.

ARNOULT, M. D., 'Transfer of predifferentiation training in simple and multiple shape discrimination', *J. exp. Psychol.*, 1953, **45**, 401–9.

ATWATER, S. K., 'Proactive inhibition and associate facilitation as affected by degree of prior learning', *J. exp. Psychol.*, 1953, **46**, 400–5.

BABB, H., 'Proportional reinforcement of irrelevant stimuli and transfer', *J. comp. physiol. Psychol.*, 1956, **49**, 586–9.

BAKER, K. E. and WYLIE, R. C., 'Transfer of verbal training to a motor task', *J. exp. Psychol.*, 1950, **40**, 632–8.

BATTING, W. F., 'Transfer from verbal pretraining to motor performance as a function of motor task complexity', *J. exp. Psychol.*, 1956, **51**, 371–8.

BESH, N. F. and REYNOLDS, W. F., 'Associate interference in verbal paired-associate learning', *J. exp. Psychol.*, 1958, **55**, 554–8.

BITTERMAN, M. E., CALVIN, A. D. and ELAM, C. B., 'Perceptual differentiation in the course of non differential reinforcement', *J. comp. physiol. Psychol.*, 1953, **46**, 393–7.

— ELAM, C. B. and WORTZ, E. C., 'Perceptual differentiation as a function of non differential reward and punishment', *J. comp. physiol. Psychol.*, 1953, **46**, 475–8.

— FEDDERSEN, W. E. and TYLER, D. W., 'Secondary reinforcement and the discrimination hypothesis', *Amer. J. Psychol.*, 1953, **66**, 456–64.

— MCCONNELL, J. V., 'The role of set in successive discrimination', *Amer. J. Psychol.*, 1954, **67**, 129–32.

— ELAM, C. B., 'Discrimination following varying amounts of non differential reinforcement', *Amer. J. Psychol.*, 1954, **67**, 133–7.

BORING, E. G., 'The control of attitude in psychophysical experiments', *Psychol. Rev.*, 1920, **27**, 440–52.

BRAUN, H. W. and BENDIG, A. W., Supplementary report: 'Effect of addition of irrelevant verbal cues on perceptual motor learning', *J. exp. Psychol.*, 1958, **55**, 301–2.

BRAY, C. W., 'Transfer of learning', *J. exp. Psychol.*, 1928, **11**, 443–67.

BRUCE, R. W., 'Conditions of transfer of training', *J. exp. Psychol.*, 1933, **16**, 343–61.

BUGELSKI, B. R., 'An attempt to reconcile in learning and reproductive inhibition explanation of proactive inhibition', *J. exp. Psychol.*, 1948, **3**, 670–82.

— CADWALLADER, T. C., 'A reappraisal of the transfer and retroactive surface', *J. exp. Psychol.*, 1956, **52**, 360–6.

BUNCH, M. E. and ROGERS, M., 'The relationship between transfer and the length of the interval separating the mastery of two problems', *J. comp. Psychol.*, 1936, **21**, 37–52.

— MACCRAVEN, 'The temporal course of transfer in the learning of memory material', *J. comp. Psychol.*, 1938, **25**, 481–96.

— 'A comparison of retention and transfer of training from similar material after relatively long interval of time', *J. comp. Psychol.*, 1941, **32**, 217–31.

CANTOR, J. H., 'Amount of pretraining as a factor in stimulus pre-differentiation and performance set', *J. exp. Psychol.*, 1955, **50**, 180–4.

COOK, T. W., 'Studies in cross education. I. Mirror tracing the star-shaped maze', *J. exp. Psychol.*, 1933, **16**, 144–60.

— 'Studies in cross education: III. Kinaesthetic learning of an irregular pattern', *J. exp. Psychol.*, 1934, **17**, 749–62.

— 'Studies in cross education: IV. Permanence of transfer', *J. exp. Psychol.*, 1935, **18**, 255–66.

— 'Whole and four part learning thirty-two unit spider mazes', *J. exp. Psychol.*, 1938, **22**, 439–50.

COX, J. W., 'Some experiments on formal training in the acquisition of skill', *Brit. J. Psychol.*, 1933, **24**, 67–87.

DEESE, J., *The psychology of learning*, 2nd edn., New York, McGraw-Hill, 1958.

DI VESTA, F. J. and BLAKE, K., 'The effects of instructional "sets" on learning and transfer', *Amer. J. Psychol.*, 1959, **72**, 57–67.

DRESSLAR, F. B., 'Studies in the psychology of touch', *Amer. J. Psychol.*, 1894, **6**, 313–68.

DUNCAN, C. P., 'Transfer in motor learning as a function of degree of first-task learning and inter-task similarity', *J. exp. Psychol.*, 1953, **45**, 1–11.

— UNDERWOOD, B. J., 'Retention of transfer in motor learning after twenty-four hours and after fourteen months', *J. exp. Psychol.*, 1953, **46**, 445–52.

— 'Transfer after training with single versus multiple tasks', *J. exp. Psychol.*, 1958, **55**, 63–72.

ECKSTRAND, G. A. and WICKENS, D. D., 'Transfer of perceptual set', *J. exp. Psychol.*, 1954, **47**, 274–8.

Bibliography

EWERT, P. H., 'Bilateral transfer in mirror-drawing', *J. genet. Psychol.*, 1926, **33**, 235–49.

FECHNER, G. T., 'Beobachtungen Welchezu berveisen scheinen dass durch die Uebung der Glieder der einen Seite die der andein zugleich mit geübt werden', *Ber Sächs Ges Wiss Leipzig Math. Phys. Cl.*, 1858, **10**, 70–6.

FERGUSON, G. A., 'On learning and human ability', *Canad. J. Psychol.*, 1954, **8**, 95–112.

FLORÈS, C., 'Le rôle de la similitude des éléments dans l'apprentissage et le transfert', *Année psychol.*, 1957, **57**, 399–424.

FORGUS, R. H. and SCHWARTZ, R. J., 'Efficient retention and transfer as affected by learning method', *J. Psychol.*, 1957, **43**, 135–9.

FRANZ, S. I., 'Studies in cerebral function: VIII. Training in touch perception and cross-education', *Publ. Univ. Calif. Los Angeles, Educ. Phil., Psychol.*, 1933, **1**, 121–8.

GAGNÉ, R. M., FOSTER, H. and CROWLEY, M. E., 'The measurement of transfer of training', *Psychol. Bull.*, 1948, **45**, 97–130.

— 'Transfer to a motor skill from practice on a pictured representation', *J. exp. Psychol.*, 1949, **39**, 342–54.

— BAKER, K. E. and FOSTER, H., 'On the relation between similarity and transfer of training in the learning of discriminative motor tasks', *Psychol., Rev.*, 1950, **57**, 67–79.

GAYDOS, H. F., 'Intersensory transfer in the discrimination of form', *Amer. J. Psychol.*, 1956, **69**, 107–10.

GIBBS, C. B., 'Transfer of training and skill assumption in tracking tasks', *Quart. J. exp. Psychol.*, 1951, **3**, 99–111.

GIBSON, E. J., 'A systematic application of the concepts of generalization and differentiation to verbal learning', *Psychol. Rev.*, 1940, **47**, 196–229.

— 'Retroactive inhibition as a function of degree of generalization between tasks', *J. exp. Psychol.*, 1941, **28**, 93–115.

GIBSON, J. J., 'Adaptation, after-effect and contrast in the perception of curved lines', *J. exp. Psychol.*, 1933, **16**, 1–31.

GLADIS, M., 'Grade differences in transfer as a function of the time interval between learning tasks', *J. educ. Psychol.*, 1960, **51**, 191–4.

GOSS, A. E., 'Transfer as a function of type and amount of preliminary experience with task stimuli', *J. exp. Psychol.*, 1953, **46**, 419–28.

GRAHAM, F. K., 'Conditioned inhibition and conditioned excitation in transfer of discrimination', *J. exp. Psychol.*, 1943, **33**, 351–68.

GULLIKSEN, H., 'Transfer of response in human subjects', *J. exp. Psychol.*, 1932, **15**, 496–516.

HAMILTON, C. E., 'The relationship between length of interval separating two learning tasks and performance on the second task', *J. exp. Psychol.*, 1950, **40**, 613–21.

HARCUM, E. R., 'Verbal transfer of overlearned forward and backward associations', *Amer. J. Psychol.*, 1953, **66**, 622–5.

HARLOW, H. F., 'The formation of learning sets', *Psychol. Rev.*, 1949, **56**, 51–65.

— 'Analysis of discrimination learning by monkeys', *J. exp. Psychol.*, 1950, **40**, 26–39.

HAUTY, G. T., 'Response similarity-dissimilarity and differential motor transfer effect', *J. Psychol.*, 1953, **36**, 363–79.

HAYES, R. and THOMPSON, C., 'Discrimination learning set in chimpanzees', *J. comp. Physiol. Psychol.*, 1953, **46**, 99–104.

HENDRICKSON, G. and SCHROEDER, W. H., 'Transfer of training in learning to hit a submerged target', *J. educ. Psychol.*, 1941, **32**, 205–13.

HILGARD, E. R., IRVINE, R. P. and WHIPPLE, J. E., 'Rote memorization understanding and transfer: an extension of Katona's card-trick experiments', *J. exp. Psychol.*, 1953, **46**, 288–92.

HOVLAND, C. I., 'Human learning and retention', in Stevens, S. S., *Handbook of experimental Psychology*, New York, John Wiley and Sons, 1951, pp. 613–90.

HULIN, W. S. and KATZ, D., 'Transfer of training in reading Braille', *Amer. J. Psychol.*, 1934, **46**, 627–31.

HUSBAND, R. W., 'Comparative behavior on different types of mazes', *J. gen. Psychol.*, 1931, **5**, 234–44.

— 'Positive transfer as a factor in memory', *Proc. Iowa Acad. Sci.*, 1947, **54**, 235–8.

JAFFE, R., 'The influence of visual stimulation on kinesthetic figural after-effects', *Amer. J. Psychol.*, 1956, **69**, 70–5.

JUDD, C. H., 'The relation of special training to general intelligence', *Educ. Rev.*, **36**, 28–42.

KATONA, G., *Organizing and memorizing*, New York, Columbia Univ. Press, 1940.

KEMP, E. H., COPPEE, G. E. and ROBINSON, E. H., 'Electric responses of the brain stem to unilateral auditory stimulation', *Amer. J. Psychol.*, 1937, **120**, 304–15.

KIMBLE, G. A., 'Transfer of work inhibition in motor learning', *J. exp. Psychol.*, 1952, **43**, 391–2.

KITTELL, J. E., 'An experimental study of the effect of external direction during learning on transfer and retention of principles', *J. educ. Psychol.*, 1957, **48**, 391–405.

KURTZ, K. H., 'Discrimination of complex stimuli: the relationship of training and test stimuli in transfer discrimination', *J. exp. Psychol.*, 1955, **50**, 283–92.

KUENNE, M. R., 'Experimental investigation of the relation of language to transposition behavior in young children', *J. exp. Psychol.*, 1946, **36**, 471–90.

LASHLEY, K. S., 'Studies of cerebral function in learning: V. The retention of motor habits after destruction of the so-called motor areas in primates', *Arch. Neur. Psychiatr.*, 1924, **12**, 249–76.

— WADE, M., 'The Pavlovian theory of generalization', *Psychol. Rev.*, 1946, **53**, 72–87.

LAWRENCE, D. H., 'Acquired distinctiveness of cues: I. Transfer between discriminations on the basis of familiarity with the stimulus', *J. exp. Psychol.*, 1949, **39**, 770–84.

LE NY, J. F., 'Similitude conditionnelle et illusion auditive après une association sons-lettres', *Année psychol.*, 1959, **59**, 47–60.

LUCHINS, A. S., 'Mechanization in problem solving. The effect of einstellung', *Psychol. Monogr.*, 1942, **54**, no. 6, p. 95.

MACFANN, H. H., 'Effects of response alteration and different instructions on proactive and retroactive facilitation and interference', *J. exp. Psychol.*, 1953, **46**, 405–11.

MACGEOCH, J. A. and IRION, A. L., *The psychology of human learning* (rev. ed.), New York, Longmans Green and Co., 1953.

— OBERSCHELP, V. J., 'The influence of length of transfer upon rational learning and its retention', *J. exp. Psychol.*, 1930, **4**, 154–68.

MACEK, A., 'Transfer from verbal to motor responses of different degrees of concordance', *Proc. Iowa Acad. Sci.*, 1957, **64**, 527–35.

MANDLER, G. and HEINEMANN, S. H., 'Effect of overlearning of a verbal response on transfer of training', *J. exp. Psychol.*, 1956, **52**, 39–46.

— 'Transfer of training as a function of degree of response overlearning', *J. exp. Psychol.*, 1954, **47**, 411–17.

MARTIN, M. A., 'The transfer effects of practice in cancellation tests', *Arch. of Psychol.*, 1915, **32**, 1–68.

MARX, M. H., 'The effects of cumulative training upon retroactive inhibition and transfer', *Comp. psychol. Monogr.*, 1944, **18**, no. 2, p. 62.

MELTON, A. W. and IRWIN, J. M., 'The influence of degree of interpolated learning on retroactive inhibition and the overt transfer of specific responses', *Amer. J. Psychol.*, 1940, **53**, 173–203.

MEYER, D. R., 'On the interaction of simultaneous responses', *Psychol. Bull.*, 1953, **50**, 204–20.

MILLER, G. A., 'Free recall of redundant strings of letters', *J. exp. Psychol.*, 1958, **56**, 485–91.

MILLER, N. E. and DOLLARD, J., *Social learning and imitation*, New Haven, Yale Univ. Press, 1941.

MILLER, R. B. and SLEBODNICK, E. B., 'Research for experimental investigations of transferable skills in electronic maintenance', *U.S.A.F., Personnel Train. Res. Cent. Tech. Rep.*, 1958, no. 58–2, p. 21

MONTPELLIER, G. de, 'L'inhibition rétroactive et la courbe de Skaggs-Robinson', *J. Psychol. norm. path.*, 1936, **33**, 133–47.

MORGAN, R. L. and UNDERWOOD, B. J., 'Proactive inhibition as a function of response similarity', *J. exp. Psychol.*, 1950, **40**, 592–603.

MUKHERJEE, K. C., 'The duration of cutaneous sensation (I) and the improvement of its sensible discrimination by practice', *J. exp. Psychol.*, 1933, **16**, 339–42.

MÜLLER, G. E. and SCHUMANN, F., 'Experimentelle Beitrage zur Untersuchung des Gedächtnisses', *Z. Psychol.*, 1894, **6**, 81–190.

MUNN, N. L., 'Bilateral transfer of learning', *J. exp. Psychol.*, 1932, **15**, 343–53.

MURDOCK, B. B. Jr., ' "Backward" associations in transfer and learning', *J. exp. Psychol.*, 1958, **55**, 111–14.

— 'Transfer designs and formulas', *Psychol. Bull.*, 1957, **54**, 313–26.

— 'Intralist generalization in paired-associate learning', *Psychol. Rev.*, 1958, **65**, 306–14.

— 'Response-factors in learning and transfer', *Amer. J. Psychol.*, 1960, **73**, 355–69.

NOBLE, C. E., 'Psychology and the logic of similarity', *J. gen. Psychol.*, 1957, **57**, 23–43.

OLÉRON, G., 'Récents travaux sur le transfert', *Année psychol.*, 1955, **55**, 361–79.

OLÉRON, P., *Recherche sur le développement mental des sourds-muets: contribution à l'étude du problème 'langage et pensée'*, C.N.R.S., Paris, 1957.

ORATA, P. T., 'Recent research studies on transfer of training with implications for the curriculum, guidance and personnel work', *J. educ. Res.*, 1941, **35**, 81–101.

OSGOOD, C. E., *Method and theory in experimental psychology*, N.Y., Oxford University Press, 1953, p. 800

— 'The similarity paradox in human learning: a resolution', *Psychol. Rev.*, 1949, **56**, 132–43.

PORTER, L. W. and DUNCAN, C. P., 'Negative transfer in verbal learning', *J. exp. Psychol.*, 1953, **46**, 61–4.

POSTMAN, L. and ROSENZWEIG, M. R., 'Practice and transfer in the visual and auditory recognition of verbal stimuli', *Amer. J. Psychol.*, 1956, **69**, 209–26.

RAY, W. S., 'Proactive inhibition: a function of time-interval', *Amer. J. Psychol.*, 1945, **58**, 519–29.

RESTLE, F., 'Additivity of cues and transfer in discrimination of constant clusters', *J. exp. Psychol.*, 1959, **57**, 9–14.

RIOPELLE, A. J., 'Transfer suppression and learning sets', *J. comp. physiol. Psychol.*, 1953, **46**, 108–14.

Bibliography

ROBINSON, J. S., 'The effect of learning verbal labels for stimuli on their later discrimination', *J. exp. Psychol.*, 1955, **49**, 112–14.

ROSENZWEIG, M. R. and SUTTON, D., 'Binaural interaction in lateral lemniscus of cat', *J. Neuro-physiol.*, 1958, **21**, 17–23.

SANDIFORD, P., *Educational Psychology*, New York, 1928.

SCRIPTURE, E. W., SMITH, T. L. and BROWN, E. M., 'On the education of muscular control and power', *Stud. Yale psychol. Lab.*, 1894, **2**, 114–19.

SEARS, R. R. and HOVLAND, C. I., 'Experiments on motor conflict: II. Determination of mode of resolution by comparative strengths of conflicting responses', *J. exp. Psychol.*, 1941, **28**, 280–6.

SINHA, A. K. P. and SINHA, S. N., 'Intersensory transfer in learning sequences', *J. exp. Psychol.*, 1960, **60**, 180–2.

SIIPOLA, E. M. and ISRAËL, H. E., 'Habit-interference as dependent upon stage of training', *Amer. J. Psychol.*, 1933, **45**, 205–27.

SMITH, D. E. P., 'Applicational transfer and inhibition', *J. educ. Psychol.*, 1954, **46**, 169–75.

STARCH, D., 'A demonstration of the trial and error method of learning', *Psychol. Bull.*, 1910, **7**, 20–3.

SWIFT, E. S., 'Studies in the psychology and physiology of learning', *Amer. J. Psychol.*, 1903, **14**, 201–51.

THORNDIKE, E. L. and WOODWORTH, R. S., 'The influence of improvement in one mental function upon the efficiency of other functions', *Psychol. Rev.*, 1901, **8**, 247–61, 384–95 and 553–64.

— *Educational psychology*, New York, Lemeke and Buechmer, VII, 1903, 177 p.

— *Educational Psychology*, vol. II: *The psychology of learning*, Teachers College, Columbia University, 1921, p. 452

THUNE, L. E., 'Warm-up effect as a function of level of practice in verbal learning', *J. exp. Psychol.*, 1951, **42**, 250–6.

— 'The effect of different types of preliminary activities on subsequent learning of paired-associate material', *J. exp. Psychol.*, 1950, **40**, 423–38.

UNDERWOOD, B. J., 'Retroactive and proactive inhibition after five and forty-eight hours', *J. exp. Psychol.*, 1948, **38**, 29–38.

— 'Associative transfer in verbal learning as a function of response similarity and degree of first list learning', *J. exp. Psychol.*, 1949, **39**, 24–34.

VOLKMANN, A. W., 'Über den Einfluss der Übung auf das Erkennen räumlicher Distanzen', *Ber Sächs Ges Wiss Leipzig Math. Phys.*, 1858, **10**, 38–69.

WARD, L. B., 'Reminiscence and rote learning', *Psychol. Monogr.*, 1937, **49**, no. 4.

WEBER, E. H., *De pulsu, resorptione, auditu et tactu*, Leip., Koehler, 1834; see also *Annotationes anatomicae et physiologicae*, 1851, vol. I, 1–175.

WOODWORTH, R. S. and SCHLOSBERG, H., *Experimental Psychology* (rev. edn.), New York, Holt, 1954.

WYLIE, H. H., 'An experimental study of transfer of training in motor learning', *Behav. Monogr.*, 1919, **3**, no. 16.

YOUNG, R. K. and UNDERWOOD, B. J., 'Transfer in verbal materials with dissimilar stimuli and response similarity varied', *J. exp. Psychol.*, 1954, **47**, 153–9.

YUM, K. S., 'An experimental test of the law of assimilation', *J. exp. Psychol.*, 1931, **14**, 68–82.

ZAIDI, S. M. H., 'Effect of frustration on transfer of training in an eye-hand coordination task', *Indian J. Psychol.*, 1956, **31**, 45–7.

Chapter 14

Memory

César Florès

Introduction

1 Definition

Memory, as it is studied in psychology, is not a mental faculty—power or function of the mind—that can be examined by introspection. The term memory embraces a collection of *activities*, including both bio-physiological and psychological processes, which can only happen *now* because certain things that occurred *earlier*, in the recent or remote past, have had a lasting effect on the organism.

Any act of memory consists of three phases: (*a*) *Acquisition*, when the individual memorizes certain responses evoked by the requirements of the situation. This phase is sometimes only a brief, perceptual act, but it can also involve fairly complex activity, in the case of successive repetitions, by which the task is gradually mastered; (*b*) *Retention*, extending over a short or long period of time during which the material that has been memorized is stored but latent; (*c*) *Reactivation and actualization* of responses acquired, giving rise to observable mnemonic behaviour.

The psychologist is usually directly concerned with the first and third phases only. The retention phase can only be inferred from observation of the mnemonic behaviour which proves that retention does, in fact, exist.

Generally speaking, mnemonic behaviour can be divided up into three categories. The first category concerns *recall* behaviour. This includes *reproduction* of responses acquired in an earlier situation (for example, recitation of a poem, a passage of prose, a theorem, a list of words or numbers, vocabulary in a foreign language, a drawing, or even a route leading to a particular goal), and *narration*, when an individual describes a situation or event that he has experienced, either as a participant or a spectator.

The second category is *recognition*, which means that an individual must identify a situation to which he has responded in the past; or, more often, it involves the perceptual-mnemonic identification of a previously memorized *object* which *reappears* in the subject's perceptual field.

The third category includes all *relearning*. The saving in the practice required for relearning proves the existence of a process of retention.

All the activities distinguishing recall, recognition, and relearning have one thing in common, i.e. the fact that they depend on mnemonic means for expression. Nevertheless, these activities appear in psychological situations that can be very dissimilar. The processes at work in each case and the variables that can affect the efficiency of these processes can vary from one situation to another. But, in addition to the interest of the problems they raise, these divergences form a very important source of information for the psychologist. Since recall, recognition, and relearning are all relatively distinct, they reveal specific aspects of the long-term effects of the different experiences.

2 The chapter's limits

An individual's mnemonic activity at any given moment is the result of many factors, principally conditions of learning and features of the task, the various occupations filling the time that elapses after the practice, the conditions of the actual situation in which the act of memory takes place, the nature of this act (behaviour in recall, recognition or relearning), habits acquired before learning which are likely to intervene both in acquisition and in mnemonic behaviour, and, of course, an individual's motivation, attitudes and interests. The role played by the latter can sometimes be decisive.

Of these factors, those relating to learning are of considerable importance to the problem under review: (1) Because memory is a deferred effect of learning and depends very closely on learning; (2) Because, from an explanatory point of view, memory has to be considered within the framework of theories that employ the same system of concepts to account for both phenomena of acquisition and mnemonic phenomena. Consequently, in every question studied in this chapter, an attempt will be made to establish how far and why the systematic variations, observed in learning under the restrictions of experimental control, have subsequent repercussions on the efficiency of memory.

This review will be limited to the problems posed by learning and memorizing verbal symbols (words, nonsense syllables) or numerical symbols and figures (geometrical figures). This is because most of the research has been in this field, so there are more data available and theoretical speculations are more systematic and more detailed. The review will only quote examples of research on animals or experiments in the sensori-motor field when these are necessary in order to prove or disprove a hypothesis.

1 Methodology

---

1 Methods for studying memory

Hermann Ebbinghaus (1850–1909) formulated the first experimental methods for the study of mnemonic processes. A student of philosophy, Ebbinghaus came across *Elemente der Psychophysik* by Gustav Fechner on a Paris bookstall. This book gave him the idea of studying higher, psychological processes, particularly memory, by quantitative methods, inspired by those that Fechner had invented for the study of sensations. In 1885, after several years of work, he published a basic study called *Über das Gedächtnis* in which he described the acquisition method (or method of successive reproductions) and the savings method, together with the principal results obtained by their application in the field of memory. Before he died, Ebbinghaus was to enrich psychological methodology still further by elaborating, in 1902, the anticipation or 'prompting' method.

These methods have become classical, and the various new

methods which have developed since all belong to the experimental tradition started by Ebbinghaus: for example, Bolton's method of reproduced elements (1892), the paired-associates method of Calkins (1894), the reconstruction method of Munsterberg and Bigham (1894), Woodword's method of equalizing learning (1914) and the recognition method used by Wolfe from 1886 onwards, but elaborated in its present form by Binet and Henri in 1894.

(A) THE ACQUISITION METHOD OF EBBINGHAUS

The object of this method is to enable a subject to gain complete mastery of the material that he has been asked to learn. The criterion of mastery was usually the first perfect recitation of the material or, more exacting, the first two, perfect recitations in succession. However, this method should probably be called the *method of successive reproductions*, in accordance with today's practice, since the material is presented several times in succession at a constant speed, with recitation of the elements retained interspersed between presentations.

Two figures for measuring speed of learning can be obtained by this method: the *number of trials* or the *time* needed for complete acquisition of the task. As a result, learning curves can be plotted, with trials on the abscissae and the number of elements reproduced correctly in each trial on the ordinates.

This method is adequate, in the field of memory, for the study of mnemonic behaviour, which is deferred for a long time, and so requires a high standard of learning. Nevertheless, two objections can be made: (1) As Gillette pointed out (1936), this method favours subjects who learn slowly, because they require a greater number of trials to reach the criterion than subjects who learn quickly, and they may overlearn certain elements in the material; (2) The collective application of this method to a group of subjects presents practical problems that it is sometimes difficult to solve.

(B) METHOD OF CONSTANT NUMBER OF PRESENTATIONS

This is actually a variation of the previous method. Instead of a criterion of mastery, a constant criterion of practice is adopted for all subjects. This criterion is a certain number of presentations, decided in advance by the experimenter. No reproduction of elements retained is necessary between presentations. Retention is tested by recall (oral or written reproduction of the elements learnt) or recognition, immediately after the last presentation or some time later. A subject's recall score is the number of elements he reproduces correctly, and his recognition score is the number of elements he identifies correctly. This method, which can easily be applied to large groups of subjects, is widely used. However, Gillette (1936) demonstrated that this method favours quick subjects, who retain more than slow subjects.

(C) WOODWORTH'S METHOD OF EQUALIZING LEARNING

This method reduces the disadvantages, pointed out by Gillette (1936), of the two previous methods. It consists of obtaining an equal number of correct reproductions from all the subjects during learning. Each presentation of the material is followed by the reproduction of the elements retained. But the experimenter withdraws an element from the material as soon as it has been correctly reproduced, so that the next presentation only includes material that has not yet been correctly reproduced. The experiment continues in this way until all the elements have been correctly reproduced once (although more exacting criteria may be adopted).

(D) THE ANTICIPATION METHOD OF EBBINGHAUS

The elements of the material, arranged $a \rightarrow b \rightarrow c \rightarrow d$, etc., are presented successively to the subject once or several times, after which he has to try and recite them *in the same order*. If he makes a mistake, the experimenter corrects him; and, if he falters, the experimenter 'prompts' him with the next element. This usually continues until the subject achieves his first perfect recitation of the whole series.

A different version of this method is more often used today: the various elements are presented under the control of a device, which ensures that presentation time remains constant for all the elements in the series, and that the amount of time between any two elements is always the same. For example, in the case of two consecutive elements *x* and *y*, the subject must give the response *y* to *x* before *y* appears.

Whatever version is used, four scores are obtained: (1) Total learning time; (2) Number of trials needed to reach criterion of mastery; (3) Number of responses correctly anticipated in each trial; (4) Number of mistakes in each trial.

This method, which offers a variety of possibilities, is very useful in the study of associative mechanisms of memory.

(E) THE PAIRED-ASSOCIATES METHOD OF CALKINS

In this method, elaborated by Calkins (1894), the elements of the material are arranged in pairs, as in a list of French-English vocabulary. In the memory test, the first element in each pair plays the part of *stimulus* and the second that of *response*. The learning instructions tell the subjects that they must remember the pairs, so that *they can respond with the second element when they are presented with the first*. All the pairs are presented once or several times before this memory test.

This method can be combined with the Ebbinghaus anticipation method. After one or several preliminary presentations of the pairs, the stimuli elements can be presented alone. The subject's task is to respond to each stimulus with the correct, associated element. If the subject does not respond or responds incorrectly, he is then presented, either visually or orally, with the right response. This method can be varied by always presenting the correct response (even if the subject has already given it), after the short period of time during which the stimulus is presented alone. This perception of the correct response confirms or *reinforces* the response that has just been given. This method produces the same scores as the anticipation method described in (D).

(F) THE RECOGNITION METHOD

In this memory test, the elements learnt are *rearranged in an order that the subject cannot foresee* among new elements belonging to the same family. For example, syllables will be combined with other syllables, adjectives with other adjectives, drawings with other drawings, etc. The subject then has the task of identifying the elements that he has already learnt.

In practice, the recognition test is usually organized in one of two ways; either a series of 10 stimuli, previously learnt, can be combined with 30 new stimuli to form a single list for presentation to the subject; or a *multiple-choice* technique can be employed, in which case the test is divided up into 10 distinct items consisting of *one* correct stimulus and three new stimuli, and the subject has to choose the stimulus that he thinks he learnt earlier.

The relative difficulty of a recognition test depends on two variables. When *the number of new stimuli* is increased or when *the degree of similarity* (or resemblance) between the stimuli learnt and the new stimuli becomes greater, it is more difficult to recognize the correct stimuli (Lehmann, 1888–89; Seward, 1928; Postman, 1950, 1951; Florès, 1958b; Ehrlich, Florès, Le Ny, 1960).

The experimenter must take into account the fact that the subject may choose the right stimulus *by chance* in a recognition test. Theoretically the probability that a correct choice results from luck is greater, the smaller the number of new stimuli. If 10 learnt stimuli are combined with 10 other stimuli, the subject who makes a random selection stands a two-to-one chance of being right. But he will only have a four-to-one chance when these 10 stimuli are combined with 30 new ones.

Similarly the probability of a correct choice resulting from luck is greater, the higher the number of incorrect identifications (i.e. new stimuli thought to belong to the material previously learnt). For example, two subjects A and B take a recognition test in which the 10 stimuli learnt are combined with 30 new stimuli. Subject A recognizes 3 stimuli correctly, and makes no mistakes. Subject B identifies 3 stimuli previously learnt, but he also 'recognizes' 5 new stimuli which were not included in the material learnt. It seems logical to award a higher score to subject A, who did not make any mistakes, for his 3 correct responses than to subject B, who was wrong 5 times.

Consequently the subjects' gross scores should be submitted to the following formula, proposed by Postman (1950), as a function of the two causes of error mentioned above:

$$R_c = B - \frac{M}{n-1}$$

in which B is the number of elements correctly identified, M is the number of incorrect elements chosen, n is the total number of selections and R_c is the amended, recognition score.

(G) THE RECONSTRUCTION METHOD OF MUNSTERBERG AND BIGHAM

The elements to be learnt are always arranged in the same order, and this order must be memorized. After the learning session, the subject is presented with the same elements in a different order, and his task is to put them back into their original order. The most relevant score seems to be a correlation coefficient of the correct order of the stimuli and the order given by the subject, thus making use of Spearman's 'rho' and Kendall's 'tau'.

(H) THE SAVINGS METHOD OF EBBINGHAUS

The object of this method is to study the development of memory in time and, in particular, of forgetting. It is also very important in research relating to phenomena of transfer and interference between tasks.

The psychometric measurement of a subject's memory varies considerably as a function of the methods of testing employed. For example, the recognition score is nearly always higher than the recall score, although, some time after learning, a subject may occasionally prove incapable of reproducing, or even identifying, a single stimulus that he has learnt. However, it would be wrong to assume that total forgetting has taken place unless the subject has taken a relearning test. If such a test reveals saving in practice this will result from the durability of a latent, mnemonic residue.

A relearning test must fulfil two conditions: (*a*) the method used in learning must be used again; (*b*) the subject must reach the same criterion of mastery as before.

The difference between the number of trials in learning and the number in relearning is the amount of *absolute savings in* practice. But this absolute saving has little meaning when it is compared with the savings scores of several subjects. If subject A finished learning in 20 trials and relearning in 15 trials, there is an absolute saving of 5 trials. If subject B accomplishes learning in 16 trials and relearning in 11, he will have the same absolute score of 5 trials. But a gain of 5 in 20 is not the same as a gain of 5 in 16, so the percentage of *relative savings* must be worked out. Various formulae have been proposed, but the best seems to be Hilgard's (1934), because all the scores can be calculated in percentages from 0 to 100. If E_a is the number of trials in learning, E_r the number of trials in relearning and J the number of correct trials meeting the experimenter's requirements for mastery (J equals 1 when this criterion is the first correct recitation of the material), the relative saving E_c will be:

$$E_c = \frac{100(E_a - J) - (E_r - J)}{(E_a - J)} = \frac{100(E_a - E_r)}{(E_a - J)}.$$

This formula rectifies the relative savings score by abstracting the correct trial (or trials) J, which is the criterion of mastery common to both learning and relearning. A subject whose memory is perfect will perform the first relearning trial correctly. However, it is obvious that his savings score will not be 100 per cent unless it is amended in accordance with Postman's formula.[1]

2 Determination of the degree of learning and amount of over-learning

The relative accuracy of the retention of any material or of the skill with which an acquired task will subsequently be performed depends largely on the amount of practice. When a subject's retention is examined, the degree of acquisition already attained by him must be measured by means of well-defined criteria.

Various indications of the level of learning have been used by researchers. For example, if, in the last learning trial, the subjects in the first group give a larger *number of correct responses* or make a smaller *number of mistakes* than the subjects in the second

---

[1] But the saving obtained in this way is *only* partially produced by memory. A second phenomenon, dissimilar to the phenomenon being measured, intervenes in relearning and tends to result in an unduly high savings score (Bunch, 1941). This is because certain effects are transferred from the original learning to relearning. The subject has 'learnt to learn' under specific, experimental conditions, and he has become familiar with the material and the method, all of which help to reduce the number of trials needed for re-acquisition. This transfer effect should be eliminated as far as possible from the assessment of genuine, mnemonic savings. Thus the number of trials E_a, needed in learning, should be replaced by the number of trials E'_a, required to learn new material, of an identical nature and standard, to the same criterion (see p. 318).

group, the first group is considered to have attained a higher degree of learning than the second. Levels of learning, defined in this way, vary as a direct function (in the case of correct responses) or as an inverse function (in the case of errors) of the amount of practice or number of repetitions.

Overlearning occurs when the number of repetitions or amount of learning are such that the task is prolonged beyond the point at which it is completely mastered. Luh (1922) suggested a way of measuring overlearning by comparing the number of additional repetitions with the precise number needed to master the task. If, for example, learning was achieved in 16 repetitions, but the task went on for a further 8 repetitions, there would be 50 per cent overlearning; if there were 12 additional repetitions, there would be 75 per cent overlearning, etc. Usually S, the amount of overlearning, is said to equal $100n/N$, when N is the number of repetitions needed to reach the criterion of mastery and n the number of additional repetitions.

Nevertheless, as Hilgard pointed out (1951), there is one serious drawback to this formula. If B achieves learning in 10 trials, while F takes 30 trials to do the same thing, 5 trials will have to be added to B's task and 15 to F's to obtain 50 per cent overlearning in both cases. However, F, slower than his companion, will already have 'overlearnt' some elements of the material in his first 30 trials, which will give him an advantage over B. Luh's formula would give him an even bigger advantage, since he would have three times as many supplementary trials in order to reach a comparable degree of overlearning.

Hilgard (1951) suggested a new way of assessing overlearning which would avoid this problem. He assumed that overlearning an element in the material is proportional to the number of times y has been reproduced during the task. Thus a subject X's overlearning score on the whole task would be:

$$S_x = 100\frac{T_r}{T_{r'}}$$

in which S_x is the overlearning score, T_r the total number of correct responses during the task and $T_{r'}$ the maximum number of times a correct response *could be* given in the task.

3 Categories of material

The material used by psychologists in research on mnemonic processes can be divided up into two main groups: verbal material and non-verbal material. There are two sub-categories within these groups, depending on the amount of meaning possessed by the elements in the material: meaningful material and so-called 'meaningless' material.[1] Here are the principal examples of each of these types of material.

Meaningful, verbal material: series of nouns, adjectives, verbs or names, prose passages, poems or stories;

'Meaningless' verbal material: series of three-consonant syllables (RTL, SBN, KCP), other syllables (RUV, KAF, TEG), meaningless two-syllable words (ESOJ, ARIL, UKEB). One special case in this category is the verbal material used by Miller and Selfridge (1950), which bears varying degrees of resemblance to real language (see p. 246);

Meaningful non-verbal material: traditional geometrical shapes (circles, squares, rectangles, etc.), drawings, paintings or photos of objects, people or scenes;

'Meaningless' non-verbal material: unorthodox geometrical shapes or ink-blots.

Series of words are widely used, not because they present more interesting psychological problems, but for methodological reasons. They are easily reproduced by subjects, and the experimenter can establish, beyond doubt, whether these reproductions are accurate or not. With drawings and geometrical shapes, it is often difficult to decide just how accurate a reproduction is and to make a distinction between mistakes caused by faulty memory and those caused by a lack of skill in drawing. Nevertheless, the recognition method provides an adequate test of retention of this sort of material, since it does not involve a subject's ability to draw.

[1] Later in this chapter, it becomes apparent that the categories 'meaningful–meaningless' and 'verbal–non-verbal' are largely arbitrary, since 'meaningless' material always has some meaning and 'non-verbal' material can usually be expressed verbally.

2 Influence of material

1 General effects connected with the arrangement of elements in a series

The organization of material into series of successive elements has two general effects: (*a*) The formation of 'remote' associations between non-adjacent elements, described as either forward or backward, depending on their direction; (*b*) Inhibitory effects which affect retention as a function of an element's position within a series.

(A) 'REMOTE' ASSOCIATIONS

When a subject has to learn a series of elements in a given order, associations are created between the consecutive elements, so that each element becomes the stimulus to the following one and the response to the preceding one (with the exception of the first and last elements in the series, which can only be either stimulus or response). However, this happens only when a high standard of learning is achieved. An examination of the order in which various elements are reproduced by subjects during acquisition will show that this does not correspond to the original order of the series. Some elements will be given too soon (for example, 8 before 5), while others will appear too late (for example, 3 after 7). The first type of mistake is called a *forward association*, while the second is a *backward association*.

In an attempt to explain this phenomenon, it has been suggested that the response to an element *x* in a series will be associated in learning with all the other responses (different elements) which precede or follow, closely or otherwise, element *x*. Figure 1 gives these hypothetical connections.

Fig. 1. Hypothetical schema of adjacent and 'remote' associations between elements in a series. (After McGeoch and Irion, *The Psychology of Human Learning*, New York, Longmans Green and Co., 1952, p. 91.)

Various methods have been used to study these 'remote' associations in learning and memory. Ebbinghaus used a method known as the 'derived-lists' method. He learnt a series of 16 nonsense syllables, arranged in a certain order which remained the same (1, 2, 3, 4, 5, 6, . . . 14, 15, 16). Twenty-four hours later, he relearnt the same syllables in a different order. He varied this order systematically from one experiment to the next. For example, he would place next to each other syllables that had been separated by one intermediate syllable in the original series (giving the following order: 1, 3, 5, 7, 9, 11, 13, 15, 2, 4, 6, 8, 10, 12, 14, 16) or by two intermediate syllables (1, 4, 7, 10, 13, 16, 2, 5, 8, 11, 14, 3, 6, 9, 12, 15) or even by three or seven syllables. In addition, he learnt another series, containing the same stimuli arranged at random, as a control list. The hypothesis of his study was that, if *first-degree* associations (which 'jump' one syllable) and *second-degree* associations (which 'jump' two syllables) and associations to the nth degree, are established in learning the first series, they will produce a greater saving than that resulting from series arranged at random.

The results obtained by Ebbinghaus (Table I) show that the percentages of savings in practice, resulting from learning derived lists, diminished as an inverse function of the number of intermediate syllables that were 'jumped' in the formation of the various lists. These percentages tended to decline progressively as the series became more random, with practically no savings for the totally random list.

Nevertheless, the derived-lists method provides only indirect data on the presence and role of 'remote' associations, and the decrease in savings percentages, as a function of the increase in distance between stimuli, can be interpreted in two ways which, although they are quite different, are not necessarily contradictory: remote associations are less efficient in relearning than near associations because (1) they are weaker, and (2) they are less numerous.

Other researchers followed Ebbinghaus and contributed to a better understanding of this question by means of the association method (Wohlgemuth, 1913):[1] after a series of stimuli has been

---

[1] Wohlgemuth (1913) introduced the association method into the study of this problem, but he was only concerned with *adjacent*, backward and forward associations.

learnt in a previously arranged order, each stimuli is taken at random from the list and presented to the subject, who is asked to respond quickly with the first response he thinks of. It is then possible to establish at what distance and in which direction the element (given as the response) is situated in relation to the stimulus presented.[1] The use of this method has revealed several interesting facts.

TABLE I

Time needed to learn the original series and the
derived series and the resultant savings

Number of intermediate syllables 'jumped' in forming the derived lists	*Learning the original series (time in seconds)*	*Learning the derived lists (time in seconds)*	*Savings percentages*
0	1,266	844	33·3
1	1,275	1,138	10·8
2	1,260	1,171	7·0
3	1,260	1,186	5·8
7	1,268	1,227	3·3
Series arranged at random	1,261	1,255	0·5

From the results obtained by Ebbinghaus (1885), in McGeoch and Irion, *The Psychology of Human Learning*, p. 93.)

(1) *Forward and backward associations, covering all the distances between the stimuli in the series learnt, can be efficiently obtained*: (McGeoch, 1936; Raskin and Cook, 1937; Hertzman and Neff, 1939; Wilson, 1943, 1949), Table II gives the actual numbers of such responses, obtained by Hertzman and Neff (1939) from four groups of subjects who had memorized the same series of 8 nonsense syllables by the anticipation method, to different levels of learning and overlearning. The 22 subjects in group I did not achieve one completely correct repetition. The 27 subjects in group II achieved two to three perfect repetitions, while

[1] This method eliminates from the second phase of the experiment the first stimulus in the original series (because it cannot suggest backward associations) as well as the last stimulus (because it cannot suggest forward associations), but the subject can still give these elements as responses to other stimuli.

Table II

Number of forward and backward associations as a function of the distances between stimuli and the degree of learning

Degrees of learning	Forward associations				Backward associations			
	Gr. I	Gr. II	Gr. III	Gr. IV	Gr. I	Gr. II	Gr. III	Gr. IV
	1	2–3	4–6	7–9	<1	2–3	4–6	7–9
Adjacent associations	80	134	250	206	74	66	116	102
1st-degree associations	70	84	85	68	51	73	72	65
2nd-degree associations	26	42	38	22	27	35	27	23
3rd-degree associations	26	22	25	23	15	25	30	20
4th-degree associations	21	21	16	8	26	19	16	9
5th-degree associations	9	20	10	16	10	16	15	10
6th-degree associations	4	9	3	3	10	15	17	26
TOTAL	236	332	427	346	213	249	293	255

(After Hertzman and Neff, *J. exp. Psychol.*, 1939, **25**, 393.)

the 32 subjects in group III achieved four to six repetitions, and the 26 subjects in group IV seven to nine repetitions. The association test consisted of a series of 24 stimuli, made up of the 8 original stimuli arranged in such a way that each stimuli appeared three times, although the same two stimuli were never repeated together.

When the numbers of backward associations in each group were compared with those of forward associations, the latter always predominated, regardless of the degree of learning (213 and 236 for group I, 249 and 332 for group II, etc.). Other authors (in particular, McGeoch, 1936; Ruskin and Cook, 1937) obtained the same result.

(2) *Adjacent associations were also found to be more numerous.* The percentages of these associations (calculated from the *total* number of forward *or* backward associations) increased with the degree of learning, resulting in a decrease in the percentage of remote associations (1st, 2nd, 3rd, 4th, . . . , 6th degree). Thus, with learning below the criterion of perfect mastery (group I), adjacent, forward associations only represented 33·9 per cent of all forward associations (i.e. 80/236), while this percentage rose to 59·2 (i.e. 206/346) when the task was continued until a high level of overlearning was attained (group IV). This phenomenon seemed to be more marked in the case of forward associations.

(3) Finally an examination of the numerical data contained in Table II suggests that, in general, *the number of remote associations diminished as an inverse function of their remoteness.* However, this must be qualified by the fact that sixth-degree, backward associations (*first* stimulus in a series given in response to the *last* stimulus) revealed a phenomenon previously discovered by Raskin and Cook (1937). The figures given in the last line of Table II show that, in fact, these associations were relatively more numerous than forward associations of the same degree. In addition, *they tended to increase with the degree of learning* (10, 15, 17, 26) until they were more numerous than the remote associations of a lower degree (see last column in Table II). Any explanation of this phenomenon must presume that, as a result of successive repetition, *the last stimulus in a series is associated forwards with the stimulus most closely following it, i.e. the first stimulus in the same series.* This being so, the circular effect will complicate considerably the problem of internal associations; for,

César Florès

even though it is particularly concerned with the two stimuli at either end of the series, it will certainly not be limited to these two.[1]

(B) INTERNAL INHIBITIONS

When the material for memorization is composed of elements in series, the elements at the beginning and end are learnt more quickly than those in the middle. The least favourable position for an element has proved to be slightly towards the end of the series in relation to the middle element.

Ebbinghaus (1885) observed this fact, which has been confirmed by many psychologists, including Robinson and Brown (1926), Foucault (1928), Lepley (1934), Ward (1937) and Hovland (1938a, 1938b). It can be demonstrated easily by a group of subjects who learn, by the anticipation method, a series of verbal stimuli. For each successive stage in learning, curves of percentages of correct anticipations of stimuli in positions 1 to *n* of the series can be plotted (Fig. 2).

Foucault (1928) explained this phenomenon as a result of two processes of inhibition, acting simultaneously during learning, and delaying it. The first, *progressive internal inhibition*, he regarded as effects of interference by responses to earlier stimuli on responses to subsequent stimuli, while the second, *regressive internal inhibition*, would be interference in responses to earlier stimuli by responses to subsequent stimuli. The conclusion to be drawn from this theory is that the action of progressive *or* regressive inhibition on the response to a particular stimuli will

---

[1] In an endeavour to simplify the whole problem, this analysis has been limited to the *actual* number of associations. In practice, the number of remote associations actually *reproduced* by the subjects should be compared with the total number of remote associations *possible*. These total numbers will vary with the degrees of distance between stimuli. For example, stimuli in places 1, 2, 3, 4, 5 and 6 can all provoke first-degree, forward associations ($1 \rightarrow 3$; $2 \rightarrow 4$; . . . $6 \rightarrow 8$). If each stimulus in the experiment is presented three times in the association test, the total number of first-degree associations possible is $6 \times 3 = 18$ for any one subject, and $18 \times N$ for N subjects. However sixth-degree, forward associations can only be produced by the first stimulus, and the total number possible is only $3 \times N$. Consequently *the decrease in the number of remote associations as distance increases must be partly due to the decrease in the number of associations possible.* From these possible totals, Hertzman and Neff calculated the percentage of remote associations for each degree of distance. Their calculations clearly confirmed the existence of a circular process of association.

be greater, the higher the number of stimuli preceding it (in the first case) or following it (in the second).

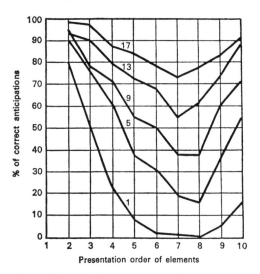

Fig. 2. The effect of the position of elements in the series on memorization of lists of 10 three-figure numbers. There were 8 lists and 11 subjects. The curves numbered 1, 5, 9, 13 and 17 correspond to trials 1, 5, 9, 13 and 17. Each of the points forming the curves are percentages of successes obtained in 8, 11 and 88 attempts to anticipate a number from the number preceding it. (After Robinson and Brown, *Amer. J. Psychol.*, 1926, **37**, 547.)

Foucault (1928) confirmed this hypothesis in research on series of 3, 4, 6 and 7 words that subjects (children from 10 to 14 years) had to reproduce immediately after reading the list through once. Table III shows the number of times the first stimulus (affected by regressive inhibition only) and the last stimulus (affected by progressive inhibition only) could not be recalled. The changes in these figures as a function of the number of stimuli in the series would seem to confirm the hypothesis.

Another hypothesis put forward by Foucault suggests that progressive inhibition, by weakening the responses that it affects, increases their susceptibility to the action of regressive inhibition. Thus this combination of the two inhibitory processes should show (in the case of all responses to stimuli preceded or followed by other stimuli) greater, overall inhibition than the sum of the two processes could be expected to produce. This hypothesis has been verified as follows: if the total effect of these two types of inhibition is merely their effects added together, forgetting the 4th element in a series of 7 words should equal the sum of forgetting the 1st and 4th elements in a series of 4 words; for, in both cases, progressive inhibition results from the presence of 3 words

TABLE III

Number of times that the first and last stimulus
in each series could not be reproduced as a function
of the length of the material to be retained

Stimulus not reproduced	Length of the series in number of words				
	3	4	5	6	7
First stimulus	2	12	26	37	47
Last stimulus	2	9	39	34	33

(After Foucault, *Année psychol.*, 1928, **29**, 100.)

prior to the word in question, and regressive inhibition from the presence of 3 words after it. In fact the 4th word in a series of 7 elements was forgotten by 81 subjects out of 100, while the first and last word in a series of 4 elements were only forgotten 21 times out of 100 (12 subjects forgot the first word and 9 subjects the last). Clearly the combined action of the two processes is more efficient than could be supposed from the sum of their separate actions. This could account for the maximum amount of interference affecting responses to stimuli situated in the middle of a series, which is where its effect should be most marked. However, Foucault's hypothesis really only skirts the truth, since the element most likely to be affected by internal inhibition occurs slightly after the middle of a series.[1]

[1] Hull (1935) developed a hypothesis (first formulated by Lepley in 1934) which tries to explain the effect of position in terms of conditioning. This hypothesis assumes that each stimulus in a series is associated forwards, during learning, with each of the following stimuli by means of a process similar to that of trace conditioning. Each association has an *excitation potential* for evoking the response and an *inhibition potential*, similar to Pavlov's delayed inhibition; so, in a series of stimuli, A, B, C, D, E, . . . N, the direct associations between A and B, B and C, C and D, etc. should favour the reproduction of

The first and last elements in a series also have a favourable position from the point of view of *deferred memory*. The curve in Fig. 3 shows the correct reproductions of nonsense syllables, as a function of their position in the series, 24 hours after learning to a criterion of one perfect recitation (Underwood and Richardson,

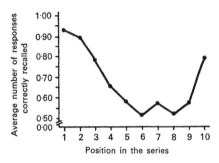

Fig. 3. Average number of elements recalled as a function of their position in the series. (From Underwood and Richardson, *J. exp. Psychol.*, 1956, **52**, 122.)

1956). Postman and Rauh (1957) obtained similar results 24 and 48 hours after learning series of English words. There are probably several reasons for this long-term effect. Responses to the first and last stimuli are retained better because, being memorized first, the subject reproduces them more often during learning. Responses to stimuli, lying in the middle of a series, may be more susceptible to proactive and retroactive interference (see pp. 319 *et seq.*) than the other responses, because they are not so well established and they are affected to a greater extent by internal inhibition.

---

these stimuli. On the other hand, the remote associations between A and C, A and D, A and E, A and N, B and D, etc. should tend to inhibit the reproduction of the stimuli occurring in between. Therefore the more remote associations there are 'over' a stimulus, the less likely it is to be reproduced. But this hypothesis, only briefly outlined here, is no more satisfactory than Foucault's, since it assumes that the stimulus most susceptible to inhibition lies in the middle of a series. Hull and his collaborators (1940) revised their explanation in an attempt to overcome this problem. Their revised formula does offer a more adequate explanation of the internal effects; but, in addition to the fact that it is purely hypothetical, it makes hypotheses that are not in accord with the development of other, related phenomena, such as the effects of distribution of practice on learning efficiency. In this connection, see Osgood (1953).

2 Length of material, learning time and memory

When the number of elements in the material extends beyond the apprehension span,[1] a greater number of trials are required for learning, and the overall practice time is longer. This applies to all types of material and methods of learning. Studies on series of syllables (Ebbinghaus, 1885; Neumann, 1913; Lyon, 1914; Henmon, 1917; Hovland, 1940), words (Foucault, 1913) and numbers (Lyon, 1913), and on prose passages (Lyon, 1914), all of which were gradually increased in length, showed that the time needed to learn material increased more rapidly than its length, with the result that the time per element increased. The numerical data in Table IV comes from research carried out by

TABLE IV

Time taken to learn material of varying lengths

Syllables		Prose	
Number of syllables	*Time in minutes*	*Number of words*	*Time in minutes*
8	0·13	50	2·25
12	1·50	100	9·00
16	3·67	200	24·00
24	5·00	600	84·00
32	6·00	1,000	165·00
48	14·00	3,000	780·00
72	25·00	5,000	1,625·00
104	37·00	7,000	2,065·00
200	93·00	10,000	4,200·00
300	195·00	15,000	5,475·00

(After results obtained by Lyon, *J. educ. Psychol.*, 1914, **5**, 85–91, and McGeoch and Irion, *The Psychology of Human Learning*, 1952, p. 489.)

Lyon (1914) on the memorization of series of syllables and prose passages. The increase in the time taken did not correspond to the rise in the number of elements to be memorized in either case.

[1] The apprehension span is the number of stimuli that can be correctly reproduced when they have been perceived once only. Stimuli reproduced in this way are not necessarily memorized. In this connection, see the research done by Fraisse and Florès (1956).

For example, the time taken to learn a passage of 200 words was about 10 times longer than the time needed for a passage of 50 words. In other words, the difficulty of a task is not directly proportional to its length.[1] Learning a series of 48 syllables is not the same as memorizing two series of 24 syllables. Foucault's hypotheses (1928) on progressive and regressive inhibition (see p. 233) provide an adequate explanation of this phenomenon.

As far as length of material and deferred retention are concerned, the various studies made of this subject (in particular, by Robinson and Héron, 1922, and Robinson and Darrow, 1924) all proved that, with identical learning criteria, longer material was retained better than shorter. The data in Table V were obtained 20 minutes after 10 subjects had learnt syllables until they achieved one perfect recitation by the anticipation method.

TABLE V

Deferred retention as a function of the length of material

Length of the series (Number of syllables)	Average percentage of elements recalled	Average percentage of savings
6	71·3	68·7
9	78·3	78·8
12	78·7	78·1
15	77·0	80·7
18	81·7	86·3

(After Robinson and Heron, *J. exp. Psychol.*, 1922, **5**, 443.)

Longer series are probably retained better, because they require a longer learning session to reach the same criterion of mastery than shorter series.[2] Using Woodworth's method of equalizing learning (see p. 220), Sand (1939) verified this hypothesis by showing that, when, during a task, a subject made the same number of correct anticipations for each stimulus, no matter

[1] Foucault (1913) estimated that the total time for learning a series was proportional to the square of its length. But, as Piéron (1934) pointed out, this can only be an approximate estimate, since there are considerable variations between different types of materials.

[2] This conforms with another hypothesis, i.e. the longer the series, the more likely the subject is to encounter elements with which he is familiar and which, consequently, he can memorize more easily.

how long a series was, retention of the longer series was not favoured in comparison with the shorter one (deferred memory of 10 minutes).

3 Degree of homogeneity between elements in material

The degree of resemblance or difference between elements in material plays an important role in many psychological processes, particularly in perceptual learning, conditioning, learning by repetition and memory. This problem has been the subject of many works by psychologists who have treated it either in a neo-associationist perspective (Gibson, Underwood) or within the framework of the theory of form (von Restorff).

(A) THE ROLE OF SIMILARITY IN MEMORIZATION[1]

On the subject of memorizing tasks, the work done by Gibson (1942), with meaningless shapes associated with syllables, and by

---

[1] When two or several stimuli possess common features, they are said to be similar. Deciding in what respect and to what extent different stimuli are similar is a delicate question, and all the answers proposed so far have been of a highly empirical nature. The following criteria, used by psychologists in their search for a solution, are worth mentioning:

(a) Any two stimuli of the *same nature* are generally more similar than two stimuli of a different nature. For example, two words are more similar than a word and a colour. Stimuli that can be grouped together in one homogeneous, physical continuum represent a special category from the point of view of measurement, since their degree of similarity will be higher, the closer (physically) they are together. For example, a sound of 1,000 Hz is more similar to one of 2,000 Hz than to one of 5,000 Hz, when they are all of equal intensity.

(b) Two stimuli are more similar, the greater *the number of identical elements* they have in common. For example, the syllables FED and NED have a greater degree of similarity than the syllables FED and REJ, which are, in turn, more similar than FED and XON.

(c) Two stimuli are similar when their respective *structures* bear a strong resemblance to one another; for example, two squares of different sizes or one tune transposed into two different keys.

(d) Two stimuli are similar when they belong to *the same semantic family*. For example, table, chair, cupboard and sideboard resemble each other more than table, apricot, horse and sun. The greatest similarity in this category lies between synonymous words (ship, vessel) associated with the same object.

(e) Finally two stimuli are similar when they produce responses which are *identical* or *close together*; for example, two words which are different, but which both sound disagreeable, produce psycho-galvanic reactions.

The categories included in this list, which is not exhaustive, are all different in nature and in the psychological processes they provoke in subjects: semantic

Underwood, with series of adjectives (1951),[1] paired adjectives (1951), series of nonsense syllables (1952) and series of triads of consonants (1955) showed that *the number of trials required to reach the same criterion of learning grows with the increase in similarity between elements in the material.*

Table VI illustrates this point by giving the average number of trials required to reach the criterion of mastery in learning various types of material. Two degrees of similarity were used for each type of material. In all these experiments, set up by Underwood, the anticipation method was used with 30-second intervals between successive trials.[2]

TABLE VI

Average number of trials needed to reach the criterion of mastery
as a function of the degree of similarity between elements in the material
(Underwood's experiments)

Type of material	Criterion of similarity	Degree of similarity Low	High
Series of:			
14 adjectives (1951)	Semantic	13·21	17·00
14 syllables (1952) (2)	Number of common letters	24·00	32·00
10 pairs of adjectives (1951)	Semantic	9·30	15·44
10 pairs of syllables (1953)	Number of common letters	22·42	32·89

There is still very little information available on deferred retention of material as a function of degrees of similarity. In accordance with Gibson's theory of generalization and differentiation (1940), the most probable hypothesis seems to be that

[1] In collaboration with Goad.

[2] In the case of the 14-syllable series, the averages are approximate estimations taken from a graph included by the author in his publication on his research.

similarity is the result of verbal learning, while similarity between two sounds involves sensory discrimination. In addition, they can be combined: two words can be similar from the point of view of meaning, phonetic composition and the reactions they produce.

retention will be lower, the more similar the elements learnt (see p. 336). Underwood and Richardson (1956) verified this hypothesis with syllables of a low association value. One hundred subjects, who had learnt a series of 10 very similar syllables to a criterion of one perfect recitation, were able to recall an average of 6·33 syllables 24 hours later. The same number of subjects, who had learnt a series of 10 syllables that were only slightly similar, were able to recall an average of 7·10 syllables. The authors found that this difference was significant.

(B) HETEROGENEITY OF MATERIAL AND VON RESTORFF'S EFFECT

What happens when the elements making up a piece of material are not all of the same type, for instance, when numbers are combined with syllables or colours in varying proportions? A pupil of W. Köhler, H. von Restorff, discovered the answer in some research he did in 1933. Initially he used five categories of material: syllables, geometrical figures, numbers, letters and colours. These were arranged into series, each including 4 similar and 4 dissimilar elements: for example, 4 pairs of syllables, 1 pair of letters, 1 pair of colours, 1 pair of numbers, or 4 pairs of letters and 1 pair of each of the other categories, etc. He made use of every possible combination.

These series were presented two or three times to the subject, followed by an interval of a few minutes, during which he carried on some neutral occupation, before he was given a retention test using the paired-associates method. Table VII shows the absolute and relative numbers of correct responses given by 22 subjects for the different types of pairs and for the whole experiment.

For example, when the 4 homogeneous pairs in the series were geometrical figures, only 33 per cent of the responses relating to them were correct; but this percentage was 74 when there was only 1 pair of geometrical figures in the series (8 pairs in all). The general rule which emerged from these experiments was that *when heterogeneous elements are combined with a greater number of homogeneous elements the former are remembered better that the latter, regardless of the type of material used.*

However, if all the elements in a series are equally dissimilar, this constant difference between elements endows the whole series with a certain homogeneity. Remembering an element in a series like this is much the same as remembering an element

TABLE VII

Reproduction of pairs of stimuli in von Restorff's experiment

Types of pairs	Syllables		Figures		Numbers		Letters		Colours		Total	
	H	*I*	*H*	*I*	*H*	*I*	*H*	*I*	*H*	*I*	*H*	*I*
Absolute numbers	36	61	29	65	23	55	52	65	49	82	189	328
Percentages	41	69	33	74	26	63	59	74	56	93	43	75

H: homogeneous pairs in series; I: heterogeneous pairs (isolated) in series.
(After H. von Restorff, *Psychol. Forsch*, 1933, **18**, 302.)

placed among other, similar elements. Von Restorff (1933) demonstrated this in an experiment with three types of series, presented at daily intervals:
Series   I: 1 number followed by 9 syllables;
Series II: 1 syllable followed by 9 numbers;
Series III: 1 number, 1 syllable, 1 colour, 1 letter, 1 word, 1 photograph, 1 punctuation mark, 1 chemical formula, 1 button and 1 graphic symbol.

The subjects had to reproduce as many elements as they could remember 10 minutes after the presentation of each series. Their results showed:
(1) That the highest percentage of correct reproductions was of elements isolated in their series (the number in series I, the syllable in series II). This was 70 per cent;
(2) That correct reproductions of the same elements in series III came next (40 per cent);
(3) That correct reproductions of homogeneous elements in series I (syllables) and series II (numbers) only represented 22 per cent.

Other researchers, i.e. Pillsbury and Raush (1943) and Siegal (1943), have verified von Restorff's findings by more complicated techniques.

Von Restorff's effect is an extreme example of the more general problem posed by relations of similarity between stimuli. This problem occurs when the degree of similarity between certain stimuli combined with other stimuli, which are more numerous and more similar, becomes *minimal*.

This effect can be explained by hypotheses common to it and to the other phenomena described here. In a neo-associationist context, it can be predicted from the principles of generalization and differentiation that learning will be slower and retention less, the higher the degree of similarity (see p. 336). A heterogeneous stimulus, isolated in a group of homogeneous stimuli, is quickly differentiated, and so retained better than the stimuli around it. The explanation offered by theoreticians of the *Gestalt* school arrives at the same conclusion. Generally speaking, the difficulty of learning and remembering a task depends on the properties of its global structure. The organization of a task composed of closely connected stimuli (such as syllables) will not have many prominent features, and its corresponding field of mnemonic traces will be of an unstable equilibrium, dominated by slight, internal tensions. The individual traces[1] of the stimuli will tend to *agglutinate* in a confused manner before finally disintegrating, thus rendering all memory impossible. The greater retention of 'isolated' stimuli is an argument in favour of this thesis, since these stimuli, by their very isolation, have properties similar to those of a figure standing out from its background. Traces of such stimuli are less likely to be confused with other traces, so they will be more stable and last longer.[2]

4 The role of familiar stimuli

An individual's behaviour is governed, to a great extent, by habits acquired in past experience. These habits are responses or schemes of responses, available to the individual, with which he reacts in concrete situations. Verbal responses represent a special and very important example of these habits. As a stimulus, the word *chair*

[1] The Gestalt psychologist Katona (1940) made a distinction between *individual traces*, corresponding to specific stimuli, and *structural traces*, relating to the task as an integrated whole. Structural traces should be more stable and less rigid than individual traces, but this is pure speculation.

[2] Consult Guillaume (1937) for a more complete account of the theory of form. Also see p. 312 of this chapter.

can produce perceptual, auditory or visual responses: while, as a response, it can be used as a means of spoken or written communication with other individuals. A subject does not *use* or *encounter* all the words in his vocabulary the same number of times, i.e. with the same or similar frequency. Generally speaking, a word is a *familiar stimulus* when it is encountered frequently, and a *familiar response* when it is used frequently.

(A) RELATIONS BETWEEN FREQUENCY, LEARNING AND MEMORY

Experimental studies of relations between frequency of words and learning have shown that, when the number of trials is constant, the number of verbal stimuli learnt varies according to the frequency with which these stimuli appear in written language.

Hall (1954) verified this relationship, using material composed of 4 series, each series consisting of 20 words of the same length (7 letters). Each series was entirely composed of words of a particular frequency (following the Thorndike–Lorge tables, 1944). The frequencies were 1/1,000,000 for the words in the first list, 10/1,000,000 for the second list, 30/1,000,000 for the third list and from 50 to 100/1,000,000 for the fourth list. The series were presented to the subjects 5 times, 5 seconds per stimulus. Immediately after learning each list, the subjects were told to write down as many words as they could remember (time allowed: 5 minutes). Table VIII gives their results.

TABLE VIII

Relation between learning words and their frequency

Frequency of words	Number of subjects	Average written recall
1/1,000,000	76	12·04
10/1,000,000	52	13·31
30/1,000,000	44	15·02
50 to 100/1,000,000	55	15·04

(After Hall, *Amer. J. Psychol.*, 1954, **67**, 140.)

Underwood and Schulz (1960, experiment 8) gathered together all the similar data by using series of 13 three-letter syllables belonging to English words of which they knew the approximate frequency of appearance in written language. The graph in Fig. 4 shows how the efficiency of learning evolved as a function of the frequency of the stimuli used in the series.

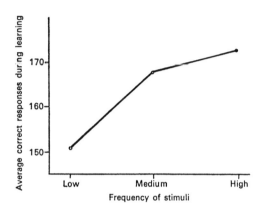

Fig. 4. How learning efficiency (measured by the average number of correct responses in an exercise of 20 trials) evolved as a function of the frequency of the stimuli (three-letter syllables). Each dot represents a series of 13 stimuli. (After Underwood and Schulz, *Meaningfulness and Verbal Learning*, Lippincott Co., p. 159.)

However, considerable variations in frequency were necessary to produce even a relatively small improvement in learning speed. Thus, in order to obtain a 24·7 per cent increase in recall, the frequency of the words had to be multiplied 30 times (Hall's experiment). A 15 per cent[1] improvement in learning efficiency would require stimuli that appear 33·7 times more frequently (experiment carried out by Underwood and Schulz). These effects seem very small, considering how frequently the stimuli used appear. There are probably several reasons for this phenomenon, which has not yet been adequately explained. For example, many words of a relatively low frequency remain readily available to the subject, probably because they belong to

[1] Estimated from the graph in Fig. 4.

his familiar repertoire, i.e. to vocabulary specifically used by him in a particular situation which recurs in his daily life.[1]

(B) FAMILIARITY AND THE DEGREE OF APPROXIMATION TO LANGUAGE

Frequency of words is only one of the various statistical aspects of written or spoken language. For example, a study can be made of the frequency with which one specific verbal unit is followed by another of the same type, i.e. one word after another, one syllable after another, or one phoneme after another. This approach leads to an analysis of the statistical properties of the verbal sequences occurring in language. Such an analysis touches on the question under consideration here, since the connections between words in language sequences give rise to language habits (in individuals) belonging to this linguistic field. Thus it becomes possible to study the role of these habits in mnemonic processes.

On this basis, C. E. Shannon (1948) built up *artificial verbal sequences*, which are called 'approximations to language', and classified as zero-order,[2] first-order, second-order, third-order etc., depending on how similar or dissimilar they are to actual language. Thus material of a zero degree of approximation would be unfamiliar and meaningless, while material of an nth degree of approximation would be considerably more familiar and meaningful and would be closer to the language habits created by connections between words.

[1] Certain, very familiar words, featured in the table of frequency of French words compiled by Gougenheim and his collaborators (1956), did not appear once in ordinary, recorded conversations.

[2] A *zero-order approximation* would be a sequence composed of verbal units, in any order, taken at random from a language repertoire, such as a dictionary. The frequency with which these units appear in language is not respected.

A *first-order approximation* would be obtained by choosing verbal units at random from a repertoire which takes into account their frequency. As in the previous case, the connections between the successive, verbal units would be practically zero, although a familiar sequence might appear by chance.

In theory, the experimenter who wishes to construct a *second-order approximation* should have a table of all the pairs of words in existence, together with their frequency. He could then choose any pair (for example, 'walk on'), followed by any pair beginning with the second word of the first pair ('on my'), and so on. The same technique may be used to obtain *third-order, fourth-order, etc. approximations* by choosing at random groups of 3, 4, etc. words which actually follow each other in language.

In 1950, Miller and Selfridge investigated how memory evolved as a function of these degrees of approximation. Their material was composed of two groups of 32 series of artificial words which differed in length (series of 10, 20, 30 and 50 words) and in degree of approximation (approximations of the order of 0, 1, 2, 3, 4, 5, 6 and 7). In addition, they used coherent passages drawn from English texts (10, 20, 30 and 50 words). Two groups of 10 subjects (one group per 32 series) took part in the experiment. Their task was to write down the words in each series as soon as the experimenter had read them out. The curves in Fig. 5 show the results obtained. The subjects' recall was more

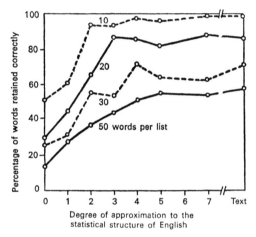

Fig. 5. How memory evolves as a function of the order of approximation to the structure of the English language of the stimuli used. The 4 curves represent lists of 10, 20, 30 and 50 stimuli, respectively. (After Miller and Selfridge, *Amer. J. Psychol.*, 1950, **63**, 181).

efficient when the approximation to language was of a higher order, regardless of the length of the material. However, one qualification must be made to this statement, since the plateaux of the curves show interaction between length of material and order of approximation. In the case of the 10-word series, there was rapid progress up to the second-order approximation, after which the gain became slight. In the case of the 20-word lists, retention of the third-order words was the same as that of the passage from an ordinary text. This also applied to the fourth-order approximation of 30 words and the fifth-order approximation of 50 words.

In other words, the longer the task and the higher the degree of approximation, the closer the retention of artificial words comes to the level of retention of ordinary texts. This increasing dependence of memory on degrees of approximation, as the task grows more difficult, can be explained by the presence of connections with familiar words which increase in number as the sequences become more like language. These connections between words favour learning, because the subject has already acquired them and uses them constantly. When they are sufficiently numerous, they ensure that the retention of artificial material is as efficient as that of meaningful material. As a result, Miller and Selfridge stated that: '*A basic distinction must be made, not between meaningful and meaningless material, but between material which allows the subject to use positive transfer from previous learning and material which does not do this.*'[1] It is easy to learn material which preserves the associations in current use in English. Similarly meaningful material is easy to learn, not because it has meaning, but because it contains associations with which the subject is familiar.' This interpretation covers all the phenomena connected with the frequency of stimuli, studied in the preceding paragraph.

5 Meaning, learning and memory

Ebbinghaus thought that the meaning of stimuli could alter the results of experiments on memory. He therefore established verbal material of a 'meaningless' nature, composed of 'nonsense' syllables, which he regarded as *simple, of a uniform standard of difficulty and measurable*, and so likely to produce *responses which were quite distinct and, in turn, measurable*. However, even if these meaningless syllables do make easily measurable stimuli, they do not possess the qualities of simplicity and homogeneity with which Ebbinghaus credited them. But they have a certain degree of meaning, which varies from syllable to syllable, in so far as they often suggest meaningful verbal associations (words, groups of words, verbal expressions, etc.) or associations that can be verbalized. Psychologists have perfected

[1] Our italics.

techniques for the establishment of degrees of meaning in material of this kind. Consequently they can make use of this variable in their research on learning and memory.

(A) STUDY OF THE ASSOCIATION VALUE OF VERBAL MATERIAL

The relative frequency with which a meaningless, verbal stimulus produces meaningful associations, when it is presented to subjects for the express purpose of establishing this frequency, is known as its degree of meaning or, more usually, its 'association value'. Only one of the methods used to determine the association value of meaningless verbal stimuli will be described here.[1]

The method used by Glaze (1928), to grade syllables, and by Witmer (1935), to grade three-consonant syllables, consisted of presenting series of stimuli to a group of subjects who were asked to say briefly what each stimulus suggested to them. The presentation time per stimulus was kept fairly constant (Glaze: 2 to 3 seconds; Witmer: 4 seconds), as were the intervals between stimuli. By this method, the association value of a stimulus α equals the percentage of subjects who, under experimental conditions, associate it with a word or verbal expression. The association value of a stimulus associated in this way by all the subjects is 100 per cent, while that of a stimulus not associated by any of the subjects is 0 per cent.[2]

(B) THE EFFECT OF THE MEANING OF MATERIAL ON LEARNING AND MEMORY

As a general rule, it is easier to learn meaningful material than material which has little meaning. Research into relations between the meaning of material and the efficiency of learning revealed the following facts:

(a) *Given a constant practice time, the number of stimuli memor-*

[1] There is a distinct relationship between the association value of verbal stimuli, obtained by these methods, and the frequency with which they form part of words in language (Underwood and Schulz, 1960).

[2] In another method, used by Noble (1952), a given verbal stimulus (a real word or a nonsense syllable) is assumed to possess an association value which will be greater, the larger the number of associative responses it suggests in a given time. The work by Underwood and Schulz (1960) contains a critical review of this question.

248

ized is higher, the greater the degree of meaning possessed by the stimuli. In research carried out by McGeoch in 1930, groups of subjects memorized series of 10 three-letter words and of 10 nonsense syllables with association values of 0, 53 and 100 per cent (taken from Glaze's standardization, 1928). Length of time allowed for learning was 2 minutes per series, and the subjects were asked to reproduce the series from memory immediately after learning. Table IX gives the principal results obtained from this experiment. The average number of correct responses increased, while intrusions diminished, as a function of degree of meaning.

TABLE IX

Average number of correct reproductions as a function of degree of meaning (practice time constant)

	Average	σ
10 words	9·11	1·12
10 syllables (100%)	7·35	1·96
10 syllables (53%)	6·41	2·37
10 syllables (0%)	5·09	2·60

(After McGeoch, *J. genet. Psychol.*, 1930, **37**, 425.)

(*b*) *It follows that meaningless material will require a longer period of practice than meaningful material in order to reach the same degree of learning.* The subjects who took part in a study by Guildford (1914) required an average of 20·4 trials to memorize 15 nonsense syllables, but only 8·1 trials to learn a series of 15 independent words, and only 3·5 trials for 15 words similar in meaning. Other studies (Postman and Raugh, 1957) have confirmed this general rule which is equally valid when the association value of meaningless verbal material is adopted as a measure of its degree of meaning (Noble, 1952; Underwood and Richardson, 1956; Dowling and Braun, 1957; Braun and Heymann, 1958).

(*c*) This relationship between speed of learning and degree of meaning remains when *material is organized into S–R pairs, and when the association value of both elements in each pair is identical or nearly so* (Mandler and Huttenlocher, 1955; Kimble and

Dufort, 1955; Noble and McNeely, 1957). However, if there is a difference between these association values, *learning will be faster, when the second element (response) has a high-association value and the first element (stimulus) a low one, than in the reverse situation.* In 1929 Stoddard conducted a study in which 328 subjects, who did not know a word of French, learnt 50 pairs consisting of one French and one English word. The French word was the stimulus for half the subjects (i.e. the stimulus had little meaning, while the response had a lot) and the English word was the stimulus for the other half (i.e. the stimulus had a lot of meaning, while the response had very little). All the subjects had 20 minutes in which to study the material. The recall test consisted of reproducing the response to each stimulus, and the result was that the average number of correct responses given by the subjects in the first group was 15·1, but it was only 8·0 for the subjects in the second group. Other studies have confirmed this law (Kimble and Dufort, 1955; Cieutat, Stockwell and Noble, 1958; L'Abate, 1959; Hunt, 1959).

These results, which had always demonstrated the positive effect of meaning on speed of learning, led psychologists (Hovland, 1951; McGeoch and Irion, 1952; Woodworth and Schlosberg, 1954) to believe that meaningful material was always retained better than meaningless material. However, research carried out by Underwood and Richardson (1956) showed that, *when the criterion of learning was the same*, there was little difference in recall between syllables of a high association value and those of a low one. One of their experiments used 2 series of 10 syllables, each memorized by a different group of 100 subjects (criterion of acquisition: first correct trial). The association values of the syllables in one series varied between 93 and 100 per cent. The association values in the other series were between 0 and 20 per cent. Table X gives the average recall 24 hours after learning.

One possible objection is that syllables of a high association value still do not have any real meaning, so they are too close to all the other syllables, in this respect, for the experiment to show any distinct difference between their respective retention. But, in some research already quoted (see p. 249), Postman and Rau were able to demonstrate that, *when the criterion of learning was the same*, there was no significant difference between the recall of series of 12 syllables and that of series of 12 words, after intervals of 20 minutes, 1 day and 2 days (different groups having been used for the various intervals). Nevertheless, in all the work done

TABLE X

Recall and association value

Association value	N. trials	Average recall
93–100%	19·27	6·90
0– 20%	29·18	7·10

(After Underwood and Richardson, *J. exp. Psychol.*, 1956, **52**, 120 and 121.)

by Postman and Rau and Underwood and Richardson, the retention of meaningless material could have been favoured by considerably longer learning.

(C) THEORETICAL EXPLANATION OF THE ROLE OF MEANING AND FAMILIARITY

The problem of the role of meaning in learning and retention is closely linked to that of familiarity. Meaningful, verbal stimuli (for example, words) are used fairly frequently in the practice of language. This frequency of use, which is the basis of familiarity, produces verbal habits on two levels: (*a*) *semantic*: a verbal stimulus, which is used frequently, usually has connections with a large number of other verbal stimuli; (*b*) *phonetic and literal*: the literal-phonetic combinations contained in these stimuli become better established, the more often they are used in language.

These two categories of verbal habits often act in opposition. When a series of words, which frequently occur in a particular order, has to be learnt, the fact that each of these words contains a familiar, literal-phonetic combination favours both learning and retention; but semantic associations, acquired before learning, can produce interference, either because pre-established connections already exist between these words and words not included in the material (causing a risk of intrusion), or because pre-established connections exist between non-contiguous words

251

in the series causing interference through 'forward' or 'backward' associations (see p. 227).

The same reasoning can be applied to learning meaningless, verbal material. The ease or difficulty with which such material is learnt depends on how far its literal-phonetic structures conform to literal-phonetic structures in language (see the experiments carried out by Miller and Selfridge, p. 247). For example, in extreme cases, a meaningless syllable, the literal-phonetic structure of which is very different from familiar structures, will be in a very unfavourable position for learning, since it cannot benefit from language habits acquired in the past. Indeed, if such habits do intervene during the learning or memory tasks, they will only cause interference. On the other hand, this meaningless syllable will be favoured by its lack of semantic associations and therefore will be free from interference.

Finally, with both meaningful and meaningless verbal material, the efficiency of retention depends on the relative effects of these two variables. This explains why series of nonsense syllables are sometimes remembered better than series of words. This theory has been principally elaborated by Underwood and Postman, and is confirmed by all their experimental results (Underwood and Postman, 1960; Postman, 1961).

3 The role of practice

---

1 The influence of the degree of learning on memory: overlearning

As a general rule, an increase in the level of learning (measured by the number of times the material is repeated or the length of time the practice lasts), brings about an improvement in retention which can be measured from the recall, recognition or relearning score.

Ebbinghaus (1885) learnt series of nonsense syllables, varying the number of trials from 1 to 65. Twenty-four hours after learning, he measured the amount he could remember by the savings method. Fig. 6 reveals the existence of an almost linear relationship between the frequency of repetition and the percentage of saving in relearning, under the experimental conditions that Ebbinghaus imposed on himself.

The specific aim of Kreuger's classical research (1929) was to study the influence of overlearning (using Luh's method of comparing the number of supplementary repetitions with the number required to meet the criterion of mastery, see p. 225), on memory,

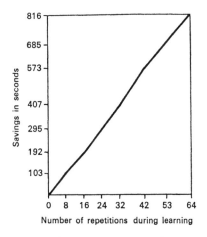

Fig. 6. Relation of degree of learning (measured by number of repetitions) to savings in relearning 24 hours later. (After Ebbinghaus, *Über das Gedächtnis*, Duncker and Humblot, 1885, and McGeoch, *The Psychology of Human Learning*, New York, Longmans Green and Co., p. 378.)

tested after increasing lengths of time. The subjects learnt series of 12 common, monosyllabic nouns until they achieved one perfect trial. In some cases, practice stopped there (0 per cent overlearning), while it went on until there was 50 or 100 per cent overlearning in other cases. The results obtained are shown in Table XI overleaf.

An examination of the figures contained in this table shows that recall and savings in relearning were greater, the higher the degree of overlearning. This applied to all the intervals of time between learning and recall. Considerable experimental research subsequently verified this conclusion.

2 Distribution of practice, learning and memory

In the acquisition of material or a skill, when perfect learning is required with the minimum amount of practice, is it better to repeat the task without interruption until the criterion of mastery is reached, rather than to space the trials out? The answer to this question is very important, both from the point of view of the practical application of psychology and of the theoretical problems that it raises. Jost (1897) made the first study of this question,

TABLE XI

Development of recall and savings in relearning as a function
of degrees of overlearning

	Degrees of overlearning					
	0	50	100	0	50	100
Interval in days	Average number of words recalled			Average saving in relearning		
1	3·10	4·60	5·83	21·73	36·15	47·10
2	1·80	3·60	4·65	13·40	33·45	42·05
4	0·50	2·05	3·30	3·40	29·75	32·30
7	0·20	1·30	1·65	1·75	23·15	27·55
14	0·15	0·65	0·90	1·65	20·80	25·45
28	0·00	0·25	0·40	1·50	20·50	25·10

(After Kreuger, *J. exp. Psychol.*, 1929, **12**, 74 and 75.)

which had already been raised by Ebbinghaus (1885). In Jost's experiment, two subjects (B and S) had to repeat series of nonsense syllables 30 times under different sets of conditions:

(1) Thirty repetitions on the same day, followed the next day by a relearning test to one perfect repetition;

(2) Thirty repetitions distributed over three successive days (10 repetitions per say), followed by the same relearning test as above on the fourth day.

The results given in the table overleaf show that the number of repetitions required for relearning the series repeated 30 times on the same day was a little higher than the number needed by the series distributed over three days.

Jost explained this result as follows: when a subject repeats series of syllables, he establishes connections between the different elements of the material; in distributed learning, repetition reactivates 'old' associations (which are 'older', the longer the interval of time between trials), while repetition reactivates the more recently elaborated associations in massed learning. Given

Number of trials for relearning

	Massed learning[1] (30 *repetitions on* *the same day*)	*Distributed learning*[1] (10 *repetitions* *per day*)
Subject B	6·5	5·5
Subject S	11·5	9·7

the greater efficiency of distributed learning, it can be postulated that, *in the case of two associations of equal strength, but unequal age, repetition increases the strength of the older more than that of the younger* (Jost's law).

(A) EXPERIMENTAL VERIFICATION OF JOST'S LAW

There have been various attempts to verify this law, and the work done by Youtz (1941) merits particular mention. The major difficulty encountered here is the definition of associations of 'equal strength', and this can only be overcome by the adoption of a operational definition. For example, the strength of the associations between elements in a series is the same as that of the associations between the elements of a previously learnt series, when the *number of trials* or the *number of errors* registered during relearning is practically the same for both sets of material; or, when the *number of elements correctly reproduced from memory is the same*. Youtz employed all three criteria of 'association strength' in order to give a rational basis to his research.

[1] The expressions 'massed learning' and 'distributed learning' only refer to the time conditions of learning. In 'massed learning', the task is executed at a uniform speed with the *minimal interval of time* between stimuli and between trials. In 'distributed learning', considerably longer intervals (so-called 'rest' periods) are interposed at regular points during the learning task. Thus there is no fundamental difference of nature between these two types of learning. They only vary in their temporal organization. Learning which is 'distributed' in relation to another learning task may be 'massed' in relation to a third.

255

The experiment was carried out under the following conditions: 15 subjects learnt series of 12 nonsense syllables by the anticipation method. The research scheme provided for three degrees of learning and various intervals of time (see the summary below).

	Length of time before relearning
Degree of learning 1: Criterion of first perfect recitation	6 secs., 10 mins., 20 mins., 40 mins., 60 mins., 2 hrs., 24 hrs.
Degree of learning 2: Criterion of 7 correct anticipations	6 secs., 10 mins., 20 mins., 40 mins., 60 mins.
Degree of learning 3: Criterion of 4·5 correct anticipations	6 secs., 10 mins., 20 mins., 40 mins., 60 mins.

Relearning was continued to the criterion of the first perfect trial without errors or omissions. The number of correct anticipations in the first trial in each relearning session provided the recall score.

Fig. 7 shows how retention evolved when measured by the average number of mistakes made in relearning. Curves I, II and III correspond to the degrees of learning 1, 2 and 3. An examination of these curves will reveal the various points at which the number of errors made in relearning was the same, or nearly the same, although the amount of time between learning and relearning was different. These points lie close to where the curves intersect the two lines A and B (running parallel to the abscissa) which show the two levels of errors. Point $III_{6'}$ (series relearnt after 6 seconds), point $II_{40'}$ (series relearnt after 40 minutes) and point $I_{120'}$, whose average errors numbered 29·71, 32·37 and 31·33 respectively, all lie on level A. The three points on level B represent the series relearnt with 35·05 mistakes (point L), 35·77 mistakes (point III_{10}) and 34·60 mistakes (point II_{60}).

This verification of Jost's law shows that, when the same number of mistakes is made, the progress in retention shown by the first relearning trial must be greater for the series of 'older'

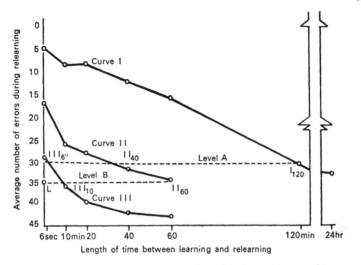

Fig. 7. Curves I, II and III correspond to the three degrees of learning used by Youtz in his experiment. The dotted lines A and B represent two levels in errors in relearning. On level A, Points $III_{6''}$, $II_{40'}$ and $I_{120'}$ represent relearning with almost the same number of mistakes. Points L, III_{10} and II_{60} on Level B show the same thing. (After Youtz, *Psychol. Monogr.*, 1941, **53**, 17.)

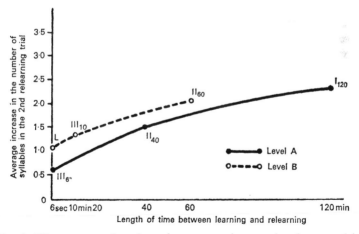

Fig. 8. These curves show how the progress in retention (measured by the difference between the number of correct responses given in the first and second trials developed as a function of the length of time between learning and relearning. (After Youtz, *Psychol. Monogr.*, 1941, **53**, 19.)

acquisition than for series acquired more recently. This is precisely what emerges from an examination of the curves in Fig. 8, since they show that the gain in retention (measured by the difference between the number of syllables correctly anticipated in the first and second trials) increases as a function of the increase in the length of time between learning and relearning. Youtz also arrived at the same conclusion when, in a similar analysis, he used both the number of trials needed for relearning and the number of elements correctly anticipated in the first relearning trial as criteria of 'equal strength'.

(B) DIFFERENT WAYS OF DISTRIBUTING PRACTICE

Jost's law can be expressed in a different way: *fewer trials are needed for learning by the distributed method than for learning by the massed method.*[1] However a distinction must be made initially between the two different ways of distributing practice: (1) intervals of time between the elements which form the task; and (2) intervals of time between the successive trials.

(*a*) *The role of intervals of time between the elements in the task.* A series of 12 nonsense syllables can be presented with regular intervals of 2 (or 4) seconds between each syllable, while the interval between successive presentations remains constant at 6 seconds. In this way, Hovland (1938) demonstrated that there were fewer errors with the 4-second rhythm. Curves II and II' in Fig. 9 show that the drop in the number of errors was particularly marked in the case of the elements situated near the middle of the series. It has already been demonstrated that these are the most difficult elements of a series to memorize (see p. 232).

(*b*) *The role of intervals of time between successive trials.* Distributed learning is still more efficient when the amount of time between successive trials varies, while the length of the interval between successive elements in the material remains constant.

---

[1] This law has been verified by a wide variety of research, both on animals (mice, Yerkes, 1907; hens, Katz and Revesz, 1908; fresh and sea water molluscs, Piéron, 1913; rats, Ulrich, 1915; Lashley, 1918; Warden, 1923; Mayer and Stone, 1931, among many others) and on humans, with a large selection of different tasks (mirror drawing a star, Lorge, 1930; typewriting, Book, 1908; Pyle, 1914; series of numbers, Piéron, 1913; stylet maze, Carr, 1919; nonsense syllables, Jost, 1897; Muller and Pilzecker, 1900; Piéron, 1913; Hovland, 1938, 1940; Underwood, 1951, etc.).

Hovland (1938) employed different experimental conditions in his research. In one case, the interval *between trials* was 6 seconds, while it was 2 minutes and 6 seconds in the other. When there was a constant 2-second interval between adjacent syllables, there appeared to be fewer errors with 2 minutes 6 seconds between trials than with 6 seconds between trials (curves I and II' in Fig. 9).

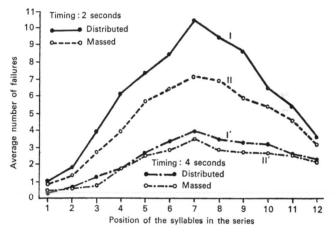

Fig. 9. Comparison of massed learning (6 seconds between trials) and distributed learning (2 minutes and 6 seconds between trials) when the rhythm of presentation was timed differently (2 seconds *or* 4 seconds between successive elements). (After Hovland, *J. exp. Psychol.*, 1938, **23,** 178.)

However, the apparent superiority of distributed practice over massed practice does have certain limitations. In fact, the relative efficiency of learning depends on a precise balance between the intervals separating the trials and the intervals separating the elements in the material. In the same experiment, Hovland showed that there was practically no difference between massed learning and distributed learning when the intervals between adjacent syllables always lasted 4 seconds (curves I' and II' in Fig. 9).

(C) THE PROBLEM OF ESTABLISHING WHAT IS THE
   BEST TIMING FOR THE PRACTICE PERIOD

This problem can be approached in two different ways: either the practice periods can be kept constant, while the rest periods vary in length; or the rest periods can be kept constant, while the practice periods vary.

(*a*) *The effect of varying the rest periods.* If the length of the practice periods is kept constant, while the intervals of time between them are varied systematically, the best time (which sometimes varies considerably) can be obtained for the smallest possible number of practice periods.

Using a motor test, Travis (1937) studied the influence of intervals of 5 minutes, 20 minutes, 48 hours, 72 hours and 120 hours interposed between continuous practice periods lasting 5 minutes. The best interval was that of 20 minutes, but this depended very much on the nature of the task, and it could even vary considerably for the same task. Piéron (1913) made a subject learn series of 18 nonsense syllables. They were read through at intervals of 30 seconds, 1, 2, 5, 10 or 20 minutes, 24 hours or 48 hours. The practice period occurred after each time interval until the first correct recitation of the material was achieved. Here are the results obtained:

Length of the interval between each reading

	30 secs.	1 min.	2 mins.	5 mins.	10 mins.	20 mins.	24 hrs.	48 hrs.
Number of times the material was read before the criterion was reached	14	8	7	5	4	4·5	4	7

As the author himself remarked, 'From an interval of half a minute to an interval, twenty times greater, of ten minutes, the number of times the material has to be read is reduced by nearly two-thirds'. The best interval appeared to be from 10 minutes upwards, but both 20 minutes and 24 hours seemed to be favourable from the point of view of the efficiency of learning.

Using three different tasks (mirror drawing, mirror reading and a code test), Lorge (1930) studied the effect on the speed of acquisition of 20 massed trials and 20 trials separated by intervals of 1 minute or 24 hours. Distributed learning was clearly faster in both cases. But it also emerged that the difference between the intervals of 1 minute and 24 hours was only slight (see Fig. 10).

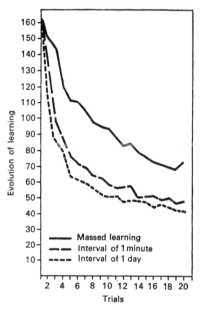

Fig. 10. Learning curves of a mirror-drawing task when the exercise was spaced out in two different ways. (After Lorge, *Teach. Coll. Contr. Educ.*, 1930, no. 438, 16.)

(*b*) *The effect of varying the practice periods.* What length of practice period (when the intervals in between remain constant) produces the best results? In Jost's experiments (1897), the subjects learnt nonsense syllables under the following conditions:

Condition A: series learnt for 3 days, 8 repetitions a day; memory test on the fourth day;

Condition B: series learnt for 6 days, 4 repetitions a day; memory test on the seventh day;

Condition C: series learnt for 12 days, 2 repetitions a day; memory test on the thirteenth day.

An examination of the number of syllables reproduced correctly showed that the shortest practice periods (2 trials a day) produced the highest retention, and that memory efficiency diminished as the number of trials per practice period increased.

Number of correct responses 24 hours after the end of the task (after Jost)

	Condition A (8 *trials a day*)	Condition B (4 *trials a day*)	Condition C (2 *trials a day*)
Subject B	18	39	53
Subject M	7	31	55

All the results obtained by other authors confirm the existence of an optimum practice period which varies in accordance with the nature and difficulty of the task and the skill of the subjects.

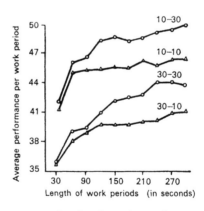

Fig. 11. Learning curves showing how the performance of 4 groups of subjects progressed as a function of the length of the work period (10 seconds *or* 30 seconds) and of the length of the rest interval (10 seconds *or* 30 seconds). The first number on each curve refers to the length of the work period and the second to the length of the rest interval. (After Kimble and Bilodeau, *J. exp. Psychol.*, 1949, **39**, 153.)

This also applies to tasks in the psychomotor field. Kimble and Bilodeau (1949) compared learning curves when a motor task was acquired in *practice periods of 10 seconds*, separated by 10-second or 30-second intervals, or *of 30 seconds*, spaced out in the same way. The curves in Fig. 11 show the superiority of 10-second work periods over those of 30 seconds, regardless of the length of the intervals separating them. However, the curves also show that, under the conditions of this experiment, the more distributed work periods (30 seconds of rest) produced the best performances (when the work periods were of equal length).

(D) DISTRIBUTION OF PRACTICE AND RELATIVE DIFFICULTY OF THE TASK

The optimum length for practice periods and rest periods depends upon the nature of the task, and so varies considerably from one task to another. However, if a task remains the same, but is made progressively more difficult by being increased in length, *learning by distributed practice appears to keep pace with the increasing difficulty of the task*. This has been verified in studies made by Lyon (1914) and Hovland (1940). The object of Hovland's research was to compare the efficiency of distributed practice (2-minute intervals between trials) with that of massed practice (6-second intervals between trials) on the memorization of series of 9, 12 and 15 meaningless syllables. The numerical data in Table XII shows that the savings in practice, which resulted from distributed learning, increased progressively (both in relative and in absolute value) with the number of elements to be learnt.

It has also emerged that the superiority of distributed learning over massed learning (amply proved by several decades of research) is, in fact, only relative, since it tends to diminish if the task becomes easier. Underwood (1951, together with Richardson, 1955 and 1958, and Schutz, 1959) gathered together all the data which seemed to confirm that the acquisition of verbal material, composed of very similar elements (which are difficult to memorize on account of the interference arising from their similarity), is favoured by spacing out the practice. However, there is very little difference between massed practice and distributed practice when it comes to learning series of the same length but composed of dissimilar elements.

Finally a subject's skill, in relation to what the task requires of him, must be considered. One subject examined by Jost (1897) was capable of learning 12 nonsense syllables after reading them an average of 18·5 times (4 times a day). He only needed to read them through 17·9 times when he did it twice daily, but he managed the same performance after reading them only 7 to 9 times when the task took place without interruption.

TABLE XII

Number of trials needed to learn series of different lengths by massed practice and by distributed practice

	Series of 8 syllables		Series of 11 syllables		Series of 14 syllables	
	Average	σ	Average	σ	Average	σ
Massed learning	7·00	0·28	11·64	0·68	17·14	0·80
Distributed learning	5·93	0·36	9·43	0·59	12·14	0·76
Difference	1·07		2·21		5·00	
Average savings in practice in relation to massed learning	15·2%		18·9%		29·1%	

(After Hovland, *J. exp. Psychol.*, 1940, **27**, 272.)

Jost's conclusions still seem valid in the light of more recent experiments: when a task can be learnt with few repetitions, the massed learning method is more efficient; but, if a large number of repetitions is required, the distributed method is indubitably better.

(E) THE EFFECT OF THE DISTRIBUTION OF PRACTICE ON DEFERRED MEMORY

Jost's research (see p. 254) proved that retention (measured by the relearning method 24 hours after the original task) was greater when the material was acquired by distributed learning than when it was acquired by massed learning, *with the same number of repetitions* in both cases. A more detailed approach to this problem seeks to establish the relative efficiency of deferred retention when the subjects reach *the same criterion of mastery* (for example, the same number of correct responses) by both methods of learning. Two different categories of experiments have been used.

(*a*) *The effect of intervals of time introduced between practice periods.* In research carried out by Cain and Willey (1939), six groups of subjects (well trained in advance) memorized a series of 12 nonsense syllables by the anticipation method. Each group worked under one of the six conditions provided for in the experimental plan, which combined 2 *conditions of practice* (*massed learning*: a single work session, criterion of acquisition: 12 correct anticipations; *distributed learning*: 3 work sessions, separated by intervals of 24 hours, criterion of acquisition: 6 correct anticipations the first day, 9 the second day and 12 the last day) and *3 intervals of time* between the end of learning and the memory test (24 hours, 3 days and 7 days). The results show that there was very little difference between the total number of repetitions required to achieve 12 correct anticipations in either learning situation (an average of 35·6 trials with distributed practice and 33·5 trials with massed practice). The first trial in relearning provided each subject's recall score (number of responses correctly anticipated). Fig. 12 shows how the average, recall percentages developed. The decline in retention was clearly slower after memorization in several work sessions than after memorization in a single session.

(*b*) *The effect of intervals of time between trials.* When the successive trials in learning are separated by short, rest periods, rather than longer intervals of time between blocks of massed practice, the results obtained confirm those of the research carried out by Cain and Willey, although one important qualification must be made: retention after distributed learning is, in fact, greater than that resulting from massed learning, *but only when a high risk of interference makes the task more difficult.* Indeed, if the risk of interference is only slight, massed learning can produce retention which is as efficient as, and sometimes more efficient than, retention after distributed learning.

In an experiment carried out by Underwood and Richardson (1955), 168 subjects' first task was to learn a series of 6 three-consonant syllables, 84 by massed practice and 84 by distributed practice. Twenty-four hours after acquisition, the average recall of these two groups showed nothing to prove the superiority of distributed learning on the efficiency of deferred retention, i.e. there was no appreciable difference in recall.

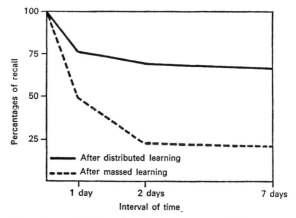

Fig. 12. How the recall of a series of 12 nonsense syllables developed with the passage of time, according to whether the series had been learnt by the distributed method or the massed method. (After Cain and Willey, *J. exp. Psychol.*, 1939, **25**, 211.)

All the subjects then learnt 5 new series by the massed method. The object of this learning sequence was to give rise to interference of a proactive nature in the acquisition of the last critical series (series 7). This seventh series was learnt by distributed practice by half the subjects (divided up into 3 sub-groups on the

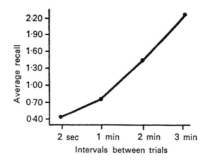

Fig. 13. How recall of series 7 developed as a function of the intervals between trials during learning. (After Underwood and Richardson, *J. exp. Psychol.*, 1955, **50**, 42.)

basis of the length of the interval between trials: 1 minute, 2 minutes or 3 minutes). The other half learnt this same series by a massed practice. The curve in Fig. 13 shows how recall of series 7 evolved as a function of the length of the intervals between trials. It shows that, 24 hours after the end of the task, the recall resulting from distributed learning was higher than that from massed learning. The difference was greater, the longer the intervals between trials; so distributed practice improves long-term retention when interferences disturb the fixation of the task (as was the case in series 7), but this positive effect does not appear when the likelihood of interference is less probable.[1]

(F) THEORIES OF THE EFFECTS OF THE DISTRIBUTION
OF PRACTICE

The principal theories, which offer an explanation of the effects of the distribution of practice on learning and retention, can be divided into two groups. Some hypotheses (for example, those of mental revision and perseveration put forward by Muller and Pilzecker) assert that processes of reactivation or consolidation of mnemonic responses take place during the intervals between trials. Others (for example, Hull's theory of fatigue and of reactive inhibition, and McGeoch's theory of differential forgetting) suggest that these intervals provide opportunities for the dispersion of these inhibitory processes, which tend to weaken the availability of mnemonic responses.

The theory that distributed learning is more efficient than massed learning, because the subject must mentally revise the task during the rest period that he is allowed, is based on a phenomenon that may occur in human beings; but this phenomenon can hardly account for the fact that distributed practice has the same favourable effect on learning in animals.

The theory formulated by Muller and Pilzecker (1900) is more satisfactory, because its application is more general. It suggests that the biophysiological processes at work during the practice persevere for some time after learning. This perseveration will

---

[1] However, this research does explain some apparently contradictory results obtained earlier. See Hovland's studies (1940), which showed that recall was more efficient after distributed learning, and Underwood's research (1952*a*, 1952*b*, 1953), which did not produce the same result.

consolidate the mnemonic traces, provided that no other activity disturbs it. It follows that the consolidation of the responses in a particular trial will depend upon the length of the rest period. Since the rest period is always longer in distributed learning, the phenomenon of consolidation must be more efficient in this case, because it will always be restricted in massed learning by the rapid succession of the trials. The possibility that such a phenomenon of consolidation may exist cannot be disregarded (see the discussion of this hypothesis in connection with theories of forgetting, p. 339), but its explanatory value is very limited, since it cannot account for those experiments in which massed learning is as efficient as distributed learning.

The fatigue theory suggests that distributed learning is faster than massed learning, because the fatigue produced by the subject's activity in performing the task can be eliminated during the rest periods. But, in addition to the fact that the notion of fatigue is very vague (what is the exact nature of this fatigue and how can it be defined?), this theory does not explain the improvement in performance when rest periods, introduced between trials, prolong the first phase of a practice period which is still too short to produce any fatigue. For similar reasons, Hull's theory of reactive inhibition (1943) is equally unsatisfactory.[1]

Finally McGeoch's theory of differential forgetting (in McGeoch and Irion, 1952) suggests that a subject associates, not only correct responses, but also incorrect ones, with any learning task. These incorrect responses, which arise either within the task itself or from the intrusion of previously acquired responses into the task, conflict with the correct responses, delay their acquisition and interfere with them when they are recalled.[2] Their connections with the task are weaker than those of the

[1] Hull (1943) assumed that the responses given by an organism in a learning situation must produce some fatigue, which would be greater, the longer the task. This phenomenon, which he called reactive inhibition (I_R), would be capable of weakening, and even temporarily neutralizing, the reaction potential determining the appearance of responses. Reactive inhibition would disappear during the rest periods. This theory does account for certain phenomena in distributed learning and reminiscence, but its explanatory value is far from general.

[2] McGeoch's theory of differential forgetting is really part of his general theory of interference which will be discussed in connection with forgetting (see p. 335).

correct responses,[1] and so they are forgotten more quickly than the latter, which can survive for some time without practice. Consequently distributed learning must be superior to massed learning, because it affords the opportunity for incorrect responses to be forgotten.

This theory is compatible with quite a lot of experimental data. In particular, it predicts that the advantage of distributed practice will become greater as the growing difficulty of a task increases the probability of interference (either the number of elements to be memorized rises or these elements become more similar). It also covers the fact that the superiority of distributed learning is only relative: massed learning can be just as efficient when the risk of interference is only slight. However, it is based on the assumption that incorrect associations are weaker, and this has not been experimentally verified.[2]

One qualification must be made. It has not yet been possible to explain the whole group of effects of distributed practice by one single theory. Indeed the theories just reviewed are not necessarily incompatible. The reactivation of responses by mental revision, their consolidation by the perseveration of underlying biophysiological processes, the dispersion of inhibition created by fatigue and the phenomena of conflict between

[1] McGeoch has not explained very clearly *why* he assumes that these connections are weaker. However, this is readily understandable in view of the fact that, unlike correct responses, incorrect responses are not reinforced during learning.

[2] Thus, by adopting the latency of responses or the speed with which they disappear as a function of the passing of time, as working criteria for this supposed weakness, it should be possible to show that 'remote' associations (which are said to be incorrect in a situation in which a series of syllables or words have to be memorized in a given order, see p. 227) have longer latencies and are affected more quickly by forgetting than forward associations between adjacent elements (correct associations). However, the work done by McGeoch (1936) and Wilson (1943) to verify this logical conclusion of the theory of differential forgetting did not confirm it. On the contrary, the tendency to give incorrect responses seemed to be stronger than the tendency to give correct responses when learning first began. Underwood (1961) has recently formulated a new theory from this point (confirmed by certain experimental results), which is based on the the the phenomenon of concurrence of responses. This theory presumes that distributed learning increases the probability of interfering responses appearing during practice, whereas massed learning makes this less probable. But, by acting in this way, distributed learning must favour differentiation of correct and incorrect responses (as well as the inhibition of incorrect responses) more than massed learning does. However, there is not enough experimental data to estimate the value of such a theory.

responses may all be partly responsible, and the extent of this responsibility has to be decided in each individual case. This is doubtless an eclectic conclusion. Nevertheless, many authors of more ambitious theories would not disagree.

3 Whole and part learning

When a task (for example, a lesson or a poem) is too long or too difficult to learn as it stands, it can be divided into shorter parts, which can be memorized successively, and then learnt as a whole in additional trials (part method of learning). However, the whole task can be attempted in the first place by running through it a number of times until complete acquisition is achieved (whole method of learning).

The first psychologist to experiment with whole or part methods was Lottie Steffens (1900). After she had observed the procedure adopted by several highly educated adults for learning a short piece of poetry, she did some research with poems of 8 to 9 lines and series of 12 to 20 nonsense syllables. The results obtained from 5 adults and 2 children showed that the task could be accomplished by the whole method with an average saving of 12 per cent compared with the part method (average taken over several experiments).

Her work was followed by considerable research which, unfortunately, was largely carried out under conditions which did not lend themselves to comparison, nor were they really adequate from a methodological point of view. Consequently it has not been possible to work out any systematic relationship between the whole and part methods and speed of learning.[1] The variety of results obtained suggests that the approach was wrong. Today it is no longer regarded as a question of proving which method is the better one, but of establishing the conditions which determine the efficiency of both methods. This new perspective calls for an analysis of the variables capable of producing systematic short- and long-term effects on the subjects' results.

---

[1] G. O. McGeoch (1931) wrote an interesting, critical review of this problem, which is particularly valuable for the study of the earliest work in this field.

(A) DIFFERENCES BETWEEN INDIVIDUALS

The efficiency of the whole method does seem to increase with chronological age and intelligence quotient or, more simply, with *the level of intellectual* development. Everything observed in the various studies by Larguier des Bancels (1902), Pentschew (1903), Neumann (1907), Pechstein (1926) and Sawdon (1927) seems to confirm this.

G. O. McGeoch (1931) compared the performances of 31 gifted children (average I.Q.: 151·2) and 32 normal children (average I.Q.: 99·4), all aged about 10 years, in learning by the part method and the whole method. The children's learning consisted of tasks of the following material: words from an English–Turkish vocabulary, pairs of nonsense syllables and English words, poems of 12 lines. The experimenter tested the children's immediate recall and also their deferred retention 24 hours after each task.

The whole method only proved to be more efficient than the part one (with a constant number of presentations) for learning the vocabulary and the pairs of words and syllables. *In addition,*

TABLE XIII

Average immediate recall scores and deferred recall scores obtained by gifted subjects and normal subjects using the whole and part methods (English-Turkish vocabulary)

| Groups of subjects | N | Whole method | | Part method | | Comparison |
		Average	Standard deviation	Average	Standard deviation	(Part/ whole) × 100
			Immediate recall			
Gifted	31	5·06	1·55	2·53	1·27	50%
Normal	32	2·42	1·32	1·48	0·87	61%
Comparison normal/gifted		48%		58%		
			Deferred recall			
Gifted	31	4·12	1·49	2·17	1·36	52%
Normal	32	1·76	1·21	0·78	0·74	44%
Comparison normal/gifted		43%		36%		

(After McGeoch, *J. exp. Psychol.*, 1931, **14**, 343.)

this efficiency was greater in the gifted subjects than in the normal subjects. Table XIII gives the results obtained from learning the English–Turkish vocabulary.

As far as the poems were concerned, the gifted children retained their superiority over the normal children, but it was not possible to discover any systematic advantage of one system over the other.

(B) FAMILIARITY OF METHOD: THE ROLE OF PRACTICE

Considerable work, showing the superiority of the whole method over the part method or over mixed methods, has been done with multiple series (series of elements arranged in sequences or in pairs) memorized by the *same* subjects. An analysis of the development of successive performances as a function of training, i.e. the number of series already learnt, shows that this training apparently favours the whole method as opposed to the part method. This phenomenon came to light in the earliest work on the problem by Steffens (1900), Ephrussi (1904) and Neumann (1907), and was confirmed by Wylie's research (1928) on 162 subjects. It can be partly explained by the relative 'novelty' of the *pure*, whole method, as it is applied in the laboratory. In fact, this type of learning is rarely used in actual teaching.[1] Consequently the subject has to become familiar with it before he can obtain the maximum results from it.

Other studies have shown that distributed learning tends to favour the whole method, whereas massed learning improves the part method. This has been verified in a variety of tasks: maze (Pechstein, 1917), verbal material (Winch, 1924; Sawdon, 1927) and code tests (Crafts, 1930).

(C) THE DIFFICULTY OF THE TASK AND THE PART
    PLAYED BY THE LENGTH OF THE MATERIAL

Pentschew (1903) found that the whole method was more efficient in learning poems of 16 lines than the part method, but that

---

[1] Steffens noted that highly educated adults spontaneously chose mixed methods. There are two mixed methods: (*a*) the progressive method by which a task is broken up into parts A, B, C, D, etc.; A is learnt separately, then B; A–B are repeated; then C is learnt and A–B–C are repeated, and so on; (*b*) the repetitive method: A is learnt, then A–B, then A–B–C, etc.

the latter became more efficient when poems of 24 or 32 lines had to be learnt. Similarly the whole method often proved to be quicker for the memorization of series of 8 to 24 nonsense syllables (Steffens, 1900; Pentschew, 1903; Wylie, 1928), but it lost its advantage when the series contained 32 syllables (Pechstein, 1926). However, these results can only provide a guide, since the research which produced them was often carried out under widely differing, experimental conditions with limited numbers of subjects.

Orbison (1944) was the only experimenter to vary the length of the task in a systematic way. Several groups of subjects learnt series of 8, 12, 16 and 24 pairs (word-nonsense syllable). These pairs were presented in a different order (which could not be predicted) each time so as to avoid effects connected with the position of a pair within the material. For whole learning, the entire series was presented each time, and the task continued until one perfect recitation was achieved. For part learning, the series were split in half (4–4, 6–6, 8–8, 12–12), and the subjects memorized the pairs, following the same procedure for both halves, until they could repeat them once perfectly. The experimenter then mixed up all the pairs, and carried out additional trials until he obtained the first perfect recitation of the entire task.

Table XIV gives the average calculated from the number of times the pairs had to be presented to reach the criterion marking the end of learning.

TABLE XIV

Average number of times the pairs had to be presented
in order to reach the criterion of one perfect recitation

Number of pairs in the series	Whole method Averages	Part method Averages	Differences
8	18·75	18·67	0·08
12	20·58	16·96	3·62
16	28·75	23·42	5·33
24	38·50	25·21	13·29

(After Orbison, unpublished Ph.D. thesis, Yale University, 1944, and Hovland, in Stevens, *Handbook of Experimental Psychology*, p. 641.)

The two methods were equally fast for learning series made up of 8 pairs. But, as the material increased in length, the part method gained in efficiency, and produced greater savings in relation to the whole method.

(D) RELATIONSHIP BETWEEN THE LENGTH OF THE WHOLE OR PARTS AND THE TIME NEEDED FOR ACQUISITION

Orbison's research[1] was inspired by a theoretical analysis by McGeoch (1942, pp. 188–95), based on the relation between the length of the material and the time it takes to learn it.

Imagine a series X composed of N elements and split into two parts, A and B, each of N/2 elements. In a part-learning situation, the total length of time for the acquisition of X will be made up of t_A (memorization of part A), t_B (memorization of part B) and some additional time t_S for the supplementary trials which seek to accomplish the task by joining A and B together. Let t_X be the length of time taken to acquire the task by whole learning. McGeoch's reasoning would then be as follows: the time needed to learn material increases more quickly than its relative length (see p. 236), so (given a certain value for N) the time t_X needed to learn the entire task by whole learning will be greater than the sum of the times t_A and t_B taken to acquire the two parts of N/2 elements each. It follows that, when the difference $t_X - (t_A + t_B)$ = D is higher than t_S, the part method produces greater savings than the whole method, but the reverse is true when $t_S > D$. It would, therefore, seem that the relative efficiency of the two methods depends on variables systematically affecting D, t_S and the relations between them.

Apparently based on this analysis, Orbison has postulated that, when the total number of elements N in a task X increases and the relation between N and the number of elements in one of the parts remains constant,[2] saving D will increase rapidly. *It will increase more rapidly than the time t_S for the two parts joined together*; for, given the same criterion of mastery, the elements in

---

[1] Orbison's research is contained in an unpublished thesis for a doctorate. We learnt of this work from accounts of it by Hovland (1951) and Osgood (1953, pp. 540–2).

[2] In this author's experiments, the ratios were 8 : 4, 12 : 6, 16 : 8 and 24 : 12.

these parts will be better memorized, the larger their number (see p. 237), since this must have the effect of reducing the interference between the two parts when they are joined together.

The graph in Fig. 14 shows how D and T_C developed as a function of N (Orbison's research). The curves coincide exactly with his predictions. While curve D (being the difference between the time t_X taken to master the task by the whole method

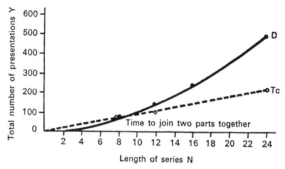

Fig. 14. Curves showing the increasing superiority of the part method over the whole method as the material grows longer. The time taken to join the two parts (the dotted line) increases more slowly than the saving D (difference between learning the task by the whole method and learning the two parts). (After Orbison, unpublished Ph.D. thesis, Yale University, 1944, and Osgood, *Method and Theory in Experimental Psychology*, New York, Oxford University Press, p. 541.)

and the sum of $(t_A + t_B)$ taken to learn the parts separately) rises rapidly, curve t_S (time for joining the two parts together) is a practically linear function. The deviation between the two, zero at N = 8, is greatest at N = 24.

(E) OTHER FACTORS AFFECTING WHOLE AND PART
    LEARNING

The conclusions that can be drawn from Orbison's work clearly demonstrate the part played by the length of the material in the relative efficiency of the part and whole methods, at any rate in the case of the verbal pairs used in this research. Nevertheless, many other variables, which have not yet been satisfactorily studied, do intervene. Only three of these points, requiring further elucidation, will be included here.

The first concerns the phenomena of transfer and interference which may occur in part learning, *particularly when the subject is not familiar with the task given to him.* When a task is divided into several parts A, B, C, . . . N, which are learnt in succession, the experimenter must expect to find between these parts the pro-active and retroactive effects of facilitation and inhibition, usually studied by psychologists in connection with the theory of transfer (see Chapter 13 of this manual). These effects vary as a function of the number of parts, their length and their similarity. One would be quite justified in thinking that the overall result (either positive or negative) of these phenomena must influence the relative efficiency of the part method as compared with the whole method.[1]

The second question directly concerns the joining up of the various parts to form a whole. Whatever the nature of the task, it is reasonable to suppose that the last phase in the part method (i.e. the repetition of A–B–C–D after A, B, C and D have been learnt separately) must involve a certain amount of reorganization of the task, which may prove difficult. The length of time taken over this final phase (or the number of mistakes made in it) may even be greater than the total length of time taken (or the number of mistakes made) in learning the separate parts.[2] It is an established fact that considerable additional practice is required to achieve the criterion of mastery after the various parts have been suitably memorized, and this suggests that the parts do not retain all their individual features when they are integrated into a whole.

Pechstein (1917) studied maze learning by the part method, and he noted that, when the two parts were joined together, what had been the 'beginning' of the second part was no longer the

---

[1] In a study of maze learning by humans, Pechstein (1917) suggested that transfer could account for those cases in which part learning proved to be more efficient than whole learning (results of his research). But Pechstein, in his experiment, used subjects who were not familiar with the task. Using *previously trained* subjects (rats and humans), Hanawalt (1931, 1934) proved that whole learning was more efficient than part learning in this situation.

[2] In one of his experiments on maze learning by humans, Hanawalt (1934) divided the overall exercise time into two unequal portions: 36·9 per cent of the time was spent learning the four parts of the course separately, while 63·1 per cent of the time was used for learning all the parts together. Also in maze learning, Pechstein (1917) demonstrated that 80 per cent of the errors in the part method occurred in this final phase.

familiar 'entry' into a maze that the subject had already crossed, nor did the 'end' of the first part still constitute the 'goal', i.e. the end of the course for humans or the place where the animals found their reward. When the experimenter joins the two parts together, he alters some of the aspects with which the subject has become familiar. As a result, the structure of the whole possesses certain new features which necessitate the adaptation of behaviour. In an extreme case, the task may resemble a new task of a similar nature, rather than a complex composite of portions of the original task.

On the other hand, the whole method ensures a permanent structure of the task from the beginning of learning, and correct responses, once acquired, continue to be the 'right responses' until mastery is attained.

The third point is that of the part played by motivation in whole and part learning. In the case of whole learning, a task often has to be repeated several times before there is any appreciable improvement in retention. Mastery of the whole task is always a more difficult and more distant goal than mastery of the parts. In other words, a subject gains a feeling of satisfaction (which can reinforce correct responses) more quickly from memorizing parts than from memorizing the whole. The principle of reinforcement leads to the prior assumption that the part method will be more efficient (Kingsley, 1946). However, reorganization of the parts within a much larger whole eliminates the 'less distant goals' previously attained. This may result in reactions of frustration, which temporarily reduce a subject's ability and slow down his performance. Of course, in the case of a human being who adopts the part method in order to work progressively up to perfect acquisition of the task, the successive stages present him with secondary goals, which all eventually lead to the final goal.

4   The effect of recitation

In 1907, Witasek observed that learning was faster when a subject recited the material during the exercise, rather than just read it through until he could achieve a perfect oral recitation. Gate (1917) verified the superiority of the recitation method over the reading method in an experiment with children (of 8 to 13 years), who had to learn by heart 16 nonsense syllables and prose passages (short biographies). Each task lasted 9 minutes and was made up, in varying proportions, of a reading time, followed by a recitation time, when they were prompted if they could not remember. In one of the conditions reading took up the whole period. The material was recalled immediately after learning was over and again four hours later.

The results obtained (Table XV) reveal two basic facts: (1) lower percentages of recall by the reading method, which was obviously less efficient than the method combining reading and recitation; (2) recall percentages increased progressively as a function of the length of time allowed for recitation; this applied to both immediate and deferred recall.

TABLE XV

Effect of recitation on memory

	Type of material			
	16 nonsense syllables (Recall percentages)		5 short biographies of about 170 words each (Recall percentages)	
	Immediate	After 4 hours	Immediate	After 4 hours
Whole time devoted to reading	35	15	35	16
Recitation:				
1/5 of the time	50	26	37	19
2/5 of the time	54	28	41	25
3/5 of the time	57	37	42	26
4/5 of the time	74	48	42	26

(After Gates, *Arch. Psychol.*, 1917, **6.**)

However, the reading-recitation method does not seem to have been as efficient in retention of the prose passages. When four-fifths of the practice time was devoted to recitation, recall of the nonsense syllables (4 hours later) was 3·2 times higher than the recall after learning by reading only (also after 4 hours). But this recall was only 1·63 times higher in the same situation for the memorization of the prose passages.

According to Woodworth (1949), this relative inferiority of the reading-recitation method for learning texts can be explained by the difficulty that a subject experiences in distinguishing clearly between reading and recitation: when he rereads a coherent text, he inevitably anticipates what comes next, and so he recites it as he reads it.

There are several reasons for the efficiency of recitation:

(1) the subject who recites the material participates more actively than the subject who merely reads the material passively;

(2) recitation provides a more immediate goal, and so greater incentive for learning, than reading;

(3) recitation gives the subject more control over his own progress, the mistakes he makes and the gaps in his memory. Consequently he can organize his efforts and direct them towards the parts that he has not learnt properly;

(4) recitation also favours the organization of responses by facilitating their formation into groups on the basis of accent or rhythm and by activating meaningful associations. This probably explains why recitation is a more efficient means of learning nonsense syllables (material of an unorganized nature) than of learning texts (highly organized material);

(5) finally, recitation places the subject in a situation, very similar to that of recall (or relearning), in which he will eventually find himself when he takes a retention test.

4   The part played by attitudes, motivation and emotive
    reactions

---

1   Incidental and intentional learning

It is generally accepted that a person can perceive an object, in which he has no interest, many times without remembering any of its characteristics.[1] A person's interest in specific objects

---

[1] The psychologist Sandford (1917) remarked that, although he had read a prayer of 124 words about 5,000 times in the previous 25 years, he could not recite it without a mistake, and he had to be 'prompted' 44 times before he could recall it once perfectly.

largely determines the efficiency of learning, because it produces and maintains a positive attitude towards the requirements of the task.

In daily life, this attitude is encouraged by the subtle play between rewards and punishments accorded, intentionally or otherwise, by teachers, parents or anybody else who upholds standards of social behaviour. An attitude may be self-imposed for a particular, personal reason. For example, a person will learn, of his own accord, to drive a car or will memorize a poem or a song.

However, in many cases, a particular event (a scene from a film, something that happened on holiday, a beautiful view, etc.) may be memorized and retained, apparently unintentionally, i.e. without any *specific* intention of remembering it. This kind of learning occurs in all sorts of situations and tasks. A subject, entering a laboratory for the first time to take part in an experiment, will remember certain features in the room (a photo on the wall, the experimenter's face, etc.), which make up the situation in which he finds himself, but which have nothing to do with the task he is given. When psychologists first studied this question, they used the expression 'incidental learning' to describe memories acquired in this way.

(A) COMPARISON OF THE RELATIVE EFFICIENCY OF INCIDENTAL AND INTENTIONAL LEARNING: THE ROLE OF DEGREES OF ACQUISITION

Intentional learning is usually more efficient than incidental learning in a specific task. Twenty-four pairs of students took part in an experiment conducted by Jenkins (1933). One student in each couple played the 'experimenter', while the other was the 'subject'. All the 'experimenters' had to do was to read a series of 20 nonsense syllables, presented successively and at a regular rhythm (by means of a special device), to the 'subject', who could not see them. The 'subject' was told to learn the material 'by heart'. Once he had achieved the criterion of one perfect recitation, he was asked to return the next day with the 'experimenter' to finish the experiment. The next day they were both asked to reproduce as many syllables as they could remember. The 'experimenters' (incidental learning) recalled an average of 10·8 syllables correctly, while the 'subjects' (intentional learning) recalled 15·9. This superiority of intentional learning over incidental learning has been verified by considerable research, particularly in the study programme undertaken by Postman and his collaborators (with Phillips, 1954; with Adams and Phillips, 1955; with Adams, 1956*a*, 1956*b*, 1960; with Adams and Bohm, 1956*c*).

The first hypothesis which springs to mind in an attempt to explain the greater efficiency of retention resulting from intentional learning is that the instructions given to subjects in this situation engender a learning set, which gives these subjects an advantage over subjects in an incidental, learning situation. The material, used by Biel and Force (1943) in their experiment, consisted of 12 nonsense syllables, printed in six different types. One group of subjects (in the intentional learning situation) were instructed to learn these syllables 'by heart' in 5–6 presentations. Another group (in the incidental learning situation) had the task of estimating the degree of legibility of the different typographical forms during 12 presentations. Immediately afterwards, all the subjects had to reproduce from memory as many syllables as possible. Then, in order to make the two groups equivalent in amount of learning, the subjects in the first group were paired with subjects in the second group who had a similar recall score. This produced two equal groups of 48 subjects whose retention was examined 19 days later by the recall and recognition methods. Table XVI shows the results of the experiment: there was no

TABLE XVI

Recall and recognition resulting from intentional learning and incidental learning

	Intentional learning		Incidental learning	
	Average	σ	*Average*	σ
Immediate recall	6·08	0·36	6·08	0·35
Recall after 19 days	1·92	0·26	2·08	0·22
Recognition after 19 days	7·88	0·26	8·52	0·22

(After Biel and Force, *J. exp. Psychol.*, 1943, **32**, 60.)

significant difference between the mnemonic behaviour resulting from incidental learning and that produced by intentional learning when the amount of learning in both conditions was equal.

(B) INCIDENTAL LEARNING AND ATTITUDES

The amount of learning constitutes a variable which affects both incidental and intentional learning, and the mnemonic behaviour resulting from both types of learning. Other similarities in this behaviour have been discovered in various experiments. One experiment by Postman and Phillips (1955) showed that the curves (relating to the temporal evolution of retention) produced by any sort of learning are always practically parallel. Two other studies by Prentice (1944) and Postman and Adams (1956) verified that retention produced by incidental learning is affected by phenomena of proactive and retroactive interference. The same thing had already come to light *vis-à-vis* material retained after intentional learning.

However, although these similarities show that the same mechanisms function in both cases, they do not explain how or why subjects retain certain elements without being told to do so.

A possible clue to the explanation lies in the hypothesis that attitudes favourable to learning can arise from interaction between the subject and the task he is given. The introspective accounts given by the 24 subjects, who took part in Jenkins's (1933) research (see above) as 'experimenters' in incidental learning, show that 10 of them consciously imposed upon themselves the task of memorizing the syllables at some stage of the experiment. Of course these are *explicit attitudes* which only differ in origin from learning attitudes induced by specific instructions. However, other attitudes, which are to a lesser or greater extent implicit, can also play a part here, but such attitudes are unknown to the subject and, consequently, to the experimenter. As far as it is possible to tell, such *implicit attitudes* can be defined as the 'predisposition to respond selectively to certain aspects of the task, probably acquired in the individual's past' (Postman and Sender, 1946). Far from appearing at random, these attitudes depend on considerable interaction between the subject in an incidental, learning situation and features of the stimuli and the way in which the task develops. By an analysis of the introspective accounts given by the 8 'experimenter' subjects, who felt that they definitely did not try to learn, Jenkins (1933) was able to show that some stimuli had to be noticed, due either to the effect of their position (the first and last syllables in a series) or to the effect of perceptual frequency or frequency of use in the past (a syllable was retained because it seemed more familiar) or to an associative effect (a syllable evoked a meaningful word) or to discrimination on the basis of the partner's behaviour (a particular syllable was always forgotten or reproduced incorrectly by the subject under supervision, this attitude of supervision being linked to the role of 'experimenter'.[1]

The subject's preference for one part of a task is not entirely independent of the dominant attitude induced by the instructions given to him. This emerged from some research done by Postman and Senders (1946). They used a passage from Chekov with 6 groups of subjects. In their instructions, they described the task either as a test of reading speed (condition A: classical, incidental, learning situation) or as material for a memory test to be taken at some later date (conditions B, C, D, E and F). In the second case, features of the task varied from one condition to another, thereby inducing different dominant attitudes. The instructions indicated that the following would be examined:

general understanding of the story (condition B);
retention of the sequence of events (condition C);
details of the contents (condition D);
specific details of vocabulary (condition E);
features of the way the passage was printed (condition F).

After reading the passage, the subjects in all 6 groups answered the same questionnaire of 50 questions (10 questions on each condition). There was a choice of 4 answers to each question, one of which was the correct one. The curves in Fig. 15 represent the performances obtained for each group of 10 questions under all 6 experimental conditions. They show that implicit attitudes

[1] Postman, Adams and Phillips (1955) emphasized this selective aspect of incidental learning in an experiment in which they used nonsense syllables with association values of 0, 33, 66 and 100 per cent. A memory test immediately after the exercise, followed by another 20 minutes later, showed that there was no difference between incidental learning and intentional learning when the association values were high, but a difference favouring intentional learning appeared and increased when the association values were lower.

are compatible with some dominant attitudes, and not with others. For example, general comprehension was favoured when the dominant attitude concerned details of the contents (D),

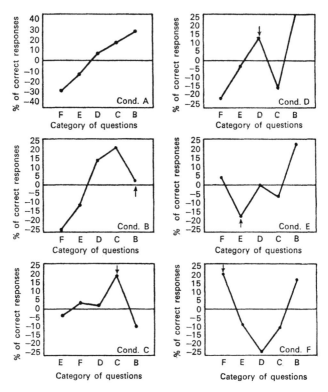

Fig. 15. Variations in relative percentages of correct responses to each category of questions as a function of the dominant attitude induced by the instructions given in the various, experimental conditions. (After Postman and Senders, *J. exp. Psychol.*, 1946, **36**, 157.)

vocabulary (E) and printing (F), but it was not favoured under condition C (retention of the sequence of events), which meant that subjects had to analyse the whole passage, thereby breaking it up into individual pieces. This implicit attitude occupied the same favoured position in incidental learning (condition A). The implicit attitude of retaining details of printing was favoured by the dominant attitude of memorizing details of vocabulary, although the reverse was true of all the other situations. However, the dominant attitude of learning the printing details did not favour the retention of the vocabulary.

Numerous observations of this sort can be made; but none of these effects can be described as 'incidental', if this is taken to mean fortuitous and entirely due to chance. On the contrary, in the light of these experiments, 'incidental' learning would seem to be determined by selective processes through which the subject contrives to retain some other aspect of the task or, more often, by the situation in which he finds himself. Therefore the problem is to find out under what conditions these selective processes, which are really acquired attitudes, can occur and operate. However, this leads to other problems, notably that of the phenomena of 'filtering' on the perceptual and mnemonic level. These phenomena directly concern the questions, raised by Postman and his collaborator, about the constraints exercised by behaviour linked to dominant attitudes (which make the subject concentrate on specific features of the situation) over secondary behaviour (involving other features also present in the situation) which proves to be compatible with the situation's principal activity.

2   A subject's involvement in the task

When a subject is presented with a task and asked to learn it, he can react in a variety of different ways. If the task seems pointless or forbidding to him, he may adopt a passive attitude towards it, or he may even refuse to do it. On the other hand, he may demonstrate a very positive attitude, either because he wants to rid himself of something irksome, or because he really wants to please the teacher, his parents or the experimenter. A subject often feels that he is personally involved in a task, either because he is afraid he will be judged by his performance, or because he hopes to gain some material or moral advantage from it, or because his participation in it conflicts with habits or attitudes which are important to him, etc.

Consequently, experimental research has been into three categories of problems:

(1) The connection between the degree of motivation, learning and memory;

(2) The effect of interrupting a task on its subsequent retention;

(3) The effect of conflict between attitudes acquired and the task's contents on memory.

(A) RELATIONS BETWEEN THE DEGREE OF MOTIVATION, LEARNING AND MEMORY

When the degree of motivation inducing a subject to learn a task increases, the long-term efficiency of memory tends to improve.[1] Heyer and O'Kelly (1949) succeeded in verifying this connection between the degree of motivation and the efficiency of retention. Two groups of subjects (students) participated in the experiment, and their task was to learn a series of 20 nonsense syllables in 5 presentations. The instructions given to one group (low motivation) indicated that the object of the experiment was to standardize the material, while the subjects in the other group were allowed to think that their individual performances would be of interest for the study of the effects of motivation in learning. They were given a memory test immediately after the task, followed by another a week later. The results show that the number of errors was lower and the number of correct reproductions higher when there was strong motivation (Table XVII).

What is the reason for this? The answer is probably that the problems concerning the relations between degree of motivation and efficiency of learning and retention should be compared to the problems produced by the influence of the *general level of activity* of the organism on the speed of acquisition. There is a definite connection between degree of motivation and activity of the organism, since the level of activity rises and performance improves as motivation increases.

Bills (1927) demonstrated that fewer repetitions were required for learning a series of 9 syllables when the task was carried out in a state of muscular tension (experimental group) than when it took place in a normal situation (control group). This facilitation was still obvious three hours after learning, for this group's

---

[1] This connection has been confirmed by a considerable amount of work in animal psychology, although some contradictory results have been obtained. See Hilgard and Marquis (revised by Kimble, 1961) on this subject.

recall scores and savings in relearning were still considerably higher than those of the control group.

TABLE XVII

Development of retention as a function of degrees or motivation during learning

	Weak motivation		Strong motivation	
	Average	σ	Average	σ
Number of errors:				
After learning	8·72	4·92	6·87	5·32
One week later	15·25	4·92	12·52	4·79
Number of syllables correctly				
reproduced				
After learning	13·89	3·96	14·65	4·12
One week later	7·28	5·01	9·41	4·63
Percentages of deferred				
retention	52·40		64·20	

(After Heyer and O'Kelly, *J. Psychol.*, 1949, **27**, 147.)

Nevertheless, in any given task, the favourable effect of the level of activity does not increase indefinitely beyond a certain point. In other words, there is an *optimal* degree of muscular tension beyond which efficiency decreases (Courts, 1939).

An analysis of the relation between degree of motivation and learning and memory would very likely produce the same conclusion. When motivation is too strong, it often brings into play emotive mechanisms, which can disorganize the subject's activity within the task by means of excitation that the organism can no longer integrate, and which can even result in the abrupt cessation of all psychological activity. Obviously learning and memory are at a distinct disadvantage in these circumstances.

(B) THE EFFECT OF INTERRUPTING THE TASK ON MEMORY

In 1927, Zeigarnik undertook a series of studies to verify the hypothesis (put forward by Lewin) that any motivation to perform a task gives rise within the individual to a system of tension which is maintained until the task is accomplished. Thus, if a task is interrupted before the subject has completed it, the system of tension will persist, causing perseveration of the system of mnemonic traces belonging to the task. However, once the subject has completed the task, satisfaction of the need will be accompanied by reduction in tension, and the system of mnemonic traces will have little chance of survival in the absence of tension. This reasoning leads to the assumption that *interrupted tasks will be remembered better than completed tasks.*

In Zeigarnik's experiments, the subjects had to perform a series of 18 to 22 successive tasks 'as quickly and as accurately as possible'. The tasks were very varied, including small mathematical problems, riddles and manual tasks such as modelling clay figures, making cardboard boxes, etc. Half these tasks, chosen at random, were interrupted before the subjects had had time to complete them. At the end of the session, the experimenter asked them to enumerate as many tasks as they could remember. In one group, 26 of the 32 subjects recalled the interrupted tasks better than the completed ones, 3 recalled the completed ones better, and the other 3 recalled them all equally well. A comparison of $\dfrac{\text{the number of interrupted tasks recalled}}{\text{the number of completed tasks recalled}}$ produced an average of 1·9 for a group of 49 students, 2·1 for a group of 45 schoolchildren and 2 for a group of 14 adults, i.e. retention of interrupted tasks exceeded that of completed tasks by 90, 110 and 100 per cent respectively, so these results fulfilled Lewin's predictions.

Taking over Lewin's general theory that an uncompleted task creates in the subject a state of psychological tension, which causes the task to be remembered, Nuttin (1953) put forward the theory that responses to stimuli will be recalled better when their connections have been established within the framework of an uncompleted, composite task than when they have been elaborated in the course of the same task, pursued to completion.

In order to verify his hypothesis, Nuttin gave 71 subjects, whose mother tongue was Flemish, a French text to translate. The text contained several words that the subjects would not know, and they had to ask the experimenter to translate them.

The subjects were divided into two groups of equal, scholastic ability. The subjects in the first group were allowed to finish.

288

their translation, but the experimenter interrupted the work of the subjects in the second group when they reached the third line from the end. These three lines, containing the end of the story, did not include any of the words with which the subjects would not be familiar.

For the next 5 minutes, the subjects in both groups assisted the experimenter in some work he had undertaken. This new occupation provided the excuse for the *temporary* interruption of the second group's work. Each subject was then given a piece of paper on which were written the words whose meaning he had had to ask the experimenter. The subject's task was to reproduce from memory the Flemish words for these French words.[1] The results showed that the percentage

$$\frac{\text{translation reproduced}}{\text{translations requested}} \times 100$$

was 47 per cent for the first group (complete task), whereas it was 77 per cent for the second group (incomplete task), so this author's hypothesis was confirmed.[2]

The Zeigarnik effect has been verified in numerous studies (Ovsiankina, 1928; Pachauri, 1935; Marrow, 1938*a*, and many others), which demonstrated that chronological age (Sanford, 1946), the ratio of completed tasks to incomplete tasks (Prentice, 1943), the time allowed for each task (Pachauri, 1935), the relative difficulty of the tasks (Marrow, 1938) or the positive, negative or neutral significance of the interruptions (Marrow, (1938) are all variables that systematically affect this phenomenon. Nevertheless, the most important variables seem to be those of motivation, together with features of a subject's character and his involvement in the task.

In an experiment conducted by Rosenzweig (1943), the subjects were given two different sets of instructions: while the subjects in one group (low motivation) were told that the object of the experiment was merely for them to gain a better knowledge of some material to be used again later, the instructions given to

---

[1] It should be emphasized that, at this point, the part of the task containing these words had *already* been completed by *all* the subjects. The basic difference between the two groups lies in the fact that the connections (French words–Flemish words) belonged to a task *entirely completed* by the first group, whereas they belonged to a task *that still had to be completed* by the second group.

[2] Two other experiments by the same author (1953), carried out in collective sessions with intervals of 1 and 24 hours, produced similar results.

the other group (high motivation) stressed that an intelligence test would follow. The *results showed that the interrupted tasks were retained better than the completed tasks when motivation was low*, but the performances of the highly motivated subjects showed a slight tendency in the opposite direction, i.e. completed tasks were retained better than interrupted tasks. Glixman (1949) reached a similar conclusion when he introduced three degrees of involvement into the task: the number of interrupted tasks recalled decreased significantly as the subject's involvement increased.

In an attempt to combine all this data in one explanatory system, Rosenzweig (1943) postulated the existence of a double process: motivation related to the accomplishment of the task and motivation related to the defence of the Ego. When the Ego did not feel that it was threatened in a situation, *the tendency to complete the task* predominated and acted in accordance with Lewin's predictions (Zeigarnik's experiment). However, when the individual felt that he was *personally involved* in the performance of the task, *the defence mechanisms of the Ego* intervened to repress the memory of disagreeable experiences, hence the low recall of interrupted tasks which the subject had perceived as failures (for example, the experiments by Rosenzweig, 1943, and Glixman, 1949).

Nevertheless, it would be unwise to assume, on the basis of such an analysis, that a subject always forgets an unfinished task in which he has been *strongly implicated*. A mature individual's natural reaction to failure is to try and succeed by overcoming the obstacles. Sanford (1946) noted a wide variety of reactions to an unfinished task that had been perceived as a failure: repressive mechanisms predominated in some subjects, while the same situation produced a feeling of indignation in other subjects. The latter reaction usually takes the form of the spontaneous resumption[1] of the activity in which the subject felt he failed, in search of the solution (observed by Ovsiankina, 1928; Harrower, 1932). Thus, whether or not involvement in the task is a determining factor of the Zeigarnik effect[2] depends on the character of the individual.

---

[1] The subject returns to the unfinished tasks without being told to do so.

[2] The interested reader will find critical reviews of this question in the works of Prentice (1944), McGeoch and Irion (1952) and Osgood (1953).

(C) THE EFFECT ON MEMORY OF THE CONFLICT
BETWEEN ATTITUDES ACQUIRED AND THE TASK'S
CONTENTS

All the experimental work done so far seems to indicate that learning is slower and forgetting faster when the contents of the task conflict with previously acquired attitudes.

In some research done by Levine and Murphy (1943), two groups of subjects (one pro-communist and the other anti-communist) had to learn two texts, one favourable to the Soviet Union and the other unfavourable to it. The order in which the texts were presented depended on the group of subjects, who had to memorize the two texts in 5 separate sessions, with a week between sessions. At each session, they read the text through twice, and reproduced it 15 minutes later. The development in the retention of the texts was later examined in 5 daily sessions. Table XVIII gives the results obtained.

When the contents of the task conflicted with the subjects' attitude (pro-Soviet text/anti-communist subjects; anti-Soviet text/pro-communist subjects) learning was faster than in the reverse situation (pro-Soviet text/pro-communist subjects; anti-Soviet text/anti-communist subjects), while forgetting seemed to be greater. For example, of the 24·6 ideas in the anti-Soviet text correctly reproduced by the pro-communist subjects at the end of the learning session, only 5·8, i.e. 23·5 per cent, were still retained 5 weeks later; but this percentage was 54 for the anti-communist subjects. The results were confirmed in the case of the pro-Soviet text, and other studies have arrived at the same conclusion (Watson and Hartmann, 1939; Edwards, 1941).

3 The effect of affective reactions on memory

In 1898, Colgrove put the following question to a number of adults: 'Which do you remember more clearly, pleasant or unpleasant experiences?' The replies indicated that pleasant experiences were retained better than unpleasant ones. But this result (which happens to agree with a widely held belief) represents little more than the personal opinion of the subjects questioned, and so has little scientific value.

Several other methods have been employed in the study of

TABLE XVIII

Average number of ideas reproduced correctly as a function of the attitude of the subjects

	Learning					Retention				
	15 min.	1 week	2 weeks	3 weeks	4 weeks	1 week	2 weeks	3 weeks	4 weeks	5 weeks
Anti-Soviet texts										
Pro-communist subjects	6·2	10·0	13·2	16·0	24·6	20	17·6	12·8	8·6	5·8
Anti-communist subjects	10·0	14·8	20·2	26·0	34·4	30	27·2	24·0	20·6	18·6
Pro-Soviet texts										
Pro-communist subjects	16·8	28·4	34·8	42·0	48·0	37	30·6	26·4	22·6	18·8
Anti-communist subjects	14·2	24·4	29·0	35·0	41·0	31	23·4	18·0	15·4	11·4

(After Levine and Murphy, *J. abnorm. soc. Psychol.*, 1943, **38**, 511 and 512.)

this problem. One technique consists of asking subjects to recall all the events that have occurred recently in their personal life, and then to say whether each was accompanied by an agreeable or disagreeable feeling or by a feeling of indifference. Retention of these events is tested several days later. The value of this method, first practised by Kowalewski (1908), is highly debatable, largely because there can be a considerable discrepancy between the affective reaction when the event actually takes place and the affective nature of the memory of it. Consequently the qualitative judgment of the event, when it is recalled, cannot be exactly the same as its hedonic quality, when it was actually experienced. In addition, particularly pleasant or unpleasant events are probably rememorized in the interval preceding the memory test. This would partly explain why they are retained better.

In spite of all the criticisms that can be made of this line of research, it is possible to draw two general conclusions from it:

(*a*) In most cases (Meltzer, 1930; Koch, 1930; Jersild, 1931; Stagner, 1931; O'Kelly and Steckle, 1940), events regarded as pleasant are remembered better than unpleasant events, which are themselves recalled better than neutral events;[1]

(*b*) Generally speaking, pleasant or unpleasant events are recalled better than neutral events.[2]

Two other lines of research have been pursued in the investigation of this problem in traditional, laboratory situations.

The first method (practised initially by Gordon (1905) in the work he did at Würzburg in Kulpe's laboratory) consists of pairing pleasant, unpleasant or neutral sensory stimulations (sounds, smells, colours) with elements that are assumed to be neutral from an affective point of view (words, nonsense syllables, numbers). The subject's task is to associate the appropriate response with each sensory stimulus by means of one of the classical experimental techniques for learning. Retention is tested after a previously determined interval of time. The information obtained by this method has been very disappointing

---

[1] Some experiments (for example, Wohlgemuth, 1930; Cason, 1932) showed no difference between the memory of pleasant events and that of unpleasant events.

[2] In support of this statement, Smith (1921), Jones (1929) and Linch (1932) demonstrated that words producing psychogalvanic reactions of considerable amplitude are usually remembered better than other words. This agrees with Cason's results (1932), but it does not throw any light on the part played by the pleasant or unpleasant affective tone in memory.

(Gordon, 1905, 1925; Heywood and Vortried, 1905; Harris, 1908; Bolger and Tichener, 1907; Ratliff, 1938), since no significant difference has appeared to prove unequivocally that the quality of sensory stimulation has either a favourable or unfavourable effect on memory.

The second line of research concerns meaningful verbal material only: words which are judged to be pleasant, unpleasant or neutral are arranged in series or in pairs.[1] Long-term or short-term retention is examined in recall, recognition or relearning tests. The results obtained show that, in the case of immediate recall, there is little or no difference between the retention of pleasant words and that of unpleasant words (Balken, 1933; Silverman and Cason, 1934), probably because learning is too recent for the selective effect, linked to affective quality, to be produced. However, in the case of deferred recall, most of the results reveal greater retention of pleasant words (Thomson, 1930; Bunch and Wientge, 1933; White and Ratliff, 1934; Barrett, 1938).

The work done by Barrett is particularly interesting in this respect. The author compiled series of 26 words (13 pleasant and 13 unpleasant words), taking great care to choose words of equal frequency (following Thorndike and Lorge). Thirty subjects were given the following tasks in succession: (1) they had to group the words into two categories, depending on whether their affective tone was pleasant or unpleasant; (2) they had to give the 'free' associations suggested by these words (30 seconds allowed for each word); (3) they had to divide the words up again, but into *three* categories this time (pleasant, unpleasant and neutral) on the basis of the context associated with each stimulus; (4) finally, they had to note down the words on a four-

---

[1] Several methods have been used to determine the affective tone of words: arbitrary judgment by the psychologist (Tait, 1913-14; Tolman, 1918), judgment by an independent group of people who do not take part in the experiment (Chaney and Laner, 1929) or judgment by the subjects participating in the experiment (White and Ratliff, 1934; Carter, Jones and Schock, 1934; Carter, 1935, 1936; White, 1936; White and Powell, 1936; Carter and Jones, 1937); some psychologists have even asked the subjects to draw up their own individual lists, either by selecting pleasant or unpleasant words from their normal vocabulary (Thomson, 1930) or by taking words from a list drawn up by the experimenter (Bunch and Wientge, 1933; Cason and Lundgren, 1932). The individual merit of these methods varies considerably. Barrett (1938) combined several of these techniques very intelligently in his research.

point scale as a function of the intensity of their affective tone. One week after this *incidental learning* the experimenter tested their retention. The subjects recalled 54·9 per cent of the pleasant words correctly, but only 39·2 per cent of the unpleasant words.

Some psychologists[1] have used Freud's theory of repression to explain why responses with a pleasant, affective tone are retained better. According to this theory, the inhibition of certain memories results from the activity of the Ego's defence mechanisms. Memories connected with emotions, which are painful or dangerous for the Ego, are thrust out of the consciousness and become unconscious; but they may be reactivated later, if the Ego relaxes its defence mechanisms (for example, during psychoanalysis).

Experimental verification of this hypothesis suggests: (1) that mnemonic responses, which are acquired in a situation likely to engender reactions of anxiety, will be inhibited when recall is attempted in a situation in which the Ego remains alert; (2) that these same responses will be successfully evoked in another situation, which can reduce the efficiency of the Ego's alertness; (3) that there will be no difference in recall when the mnemonic responses are acquired in a situation which does not engender anxiety.

Several experiments, described in a work by Rosenthal (1944), fulfilled all these predictions. In one experiment, 13 adults had to remember lists of verbal stimuli in which 'neutral' words (grass, house, etc.) were combined with nonsense syllables. The subjects took a recall test as soon as they had learnt one list (2 presentations), before proceeding to the next list. The learning sessions were conducted in one of the two following situations: (a) *normal situation:* tasks presented as part of a classical research experiment; (b) *situation engendering anxiety:* tasks presented as intelligence tests. In the second case, the subjects were told whether they had 'passed' or 'failed' in the recall test on the basis of pseudo-norms, ostensibly obtained from subjects in the same population.

A quarter of an hour after each learning situation, the subjects again took two recall tests in succession under one of the following conditions: (1) *experimental condition:* first recall test taken

---

[1] Consult Rapaport (1942) on this subject.

TABLE XIX

Comparison of recall resulting from a situation which engendered anxiety
with recall resulting from a situation which did not engender anxiety

Learning	Experimental condition		Control condition	
	Recall 1 (awake)	Recall 2 (hypnotized)	Recall 1 (awake)	Recall 2 (awake)
Normal situation	9·47	9·69	8·92	9·22
Situation engendering anxiety:				
(a) 'Successful' learning	4·90	5·00	5·00	5·20
(b) 'Unsuccessful' learning	3·30	4·80	3·10	3·30

(After Rosenthal, *J. exp. Psychol.*, 1944, **34**, 375 and 376.)

awake, second test taken under hypnosis; (2) *control condition:* both recall tests taken awake.

Table XIX gives the results obtained in this experiment. Obviously there was very little difference between the average recall figures from learning in the normal situation.

This also applies to the four average figures of recall in the 'successful' tests: the second recall test under hypnosis (experimental condition) did not improve memory any more than the second test taken awake (control) did. On the other hand, with all the subjects awake, recall of mnemonic responses after 'unsuccessful' learning was relatively lower than that following 'successful' learning; but *responses connected with 'failures' increased significantly under hypnosis* (experimental condition: from 3·30 to 4·80). The second recall test taken awake did not produce a corresponding increase (control condition: 3·10 to 3·30).

If the elimination of anxiety under hypnosis really does make the Ego less alert, all the data can be explained by Freud's theory: mnemonic responses, associated with reactions of anxiety, can be inhibited while the Ego remains alert (awake), but they are rendered available again by situations in which the Ego relaxes its vigilance (hypnosis).

5 The role of the organization of the task by the subject

1 The organization of responses into 'groupings'

When a subject is learning a task, he can organize the responses acquired into several separate groups, each containing a certain number of responses. It is as if each group is a cluster of responses, enjoying relative autonomy within the task as this has actually been memorized by the subject. The distinctive feature of this kind of organization is the fact that connections between responses in the same group usually possess a higher power of evocation than connections between responses in different groups. Three kinds of organization, which lead to the formation of groups of responses, will be studied here.

César Florès

When the elements of material are arranged in a monotonous succession, with no apparent organization other than the order in which they follow one another, the subject's activity can consist of regrouping adjacent elements into rhythmic readings of the series. Müller and his collaborators (1894, 1900, 1911, 1913, 1917) were the first to study the properties of these rhythmic groups. Three important empirical rules were discovered:

(*a*) *Associations between elements in the same group are stronger than those between elements in different groups.* In one of Müller's experiments, a series of nonsense syllables was memorized by stressing all the uneven syllables (Á B Ċ D É F Ġ H İ J, etc.).[1] Here the accentuation reorganized the series into successive pairs as follows: Á B/Ċ D/É F/Ġ H/İ J/, etc. After the learning session, the experimenter asked the subject to evoke the syllable directly following each uneven stimuli Á, Ċ, É, Ġ, İ: 50 per cent of the responses were correct and their average latency was 3·1 seconds. However, in the case of the syllables following the even stimuli B, D, F, H, J, only 7 per cent of the responses were correct and the average latency was 7·4 seconds. The logical conclusion seems to be that the pairs AB, CD, EF, GH, IJ, etc. constitute groups whose internal connections are stronger, i.e. more efficient from the mnemonic point of view, than those of the pairs BC, DE, FG, HI, etc.

(*b*) *The evocation of one element in a group tends to favour the reproduction of the other elements in this group.* An analysis of the mistakes made during Müller's experiment (described above) provides data in support of this second rule. When the induction stimulus occupied an *uneven* position in the series, the syllable just before it, which belonged to an earlier group, was only given in error 4 per cent of the time with an average latency of 6·5 seconds. However, when the induction stimulus occupied an *even* position, the syllable just before it, which belonged to the same group, was evoked 38 per cent of the time with an average latency of 3·4 seconds.

The experiment was repeated with lists of syllables in which the stress lay on every third syllable

[1] The letters stand for syllables.

(A B Ċ D E Ḟ G H İ J K L̇, etc.),

producing groups of three. In this case, the presentation of the last element in a group often resulted in the reproduction of all three parts of the group (Ċ→A B C; Ḟ→D E F; İ→G H I).

(*c*) *Groups often possess their own associations which may be different from those existing between their elements.* The experiment which best illustrates this rule employed the derived-lists method of Ebbinghaus. After the subjects had learnt two series of nonsense syllables with trochaic stress $A_1\dot{A}_2A_3\dot{A}_4A_5\ldots A_{11}\dot{A}_{12}$ and $B_1\dot{B}_2B_3\dot{B}_4B_5\ldots B_{11}\dot{B}_{12}$, they had to memorize the following series:

$$(1)\ A_1\dot{A}_2B_3\dot{B}_4A_5\dot{A}_6B_7\dot{B}_8A_9\dot{A}_{10}B_{11}\dot{B}_{12}$$
$$(2)\ A_3\dot{A}_4B_1\dot{B}_2A_7\dot{A}_8B_5\dot{B}_6A_{11}\dot{A}_{12}B_9\dot{B}_{10}$$

Series (1) alternated the pairs in the two original series, but maintained their original positions. The second derived series (2) was composed of the same alternate pairs, but their order had been altered, with the result that savings in series (1) were greater than in series (2). In fact, the number of times the original series had to be read in learning averaged 10·9, while it was 8·6 for series (1) and 10·1 for series (2). This result can be explained by the fact that learning the original series created a connection between each group of syllables and its position in the material. When it retained its position in the derived list, this list was memorized more quickly than when the group occupied a new position.

(B) THE ORGANIZATION OF RESPONSES INDUCED BY THE ARRANGEMENT OF THE MATERIAL

Grouping effects, similar to those just described, can also appear as a function of the material's previous arrangement. Thorndike (1931, 1932) asked his subjects to listen to a long list of 1,304 pairs of words and numbers. Four of these pairs, repeated more frequently than the others, were always *preceded* by the same number: the experimenter always read the number 42 before the pair *Dregs* 91, 86 before *Charade* 17, 94 before *Swing* 62 and 97 before *Antelope* 35. After reading through the 1,304 pairs once, he asked the subjects the following questions: which word came just after 42 or which number came after *Dregs?* The first question, to which the answer was the first part of the following pair, i.e. a word, resulted in only 0·5 per cent of the responses being correct. However, when the stimulus in the question was a word and the response a number, i.e. the second half of the same pair, 35·7 per cent of the responses were correct.

Thorndike obtained the same result in another experiment using phrases: the probability of obtaining from the penultimate word the evocation of the last word in a phrase was significantly higher than the probability of obtaining the evocation of the first word in a phrase from the last word in the preceding phrase.

Other ways of organizing responses, which result from the materials' arrangement, have also been studied. Some psychologists (Binet, 1894; Fernald, 1912; Müller, 1917; Ogden, 1926) presented their subjects with stimuli arranged in squares (squares of letters, numbers or syllables), and their task was to learn the stimuli by reading them in a particular direction (for example, from left to right, one line after another). Having learnt them, the subjects were asked to recite the stimuli in a different order (for example, in columns or oblique lines). This proved to be very difficult and took much longer than reciting the responses in their original order, because the responses to each line of stimuli constituted a group with internal connections which were stronger than the connections between these responses and the responses to the stimuli in the other lines.

(c) THE ORGANIZATION OF RESPONSES BY SEMANTIC
     REGROUPING

This kind of organization results from the subject's verbal habits and consists of regrouping the elements on the basis of common semantic features. Research into this question began comparatively recently, partly because of the increasing interest in linguistic problems in the last few years.

In their study in 1944, Bousfield and Sedgewick had found that, when subjects were asked to give a series of words belonging to a given, semantic category (names of birds or of towns in the United States), sequences of words of similar meaning could be detected within the series of responses reproduced. For example, the series of birds' names contained two sequences, 'hawk, eagle, vulture' (all birds of prey), and 'chicken, turkey, duck, goose' (all domestic birds).

In some later research, Bousfield (1953) wanted to verify whether or not learning and retention of series of words were accompanied by reorganization of the material into sequences of this kind. His material consisted of 15 names of animals, 15 names of people, 15 names of professions and 15 names of vegetables, making a total of 60 words. The average frequencies of use in language of the 4 groups of words were the same (taken from the Thorndike–Lorge tables, 1944). These 60 words were then combined in an 'unpredictable' order, so that the total number of words together, which belonged to the same semantic category, equalled what could reasonably be expected to result from a random selection. This series was read aloud once to a hundred students at the rate of 1 word every 3 seconds. This was followed by a written recall test which lasted 10 minutes. In this test, the subjects were instructed to reproduce the words in the order in which they occurred to them.

The results were analysed by taking the number of 'isolated' words and the number of sequences of several, semantically similar words from each recall sheet. Table XX gives these

TABLE XX

Results of Bousfield's experiment

		Sequences of					
	Isolated words	2 *words*	3 *words*	4 *words*	5 *words*	6 *words*	7 *words*
Subjects	810	261	164	85	38	18	5
Chance	1,452	343	87	18	4	1	0

(After Bousfield, *J. gen. Psychol.*, 1953, **49**, 234.)

results. The first line shows the total number of isolated words and the total number of sequences of 2, 3, 4, . . . , 7 semantically similar words. These figures have to be compared with the figures on the second line, which are estimations of what chance alone would have produced.[1] This comparison suggests:

(1) that the number of isolated words and the number of

[1] Obviously the subjects' regroupings are only of psychological significance

sequences containing two words were lower than the corresponding numbers produced by chance, but that the figures for sequences of 3, 4, 5, 6 and 7 words were clearly higher;

(2) that the difference between the number of groups formed by the subjects and those produced by chance increased more rapidly than the length of the sequences: thus the ratio

$$\frac{\text{number of sequences in recall}}{\text{number of sequences due to chance}}$$

is 1·8 for sequences of 3 elements, but this figure is as high as 18 for sequences containing 6 elements.

Other work in this field has shown that the variation in the relative size of regroupings is directly related both to the duration of learning (Bousfield and Cohen, 1953) and to the words' frequency of usage in language (Bousfield and Cohen, 1955).[1]

2 *Perceptual organization of stimuli: the role of the mode of apprehension in memory*

Obviously every act of memory must result from a perceptual act, since a person can only recall or recognize what has previously been perceived. But perception is not merely a replica of physical reality. A perceptual act usually attributes properties to the stimulus which increase the immediate sensory information. When a person perceives an orange or a tennis ball on a table, it is not just a coloured, spherical shape to him. By identifying an object in this way, the perceptual act places it in a particular category[2] of familiar objects and distinguishes it from objects in

---

[1] The reader who is particularly interested in this problem will find a review of it in the work by Bousfield and Cohen (1955*b*).

[2] Bruner (1958) has been largely responsible for this notion of perception as a process of categorization and inference.

---

in so far as they differ statistically from regroupings produced by chance. Bousfield conducted an artificial experiment in order to obtain estimated figures of what chance would have produced. This consisted of picking series of capsules out of a jar containing 15 blue capsules, 15 red capsules, 15 orange capsules and 15 white capsules. One hundred series were drawn out in this way. The series of capsules were then paired with the series of words evoked by the subjects on the basis of length, so that there were as many series of 12, 13, 14, . . . , 36 capsules as there were series of 12, 13, 14, . . . , 36 words reproduced by the subjects. Finally he took the total number of isolated capsules and of sequences of capsules of the same colour from the series of capsules (100), and these figures appear in the second line of Table XX.

other categories. This process of categorization (or classification of the thing perceived) is of fundamental importance to memory, because it favours the mnemonic integration of the stimulus by associating it with a response or group of familiar responses which form an organized mental scheme; and this scheme, in turn, can partly determine the reproduction of the stimulus. Consequently the 'coloured, spherical' shape will be recalled differently, depending on whether it is perceived as an orange or as a tennis ball.

Most of the work on this question has used visual figures (geometrical forms, drawings of objects, etc.). Bartlett (1916) presented Fig. 16 to his subjects for a short time.

Fig. 16

Immediately after the presentation of this stimulus, one subject, who had assimilated it to 'two carpenter's squares put together', could reproduce it correctly. However, two other subjects, who had perceived it as a 'picture frame', reproduced it as in (*a*) and (*b*).

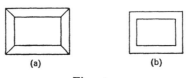

(a)   (b)

Fig. 17

Similar examples, which Gibson obtained with adults (1929), are given in Fig. 18. In all these examples, the reproduced stimuli resembled the objects evoked mentally more closely than they resembled the original stimulus. Similarly, when a geometrical figure with gaps is perceived as a complete form, the gaps are sometimes closed up in reproduction (phenomenon of closure). The phenomenon of the reorganization of the stimulus, due to the mental scheme with which it has been associated, has been given various names by different authors: 'normalization'

303

(Wulf, 1922), 'reduction to a conventional form' (Bartlett, 1932) and 'assimilation to an object' (Gibson, 1929). This phenomenon appears in the results of the quantity of research into modifications in memory with the method of reproduction.[1]

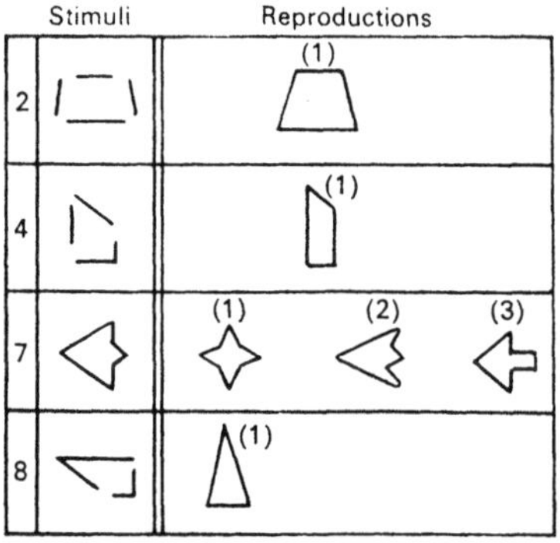

Fig. 18. Examples of assimilation to an object in mnemonic reproductions of figures:
    Stimulus 2: assimilation to a 'lamp-shade';
    Stimulus 4: assimilation to 'a letter-box';
    Stimulus 7: assimilation to 'a star' (1), 'a bird' (2), 'an arrow' (3);
    Stimulus 8: assimilation to 'an acute-angled triangle'.
    Note the phenomenon of 'closure' in the reproductions of stimuli 2, 4 and 8. (After J. J. Gibson, *J. exp. Psychol.*, 1929, **12**, 13.)

Rather than attributing a global signification to a stimulus, which tends to assimilate it to a familiar object, an analytical approach can be adopted. When a figure lends itself to this kind of approach, the subject is induced to analyse the stimulus in geometrical terms. Several authors (including Kuhlmann, 1906; Gibson, 1929) discovered, by studying their subjects' introspective reports, that this mode of apprehension favoured retention of the analysis rather than the actual figure. Consequently the relative accuracy of the mnemonic reproduction was largely determined by how adequate the analysis was (in relation to the features of the figure) and how precisely the subject remembered it.

If a figure is too complex and too far removed from any familiar

[1] The works of Philippe (1897), Kuhlmann (1906), Meyer (1913), Brown (1935), Zangwill (1936) and Hanawalt (1937), among many others, should be quoted in addition to the research already mentioned.

figure or object for the immediate establishment of a schema, its memorization will require the maximum effort in perceptual structuration. Piéron's research (1914-19) showed the problems encountered in the apprehension of stimuli of this kind. His subjects had to learn one figure composed of 10 straight lines which intersected at various points (Fig. 19). The figure was

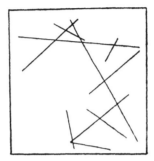

Fig. 19. Diagram of lines used by Piéron for the study of learning and retention. (After Piéron, *Année Psychol.*, 1914-19, **21**, 134.)

successively presented for periods of 5 seconds, while the subjects had to try and draw it in the 2-minute intervals between presentations. The task was pursued until the first correct reproduction of the stimulus. Piéron observed how complex a subject's activity was, when faced with a task of this kind. The subject usually located the figure's most obvious features (the long lines) which he organized into a 'frame' for all the secondary elements (the short lines). After numerous additions, omissions and corrections, the reproductions gradually attained a high degree of likeness to the original stimulus (see Fig. 20). The subsequent memory of the figure depends both on conserving the visual image and on remembering the verbal analysis, as well as the exploratory movements of the eyes and the kinaesthetic movements associated with drawing. (The relative importance of these factors varies from one subject to another.) Finally, no matter what mode of apprehension a subject uses, his reproduction of the stimulus must gradually become a reconstruction, based only on what is still available, as his memory of the original figure fades. The first reconstruction is based on the principal elements remembered, but the following reproductions will diverge from the original. There will be various alterations (lines evened out, reversed, transposed or left out altogether), which may simplify or complicate the original figure. Then, as time passes and the memory of the structuration activity fades, the number of details recalled will decrease. The subject will

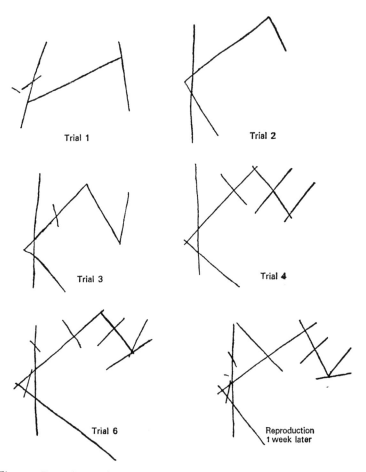

Fig. 20. Learning and mnemonic reproduction of the diagram of lines in Fig. 19. Note the appearance of a simple schema in the second trial. In the following trials, the subject has added lines to this basic schema. By the 6th trial, all 10 lines have been acquired and only minor alterations are needed to achieve maximum likeness to the original. (After Piéron, *Année Psychol.*, 1914–19, **21**, 141 and 143.)

fumble, begin again, and work very slowly with numerous stops, because he is not sure, with the result that the reproduction gradually disintegrates and becomes unrecognizable.

3 Associative behaviour and changes in memory

A cause-and-effect relationship between a subject's perceptual activity and the phenomena of mnemonic distortion has been established from the study of the learning and memorizing of visual figures. But these phenomena of distortion may have a completely different origin: a subject's habits, attitudes, interests and traits of character probably alter memory to an equal degree, either because they already have a distorting effect on the perceptual act, or because they act *a posteriori* at the moment when the mnemonic behaviour actually occurs.

On the level of associative behaviour in classical, verbal learning, Florès (1964) has demonstrated that, when words from everyday language are associated with meaningless, verbal stimuli, *the acquired habits, represented by the literal-phonetic properties of these words, partly determine mnemonic recognition,* either positively by favouring the choice of the correct stimuli, or negatively by inducing the choice of the wrong stimuli. In this experiment, 41 adult subjects had to memorize a series of 23 meaningless, two-syllable words by trying to associate them with words in the French language that had the same literal and phonetic characteristics. Each stimulus was presented four times for 6 seconds. The subjects wrote down the French word evoked by each stimulus, or R, standing for *rien* (nothing), if they could find no association. After the task, the subjects spent 5 minutes doing a different task before they took a recognition test. Each item in this test was composed of 6 stimuli of the same type, only one of which belonged to the verbal series learnt. In some of these items, the correct stimulus (for example, TAJER) was placed near another stimulus, identical or very similar to it phonetically, but with one different letter (for example, TAGER), while all the other stimuli were new to the subjects (for example, BIJOZ, BIGOZ, JENAK, JEMAK). The results of this recognition test (Table XXI) show (*a*) that identifications of correct stimuli were highest when an association's literal structure included the literal element distinguishing the correct stimulus from the incorrect stimulus most similar to it (the word '*trajet*', associated in learning with the stimulus TAJER, favoured recognition of this stimulus, because 'trajet' contains the letter J which distinguishes it from the incorrect stimulus TAGER);

TABLE XXI

Distribution of choice of stimuli in the recognition test as a function of their associations

Relation between association and stimuli	Recognition percentages		
	of correct stimuli	*of similar stimuli*	*of different stimuli*
Association included:			
(a) Letter distinguishing correct stimulus	95·6	2·3	2·3
(b) Letter distinguishing similar stimulus	68·7	29·5	1·7
Stimuli not associated with anything in learning	75·2	11·1	13·6

(b) that correct identifications of stimuli were significantly less when an association's literal structure included the literal element distinguishing the similar stimulus from the stimulus actually memorized; this decrease in the number of correct choices was accompanied by an increase in the number of mistaken recognitions involving the similar stimulus (the word '*étagère*', associated in learning with the stimulus TAJER, acted against recognition of this stimulus, favouring instead the incorrect identification of TAGER, because '*étagère*' contains the letter G, which belongs to TAGER); (c) between these two extreme cases came the percentage of correctly identified stimuli which had not been associated with anything in the task; while the proportions of stimuli similar to correct stimuli and entirely new stimuli in the incorrect identifications made were roughly the same as in (a) and (b).[1]

[1] The information obtained from this research has been confirmed by another study (Florès, 1964) in which the subjects did not find their own associations. Instead associations were imposed upon them in a learning session (prior to the experiment). The object was to make available to the subjects words in their own language, which they could later associate with stimuli (nonsense syllables) that they had to memorize.

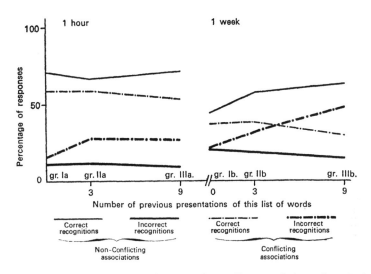

Fig. 21. Graphs showing influence of specific associations (words in language) presented with verbal stimuli (nonsense syllables) on mnemonic identification (recognition) of these stimuli after 1 hour and 1 week. The experiment was conducted as follows: 6 groups of subjects were given the task of memorizing 16 syllables (1 presentation only). In learning, the subjects in 4 of these groups (II*a*, III*a*, II*b* and III*b*) had to associate these syllables with 16 French words, *previously* made available by means of 3 oral presentations (II*a* and II*b*) or 9 oral presentations (III*a* and III*b*). The process of association was directed by the experimenter who read out the corresponding word as each syllable appeared on a screen. Eight of the words incorporated the stimulus (FIC difficulty, PEK Pekin), while the other 8 conflicted with it (ZEN xenophobe, DEB adept). Groups I*a* and I*b* were observers with no instructions to form associations. All 6 groups' retention was examined in the same recognition test 1 hour *or* 1 week after learning the syllables.

The results in the graphs show that: (1) when there was a literal conflict between the given association with a stimulus, there was a tendency to identify incorrectly the stimulus whose literal features were most like those of the association (XEN instead of ZEN, DEP instead of DEB); this effect increased significantly after 1 week as a function of the degree of availability of the associations, measured indirectly by the number of previous presentations of the words; (2) when the given association with a stimulus included its literal features, correct recognition was more favoured by the association, the longer the interval of time (better after 7 days than after 1 hour) and the more readily available the association. (After Flores, 'Intermediary processes in memory', unpublished research thesis.)

It has proved possible, as a result of this demonstration of the determining influence exerted by association on mnemonic choice of stimuli, to predict how this phenomenon should evolve in time. In the research just described, *newly memorized responses* (syllables) were associated with *familiar responses* (words), acquired by the individual in the distant past and used frequently since. Therefore these two categories of responses must evolve differently, since the learning of syllables in a relatively short task can only produce unstable, mnemonic responses which tend to become less available as time passes; whereas words (associations) are stable language habits, which can be reproduced easily in response to adequate, external excitation, i.e. perception in the recognition test of the stimuli with which they had been associated previously or similar stimuli with similar features. Since this reactivation of the association in the presence of the stimulus concerned acted, in turn, on the subject's choice of stimuli, it seemed probable that the positive effect (identification of the correct stimulus) or the negative effect (identification of the incorrect stimulus) of this process would increase in time through the interaction of a double phenomenon: the growing probability of the evocation of the associations in the recognition test, combined with the fading retention of the stimuli. This hypothesis has been experimentally verified in some further research by the same author (see the note to Fig. 21).

4 Intellectual habits and memory

In his work, *Organizing and Memorizing*, Katona (1940) made a distinction between learning acquired by repetition and learning resulting from an intellectual analysis, similar to that observed in solving problems. There is considerable basis for such a distinction, but it must not be regarded as a radical dichotomy, since activities related to these two modes of learning, far from being incompatible, can occur almost simultaneously in many tasks.

In one of Katona's experiments, the experimenter wrote the following series of numbers on the blackboard:

$$2\ 9\ 3\ 3\ 3\ 6\ 4\ 0\ 4\ 3\ 4\ 7$$
$$5\ 8\ 1\ 2\ 1\ 5\ 1\ 9\ 2\ 2\ 6.$$

The subjects in the first group (I) were told that the numbers were not presented at random, but that a rule had been observed in order to obtain the series.[1] Their task was to find out what this rule was. The subjects in the second group (II) were told to memorize the numbers in groups of three (2, 9, 3; · · · 3, 3, 6; etc.). *All* the subjects were allowed the same amount of time, 3 minutes, after which they went straight on to their first recall test (written reproduction of the numbers), followed three weeks later by a second similar test. Table XXII gives the results obtained.

TABLE XXII

| | | Percentage of subjects who made | | | |
	N	a perfect repro- duction	1 to 6 mistakes	7 to 18 mistakes	19 to 24 mistakes
Group I: Learning the rule:					
(a) Immediate recall	29	38	27	25	10
(b) Deferred recall (3 weeks)	26	23	23	39	15
Group II: Learning by rhythmed repetition:					
(a) Immediate recall	30	33	20	40	7
(b) Deferred recall (3 weeks)	23	0	0	26	74

(After Katona, *Organizing and Memorizing*, p. 189.)

In immediate recall, 38 per cent of the subjects in group I and 33 per cent of the subjects in group II reproduced the series correctly. But, when it came to deferred recall, 23 per cent of the subjects in the first group could still reproduce the series without mistakes, while none of the subjects in the second group were able to do this.

The discovery of the guiding principle behind the series favoured its long-term reproduction, but the two learning situations varied considerably in perception of the object of the task and its significance and in activities leading to acquisition and

[1] Here is the rule for obtaining the successive numbers: add numbers 3 and 4 alternately, beginning with the first number in the second line: $5 + 3 = 8$, $8 + 4 = 12$, $12 + 3 = 15$, . . . , $43 + 4 = 47$.

actualization of the responses. Mnemonic reproduction from rhythmic learning involved retention of a sequence of 24 numbers in a particular order. However, the subject who analysed the arithmetical relations within the material had only to remember the rule and the first element in the series to achieve the same result,[1] so reproduction became a *reconstruction* on the basis of the systematic application of a principle. This is one of the distinctive aspects of a very high level of mnemonic activity.

5 Changes in memory and the theory of form

According to the theoreticians of the Psychology of Form (*Gestalt*), physical, physiological and psychological phenomena can be described in terms of whole structures or complete forms with isomorphous, functional properties (Köhler, 1929; Koffka, 1935). This isomorphism is linked to the processes of equilibration, themselves isomorphous and independent of all experience, which determine the organization of structures belonging to these three levels of reality. By analogy with systems of physical forces, the general principle governing these equilibration processes would be as follows: when, within a system of forces, there exists a state of disequilibrium generating tensions, a process takes place which tends to reduce these tensions spontaneously by re-establishing the equilibrium on the basis of a realignment of forces. The law of 'good form' expresses the effects of this dynamic activity: of all the forms possible, the one perceived is the 'best', because it unites in the best way the qualities of regularity, simplicity and symmetry, all features of 'good form'.

Such a concept, in which clusters of mnemonic traces are regarded as biophysiological *Gestalten*, leads to the following hypotheses: (1) when the form learnt is perfectly balanced, so is its cluster of traces, and it has maximum stability, guaranteeing the fidelity of its long-term retention; (2) when the form learnt does not attain the criteria of 'good quality', the equilibrium of the cluster of traces will be unstable, *so it will undergo alterations to produce greater equilibrium. Gestalt* psychologists (in particular, Koffka) suggested two separate processes to explain this phen-

[1] Katona found that the mistakes made by the subjects in group I were connected with forgetting the first number in the series rather than the rule, which the subjects remembered clearly for a considerable length of time.

omenon of equilibration: (*a*) an equilibration process spontaneously generated within a cluster of traces by its own disequilibrium; (*b*) an equilibration process through interaction between the recently elaborated cluster of traces and another, older and more stable system of traces, which tends to assimilate the new one. But, in both cases, the form reproduced or recognized should contain more than the original form, since clusters of traces and mnemonic behaviour are isomorphous.[1]

However, the predictions of this theory have not been confirmed by any of the relevant studies (Gibson, J. J., 1929; Brown, 1935; Zangwill, 1937; Hanawalt, 1937, using the reproduction method; Hebb and Foord, 1945; George, 1952, using the recognition method). The results do not show any systematic compulsion towards a 'better' form on the part of the forms recognized or reproduced. When such a development did occur, it was only an isolated example of alteration among many others. In any case, most of these changes can be explained by the subject's reactions to the task, his perceptual, verbal or intellectual habits or his analytical or interpretative attitude towards the stimuli, as well as by artefacts of the experimental method used.[2]

This complex activity on the part of the subject favours the assimilation of the most recent stimuli with the most familiar schema, thus explaining the role of previously acquired experience on the level of learning and mnemonic behaviour. In the light of the information available, this explains qualitative modifications of memory and phenomena of task organization (described in the preceding paragraphs) in the most economical way. It also avoids reference to highly speculative theories of the mechanisms of a physiological reality about which very little is known.

[1] *Gestalt* psychologists explain forgetting in the same way: when the properties of a learnt form deviate considerably from 'good form', the processes of equilibration can no longer function and the cluster of traces disintegrates, producing forgetting. This makes forgetting an extreme case of learning chaotic forms.

[2] This occurs in the use of the method of successive reproductions (Wulf, 1922; Allport, 1930; Perkins, 1932; Hall, 1936) which favours systematic alterations, because, as time passes, each reproduction is increasingly based on the previous reproduction and on evocation of the mental representation made of it. But, even with this method, alterations in favour of better form do not belong to any one category (Gibson, 1929). See Woodworth (1949, p. 121) on this subject.

313

6 Memory, forgetting and reminiscence

---

1 *How memory develops in time*

(A) THE WORKS OF HERMANN EBBINGHAUS

Ebbinghaus was the first psychologist to study the effects of time intervals on memory. Ebbinghaus was a meticulous experimenter and a very enthusiastic subject. He had already prepared material on nonsense syllables (2,300 syllables according to Woodworth, 1949), and he took series at random from this material for use in his experiments. In order to establish his famous curve of forgetting, he learnt some 1,200 series, each made up of 13 syllables; he read and reread each series to the beat of a metronome (speed: 2·5 seconds per syllable) until he could recite it from memory twice in succession without hesitating. Then, after a pause of 15 seconds, he would learn another series, always keeping to the same pattern. He would carry on like this until he had learnt 8 series at each session.

After a certain length of time, he would relearn each of the 8 series until he reached the same level of proficiency as before. The unit of comparison which he used to calculate the savings in relearning was the total time taken on the learning session (after deducting the pauses of 15 seconds each). For each interval of time needed for the establishment of the curve, he began the experiment again several times with different series.

The curve in Fig. 22 shows the effect of the amount of time after learning on the savings obtained; it shows that the accuracy of retention decreased rapidly in the first hour after learning; this rapid decline was clearly followed by a phase of slowing down, and the curve levels out until the fall is very slight.

Several studies have verified this gradual slowing down, although there is some disagreement on certain points, particularly on the speed and the importance of the initial drop (Finkenbinder, 1913; Luh, 1922; Boréas, 1930) and on the precise moment at which this drop occurs (Piéron, 1913). However, it is quite likely that these divergences of opinion are only due to differences in the conditions under which the experiments were carried out, and in the material and subjects used.

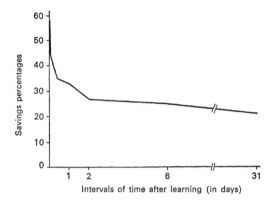

Fig. 22. Forgetting curve obtained by Ebbinghaus using the method of savings in relearning. (After Ebbinghaus, *Über das Gedächtnis*, Leipzig, Duncker and Humblot, 1885.)

The most valid objection to Ebbinghaus's research seems to have been put forward by Piéron in 1913. This objection was aimed at the method used, i.e. examining the effect of time on memory in the period immediately following learning. As Ebbinghaus memorized 8 series of 13 syllables in every learning session, each series was affected by many interferences, arising from other series learnt, with the result that, by the time the eighth had been learnt, the mnemonic responses of the first series could no longer be recalled. The rapidity and size of the immediate drop could then be explained by the inhibiting effect of interference produced by successive learnings of similar material.

To support his criticism, Piéron carried out an experiment in which a single series of 50 figures was learnt for each interval of time. There were five different intervals (7, 14, 28, 60 and 120 days), and the author used 5 series composed of the same stimuli (the 10 numbers 0, 1, 2, 3, . . . 9, repeated 5 times) in 5 different orders.

Only one subject took part in the experiment: he learnt the material in successive readings, separated by intervals of 2

315

minutes, partly spent in attempts at recitation. The task continued until the subject achieved his first perfect recitation (the 50 figures recalled in the right order). Then, after the appropriate interval of time, the subject relearnt the series, following the same procedure, after he had recited all that he could still recall.

It is interesting to compare Piéron's results (Fig. 23) with those obtained by Ebbinghaus (Fig. 22). Whereas, under Ebbinghaus's experimental conditions, the decline in retention was

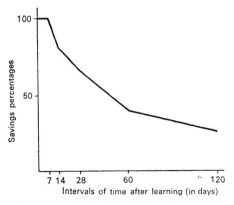

Fig. 23. Forgetting curve obtained by Piéron by means of the method of savings in relearning. (After Piéron, *Année Psychol.*, 1913, **19**, 178.)

immediate and very rapid. Piéron's research revealed a phase during which memory remained stable without apparent deterioration. The accuracy of memory only decreased at the end of this phase, rapidly at first, and then more slowly at an exaggerated and negatively accelerated rate. Piéron's results raise fewer problems than those of Ebbinghaus, since they contradict neither the phenomenon of reminiscence (see page 342) nor the studies that appear to show that the decline in retention (after a variety of tasks under different conditions) was not as immediate as that noted by Ebbinghaus.

(B) COMPARATIVE STUDY OF HOW MNEMONIC
    BEHAVIOUR DEVELOPS IN TIME

The first method used to study the development of memory in time was that of relearning, but other methods were soon employed for the same purpose, in particular, those of recall, reconstruction and recognition.

Luh's work (1922) probably constitutes the most exhaustive comparative study (to date) of the different, mnemonic behaviour resulting from these methods. Here is an outline of his experimental work: series of 12 nonsense syllables were learnt by the anticipation method to a criterion of the first entirely correct trial (each syllable presented for 2 seconds, with an interval of 6 seconds between consecutive trials). After intervals of 20 minutes, 1, 4, 24 and 48 hours, the subject's retention was examined either by the relearning method, which produced two scores, i.e. the amount of recall by the anticipation method (number of correct responses in the first relearning trial) and the time saved in relearning, or by the free-recall method (written reproduction of the responses in any order), followed by a recognition test (identifying 12 correct syllables out of 24 presented) and a reconstruction test (the correct stimuli were presented in any order and the subjects had to put them back into the right order). All the subjects participated in the experiment under all these conditions.

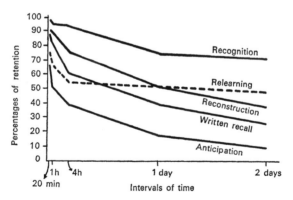

Fig. 24. Forgetting curve measured by the written recall, anticipation, recognition, relearning and reconstruction methods. (After Luh, *Psychol. Monogr.*, 1922, **31**, no. 3, 22.)

The curves in Fig. 24 were established on the results of this work. They reveal that, whatever method was used, the efficiency of mnemonic behaviour showed a negatively accelerated decrease as the length of the interval of time increased. Recognition was always higher than recall.[1] Recall efficiency varies with the method of testing: the number of responses, reproduced without regard to their associative connections (free recall), was always higher than the number of responses evoked in connection with their respective stimuli (recall by anticipation). The curve of savings in relearning is obviously very different from the other curves, since it rapidly evens out after a sudden drop (from the 4-hour intervals onwards, its fall becomes almost imperceptible). The results of a series of studies by Bunch (1936, 1941*a*, 1941*b*, with McCraven, 1938) partly explain this difference. Two different phenomena, which are closely linked in savings in relearning, are obviously quite separate in the residual effects of learning.

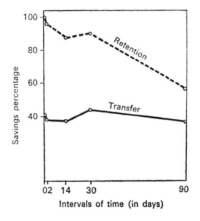

Fig. 25. The dotted curve shows the development of savings in relearning a task (Peterson's problems of rational learning). The other curve shows the development of savings in practice from learning a second similar task (transfer effect). (After Bunch, *J. comp. Psychol.*, 1936, **22**, 332.)

The first is the *mnemonic effect* of the learnt material (retention of nonsense syllables, words, path through a maze, etc.), which gradually fades as time passes; the second is a *transfer effect*, the gradual acquisition of the skill used by the subject in performing

[1] There is a positive correlation between efficiency of recall and efficiency of recognition, both for short-term retention (Achilles, 1920; Postman, Jenkins and Postman, 1948; Philip and Peixotto, 1949) and for more long-term retention (several days) (Florès, 1958*a*).

the task. The latter seems to be responsible for part of the savings in relearning. Bunch (1936) succeeded in separating these two effects by making two different groups of subjects learn tasks 0, 2, 14, 30 and 90 days after they had learnt a similar task, while other groups of subjects relearnt the original task. *The transfer effect*, unlike the mnemonic effect, apparently *remained practically constant for long periods.* This means that there is always a risk of overestimating the mnemonic phenomenon, measured by savings in relearning, thereby falsifying the pattern of its evolution in time.[1]

2 Phenomena of interference between tasks

(A) RETROACTIVE INTERFERENCE

Retroactive interference is a diminution of the retention of task A, resulting from learning another task B, interpolated between task A and the memory test. This phenomenon, discovered by Müller and Pilzecker in 1900, has been the subject of a number of studies. The experimental plan by which it can be studied follows this schema:

Experimental group	Learning task A	Learning task B	Recall and re-learning: task A
Control group	Learning task A	Rest period	Recall and re-learning: task A

A quantitative estimate of *absolute* retroactive interference can be obtained by calculating the difference: Control group recall–Experimental group recall; while *relative* retroactive interference is given by

$$\frac{\text{Control group recall–Experimental group recall}}{\text{Control group recall}} \times 100$$

[1] Woodworth pointed out quite rightly that, in order to remedy this, it would be better to calculate real mnemonic savings by comparing the number of trials (or the time) needed to relearn the task with the number of trials (or the time) taken to learn another (equally difficult) task, rather than with the number of trials required to learn the original task.

Retroactive interference is produced by the interaction of many variables. The variables that have been specifically studied are: (*a*) The similarity between the two tasks; (*b*) their respective degrees of learning; (*c*) the importance of the amount of material used; (*d*) the level of activity: memory and sleep.

(*a*) *The role of similarity between the original task and the interpolated task.* It is generally agreed that, if learning task A is followed by learning another similar task B, retention of task A will decrease to a greater extent, the higher the degree of similarity between the tasks.

Research by McGeoch and McDonald (1931) clearly illustrated this relationship. Their subjects had to learn the first task, composed of a series of 11 adjectives (5 trials), by the anticipation method. The interpolated task B (10 trials, each lasting 10 minutes) consisted of memorizing one of the following 5 sets of material: (1) a series of 11 adjectives, synonyms of the adjectives in the first series; (2) another series of 11 adjectives, antonyms of those in the first series; (3) a series of 11 neutral adjectives; (4) a series of 11 nonsense syllables; (5) a series of 11 numbers containing 3 figures. The interpolated task was followed by relearning the first task. The experiment also included an additional condition (rest), which differed from the other conditions in the nature of the subjects' occupation during this 10-minute interval (reading funny stories). Four scores per subject were obtained: (*a*) Recall 1: number of words correctly anticipated in the first relearning trial; (*b*) Recall 2: number of words correctly anticipated in the second relearning trial; (*c*) Relearning 1: number of repetitions required to attain the criterion of one perfect reproduction; (*d*) Relearning 2: number of repetitions required to attain the criterion of three perfect reproductions. Table XXIII gives the average scores and their distribution.

These figures show that *recall was lower and the number of trials for relearning higher, the greater the degree of similarity between the interpolated task and the original task.* Further research by the same authors (1931) and by Johnson (1933), employing different techniques, produced similar results.

The similarity of material in these experiments was semantic, but the results are equally valid for similarity of form on the basis of the number of common, identical elements; for example, when two tasks are composed of 3-consonant syllables, and the

TABLE XXIII

Average recall and relearning scores and their distribution

	Recall 1		Recall 2		Relearning 1		Relearning 2	
	Average	σ	Average	σ	Average	σ	Average	σ
Rest	4·50	0·83	6·50	0·63	4·58	0·66	5·17	0·72
Synonyms	1·25	0·49	4·17	0·65	7·33	0·91	9·08	1·34
Antonyms	1·83	0·55	4·42	0·45	6·67	0·80	7·00	0·89
Neutral	2·17	0·70	5·00	0·75	5·17	0·59	6·67	0·73
Syllables	2·58	0·64	5·42	0·38	4·50	0·46	7·17	1·02
Numbers	3·68	0·72	7·58	0·68	4·42	0·53	5·08	0·56

(After McGeoch and McDonald, *Amer. J. Psychol.*, 1931, **43**, 582.)

similarity between them depends on the presence or absence of common consonants (Melton and von Lackum, 1941).

Other studies, using material arranged in S–R pairs, revealed a distinction between similarity of *stimuli* in both tasks and that of their respective *responses.*

In this connection, it is worth comparing the results obtained by two researchers (Gibson, 1941, and Hamilton, 1943) who used the same material and experimental techniques. In both experiments, the stimuli in task A were meaningless drawings (material elaborated by Gibson), while their responses were nonsense syllables. The stimuli in the interpolated task B were identical to those in task A under one experimental condition (condition 1), while they had three decreasing degrees of similarity under the other three conditions (conditions 2, 3 and 4). The last condition (condition 5) for the control group incorporated a rest period between learning and relearning task A. The only difference between the two experiments lay in the responses in the interpolated task. Gibson's responses in task B were nonsense syllables, *different* from those acting as responses in task A, whereas Hamilton used *identical* syllables as responses in tasks A and B.

Fig. 26 shows the results of these experiments: *when stimuli and responses were varied in the interpolated task, there was an effect of retroactive interference which was greater, the higher the degree of similarity between the stimuli in the two tasks, and which reached its maximum point when the stimuli were identical* (Gibson's experiment, confirmed by the work of McGeoch and McGeoch, 1937, and Bugelski and Cadwallader, 1956).

However, *when (under the same conditions) the stimuli varied, but the responses remained identical in both tasks, there was an effect of retroactive facilitation which diminished as the similarity between stimuli decreased* (Hamilton's experiment).

But there have been few experiments which systematically varied the *degree of similarity of the responses*, while maintaining the identity of the stimuli. The information obtained by Bruce (1933), Osgood (1946) and Young (1955) all shows that, in this case, *the amount of retroactive interference tends to diminish as the similarity between the responses in the two tasks increases.*[1]

---

[1] Only one experiment (Bugelski and Cadwallader, 1956) produced the opposite result, but the method used may have prejudiced the results by not

Similarity of material used in the tasks is not the only feature which can produce effects of interference or facilitation. In some very interesting research, Gibson (E. J.) and Gibson (J. J.) (1934) succeeded in separating similarity relating to material from similarity connected with the *operations* of performing the tasks. The original task A (lasting 2 minutes), common to all the experimental conditions, consisted of learning 10 pairs of consonants.

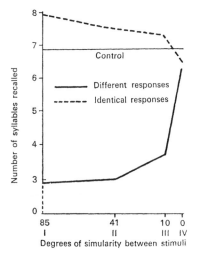

Fig. 26. Comparison of the evolution of retroactive effects when the responses in the two tasks differed (Gibson's experiment), and when they remained identical (Hamilton's experiment). Stimuli varied in degrees of similarity. (After Hamilton, *J. exp. Psychol.*, 1943, **32**, 370.)

The interpolated task B (lasting 3 minutes) involved one of the following activities: (1) learning a second series of consonants (similar material and operation); (2) learning a series of paired numbers (similar operation, different material); (3) crossing out particular pairs of consonants (different operation, similar material); (4) crossing out paired numbers (different operation and material); (5) looking at photographs (control group). Recall of the first task was lowest (37 per cent of the material) when operation and material were similar; it was highest for the control

ensuring the same degree of learning for both tasks (Postman and Riley, 1959, p. 287).

group (86 per cent). Between these two figures, percentages of recall, in ascending order, were as follows: 62 per cent (similar operation, different material); 63 per cent (different operation, similar material); 76 per cent (different operation and material); so retroactive interference was highest with joint similarity of operation and material.

Other studies have shown that retroactive interference will be greater: (1) when the material is presented in the same way in both tasks (either visually or aurally) rather than when it is presented differently (first visually and then aurally, or *vice versa*) (Nagge, 1935); (2) when the methods of memory testing are the same for both tasks (recall *or* recognition) rather than when they are different (testing the first task by the recall method and the second by the recognition method, or *vice versa*) (Jenkins and Postman, 1949); (3) when the attitude induced by the first task is used in the second rather than when it is altered in the latter (Postman and Postman, 1948); (4) when both tasks are learnt awake *or* hypnotized rather than when one task is learnt awake and the other hypnotized (Nagge, 1935). Generally speaking, it would appear that any situation which favours the 'isolation' of the two tasks (*Gestalt* school) or their differentiation (neo-associationist school) tends to reduce the amount of retroactive interference, thereby improving the relative availability of mnemonic responses.

(*b*) *Degree of learning of the original task and degree of learning of the interpolated task.* When the degree of learning the original task is increased, while the degree of learning the interpolated task remains constant, recall of the original task increases in efficiency. But, in order to obtain a satisfactory estimate of retroactive interference, this increase in recall of the experimental group should be compared with that of a control group (for whom the interpolated task has been replaced by a rest period). *The relative amount of retroactive interference will decrease steadily as the criterion of acquisition of the first task becomes higher.* This relation, known to Müller and Pilzecker in 1900, has been verified by various experiments, notably those of Robinson (1920) with series of nouns, McGeoch (1929) and Postman and Riley (1959) with series of syllables, and Briggs (1957) with pairs of adjectives. Briggs's research (1957) was comprised of 16 experimental conditions which combined 4 degrees of learning the original task A

(2, 5, 10 or 20 trials) with 4 degrees of learning the interpolated task B (2, 5, 10 or 20 trials), in addition to 4 'control' conditions, one per degree of learning the first task. The material was composed of series of 10 pairs of adjectives. Seventeen and a half minutes elapsed between learning and relearning task A. This interval was partly spent in performing task B (experimental conditions) or in a rest situation ('control' conditions). Table XXIV gives the average recall and percentages of retroactive interference obtained.

TABLE XXIV

Average number of correct responses in the first relearning trial (Recall) and percentage of retroactive interference

Number of trials for learning the interpolated task B		Number of trials for learning the original task A			
		2	5	10	20
0 (control)	Recall	3·25	4·94	7·19	9·44
2	Recall	1·94	2·38	5·44	7·88
	% RI	*40·3*	*51·8**	*24·3*	*16·5*
5	Recall	0·94	2·12	4·19	6·44
	% RI	*71·0*	*57·0*	*41·7*	*31·7*
10	Recall	0·94	2·06	3·12	4·75
	% RI	*71·0*	*58·2*	*56·6*	*49·6*
20	Recall	0·94	1·62	3·06	4·38
	% RI	*71·0*	*67·2*	*57·4*	*53·6*

(After results obtained by Briggs, *J. exp. Psychol.*, 1957, **53**, 61.)

As a function of degrees of learning task A, all these figures develop in accordance with the rule just elaborated, regardless of the criterion of acquisition of the interpolated task B (with the possible exception of the IR percentage marked by an asterisk).

If the degree of learning task A is kept constant, but the degree of learning the interpolated task B is varied, the development of retroactive interference appears to become more complex than under the previous conditions. Certainly both *absolute* and and *relative* retroactive interference tend to increase as the degree of acquisition of the second task rises. Briggs's results (given above) are a clear example of this phenomenon, which has been confirmed by McGeoch (1932, 1936), Melton and Irwin (1940), Thune and Underwood (1943) and Postman and Riley (1959), with a variety of materials.

Nevertheless, some of the results of these studies seem to suggest that, beyond a certain degree of learning (or, more precisely, of overlearning) the interpolated task, the absolute and relative differences between recall of the control and of the experimental situations tend to decrease slightly, marking a regression of retroactive interference. This phenomenon sometimes appears more clearly in the development of retroactive interference on the relearning level. Thus, in some research by Melton and Irwin (1940), several groups of subjects had to memorize a series of 18 nonsense syllables by the anticipation method in a succession of 5 trials. Then, while one group remained in a rest situation, the other groups learnt a second series of 18 syllables to various criteria (5, 10, 20 or 40 trials). Finally all the groups relearnt the first task (criterion: 2 correct trials in succession), the number of correct anticipations in the first trial providing a recall score for each subject. The figures in Table XXV show that interference on the recall level had tended to diminish slightly by the time the criterion for the interpolated task reached

TABLE XXV

Development of recall and relearning as a function of degrees of learning the interfering task

Degrees of learning task B	Recall		Relearning	
	Averages of task A	Relative retroactive interference (in percentages)	Average no. of trials	Relative retroactive interference (in percentages)
0 (rest)	5·58		12·5	
5 trials	2·04	63·4	13·6	8·8
10 trials	1·33	76·2	14·6	16·8
20 trials	0·92	83·5	14·9	19·2
40 trials	1·54	72·4	12·3	+1·6

(After the results obtained by Melton and Irwin, *Amer. J. Psychol.*, 1940, **53**, 183 and 184.)

40 trials, while interference on the relearning level had practically disappeared at this point.

A comparison of these two effects of interference is very revealing. Although the availability of responses may be considerably weakened when they have to be evoked, the action of the inhibitory processes responsible for this reduced availability rapidly disappears in relearning, since prolonged practice of the interpolated task has produced a clear distinction between the two tasks, thereby reducing the risk of confusion.

(*c*) *The importance of the amount of material.* If the number of elements in the original task is increased, while the number in the interpolated task is kept constant, retroactive interference decreases slowly, but steadily (results obtained by Robinson and Heron, 1922, with nonsense syllables, and by Robinson and Darrow, 1924, with numbers containing 3 figures). But, as McGeoch and Irion (1952) pointed out, this diminution of interference is linked to the greater difficulty encountered in memorizing long tasks, which require more practice than short tasks in order to achieve the same degree of proficiency. This means a higher degree of learning, leading to a greater resistance to interference (see p. 236).

Vice versa, the amount of retroactive interference rises when the number of elements in the original task remains constant, but the interpolated task increases in length. In an experiment by McGeoch (1936), the original task consisted of learning a series of 16 adjectives, presented 8 times. This was followed by the acquisition of a second series of 8 *or* 16 adjectives, presented 4, 8 or 16 times, depending on the experimental conditions. Recall and relearning the first task took place 20 minutes after learning. The results show that interpolation of the series of 16 adjectives diminished recall efficiency of the original series to a greater extent than interpolation of the series of 8 did. This was so, no matter how many times the series were presented.

If, instead of varying the length of the second task, several tasks of a similar nature and length are introduced, there will still be interference which will increase rapidly as a function of the number of interpolated tasks (Twining, 1940; Underwood, 1945).

(*d*) *Retroactive interference and the level of activity: memory and sleep.* Although most of the control situations, which are used for comparisons to prove the appearance and amount of retroactive interference, are called 'rest' situations, this is really a euphemism. In fact, these situations involve some occupation of an entirely different nature, entailing a new attitude and, often, a lower level of activity. Nevertheless, these occupations very efficiently fulfil their purpose, which is to 'distract' the subject during a period of time that he could otherwise use to repeat the original task. Such situations usually produce better retention than interfering situations (during which the subject has to memorize a second task, similar to the one already learnt). Even so, they do not ensure perfect memory, since some forgetting will still occur under these conditions, and this will increase with the length of the interval of time. Presumably this forgetting can be explained equally well by either the theory of the spontaneous disappearance of retention or by the neo-associationist theory of interference, provided that all the activities produced by learning are included (see p. 335). One approach to this problem consists of varying the subject's level of activity during the time separating learning from the memory test. Changes in memory have been compared in two extreme situations: during natural sleep and during wakefulness, the latter spent performing ordinary, everyday activities (Heine, 1914; Jenkins and Dallenbach, 1924; Dahl, 1928; Spight, 1928; Van Ormer, 1932).

The study made by Jenkins and Dallenbach (1924) provides an excellent summary of the most important results obtained in this field.[1] Two subjects, H and Mc, who were not aware of the object of the study, were given the task of memorizing 10 series of nonsense syllables to the criterion of the first perfect recitation. Retention was tested by the recall method after intervals of 1, 2, 4 or 8 hours which were spent either in sleeping or in everyday activities. These intervals followed the experiments in an unpredictable order. The subjects slept in the laboratory, and learning followed by sleep began between 11.30 and 1 o'clock at night, i.e. when the subjects were ready to go to bed (one experiment per night). Daytime learning took place between 8 and 10 o'clock,[2] after which the subjects were free to carry on with their

---

[1] The reader who is particularly interested in this question should consult Van Ormer's critical review (1933).

[2] With a few exceptions (one per interval and subject) when learning took place between 2 and 4 o'clock in the afternoon. The object of these exceptions was to verify the variations in performances connected with the time of day.

328

normal activities. All the experimental sessions took place in the same laboratory which was near the 'dormitory'. Each subject participated 8 times in each of the 8 conditions. The curves in Fig. 27 show how recall developed after intervals of sleep and

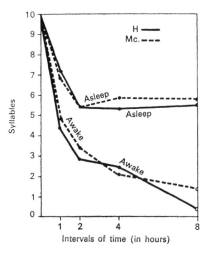

Fig. 27. Development through time of the number of syllables recalled after intervals asleep and intervals awake. (After the results obtained by Jenkins and Dallenbach, *Amer. J. Psychol.*, 1924, **35**, 609, and McGeoch and Irion, *The Psychology of Human Learning*, p. 422.)

intervals of wakefulness. Three facts merit attention: (1) there was a decline in retention under the two principal experimental conditions (wakefulness and sleep), but the efficiency of recall was always higher after a period of sleep than after the same period of time spent awake; (2) the initial drop in retention (intervals of 1 and 2 hours) was always more marked in a state of wakefulness; (3) from 2 to 8 hours after learning, recall continued to decrease in a state of wakefulness, while it appeared to remain fairly constant after a period of sleep. Van Ormer's results (1932) with the savings method confirm the third fact. Everything demonstrated by Jenkins and Dallenbach (and all the other researchers mentioned) suggests that the ordinary activities of everyday life tend to weaken the availability of mnemonic responses and to accelerate forgetting. The elimination of these activities in sleep slows down the process of memory deterioration. This theory, largely

César Florès

expounded by McGeoch and Irion (1952) is not the only one possible. Sleep may also improve memory by favouring the 'consolidation' of mnemonic traces, while everyday activities disturb this process (Woodworth and Schlosberg, 1954).[1]

(B) PROACTIVE INTERFERENCE

Proactive interference means a diminution in the retention of task A, due to previously learning task B. Whitely discovered this phenomenon in 1927. The experimental plan by which it can be studied is as follows:

| Control group | Rest | Learning A | Rest, recall and relearning A |
| Experimental group | Learning B | Learning A | Rest, recall and relearning A |

Proactive interference can be estimated by comparing recall (or relearning) in the control group with that of the experimental group.[2] This phenomenon is present whenever the first group's retention exceeds that of the second group.

There have been fewer studies of proactive interference than of retroactive interference. Nevertheless, certain general facts have emerged concerning the following variables:

(*a*) *The degree of learning in the previous task.* When the degree of learning the interfering task increases, proactive interference also increases. In a study by Underwood (1949), the preliminary

---

[1] But not one of these theories, however probable they may seem, really accounts for the drop in recall in the sleep situation. Several explanations have been suggested: that the change from wakefulness to sleep is not instantaneous, so mental activity during this transitional phase could be responsible for part of the forgetting registered (Jenkins and Dallenbach); that the subjects had to memorize numerous series (61 series for J and 62 series for Mc) between which proactive interference must have been produced (Underwood, 1957); that sleep is only a state of reduced activity which does not necessarily mean a complete absence of all psychological activity (dreams). There is one other possibility, namely, the fading of traces.

[2] Methods for calculating proactive interference are the same as for retroactive interference. Absolute, proactive interference = Control recall − Experimental recall. Relative, proactive interference =

$$\frac{\text{Control recall} - \text{Experimental recall}}{\text{Control recall}} \times 100$$

330

Memory

task B (a series of 10 pairs of adjectives) was learnt by the anticipation method to criteria of 3, 8 or 10 correct anticipations,
followed in the last case by 5 additional trials (overlearning
situation). Task A (10 pairs of adjectives whose second elements
differed from those of the preceding series) was memorized by
the same method until the subjects achieved a trial containing at
least 6 correct anticipations. Underwood conducted two experiments, identical in all the details outlined, but which varied in the
amount of time separating learning from relearning task A. This
interval was 20 minutes in experiment I and 75 minutes in
experiment II. Table XXVI shows the average amount of recall,
and an examination of these figures reveals an inverse ratio between the degrees of learning of the interfering task and the
recall averages of task A.

TABLE XXVI

Average recall obtained after 20 minutes and 75 minutes
in a situation of proactive interference

Conditions	20 minutes Recall averages	σ m	75 minutes Recall averages	σ m
Control group	4·75	0·33	2·54	0·33
3 anticipations	4·17	0·32	2·67	0·27
8 anticipations	3·33	0·36	2·38	0·29
10 anticipations + 5 additional trials	3·33	0·28	1·67	0·24

(After Underwood, *J. exp. Psychol.*, 1949, **39**, 29.)

Another study by Atwater (1953), also on learning pairs of
adjectives, but to more demanding criteria of learning, supple-
mented Underwood's findings by showing that proactive interference could appear on the level of the relative speed of relearning (relearning was slower, the higher the degree of acquisition of B).

The introduction of an increasing number of preliminary tasks
(rather than the variation of the degree of learning task B) produces similar results. In fact, *proactive interference will be higher,
the larger the number of preliminary tasks* (Underwood, 1945).

331

(*b*) *The degree of learning in the principal task.* Postman and Riley (1959) demonstrated with nonsense syllables that, when the degree of learning the preliminary task B[1] remained constant, the number of correct anticipations in the first relearning trial of task A increased as a function of this task's degree of learning (5, 10, 20 or 40 trials). This improvement in retention corresponds to a decrease in proactive interference.

(*c*) *Similarity of the two tasks.* The research carried out by Melton and von Lackum (1941), already described in connection with retroactive interference (see p. 320) included a study of proactive interference. They compared recall in the first relearning trial of a series A of 10 three-consonant syllables without any preliminary learning (control situation) with recall of this same series A when it had been learnt either after a series B of similar syllables or after a series B of dissimilar syllables.[2] Practice (5 trials) remained the same for all the experimental conditions. Retention was tested 20 minutes after learning A. Proactive interference appeared to be higher when A and B were similar (relative proactive interference: 51 per cent) than when they were dissimilar (relative proactive interference: 25 per cent). This difference in interference was maintained throughout the first 4 relearning trials.

None of the studies carried out so far seem to have systematically modified the relative similarity of the stimuli, while retaining the same responses (experimental schema: learning task B $(S_1—R_1)$; learning task A $(S_2—R_1)$; relearning task A $(S_2—R_1)$, However, Morgan and Underwood (1950) varied the semantic similarity between the responses in 2 tasks (5 variations), but retained the same stimuli (experimental schema): learning task B $(S_1—R_1)$; learning task A $(S_1—R_2)$; relearning task A $(S_1—R_2)$. The two tasks, composed of 12 pairs of adjectives, were learnt to the criterion of 7 correct anticipations out of 12 under all 5 practice conditions. The second task was relearnt after 20 minutes. The results show that *proactive interference tended to decrease when the degree of similarity between responses increased.*

---

[1] The authors verified the general application of this law by using 4 different degrees of learning task B (5, 10, 20 or 40 trials) and by varying the degree of learning the principal task A for each of these degrees.

[2] Series A and B were similar when the three-consonant syllables were made up of the same letters. They were dissimilar when the respective syllables were composed of different letters.

Fig. 28 illustrates this relation by showing how the number of correct anticipations in the first 3 relearning trials developed as a function of degrees of similarity between responses in both tasks.

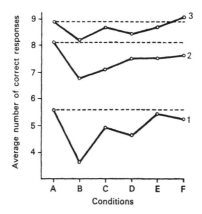

Fig. 28. How proactive interference develops as a function of similarity between responses in both tasks. Condition A is the control situation. Conditions B, C, D, E and F represent increasing degrees of similarity between responses. Curves 1, 2 and 3 correspond to the first, second and third trials in relearning. All the dots below the lines show the effects of proactive interference. (After Morgan and Underwood, *J. exp. Psychol.*, 1950, **40**, 592.)

3 General theories of forgetting

Generally speaking, there are two principal theories of forgetting.[1] The first considers that forgetting results from the inactivity of neurophysiological mechanisms brought into play in learning, so lack of practice is the main cause of the disappearance of mnemonic traces, i.e. the organic substratum of memory. Forgetting is of a spontaneous nature, and responses acquired and their connections gradually fade away if they are not reactivated by repeated stimulation. This theory, put forward by Thorndike (1921)[2] in the United States, has been severely

[1] The necessarily limited scope of this chapter does not allow a detailed account of the various theories elaborated. The reader should consult the more specialized works of McGeoch and Irion (1952), Hilgard (1956) and Osgood (1953). Gomulicki's monograph (1953) traces the historical development of the theory of mnemonic traces from ancient times to the present day.

[2] This is implied by a corollary of Thorndike's law of exercise: 'When, for

criticized as a result of psychological observations made since (Cason, 1924; McGeoch, 1932). The major criticism has been its lack of generality; retention can sometimes remain efficient for long periods without practice, or there may even be an improvement in memory (phenomenon of reminiscence), and a decrease in the availability of mnemonic traces and forgetting may be explained by factors other than inactivity.

However, these criticisms are not sufficient to invalidate the theory, even though they emphasize its limitations by pointing out that other mechanisms probably intervene in forgetting. Nine decades of research have not produced any other theory which offers a complete explanation of the development of memory. As far as contemporary studies are concerned, a dispersion process of the biophysiological after-effects of learning does not seem to be incompatible with the processes of inhibition, reactivation or maintenance which accelerate or slow down the deterioration of a mnemonic trace. Indeed this possibility is not discounted by many neurophysiologists and psychophysiologists who are concerned with the problem today.

The second theory postulates that forgetting results from active processes which have the effect of lessening the availability of mnemonic responses. A distinction has to be made between two sub-classes within this general theory. One group contains *psychological* theories elaborated on the level of behaviour: for example, neo-associationist theories which suggest that the causes of forgetting lie in internal interference from within the task or from activities before or after (proactive or retroactive interference) learning the responses whose development is being studied. The other group incorporates *psychophysiological* theories which deduce the nature of the neurophysiological processes in memory from observations on the behavioural level. Most of these theories seem a little premature in view of the limited information available on neurophysiology in this field. Nevertheless, the theory proposed by Müller and Pilzecker (1900) merits consideration.

An examination of the fundamental hypotheses, arising from these theories, follows.

---

a time, a connection of a modifiable nature is no longer made between a situation and a response, the strength of this connection decreases so that, when this situation recurs, this response is less likely to be associated with it.'

(A) PSYCHOLOGICAL THEORIES OF INTERFERENCE

(a) The theory of competition between responses. McGeoch's theory, reviewed by Melton and Irwin (1940), postulates that effects of interference (and, consequently, of forgetting) result solely from competition between the responses belonging to the two tasks. This competition occurs on two levels:

(1) In a situation of retroactive interference, when the first task A is recalled and relearnt, the responses belonging to the second task B intrude and are substituted for the correct, mnemonic responses. These intrusions account for *some* of the retroactive interference. Similarly proactive interference is caused by the intrusion of preliminary task B's responses when the principal task A is recalled and relearnt.

(2) Still in a situation of retroactive inhibition, responses from the first task are given incorrectly in learning the second task B. Since they are no longer correct in B, they are not reinforced as they were in A. *The non-reinforcement of these responses favours their inhibition, thereby diminishing the probability of their being evoked later.* This phenomenon would only account for a part of retroactive interference and would play no role at all in proactive interference.[1]

Both these cases of intrusion have been observed under experimental conditions. As far as retroactive interference is concerned, McKinney and McGeoch (1935) demonstrated that the number of intrusions was clearly higher in the direction: interpolated task (B)→recall of original task (A) than in the direction: original task (A)→learning interpolated task (B).

Intrusions of the first type (B→recall A) only account for a relatively small part of the total forgetting resulting from retroactive interference (25 per cent in the experiment mentioned). When the degree of learning the interpolated task B varies, the number of intrusions increases, and very quickly reached its maximum before *diminishing* as the acquisition criterion for B

---

[1] Logically, when tests are arranged in the order B A A (situations of proactive interference), the appearance of responses from the interfering task B in learning the principal task A should also result in the inhibition of the responses from B. In fact, these interfering responses are inhibited, which reduces the probability of their appearing later, i.e. when responses from A are recalled. Consequently this phenomenon helps to reduce the total amount of proactive interference.

becomes higher (Melton and Irwin, 1940; Thune and Underwood, 1943; Underwood, 1945). However, when task B is overlearnt (see p. 325), the total amount of retroactive interference *continues to increase*, under the same conditions, and then sometimes diminishes. This difference between the total amount of retroactive interference and the number of intrusions observed (substitutions for correct mnemonic responses) poses a problem for theoreticians who have had to admit that the number of intrusions actually observed forms only part of the total, *implicit* intrusions (responses from task B, mentally evoked by the subject, but not uttered, because he realizes that they are wrong) constituting the other part.

Intrusions of the second type (A→learning B) appear in the first learning trials of the interpolated task B. There are not very many of them, and they soon disappear (Thune and Underwood, 1943; Osgood, 1948). Some experimental results (Melton and von Lackum, 1941; McGeoch, 1943; Underwood, 1945; Bugelski, 1948) suggest the existence of an inhibitory process through non-reinforcement, connected with these intrusions. This idea seems worth retaining as a hypothesis.

Melton and Irwin (1940) had already postulated that such a process ('factor X') must account for that part of retroactive interference which cannot be explained by explicit intrusions in the memory test. But this mechanism must play a secondary role, since it is only capable of causing a very limited number of unstable intrusions.

(b) *The theory of generalization-differentiation.* The theory of competition between responses demonstrates the psychological processes that actually occur in situations of retroactive interference, but it does not make use of all the information available. In this respect, Gibson's theory (1940) is certainly an improvement, not only because it is better conceived, but also because it has proved better able to predict what actually happens in experiments.

This theory applies the concepts of generalization and differentiation (see Chapter 11), by analogy with conditioning, to the phenomena of learning and retention of series of successive stimuli or S–R pairs. Considered in this perspective, the risk of interference between stimuli belonging to a task or between stimuli belonging to two or several different tasks would depend, in the first place, on the degree of similarity between these stimuli: the risk will be higher, the greater the similarity of the stimuli, and *vice versa*. The concept of generalization covers this probability of interference.

The second half of this theory (differentiation) would explain the elimination of generalization effects. The longer a task, the better differentiated stimuli in a series will be. Similarly one task will be better differentiated than another, the higher its degree of learning in comparison with this other task.

This theory also suggests, by analogy with conditioning, that the effects of differentiation diminish towards the end of a task as a result of the 'spontaneous recovery' of generalization effects. The speed of this recovery correlates with the amount of generalization effects in learning.

The application of these hypotheses to the phenomena of learning and memory suggests the following (all of which have been demonstrated experimentally):

(1) Learning a series will take longer and its subsequent retention will be less efficient, the greater the similarity of the stimuli. Previously used stimuli (for example, words) will be learnt faster than new stimuli (syllables), because they benefit from a certain degree of differentiation.

(2) In the case of series of successive elements, recall of task A in a situation of retroactive or proactive interference will diminish as an inverse function of the degree of similarity between the stimuli in this task and the stimuli in the interfering task B.

But the generalization effect, produced by similarity of stimuli, on the efficiency of mnemonic processes, is not necessarily a negative one; so, in situations involving retroactive interference and series of elements in S–R pairs, it can be predicted that:

(3) When similarity between stimuli is high and responses in both tasks are *identical*, the generalization effect will favour retention of the first task A, because the subject will tend to respond to the stimuli in this task with the responses he gave in task B. Consequently there will be no retroactive interference, but an effect of facilitation which will be more marked, the greater the similarity of the stimuli.

(4) However, by the same reasoning, it can be predicted that, when stimuli are similar and responses *different*, there will be an

effect of retroactive interference which will increase with the relative similarity of the stimuli.

In addition, effects resulting from the relative length of the practice period in the principal and the interfering task can be correctly predicted by this theory. Other hypotheses, relating to the development of phenomena of interference, have been put forward, but research has so far produced such contradictory results that nothing definite can really be stated at this stage.

(*c*) *The limitations of psychological theories of interference.* The theory of generalization and differentiation is compatible with the theory of competition between responses. Indeed it is really complementary to it, since it defines the conditions in which phenomena of competition should appear. As a theoretical model, it suggests a basis for the experimental study of processes of interference on the *level of reality for which it was elaborated.* In this respect, it would profit from the addition of further hypotheses on the phenomena of generalization and differentiation in the same continuum of responses.[1] But any extension of its application to more complex behaviour remains problematical. In the final analysis, it seems unlikely that more highly developed, mnemonic behaviour (e.g. memory of past events or of intellectual concepts) can be reduced to a simple, explanatory schema which was, after all, inspired by the most elementary classical conditioning.

Finally, because this theory lies strictly within the confines of behaviourism, it tends to ignore the intermediary activities with which an individual reacts in a learning situation (structural activities of a perceptual, associative or logical nature) and the subsequent effects of these activities on mnemonic behaviour. It also tends to reduce forgetting to the phenomena of interference alone, thereby neglecting the part played by psychophysiological factors in the efficiency and variation of mnemonic processes.[2]

[1] A recent evaluation of Gibson's theory can be found in the work by Cofer (1961), Chapter 8 by Underwood. Chapter 7 of the same work (by Postman) gives an up-to-date picture of the theories of interference.

[2] In this connection, it is worth noting that McGeoch, foremost exponent of the theory of competition between responses, interpreted forgetting as the basic result of the processes in retroactive *interference.* Nevertheless, none of the work inspired by him has succeeded in producing a satisfactory explanation of forgetting based solely on retroactive interference, so Underwood (1957) attempted to reformulate the problem by considering *proactive interference* as the major cause of deterioration in memory. In fact, from a statistical point of view,

(B) THE PSYCHOPHYSIOLOGICAL THEORY OF MÜLLER
AND PILZECKER

Müller and Pilzecker (1900) considered that nervous activity engendered by learning did not cease immediately after the task, but continued for a while (probably a short while), weakening all the time. Any other activity that occurred during this period would disturb it and cause forgetting.

This hypothesis has been used to explain the phenomena of reminiscence (see p. 342) and the favourable effects connected with distribution of practice and sleep and rest situations. It can also be used to predict that retroactive interference will be greatest when learning the first task is immediately followed by the interpolated task, although this has never been absolutely verified. Some researchers have found no systematic relationship between retroactive interference and the length of time between the first and the second task (Robinson, 1920; Archer and Underwood, 1951). Results obtained by other researchers seem to suggest that interference effects increase when the second task is interpolated just before retention of the first task is tested (McGeoch, 1933; Müller, 1937; Newman, 1939; Newton and Wickens, 1956).

Nevertheless, it would be foolish to dismiss the theory of Müller and Pilzecker purely on the basis of this contradictory information. It may be that the tasks generally used in laboratory experiments do not involve activities that are capable of disturbing the physiological phenomena (put forward by these authors) sufficiently to demonstrate (on the behavioural level) effects of interference which would prove the existence of such phenomena.

However, considerable clinical observation has clearly demonstrated that, when certain events producing severe repercussions on the nervous system occur *immediately* after a perceptual act, which is likely to produce a memory under normal conditions, there is a striking mnemonic deficiency: for example, in cases of

---

interfering responses are more likely to belong to the whole group of responses already available to an individual (acquired and used by him in the past), than to the limited number of new responses that he has been able to acquire in the short space of time between learning and memory testing under laboratory conditions. However, an even more important criticism can be made of this theory, namely that it tends to ignore all the other factors (psychological, psychophysiological, neurophysiological) that can affect the development of mnemonic behaviour.

retrograde amnesia following cerebral trauma or electric shock treatment when there is often a permanent absence of any memory of the few seconds or minutes preceding the accident or shock.[1] It seems in order to assume that these physical trauma must play a role in the etiology of such memory disturbances, because (on the neurophysiological level) they upset a phase in the establishment of memory which is essential to its permanent fixation.

A recent study by Pearlman, Sharpless and Jarvik (1961) proved very informative in this connection. Ten groups of rats were trained to press a lever in order to obtain water. After this task, the subjects from 8 of these groups (7 experimental groups and 1 control group A) were placed in a situation in which they had to learn an avoidance reaction to an electric shock which passed through the lever and the water pipe. The subjects in other groups (control groups B and C) did not receive this treatment. Instead they were anaesthetized either by ether (group B) or by pentobarbitone sodium (group C). The subjects in the 7 experimental groups were anaesthetized in the same way under *one of the following conditions*:

—Ether:
—10 seconds after the shock (Anaesthesia obtained in 35 sec-
— 5 minutes after the shock onds. Consciousness recovered in
—10 minutes after the shock about 10 minutes.)

—Pentobarbitone sodium:
—10 seconds after the shock (Given intravenously in a propor-
— 5 minutes after the shock tion of 30 mg. per kilo of weight.
—10 minutes after the shock Anaesthesia, lasting about 1 hour,
—20 minutes after the shock obtained in 10 seconds.)

Twenty-four hours *after the electric shock*, the rats from the experimental groups and the control group A (who had not been drugged) were replaced in the cage for testing their retention of the avoidance reaction. The animals from control groups B and C were treated in the same way 24 hours *after the administration of the drug* in order to find out what effect the anaesthetics had had upon conservation of the reaction of pressing the lever.

[1] Examples of these cases can be found in the works by Delay (1950) and Ritchie Russell (1959). Such cases of amnesia also occur after an epileptic fit or an anoxic state.

Table XXVII gives the percentage of reactions of pressing the lever obtained from the animals in the different groups in the last phase of the experiment. The percentages were obtained from a comparison with the average number of reactions in the last 4 training sessions (i.e. prior to the administration of the shock and

TABLE XXVII

Percentages of reactions of pressure on the lever
obtained when retention of the avoidance reaction was examined

Time between shock and anaesthetic	Ether	Sodium pento-barbitone	Control group A (Shock, but no anaesthetic)
Control groups B and C (anaesthetic, but no shock)	100	98	
10 seconds	36	76	2
5 minutes	17	48	
10 minutes	4	23	
20 minutes		1	

(After Pearlman, Sharpless and Jarvik, *J. comp. physiol. Psychol.*, 1961, **54**, 110.)

the anaesthetic). These percentages are inversely proportional to retention of the avoidance reaction. In other words, a high percentage of reactions of pressing the lever signifies that the avoidance reaction has been profoundly disturbed, while a low percentage shows that it has retained most of its strength.

An analysis of these results shows: (1) that anaesthetics had no effect on the conservation of a reaction whose acquisition had been well consolidated (control groups B and C); (2) that the avoidance was conserved perfectly when the animals who received the electric shock were not subsequently anaesthetized (control group A); (3) *that anaesthetics disturbed the avoidance reaction when they were administered after an interval of 10 seconds, and that the effect of this disturbance decreased as the length of the interval increased.* This last result conforms to the hypothesis of Müller and Pilzecker: an anaesthetic would disturb the acquisition of a response, if administered during its period of consolidation, but administration after this period would have no effect.[1]

4 Reminiscence

This term is generally understood to mean the recall of mnemonic responses, which a subject had been unable to reproduce earlier, when the intervening period has not been spent in additional practice of the task.

The phenomenon of reminiscence has been studied in connection with two specific questions, both concerning the problem of quantitative modifications in memory. The first of these questions applies to *the quantitative improvement in memory in the course of successive recalls* (Ballard's phenomenon); the second, to *the quantitative improvement in memory in the course of a period of time during which, in theory, the subject does not evoke the memory mentally*[2] (the Ward-Hovland phenomenon).

(A) BALLARD'S PHENOMENON

A quantitative improvement in memory in the course of successive recalls was first observed at the beginning of this century[3] by Henderson (1903), Binet (1904) and Lobsien (1904). It attracted the attention of psychologists, because it seemed to contradict the predictions of memory decline, based on Ebbinghaus's studies (1885).

---

[1] Recent reviews of this question can be found in the articles by Glickman (1961) and Florès (1963).

[2] These two points suggest that reminiscence is synonymous with 'quantitative improvement in memory', and it is often used in this sense. However, this probably gives it too limited a meaning, since the evocation of mnemonic responses that have never been produced before can be accompanied by the disappearance, either temporary or permanent, of other responses that had previously been correctly reproduced; in which case, the global efficiency of memory will depend on the relative strength of these two processes. Efficiency will decrease when the number of responses evoked for the first time is lower than the number of responses apparently forgotten. Nevertheless, these mnemonic responses, never previously reproduced, can justifiably be regarded as reminiscences, even though their appearance is sporadic and the final memory will be reduced as a result. Ballard accepted both cases in his studies.

[3] A bibliography of the studies on this problem during the period 1903–35 can be found in the article by G. O. McGeoch (1935).

In Ballard's famous experiment (1913), the subjects were given the task of studying a variety of material (poems, prose passages, etc.) during a period of time which was not long enough for them to attain the criterion of perfect mastery. Each subject's retention was examined *twice* by the recall method. The first examination took place immediately after learning, the second after an interval of time, varying in length from 24 hours to 7 days. The curves in Fig. 29 show the development of retention as a function of time

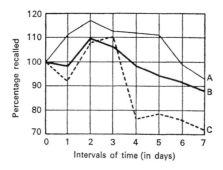

Fig. 29. Development of the retention of three different pieces of material (a poem A; a second poem B; meaningless, verbal material C) by children aged 12 years. (After Ballard, *Brit. J. Psychol. Monogr. suppl.*, 1913, **1**, 5.)

and recall percentages (immediate recall: 100 per cent). The subjects were children aged 12 years, and three different pieces of material were used. The efficiency of this process was greatest after 2 to 3 days. Huguenin (1914), Nicolai (1922) and Williams (1926) obtained similar results.

Based on his own findings, Ballard came to regard reminiscence as an opposite process to that of forgetting, *able to exert a facilitating influence upon mnemonic behaviour for several days.* Another opinion, supported by Williams (1926), was that the improvement in long-term memory obtained by Ballard was due to mental revision of the task in the time between recall tests. But a study made by G. O. McGeoch (1935) showed that subjects who had probably refrained from making any such revision produced practically the same degree of reminiscence as those who admitted to a mental revision of the task.[1] It would seem today

---

[1] Using Ballard's method, Magdsick (1936) discovered phenomena of reminiscence in rats between 1 hour and 1 week (mazes). It is difficult to explain this as consolidation by mental revision.

that a theory, put forward by Brown (1923), to explain the appearance of responses not previously evoked in successive recalls, offers a better explanation of the Ballard phenomenon. This hypothesis explains the absence of long-term forgetting by the cumulative effect of recall. Each recall consolidates the responses evoked, thereby increasing their availability, i.e. the probability of their subsequent evocation in recall. This process would favour the activation of responses, which had not been reproduced previously, but which belonged to the same task as a number of well-consolidated responses. Ammons and Irion (1954) repeated Ballard's experiment in order to find out whether this phenomenon also occurred when there was no previous recall. First the subjects learnt a poem of 24 lines (8 readings), and then they had to reproduce it from memory immediately (group I) or 2 days later (group II) or 7 days later (group III). In addition, the authors placed two other groups under Ballard's conditions: first reproduction immediately after learning, and the second either 2 days later (group IV) or 7 days later (group V). Table XXVIII gives the averages and variations in the number of lines recalled. These figures show that recall after 2

TABLE XXVIII

How recall develops in time, depending on whether or not it is preceded by earlier recall

Groups	Number of subjects	First reproduction			Second reproduction	
			Average	Standard deviation	Average	Standard deviation
I	26	Immediate	9·23	4·95		
II	26	After 2 days	6·81	4·76		
III	23	After 7 days	6·13	3·41		
IV	26	Immediate	9·73	4·43	After 2 days 10·05	5·78
V	23	Immediate	9·00	5·06	After 7 days 7·96	4·91

(After Ammons and Irion, *J. exp. Psychol.*, 1954, **48**, 185.)

or 7 days was clearly higher when preceded by immediate recall (groups IV and V).

These results show that Ballard's reminiscences were made possible by the consolidatory action of the first recall on the mnemonic responses evoked. Without this first recall (groups II and III), reminiscence is replaced by a classical process of forgetting.

(B) THE WARD-HOVLAND PHENOMENON

There is a fundamental difference between the Ward-Hovland phenomenon and the Ballard phenomenon. In the first place, the Ward-Hovland phenomenon produces an improvement in memory in the absence of any spontaneous evocation (mental revision of the task)[1] or any provocation of previously acquired responses (recall test), while the Ballard phenomenon depends on the first recall to consolidate these responses. Secondly, this improvement in memory develops for a short time only (a few minutes), whereas Ballard's reminiscence extends over periods of several days. Finally, the Ward-Hovland phenomenon apparently occurs in the use of loosely constructed verbal material (series of syllables, adjectives, etc.) or motor tasks, whereas the Ballard phenomenon particularly affects the memory of tightly constructed verbal material (poems, prose, etc.).[2]

In Ward's original experiment (1937), 30 adults had to learn series of 12 nonsense syllables by the anticipation method (presentation timing: 2 seconds per stimulus, 6-second intervals between consecutive trials). Retention was tested (recall by anticipation and relearning) after one of the following intervals: 6 seconds (immediate recall), 30 seconds, 2, 5, 10 or 20 minutes. All these intervals, with the exception of the 6-second one, were spent reading funny stories.

The curves in Fig. 30 show how recall averages developed with criteria of acquisition of 7 correct anticipations out of 12 and 12 correct anticipations out of 12. Obviously Ward's phenomenon of reminiscence was short-lived, reaching its maximum between

---

[1] In experiments on the Ward-Hovland effect, the intervals are occupied by completely different tasks, so as to ensure that the subject does not return to the original task.

[2] Williams (1926) was unable to obtain the Ballard phenomenon when he used material composed of abstract words.

César Florès

30 seconds and 2 minutes and decreasing until it disappeared completely after 10 minutes. Memory, measured by the savings method, shows a similar evolution. All this information has been confirmed by Hovland's research (1938a, 1938b).

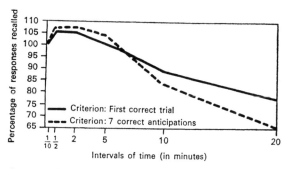

Fig. 30. Curves showing how the percentages of elements recalled developed after short intervals of time. (After Ward, *Psychol. Monogr.*, 1937, **49**, 30)

Other variables, besides the length of the rest period preceding the memory test, affect this phenomenon quantitatively: (1) the speed at which the stimuli are presented, since reminiscence increases with the speed of presentation (Hovland, 1938b); (2) massed learning favours reminiscence, while distributed learning tends to make it disappear (Hovland, 1938a); (3) the degree of learning, since reminiscence is greatest for an average criterion of mastery (neither high, nor low) (Hovland, 1938a, b). Other studies suggest that the similarity of the elements in the material (Melton and Stone, 1942) and the number of these elements (Shipley, 1939) also favour reminiscence.

Psychologists have applied to this phenomenon the theories with which they have tried to explain distribution of practice. In fact, the two problems overlap, since they both require an explanation of why retention gains in efficiency in the course of a period without practice. Consequently the theories of mental revision of the task, consolidation of mnemonic responses by a process of perseveration, dispersion of fatigue and competition between correct and incorrect responses (and all the criticisms of these theories made in connection with distributed learning, see p. 267) can be applied equally well to reminiscence.

346

Conclusion

All these studies are essentially concerned with the associative memory that results from the acquisition of stimuli, which can be isolated materially and arranged in series of successive elements or pairs. All the information obtained shows that it is almost impossible to account for the complexity of mnemonic behaviour in a single explanatory model, composed of a limited number of elementary factors. Retention of a series of words, syllables or figures cannot be explained simply by the proximity of the stimuli in space and time, combined with the mechanical processes of repetition. Of course the importance of these conditions must not be underestimated, since they favour the elaboration of associative connections and increase the long-term availability of the responses acquired. But, as far as the adult human is concerned, mechanical repetition occurs only in exceptional circumstances. It requires the collaboration of subjects who have received preliminary training and who know that they should adopt, and voluntarily maintain, an attitude of repetition to the exclusion of all other attitudes. Even so, repetition of the task and its specific features are not the only factors concerned. Unknown even to the subject, his past experience plays a role. This fact has emerged from research into the frequency, familiarity and meaning of stimuli.

An individual's motivation, his affective reactions and his dynamic activity (attitudes, habits, organizational behaviour, mode of apprehending stimuli, etc.) on the level of learning and mnemonic behaviour also play a part in determining, often decisively, the efficiency and psychological content of recall and recognition. In the final analysis, whether an association is retained or inhibited depends on the interaction of all these factors, isolated as a result of three-quarters of a century of careful and detailed research.

Finally it is obvious that the significance of all this work extends far beyond laboratory conditions. These phenomena are all features of mnemonic behaviour in everyday life. Certainly the reconstruction of the past in the form of memory is largely achieved by intellectual operations in which the individual works out the order of events experienced, situating them coherently in time and re-establishing the causal relations of their sequence. But, as Pierre Janet showed in his study of the behaviour of recitation (1928), these reconstructions are not merely deductive. They also depend on the retention of specific occurrences, and all the associative processes and dynamic activities studied in this chapter are essential to the subsequent evocation of these occurrences.

Bibliography

ACHILLES, E. M., 'Experimental studies in recall and recognition', *Arch. Psychol.*, 1920, **44**, 1–80.

ALLPORT, G. W., 'Change and decay in the visual memory image', *Brit. J. Psychol.*, 1930, **21**, 133–48.

AMMONS, H. and IRION, A. L., 'A note on the Ballard reminiscence phenomenon', *J. exp. Psychol.*, 1954, **48**, 184–6.

ARCHER, E. J. and UNDERWOOD, B. J., 'Retroactive inhibition of verbal associations as a multiple function of temporal point of interpolation and degree of interpolated learning', *J. exp. Psychol.*, 1951, **42**, 283–90.

ATWATER, S. K., 'Proactive inhibition and associative facilitation as affected by degree of prior learning', *J. exp. Psychol.*, 1953, **46**, 405–10.

BALKEN, E. R., 'Affective, volitional and galvanic factors in learning', *J. exp. Psychol.*, 1933, **16**, 115–28.

BALLARD, P. B., 'Obliviscence and reminiscence', *Brit. J. Psychol.*, 1913, Monogr. suppl. 1, no. 2.

BARRETT, D. M., 'Memory in relation to hedonic tone', *Arch. Psychol.*, 1938, **31**, no. 223.

BARTLETT, F. C., *Remembering: A study in experimental and social psychology*, Cambridge, Cambridge University Press, 1922.

BARTON, J. W., 'Smaller vs. larger units in learning the maze', *J. exp. Psychol.*, 1921, **4**, 418–29.

BIEL, W. C. and FORCE, R. C., 'Retention of nonsense syllables in intentional and incidental learning', *J. exp. Psychol.*, 1943, **32**, 52–63.

BILLS, A. G., 'The influence of muscular tension on the efficiency of mental work', *Amer. J. Psychol.*, 1927, **38**, 227–51.

BINET, A., 'Notes complémentaires sur M. Jacques Inaudi', *Travaux du Laboratoire de Psychologie physiologique*, 1892, 45–50.

— 'Sommaire des travaux en cours à la Société de Psychologie de l'enfant', *Année psychol.*, 1904, **10**, 116–30.

— HENNEGUY, F., 'Observations et expériences sur le calculateur Jacques Inaudi', *Travaux du Laboratoire de Psychologie physiologique*, 1892, 21–37.

— HENRI, V., 'Le développement de la mémoire visuelle chez les enfants', *Revue gén. des Sciences*, 15 March 1894, extract in *Année psychol.*, 1894, **1**, 402–4.

BOLGER, E. M. and TITCHENER, E. B., 'Some experiments on the associative power of smells', *Amer. J. Psychol.*, 1907, **18**, 326–37.

BOLTON, T. L., 'The growth of memory in school children', *Amer. J. Psychol.*, 1892, **4**, 362–80.

Bibliography

BOOK, W. F., *The psychology of Skill*, Missoula, Montana Press, 1908.

BOREAS, T., 'Experimental studies on memory: II. The rate of forgetting', *Praktica de l'Acad. d'Athènes*, 1930, **5**.

BOUSFIELD, W. A., 'The occurrence of clustering in the recall of randomly arranged associates', *J. gen. Psychol.*, 1953, **49**, 229–40.

— COHEN, B. H., 'The effects of reinforcement on the occurrence of clustering in the recall of randomly arranged associates', *J. Psychol.*, 1953, **36**, 67–81.

— — 'The occurrence of clustering in the recall of randomly arranged words of different frequencies of usage', *J. gen. Psychol.*, 1955a, **52**, 83–95.

— — 'General review of a program of research on associative clustering'. Technical report no. 11 under Contract no. 631 (oo) between the Office of Naval Research and the University of Connecticut, 1955b.

— SEDGEWICK, C. H. W., 'An analysis of sequences of restricted associative responses', *J. gen. Psychol.*, 1944, **30**, 149–65.

BRAUN, H. W. and HEYMANN, S. P., 'Meaningfulness of material, distribution of practice and serial position curves', *J. exp. Psychol.*, 1958, **56**, 146–50.

BRIGGS, G. E., 'Retroactive inhibition as a function of degree of original and interpolated material', *J. exp. Psychol.*, 1957, **53**, 60–7.

BROWN, W., 'To what extent is memory measured by a single recall?', *J. exp. Psychol.*, 1923, **49**, 191–6.

— 'Whole and part methods in learning', *J. educ. Psychol.*, 1924, **15**, 229–33.

— 'Growth of "memory images" ', *Amer. J. Psychol.*, 1935, **47**, 90–102.

BRUCE, R. W., 'Conditions of transfer of training', *J. exp. Psychol.*, 1933, **16**, 343–61.

BRUNER, J. S., 'Les processus de préparation à la perception', in *Logique et perception. Études d'épistémologie génétique*, vol. VI, Paris, Presses Universitaires de France, 1958.

BUGELSKI, B. R., 'At attempt to reconcile unlearning and reproductive inhibition explanation of proactive inhibition', *J. exp. Psychol.*, 1948, **38**, 670–82.

— CADWALLADER, T. C., 'A reappraisal of the transfer and retroaction surface', *J. exp. Psychol.*, 1956, **52**, 360–6.

BUNCH, M. E., 'The amount of transfer in rational learning as a function of time', *J. comp. Psychol.*, 1936, **22**, 325–37.

— 'The measurement of retention by the relearning method', *Psychol. Rev.*, 1941, **48**, 450–6.

— 'A comparison of retention and transfer of training from similar material after relatively long intervals of time', *J. comp. Psychol.*, 1941, **32**, 217–31.

— MCCRAVEN, V. G., 'The temporal course of transfer in the learning of memory material', *J. comp. Psychol.*, 1938, **25**, 481–96.

— WIENTGE, K., 'The relative susceptibility of pleasant, unpleasant and indifferent material to retroactive inhibition', *J. gen. Psychol.*, 1933, **9**, 157–78.

CAIN, L. F. and WILLEY, R. de V., 'The effect of spaced learning on the curve of retention', *J. exp. Psychol.*, 1939, **25**, 209–14.

CALKINS, M. W., 'Association', *Psychol. Rev.*, 1894, **1**, 476–83.

CARR, H. A., 'Distribution of effort', *Psychol. Bull.*, 1919, **16**, 26–8.

CARTER, H. D., 'Effects of emotional factors upon recall', *J. Psychol.*, 1935, **1**, 49–59.

— JONES, H. E., 'A further study of affective factors in learning', *J. genet. Psychol.*, 1937, **50**, 157–63.

—— SHOCK, N. W., 'An experimental study of affective factors in learning', *J. educ. Psychol.*, 1934, **25**, 203–15.

CASON, H., 'Criticism of the law of exercice and effect', *Psychol. Rev.*, 1924, **31**, 397–417.

— 'The learning and retention of pleasant and unpleasant activities', *Arch. Psychol.*, 1932, **21**, no. 134.

— LUNGREN, F. C., 'Memory for pleasant, unpleasant and indifferent pairs of words', *J. exp. Psychol.*, 1932, **15**, 728–32.

CHANEY, R. M. and LAVER, A. R., 'The influence of affective tone on learning and retention', *J. educ. Psychol.*, 1929, **20**, 287–90.

CIEUTAT, V. J., STOCKWELL, F. F. and NOBLE, C. E., 'The interaction of ability and amount of practice with stimulus and response meaningfulness (m, m') in paired associated learning', *J. exp. Psychol.*, 1958, **56**, 193–202.

COFER, C. N., *Verbal learning and Verbal behavior*, New York, McGraw-Hill, 1961.

COLEGROVE, F. W., 'Individual memories', *Amer. J. Psychol.*, 1898, **10**, 228–55.

COURTS, F. A., 'Relations between experimentally produced muscular tension and memorization', *J. exp. Psychol.*, 1939, **25**, 235–56.

CRAFTS, L. W., 'Whole and part methods with unrelated reactions', *Amer. J. Psychol.*, 1930, **42**, 591–601.

DAHL, A., 'Uber den Einfluss des Schlafens auf das Wiedererkennen', *Psychol. Forsch.*, 1928, **11**, 290–301.

DELAY, J., *Les dissolutions de la mémoire*, Paris, Presses Universitaires de France, 1950.

DOWLING, R. M. and BRAUN, H. M., 'Retention and meaningfulness of material', *J. exp. Psychol.*, 1957, **54**, 213–17.

Bibliography

EBBINGHAUS, H., *Über das gedächinis: Untersuchungen zur experimentellen Psychologie*, Leipzig, Dunker & Humblot, 1885.

EDWARDS, A. L., 'Political frames of reference as a factor influencing recognition', *J. abnorm. soc. Psychol.*, 1941, **36**, 34–50.

EHRLICH, S., FLORÈS, C. and LE NY, J.-F., 'Rappel et reconnaissance d'éléments appartenant à des ensembles définis', *Année psychol.*, 1960, **60**, 29–37.

EPHRUSSI, P., 'Experimentelle Beiträge zur Lehre vom gedächtnis', *Z. Psychol.*, 1904, **37**, 56–103, 161–82.

ERBERT, E. and MEUMANN, E. 'Über einige Grundfragen der Psychologie der Ubungsphänomene im Bereiche des Gedachtnisses', *Arch. ges. Psychol.*, 1905, **4**, 71 96, 127 56, 196-8.

FERNALD, M. R., 'The diagnosis of Mental Imagery', *Psychol. Monogr.*, 1912, **14**, no. 58.

FINKENBINDER, E. O., 'The curve of forgetting', *Amer. J. Psychol.*, 1913, **24**, 8–32.

FLORÈS, C., 'Étude sur les processus d'utilisation de la trace mnésique: le rappel, la reconnaissance et le réapprentissage', *Année psychol.*, 1958a, **58**, 25–43.

— 'Études sur les relations entre le rappel et la reconnaissance', *Année psychol.*, 1958b, **58**, 365–76.

— *Les processus médiateurs dans la mémoire*, research thesis for Ph.D., 1964.

— 'Les processus d'intégration mnémonique: Quelques données sur l'état actuel de la question', *Enfance*, 1962, **4–5**, 375–87.

FOUCAULT, M., 'Relation de la fixation et de l'oubli avec la longueur des séries à apprendre', *Année psychol.*, 1913, **19**, 218–35.

— 'Les inhibitions internes de fixation', *Année psychol.*, 1928, **29**, 92–112.

FRAISSE, P. and FLORÈS, C., 'Perception et fixation mnémonique', *Année psychol.*, 1956, **56**, 1–11.

GATES, A. I., 'Recitation as a factor in memorizing', *Arch. psychol.*, 1917, **6**, no. 40.

GERARD, R. W., 'The fixation of experience in Brain Mechanisms and learning' (Symposium), Blackwell Scientific Publications, Oxford, 1961.

GEORGE, F. H., 'Errors of visual recognition', *J. exp. Psychol.*, 1952, **43**, 202–6.

GIBSON, E. J., 'A systematic application of the concepts of generalization and differentiation to verbal learning', *Psychol. Rev.*, 1940, **47**, 196–229.

— 'Retroactive inhibition as a function of degree of generalization between tasks', *J. exp. Psychol.*, 1941, **28**, 93–115.

— 'Intra-list generalization as a factor in verbal learning', *J. exp. Psychol.*, 1942, **30**, 185–200.

— GIBSON, J. J., 'Retention and the interpolated task', *Amer. J. Psychol.*, 1934, **46**, 603–10.

GIBSON, J. J., 'The reproduction of visually perceived forms', *J. exp. Psychol.*, 1929, **12**, 1–39.

GILLETTE, A. L., 'Learning and retention: a comparison of three experimental procedures', *Arch. psychol.*, 1936, **28**, no. 198.

GLAZE, J. A., 'The association value of nonsense syllables', *J. genet. Psychol.*, 1928, **35**, 255–67.

GLICKMANN, S. E., 'Perseverative neural processes and consolidation of memory trace', *Psychol. Bull.*, 1961, **58**, 218–33.

GLIXMAN, A. F., 'Recall of completed and uncompleted activities under varying degrees of stress', *J. exp. Psychol.*, 1949, **39**, 281–95.

GOMULICKI, B. R., 'The development and present status of the trace theory of memory', *Brit. J. Psychol.*, 1953, Monog. Suppl., no. 28.

GORDON, K., 'Ueber das gedaechtnis fuer affektiv bestimmte Eindruecke, *Arch. ges. Psychol.*, 1905, **4**, 437–58.

— 'The recollection of pleasant and of unpleasant odors', *J. exp. Psychol.*, 1925, **8**, 225–39.

GOUGENHEIM, G., MICHEA, R., RIVENC, P. and SAUVAGEOT, A., *L'élaboration du français élémentaire*, Paris, Didier, 1956.

GUILFORD, J. P., *Laboratory studies in psychology*, New York, Holt, 1934, p. 122.

GUILLAUME, P., *La psychologie de la forme*, Paris, Flammarion, 1937.

HALL, J., 'Learning as a function of word frequency', *Amer. J. Psychol.*, 1954, **67**, 138–40.

HALL, V., 'The effects of time interval on recall', *Brit. J. Psychol.*, 1936, **27**, 41–50.

HAMILTON, R. J., 'Retroactive facilitation as a function of degree of generalization between tasks', *J. exp. Psychol.*, 1943, **32**, 363–76.

HANAWALT, E. M., 'Whole and part methods in trial and error learning', *Comp. Psychol. Monogr.*, 1931, **7**, no. 35.

— 'Whole and part methods in trial and error learning: human maze learning', *J. exp. Psychol.*, 1934, **17**, 691–708.

HANAWALT, N. G., 'Memory trace for figures in recall and recognition', *Arch. Psychol.*, 1937, **31**, no. 216.

HARRIS, J. W., 'On the associative power of odors', *Amer. J. Psychol.*, 1908, **19**, 557–61.

HARROWER, M. R., 'Organization in higher mental processes', *Psychol. Forsch.*, 1932, **17**, 56–120.

HEBB, D. O. and FOORD, E. N., 'Errors of visual recognition and the nature of the trace', *J. exp. Psychol.*, 1945, **35**, 335–48.

Bibliography

HEINE, R., 'Über Wiedererkennen und rückwirkende Hemmung', *Z. Psychol.*, 1914, **68**, 161–236.

HENDERSON, E. N., 'Study of memory for connected trains of thought', *Psychol. Monogr.*, 1903, **5**, 1–94.

HENMON, V. A. C., 'The relation between learning and retention and amount to be learned', *J. exp. Psychol.*, 1917, **2**, 476–84.

HERTZMAN, M. and NEFF, W. S., 'The development of intra-serial relationship in rote learning', *J. exp. Psychol.*, 1939, **25**, 389–401.

HEYER, A. W. and O'KELLY, L. I., I: 'Studies in motivation and retention'; II: 'Retention of nonsense syllables learned under different degrees of motivation', *J. Psychol.*, 1949, **27**, 143–52.

HEYWOOD, A. and VORTRIEDE, II. A., 'Some experiments on the associative power of smells', *Amer. J. Psychol.*, 1905, **16**, 537–41.

HILGARD, E. R., 'The saving score as a measure of retention', *Amer. J. Psychol.*, 1934, **46**, 337–9.

— 'Methods and procedures in the study of learning', in S. S. Stevens (Ed.), *Handbook of experimental Psychology*, New York, John Wiley, 1951.

— *Theories of learning*, New York, Appleton Century Crofts, 1956.

— MARQUIS, D. G., *Conditioning and learning* (revised by G. A. Kimble), New York, Appleton Century Crofts, 1961.

HOVLAND, C. I., 'Experimental studies in rote learning theory: I. Reminiscence following learning by massed and by distributed practice', *J. exp. Psychol.*, 1938a, **22**, 201–24.

— 'Experimental studies in rote learning theory: II. Reminiscence with varying speeds of syllable presentation', *J. exp. Psychol.*, 1938b, **22**, 338–53.

— 'Experimental studies in rote learning theory: III. Distribution of practice with varying speeds of syllable presentation', *J. exp. Psychol.*, 1938c, **23**, 172–90.

— 'Experimental studies in rote learning theory: VI. Comparison of retention following learning to the same criterion by massed and distributed practice', *J. exp. Psychol.*, 1940a, **26**, 568–87.

— 'Experimental studies in rote learning theory: VII. Distribution of practice with varying lengths of list', *J. exp. Psychol.*, 1940b, **27**, 271–84.

— 'Human learning and retention', in S. S. Stevens (Ed.), *Handbook of experimental Psychology*, New York, Wiley, 1951.

HUGUENIN, C., 'Reviviscence paradoxale', *Arch. de Psychol.*, 1914, **14**, 379–83.

HULL, C. L., 'The conflicting psychologies of learning—a way out', *Psychol. Rev.*, 1935, **42**, 491–516.

— and collaborators, *Mathematico-deductive theory of rote learning: a study on scientific methodology*, New Haven, Yale University Press, 1940.

— *Principles of Behavior*, New York, Appleton Century Crofts, 1943.

HUNT, R. G., 'Meaningfulness and articulation of stimulus and response in paired-associate learning and stimulus recall', *J. exp. Psychol.*, 1959, **57**, 262–7.

JANET, P., *L'évolution de la mémoire et de la notion du temps*, Paris, A. Chahine, 1928.

JENKINS, J. G., 'Instruction as a factor in "Incidental" learning', *Amer. J. Psychol.*, 1933, **45**, 471–7.

— DALLENBACH, K. M., 'Obliviscence during sleep and waking', *Amer. J. Psychol.*, 1924, **35**, 605–12.

JENKINS, W. O. and POSTMAN, L., 'An experimental analysis of set in rote learning: retroactive inhibition as a function of changing set', *J. exp. Psychol.*, 1949, **39**, 69–73.

JERSILD, A. T., 'Memory for the pleasant as compared with the unpleasant', *J. exp. Psychol.*, 1931, **14**, 284–8.

JOHNSON, L. M., 'Similarity of meaning as a factor in retroactive inhibition', *J. gen. Psychol.*, 1933, **9**, 377–88.

JONCKHEERE, T., 'Le procédé fragmentaire et le procédé global dans la technique de la mémorisation', in *Centenaire de Th. Ribot*, 403–13, Agen, 1939.

JONES, H. E., 'Emotional factors in learning', *J. gen. Psychol.*, 1929, **2**, 263–72.

JOST, A., 'Die Assoziationsfestigkeit in ihrer Abhängigkeit von der Verteilung der Wiederholungen', *Z. Psychol.*, 1897, **14**, 436–72.

KATONA, G., *Organizing and memorizing*, New York, Columbia University Press, 1940.

KIMBLE, G. A. and BILODEAU, E. A., 'Work and rest as variables in cyclical motor learning', *J. exp. Psychol.*, 1949, **39**, 150–7.

— DUFORT, R. H., 'Meaningfulness and isolation as a factor in verbal learning', *J. exp. Psychol.*, 1955, **50**, 361–8.

KINGSLEY, H. L., *The nature and conditions of learning*, New York, Prentice Hall, 1946.

KOCH, H. L., 'The influence of some affective factors upon recall', *J. gen. Psychol.*, 1930, **4**, 171–90.

KOFFKA, K., *Principles of Gestalt Psychology*, London, Routledge & Kegan Paul, 1935.

KÖHLER, W., *Gestalt Psychology*, New York, Liveright, 1929.

KOWALEWSKI, A., 'Studien zur Psychologie des Pessimismus', *Grenzfragen des Nerven und Seelenlebens*, 1904, **4**, 100–22.

KRUEGER, W. C. F., 'The effect of overlearning on retention', *J. exp. Psychol.*, 1929, **12**, 71–8.

Bibliography

KUHLMANN, F., 'On the analysis of the memory consciousness; a study in the mental imagery and memory of meaningless visual forms', *Psychol. Rev.*, 1906, **13**, p. 335

L'ABATE, L., 'Manifest anxiety and the learning of syllables with different associative values', *Amer. J. Psychol.*, 1959, **72**, 107–10.

LALANDE, A., *Vocabulaire technique et critique de la Philosophie*, Paris, Presses Universitaires de France, 1960.

LARGUIER DES BANCELS, J., 'Sur les méthodes de mémorisation', *Année psychol.*, 1902, **8**, 185–213.

LASHLEY, K. S. A., 'A simple maze with data on the relation of the distribution of practice to the rate of learning', *Psychobiol.*, 1918, **1**, 353–67.

LEHMANN, A., 'Über wiedererkennen', *Philos. Stud.*, 1888–89, **5**, 96–156.

LEPLEY, W. M., 'Serial reactions considered as conditioned reactions', *Psychol. Monogr.*, 1934, **46**, no. 205.

LEVINE, J. M. and MURPHY, G., 'The learning and forgetting of controversial material', *J. abnorm. soc. Psychol.*, 1943, **38**, 507–17.

LOBSIEN, M., 'Aussage und Wirklichkeit bei Schulkindern', *Beitr. Psychol. Aussage*, 1904, **1**, 26–89.

LORGE, I., 'The influence of regularly interpolated time intervals upon subsequent learning', *Teach. Coll. Contr. Educ.*, 1930, no. 438.

LUH, C. W., 'The conditions of retention', *Psychol. Monogr.*, 1922, **31**, no. 142.

LYNCH, C. A., 'The memory value of certain alleged emotionally toned words', *J. exp. Psychol.*, 1932, **15**, 298–315.

LYON, D. O., 'The relation of length of material to time taken for learning and the optimum distribution of time', *J. educ. Psychol.*, 1914, **5**, 1–9, 85–91, 155–63.

MAGDSICK, W. K., 'The curve of retention of an uncompletely learned problem in albino rats at various age levels', *J. Psychol.*, 1936, **2**, 25–48.

MANDLER, G., 'Associative frequency and associative prepotency as measures of response to nonsense syllables', *Amer. J. Psychol.*, 1956, **68**, 662–5.

— HUTTENLOCHER, J., 'The relationship between associative frequency, associative ability and paired-associate learning', *Amer. J. Psychol.*, 1956, **69**, 424–8.

MARROW, A. J., 'Goal tensions and recall', *J. gen. Psychol.*, 1938a, **19**, 3–35; *J. gen. Psychol.*, 1938b, **19**, 37–64.

MAYER, B. A. and STONE, C. P., 'The relative efficiency of distributed and massed practice in maze learning by young and adult albino rats', *J. genet. Psychol.*, 1931, **39**, 28–48.

MCGEOCH, G. O., 'The intelligence quotient as a factor in the whole-part problem', *J. exp. Psychol.*, 1931a, **14**, 333–58.

— 'Whole part problem', *Psychol. Bull.*, 1931b, **28**, 713–39.

— 'The conditions of reminiscence', *Amer. J. Psychol.*, 1935, **47**, 65–89.

MCGEOCH, J. A., 'The influence of degree of learning upon retroactive inhibition', *Amer. J. Psychol.*, 1929, **41**, 252–62.

— 'The influence of associative value upon the difficulty of nonsense syllable lists', *J. genet. Psychol.*, 1930, **37**, 421–6.

— 'Forgetting and the law of disuse', *Psychol. Rev.*, 1932, **39**, 352–70.

— 'The influence of degree of interpolated learning upon retroactive inhibition', *Amer. J. Psychol.*, 1932, **44**, 695–708.

— 'Studies in retroactive inhibition: II. Relationships between temporal point of interpolation, length of interval amount of retroactive inhibition', *J. gen. Psychol.*, 1933, **9**, 44–57.

— 'The direction and extent of intra-serial associations at recall', *Amer. J. Psychol.*, 1936, **48**, 221–45.

— 'Studies in retroactive inhibition: VII. Retroactive inhibition as a function of the length and frequency of presentation of the interpolated lists', *J. exp. Psychol.*, 1936, **19**, 674–93.

— IRION, A. L., *The psychology of Human learning*, New York, Longmans Green & Co., 1952.

— MCDONALD, W. T., 'Meaningful relation and retroactive inhibition', *Amer. J. Psychol.*, 1931, **43**, 579–88.

— MCGEOCH, G. O., 'Studies in retroactive inhibition: X. The influence of similarity of meaning between lists of paired associates', *J. exp. Psychol.*, 1937, **21**, 320–9.

— UNDERWOOD, B. J., 'Tests of the two factors theory of retroactive inhibition', *J. exp. Psychol.*, 1943, **32**, 1–16.

MCKINNEY, F. and MCGEOCH, J. A., 'The character and extent of transfer in retroactive inhibition disparate serial lists', *Amer. J. Psychol.*, 1935, **47**, 409–23.

MELTON, A. W. and IRWIN, J. MC., 'The influence of degree of interpolated learning on retroactive inhibition and the overt transfer of specific responses', *Amer. J. Psychol.*, 1940, **53**, 173–203.

— STONE, G. R., 'The retention of serial lists of adjectives over short time-intervals with varying rates of presentation', *J. exp. Psychol.*, 1942, **30**, 295–310.

— LACKUM, W. J. von, 'Retroactive and proactive inhibition in retention: Evidence for a two factors theory of retroactive inhibition', *Amer. J. Psychol.*, 1941, **54**, 157–73.

MELTZER, H., 'The present status of experimental studies on the relationship of feeling to memory', *Psychol. Rev.*, 1930, **37**, 124–39.

Bibliography

MEUMANN, E., *Vorlesungen zur Einführung in die Experimentelle Pädagogik und ihre psychologischen grundlagen*, Leipzig, Zweiter Band, Verlag von Wilhelm Engelman, 1913.

MEYER, P., 'Über die Reproduktion eingeprägter Figuren und ihrer räumliche Stellung bei Kindern und Erwachsenen', *Z. Psychol.*, 1913, **64**, 43.

MEYER, W., 'Über ganz-und Teillernverfahren bei vorgeschriebenem Rezitieren', *Z. Psychol.*, 1925, **98**, 304–41.

MILLER, G. A. and SELFRIDGE, J. A., 'Verbal context and the recall of meaningful material', *Amer. J. Psychol.*, 1950, **63**, 176–85.

MORGAN, R. L. and UNDERWOOD, B. J., 'Proactive inhibition as a function of response similarity', *J. exp. Psychol.*, 1950, **40**, 592–603.

MÜLLER, G. E., 'Zur Analyse der gedaechtnistaetigkeit und des vorstellungs verlanfs', *Z. Psychol.*, 1911, vol. I, Erbd. 5; *Z. Psychol.*, 1913, vol. III, Erbd. 8; *Z. Psychol.*, 1917, vol. II, Erbd. 9.

— PILZECKER, A., 'Experimentelle Beiträge zur Lehre vom gedachtniss', *Z. Psychol.*, 1900, Erbd. 1, 1–228.

— SCHUMANN, F., 'Experimentelle Beitraege zur Untersuchung des gedäechtnisses', *Z. Psychol.*, 1894, VI, 81–257.

MUNSTERBERG, H. and BIGHAM, J., *Psychol. Rev.*, 1894, **1**, 34–44; *ibid.*, 453–61.

NAGGE, J. W., 'An experimental test of the theory of associative interference', *J. exp. Psychol.*, 1935, **18**, 663–82.

NEWMAN, E. B., 'The temporal factor in retroactive inhibition', *Psychol. Bull.*, 1939, **36**, 543–4 (abstract).

NEUMANN, G., 'Experimentelle Beiträge zur Lehre von der Oekonomie und technik des Lernens', *D. Exp. Päd.*, 1907, **4**, 63–101; *ibid.*, 155–74.

NEWTON, J. M. and WICKENS, D. D., 'Retroactive inhibition as a function of the temporal position of interpolated learning', *J. exp. Psychol.*, 1956, **51**, 149–54.

NICOLAI, F., 'Experimentelle Untersuchung über das Haften von gesichtseindrücken und dessen zeitlichen Verlauf', *Arch. ges. Psychol.*, 1922, **42**, 132–49.

NOBLE, C. E., 'An analysis of meaning', *Psychol. Rev.*, 1952, **59**, 421–30.

— 'The role of stimulus meaning (m) in serial verbal learning', *J. exp. Psychol.*, 1952, **43**, 437–46.

— MCNEELEY, D. A., 'The role of meaningfulness (m) in paired-associate verbal learning', *J. exp. Psychol.*, 1957, **53**, 16–22.

NUTTIN, J., *Tâche, réussite et échec. Théorie de la conduite humaine*, Paris, Érasme, 1953.

OGDEN, R. M., *Psychology and Education*, New York, 1926.

ORBISON, W. D., *The relative efficiency of whole and part methods of learning paired associates as a function of the length of list*, Ph.D. Thesis, Yale University, 1944.

O'KELLEY, L. T. and STECKLE, L. C., 'The forgetting of pleasant and unpleasant experiences', *Amer. J. Psychol.*, 1940, **53**, 432–4.

OSGOOD, C. E., 'An investigation into the causes of retroactive interference', *J. exp. Psychol.*, 1948, **38**, 132–54.

— 'Meaningful similarity and interference in learning', *J. exp. Psychol.*, 1946, **36**, 277–301.

— *Method and theory in experimental Psychology*, New York, Oxford University Press, 1953.

OVSIANKINA, M., 'Die Wiederaufnahme unterbrochener Handlemgen', *Psychol. Forsch.*, 1928, **11**, 302–79.

PACHAURI, A. R., 'A study of Gestalt problems in completed and interrupted tasks', *Brit. J. Psychol.*, 1935, **25**, 447–57.

PEARLMAN, C. A., SHARPLESS, S. K. and JARVIK, M. E., 'Retrograde amnesia produced by anesthetic and convulsant agents', *J. comp. physiol. Psychol.*, 1961, **54**, 109–12.

PECHSTEIN, L. A., 'Whole vs part methods in motor learning: a comparison study', *Psychol. Monogr.*, 1917, **23**, no. 99.

— 'The whole vs part methods in learning: comparison and summary', *Stud. Educ.* (*Yearb. nat. Soc. Coll. Teach. Educ.*), 1926, **15**, 181–6.

PENTSCHEW, C., 'Untersuchungen zur Ökonomie und Tecknik des Lernens', *Arch. ges. Psychol.*, 1903, **1**, 417–526.

PERKINS, F. T., 'Symmetry in visual recall', *Amer. J. Psychol.*, 1932, **44**, 473–90.

PHILIP, B. R. and PEIXOTTO, H. E., 'Recall and recognition of nonsense syllables', *Amer. J. Psychol.*, 1949, **62**, 228–37.

PHILIPPE, J., 'Sur les transformations de nos images mentales', *Rev. philos.*, 1897, **43**, 486–92.

PIÉRON, H., 'Recherches expérimentales sur les phénomènes de mémoire', *Année psychol.*, 1913, **19**, 91–193.

— 'Recherches comparatives sur la mémoire des formes et celle des chiffres', *Année psychol.*, 1914–19, **21**, 119–48.

— 'L'habitude et la mémoire', in Dumas, G., *Nouveau Traité de Psychologie*, vol. 4, Paris, Alcan, 1934.

PILLSBURY, W. B. and RAUSCH, H. L., 'An extension of the Köhler Restorff inhibition phenomena', *Amer. J. Psychol.*, 1943, **56**, 293–8.

POSTMAN, L., 'Choice behavior and the process of recognition', *Amer. J. Psychol.*, 1950, **63**, 576–83.

— 'The generalization gradient in recognition memory', *Amer. J. Psychol.*, 1951, **42**, 231–5.

— 'Extraexperimental interference and the retention of words', *J. exp. Psychol.*, 1961, **61**, 98–110.

Bibliography

POSTMAN, L. and ADAMS, P. A., 'Studies in incidental learning: III. Interserial interference', *J. exp. Psychol.*, 1956*a*, **51**, 323–8.

—— 'Studies in incidental learning: IV. The interaction of orienting tasks and stimulus material', *J. exp. Psychol.*, 1956*b*, **51**, 329–33.

— — 'Studies in incidental learning: VI. Intraserial interference, *J. exp. Psychol.*, 1957, **54**, 153–67.

—— 'Studies in incidental learning: VIII. The effects of contextual determination', *J. exp. Psychol.*, 1960, **59**, 153–64.

— — BOHM, A. M., 'Studies in incidental learning: V. Recall for order and associative clustering', *J. exp. Psychol.*, 1956, **51**, 334–43.

— — PHILLIPS, L. W., 'Studies in incidental learning: II. The effects of association value and of the method of testing', *J. exp. Psychol.*, 1955, **49**, 1–10.

— JENKINS, W. O. and POSTMAN, D. L., 'An experimental comparison of active Recall and Recognition', *Amer. J. Psychol.*, 1948, **51**, 511–19.

— PHILLIPS, L. W., 'Studies in incidental learning: the effects of crowding and isolation', *J. exp. Psychol.*, 1954, **48**, 48–56.

— POSTMAN, D. L., 'Change in set as a determinant of retroactive inhibition', *Amer. J. Psychol.*, 1948, **61**, 236–42.

— RAU., L., 'Retention as a function of the method of measurement', *University of California Publications in Psychology*, 1957, **8**, 217–70.

— RILEY, D. A., *Degree of learning and interserial interference in retention*, Berkeley and Los Angeles, University of California Press, 1959.

SENDERS, V. L., 'Incidental learning and generality of set', *J. exp. Psychol.*, 1946, **36**, 153–65.

PRENTICE, W. C. H., 'Retroactive inhibition and the interruption of tasks', *Amer. J. Psychol.*, 1943, **56**, 283–92.

— 'The interruption of tasks', *Psychol. Rev.*, 1944, **51**, 329–40.

RAPAPORT, D., *Emotions and memory*, Baltimore, Williams & Wilkins, 1942.

RASKIN, E. and COOK, S. W., 'The strength and direction of associations formed in the learning of nonsense syllables', *J. exp. Psychol.*, 1937, **20**, 381–95.

RATCLIFF, M. M., 'The varying fonction of affectively toned olfactory, visual and auditory cues in recall', *Amer. J. Psychol.*, 1938, **51**, 695–701.

RESTORFF, H. von, 'Über die Wirkung von Bereichsbildungen im Spurenfeld' (Analyse von Vorgängen im Spurenfeld), *Psychol. Forsch.*, 1933, **18**, 299–342.

RITCHIE RUSSELL, W., *Brain, memory, learning*, London, Oxford University Press, 1959.

ROBINSON, E. S., 'Some factors determining the degree of retroactive inhibition', *Psychol. Monogr.*, 1920, **28**, no. 128.

— BROWN, M. A., 'Effect of serial position upon memorization', *Amer. J. Psychol.*, 1926, **37**, 538–52.
— DARROW, C. W., 'Effect of length of list upon memory for numbers', *Amer. J. Psychol.*, 1924, **35**, 235–43.
— HERON, W. T., 'Results of variations in length of memorized material', *J. exp. Psychol.*, 1922, **5**, 428–48.
ROSENTHAL, B. G., 'Hypnotic recall of material learned under anxiety and non-anxiety producing conditions', *J. exp. Psychol.*, 1944, **34**, 369–89.
ROSENZWEIG, S. and MASON, G., 'An experimental study of memory in relation to the theory of repression', *Brit. J. Psychol.*, 1934, **24**, 247–65.
— 'An experimental study of "repression" with special reference to need-persistive and ego-defensive reactions to frustration', *J. exp. Psychol.*, 1943, **32**, 64–73.
SAND, M. C., 'The effect of length of list upon retroactive inhibition when degree of learning is controlled', *Arch. Psychol.*, 1939, **33**, no. 238.
SANFORD, E. C., 'A letter to Dr. Titchener', *Stud. Psychol.: Titchener Commem.*, 1917, 5–10.
SANFORD, R. N., 'Age as a factor in the recall of interrupted tasks', *Psychol. Rev.*, 1946, **53**, 234–40.
SAWDON, E. W., 'Should children learn poems in "wholes" or in "parts"?', *Form. Educ.*, 1927, **5**, 182–97.
SEWARD, G. H., 'Recognition time as a measure of confidence', *Arch. Psychol.*, 1928, **16**, 5–54.
SHANNON, C. E., 'A mathematical model theory of communication', *Bell. Syst. Tech. J.*, 1948, **27**, 379–423, 623–56.
SHIPLEY, W. C., 'The effect of a short rest pause on retention in rote series of different lengths', *J. gen. Psychol.*, 1939, **21**, 99–117.
SIEGEL, P. S., 'Structure effects within a memory series', *J. exp. Psychol.*, 1943, **33**, 311–16.
SILVERMAN, A. and CASON, H., 'Incidental memory for pleasant, unpleasant, and indifferent words', *Amer. J. Psychol.*, 1934, **46**, 315–20.
SMITH, W. W., 'Experiments on memory and affective tone', *Brit. J. Psychol.*, 1921, **11**, 236–50.
SPIGHT, J., 'Day and night intervals and the distribution of practice', *J. exp. Psychol.*, 1928, **11**, 397–8.
STAGNER, R., 'The redintegration of pleasant and unpleasant experiences', *Amer. J. Psychol.*, 1931, **43**, 463–8.
STEFFENS, L., 'Experimentelle Beiträge zur Lehre vom ökonomischen Lernen', *Z. Psychol.*, 1900, **22**, 321–82, 465.

STODDARD, G. D., 'An experiment in verbal learning', *J. educ. Psychol.*, 1929, **20**, 452-7.

TAIT, W. D., 'The effect of psychophysical attitudes on memory', *J. abnorm. Psychol.*, 1913, **8**, 10-37.

THOMPSON, R. H., 'An experimental study of memory as influenced by feeling tone', *J. exp. Psychol.*, 1930, **13**, 462-7.

THORNDIKE, E. L., *The psychology of learning*, 2nd vol., New York, Teacher's College, 1921.

— *Human learning*, New York, Century, 1931.

— and others, *The fundamentals of learning*, New York, Teacher's College, Columbia University, 1932.

— LORGE, I., *The teacher's word book of 30,000 words*, New York, Teacher's College, Columbia University, 1944.

THUNE, L. E. and UNDERWOOD, B. J., 'Retroactive inhibition as a function of degree of interpolated learning', *J. exp. Psychol.*, 1943, **32**, 185-200.

TOLMAN, E. C., 'Retroactive inhibition as affected by conditions of learning', *Psychol. Monogr.*, 1917, **25**, no. 107.

TRAVIS, R. C., 'The effect of the length of the rest period on motor learning', *J. Psychol.*, 1937, **3**, 189-94.

TWINING, P. E., 'The relative importance of intervening activity and lapse of time in the production of forgetting', *J. exp. Psychol.*, 1940, **26**, 483-501.

ULRICH, J. L., 'The distribution of effort in learning in the white rat', *Behav. Monogr.*, 1915, **2**, no. 10.

UNDERWOOD, B. J., 'The effect of successive interpolations on retroactive and proactive inhibition', *Psychol. Monogr.*, 1945, **59**, no. 573.

— 'Proactive inhibition as a function of time and degree of prior learning', *J. exp. Psychol.*, 1949, **39**, 24-34.

— 'Studies in distributed practice: II. Learning and retention of paired-adjective lists with two levels of intralist similarity', *J. exp. Psychol.*, 1951, **42**, 153-61.

— 'Studies in distributed practice: VI. The influence of rest-interval activity in serial learning', *J. exp. Psychol.*, 1952a, **43**, 329-40.

— 'Studies in distributed practice: VII. Learning and retention of serial nonsense lists as a function of intralist similarity', *J. exp. Psychol.*, 1952b, **44**, 80-7.

— 'Studies in distributed practice: VIII. Learning and retention of paired nonsense syllables as a function of intralist similarity', *J. exp. Psychol.*, 1953, **45**, 133-42.

— Studies in distributed practice: XI. An attempt to resolve conflicting facts on retention of serial nonsense lists', *J. exp. Psychol.*, 1953, **45**, 355-9.

— 'Interference and forgetting', *Psychol. Rev.*, 1957, **64**, 49-60.

Bibliography

— 'Ten years of massed practice on distributed practice', *Psychol. Rev.*, 1961, **68**, 229–47.

— ARCHER, E. J., 'Studies in distributed practice: XIV. Intralist similarity and presentation rate in verbal discrimination learning of consonant syllables', *J. exp. Psychol.*, 1955, **50**, 120–4.

— GOAD, D., 'Studies in distributed practice: I. The influence of intralist similarity in serial learning', *J. exp. Psychol.*, 1951, **42**, 125–34.

— POSTMAN, L., 'Extraexperimental sources of interference in forgetting', *Psychol. Rev.*, 1960, **67**, 73–95.

— RICHARDSON, J., 'Studies in distributed practice: XIII. Interlist interference and the retention of serial nonsense lists', *J. exp. Psychol.*, 1955, **50**, 39–46.

—— 'The influence of meaningfulness, intralist similarity, and serial position on retention', *J. exp. Psychol.*, 1956, **52**, 119–26.

—— 'Studies in distributed practice: XVIII. The influence of meaningfulness and intralist similarity of serial nonsense lists', *J. exp. Psychol.*, 1958, **56**, 213–19.

— SCHULZ, R. W., 'Studies in distributed practice: XIX. The influence of intralist similarity with lists of low meaningfulness', *J. exp. Psychol.*, 1959, **58**, 106–10.

—— *Meaningfulness and verbal learning*, Chicago, Lippincott Co., 1960.

VAN ORMER, E. B., 'Retention after intervals of sleep and of waking', *Arch. Psychol.*, 1932, **21**, no. 137.

— 'Sleep and retention', *Psychol. Bull.*, 1933, **30**, 415–39.

WARD, L. B., 'Reminiscence and rote learning', *Psychol. Monogr.*, 1937, **49**, no. 220.

WARDEN, C. J., 'The distribution of practice in animal learning', *Comp. Psychol. Monogr.*, 1923, **1**, no. 3.

— 'The relative economy of various modes of attack in the mastery of a stylus maze', *J. exp. Psychol.*, 1924, **7**, 243–75.

WATSON, W. S. and HARTMANN, G. W., 'The rigidity of a basic attitudinal frame', *J. abnorm. soc. Psychol.*, 1939, **34**, 314–35.

WHITE, M. M., 'Some factors influencing recall of pleasant and unpleasant words', *Amer. J. Psychol.*, 1936, **48**, 134–9.

— POWELL, M., 'Differential reaction time for pleasant and unpleasant words', *Amer. J. Psychol.*, 1936, **48**, 126–33.

— RATLIFF, M. M., 'The relation of affective tone to the learning and recall of words', *Amer. J. Psychol.*, 1934, **46**, 92–8.

WHITELY, P. L., 'The dependance of learning and recall upon prior intellectual activities', *J. exp. Psychol.*, 1927, **10**, 489–508.

WILLIAMS, O. A., 'A study of the phenomenon of reminiscence', *J. exp. Psychol.*, 1926, **9**, 368–87.

WILSON, J. T., 'Remote associations as a function of the length of interval between learning and recall', *J. exp. Psychol.*, 1943, **33**, 40–9.

— 'The formation and retention of remote associations in rote learning', *J. exp. Psychol.*, 1949, **39**, 830–8.

WINCH, W. H., 'Should poems be learnt by school-children as "wholes" or in "parts" ', *Brit. J. Psychol.*, 1924, **15**, 64–79.

WITASEK, S., 'Uber lesen und Rezitieren in ihren Beziehungen zum Gedächtnis', *Z. Psychol.*, 1907, **44**, 161–85, 246–78.

WITMER, L. R., 'The association value of three-place consonant syllables', *J. genet. Psychol.*, 1935, **47**, 337–60.

WOHLGEMUTH, A., 'On memory and the direction of associations', *Brit. J. Psychol.*, 1913, **5**, 447–65.

WOLFE, 'Untersuchung über die Tongedachnitss', *Philos. Studien.*, 1886, **3**.

WOODWORTH, R. S., 'A contribution to the question of quick learning quick forgetting', *Psychol., Bull.*, 1914, **11**, 58–9.

— *Psychologie expérimentale* (translated from English by A. Ombredanne et I. Lézine), Paris, Presses Universitaires de France, 1949.

— SCHLOSBERG, H., *Experimental Psychology*, New York, Holt, 1954.

WULF, F., 'Über die Veränderung von Vorstellungen (Gedachtnis und Gestalt), *Psychol. Forsch.*, 1922, **1**, 333–73.

WYLIE, C. E., *Whole vs part methods of learning as dependent upon practice*, Ph.D. Thesis, Univ. Chicago, 1928.

YERKES, R. M., *The dancing mouse*, New York, Macmillan, 1907.

YOUNG, R. K., 'Retroactive and proactive effect under varying conditions of response similarity', *J. exp. Psychol.*, 1955, **50**, 113–19.

YOUTZ, A. C., 'An experimental evaluation of Jost's laws', *Psychol. Monogr.*, 1941, **53**, no. 238.

ZANGWILL, O. L., 'An investigation of the relationship between the processes of reproducing and recognizing simple figures with special reference to Koffka's trace theory', *Brit. J. Psychol.*, 1937, **27**, 250–76.

ZEIGARNIK, B., 'Das Behalten erledigter und unerledigter Handlungen', in K. Lewin (ed.), 'Untersuchungen zur Handlungs und Affektpsychologie', *Psychol. Forsch.*, 1927, **9**, 1–85.

Index